# Advances in Research on Structural Dynamics and Health Monitoring

# Advances in Research on Structural Dynamics and Health Monitoring

Guest Editors

**Shaohong Cheng**
**Haijun Zhou**

Basel • Beijing • Wuhan • Barcelona • Belgrade • Novi Sad • Cluj • Manchester

*Guest Editors*

Shaohong Cheng
University of Windsor
Windsor, ON
Canada

Haijun Zhou
Shenzhen University
Shenzhen
China

*Editorial Office*
MDPI AG
Grosspeteranlage 5
4052 Basel, Switzerland

This is a reprint of the Special Issue, published open access by the journal *Buildings* (ISSN 2075-5309), freely accessible at: https://www.mdpi.com/journal/buildings/special_issues/1Z566TF3I3.

For citation purposes, cite each article independently as indicated on the article page online and as indicated below:

Lastname, A.A.; Lastname, B.B. Article Title. *Journal Name* **Year**, *Volume Number*, Page Range.

ISBN 978-3-7258-3029-9 (Hbk)
ISBN 978-3-7258-3030-5 (PDF)
https://doi.org/10.3390/books978-3-7258-3030-5

© 2025 by the authors. Articles in this book are Open Access and distributed under the Creative Commons Attribution (CC BY) license. The book as a whole is distributed by MDPI under the terms and conditions of the Creative Commons Attribution-NonCommercial-NoDerivs (CC BY-NC-ND) license (https://creativecommons.org/licenses/by-nc-nd/4.0/).

# Contents

**About the Editors** . . . . . . . . . . . . . . . . . . . . . . . . . . . . . . . . . . . . . . . . . . . . . . . . . . . . . . . . . . . . . vii

**Shaohong Cheng and Haijun Zhou**
Buildings: Special Issue on Advancement in Research on Structural Dynamics and Health Monitoring
Reprinted from: *Buildings* 2024, 14, 3833, https://doi.org/10.3390/buildings14123833 . . . . . . 1

**Reina El Dahr, Xenofon Lignos, Spyridon Papavieros and Ioannis Vayas**
Dynamic Assessment of the Structural Behavior of a Pedestrian Bridge Aiming to Characterize and Evaluate Its Comfort Level
Reprinted from: *Buildings* 2023, 13, 3053, https://doi.org/10.3390/buildings13123053 . . . . . . 5

**Balázs Kövesdi, Dénes Kollár and László Dunai**
Temporary Structural Health Monitoring of Historical Széchenyi Chain Bridge
Reprinted from: *Buildings* 2024, 14, 535, https://doi.org/10.3390/buildings14020535 . . . . . . . 21

**Qixin Qin, Xi Tu, Yujing Hu, Zhisong Wang, Lin Yu and Shengli Hou**
Modeling and Loading Effect of Wind on Long-Span Cross-Rope Suspended Overhead Line with Suspension Insulator
Reprinted from: *Buildings* 2024, 14, 656, https://doi.org/10.3390/buildings14030656 . . . . . . . 36

**Amedeo Gregori, Chiara Castoro, Micaela Mercuri, Antonio Di Natale and Emidio Di Giampaolo**
Innovative Use of UHF-RFID Wireless Sensors for Monitoring Cultural Heritage Structures
Reprinted from: *Buildings* 2024, 14, 1155, https://doi.org/10.3390/buildings14041155 . . . . . . 56

**Javier Urruzola and Iñaki Garmendia**
Improved FEM Natural Frequency Calculation for Structural Frames by Local Correction Procedure
Reprinted from: *Buildings* 2024, 14, 1195, https://doi.org/10.3390/buildings14051195 . . . . . . 86

**Weijian Sun, Guoxin Wang and Juntao Ma**
Stability Analysis of Seismic Slope Based on Relative Residual Displacement Increment Method
Reprinted from: *Buildings* 2024, 14, 1211, https://doi.org/10.3390/buildings14051211 . . . . . . 105

**Siying Liu, Zunian Zhou, Yujie Zhang, Zhuo Sun, Jiangdong Deng and Junyong Zhou**
Theoretical and Experimental Investigations of Identifying Bridge Damage Using Instantaneous Amplitude Squared Extracted from Vibration Responses of a Two-Axle Passing Vehicle
Reprinted from: *Buildings* 2024, 14, 1428, https://doi.org/10.3390/buildings14051428 . . . . . . 122

**Xuyang Bian and Guoxin Wang**
Study of Structural Seismic Damage Considering Seasonal Frozen Soil–Structure Interaction
Reprinted from: *Buildings* 2024, 14, 1493, https://doi.org/10.3390/buildings14061493 . . . . . . 143

**Ali Ashasi Sorkhabi, Barry Qiu and Oya Mercan**
Investigating Large-Scale Tuned Liquid Dampers through Real-Time Hybrid Simulations
Reprinted from: *Buildings* 2024, 14, 2017, https://doi.org/10.3390/buildings14072017 . . . . . . 160

**Yibing Lou, Jian Zhang and Yuxin Pan**
Static and Dynamic Response Analysis of Flexible Photovoltaic Mounts
Reprinted from: *Buildings* 2024, 14, 2037, https://doi.org/10.3390/buildings14072037 . . . . . . 178

**Xuzhao Lu, Guang Qu, Limin Sun, Ye Xia, Haibin Sun and Wei Zhang**
Physically Guided Estimation of Vehicle Loading-Induced Low-Frequency Bridge Responses with BP-ANN
Reprinted from: *Buildings* **2024**, *14*, 2995, https://doi.org/10.3390/buildings14092995 . . . . . . **198**

**Xin Wang, Zhaobo Meng, Xiangming Lv and Guoqiang Wei**
Dynamic Testing and Finite Element Model Adjustment of the Ancient Wooden Structure Under Traffic Excitation
Reprinted from: *Buildings* **2024**, *14*, 3527, https://doi.org/10.3390/buildings14113527 . . . . . . **222**

# About the Editors

**Shaohong Cheng**

Shaohong Cheng is a professor in the Department of Civil and Environmental Engineering at the University of Windsor, Canada. She received her Master of Applied Science degree from Tongji University in China and obtained her PhD degree in Structural Engineering from Carleton University in Canada in 2000. She specializes in structural dynamics, bluff body aerodynamics, fluid–structure interaction, structural vibration and control, and has more than 25 years of experience in these fields. She is a Professional Engineer of Ontario, a member of the American Society of Civil Engineers, the American Association for Wind Engineering, and the International Association for Bridge and Structural Engineering. She has published over 120 peer-reviewed journal and conference articles. Over the past five years, her research publications have received close to 1,000 citations, with three of the published journal papers received awards of Key Scientific Articles from Advances in Engineering, and another one being recognized as the top cited article of 2020-2021 in the prestigious *Structural Control and Health Monitoring* journal.

**Haijun Zhou**

Haijun Zhou is a Professor and Head of the Department of Civil Engineering at Shenzhen University, China. He received his Bachelor, Master and PhD degree of Structural Engineering from Tongji University in China. He specializes in structural dynamics, structural vibration control and health monitoring, structural durability. He is an associate member of the American Society of Civil Engineers and a member of the International Association for Bridge and Structural Engineering; he also served as committee member of both ASCE EMI SHMC and ASCE EMI DYNAMIC. He is PI of six NSFC projects and has published over 120 peer-reviewed journal and conference articles. Over the past five years, He had gained the National Science and Technology Progress Award, Science and Technology Progress Award of Guangdong Province, and Natural Science Award of Ministry of Education of China.

*Editorial*

# Buildings: Special Issue on Advancement in Research on Structural Dynamics and Health Monitoring

Shaohong Cheng [1,*] and Haijun Zhou [2]

1. Department of Civil and Environmental Engineering, University of Windsor, Windsor, ON N9B 3P4, Canada
2. Department of Civil Engineering, Shenzhen University, Shenzhen 518060, China; haijun@szu.edu.cn
* Correspondence: shaohong@uwindsor.ca

Citation: Cheng, S.; Zhou, H. Buildings: Special Issue on Advancement in Research on Structural Dynamics and Health Monitoring. *Buildings* 2024, 14, 3833. https://doi.org/10.3390/buildings14123833

Received: 27 November 2024
Accepted: 27 November 2024
Published: 29 November 2024

**Copyright:** © 2024 by the authors. Licensee MDPI, Basel, Switzerland. This article is an open access article distributed under the terms and conditions of the Creative Commons Attribution (CC BY) license (https://creativecommons.org/licenses/by/4.0/).

The rapid development of engineering materials, construction technologies, and analytical approaches has made it possible to design and build more slender structures, with longer spans and taller heights. This trend in modern civil infrastructure and the increasing frequency of natural disasters brought by climate change have posed unprecedented challenges to the engineering community. For instance, the vulnerability of structures to various dynamic excitations and the control of the resulting large-amplitude vibrations have become pressing issues. In addition, for ancient and aging structures that remain in use, it is crucial to ensure their structural health so that they can continue to operate safely. Intensive research is urgently needed to examine the dynamic behavior of structures under extreme loading conditions, such as damaging wind and devastating earthquakes, and evaluate the structural health of existing structures, especially those that are aging. In addition to properly addressing the characteristics associated with loading and structural responses and evaluating the effectiveness of implemented vibration control solutions, monitoring the actual structural parameters to accurately assess the structural health of a building during its service life is imperative to ensure the safe performance and serviceability of structures during their lifespan.

This Special Issue has collected twelve recent studies to showcase the latest developments in the dynamic analysis and health monitoring of civil structures, with the objective of reflecting the current research trends and challenges in these fields.

As a vital component of the transportation system, bridges play an important role in facilitating global and regional economic development and social communication. With the aging of bridges worldwide, how to diagnose their structural health and identify possible damage becomes an urgent issue. This is tackled by Liu et al. in "Theoretical and Experimental Investigations of Identifying Bridge Damage Using Instantaneous Amplitude Squared Extracted from Vibration Responses of a Two-Axle Passing Vehicle", where the feasibility of employing an ordinary two-axle passing commercial vehicle to indirectly detect possible damage in a bridge structure was explored. This approach uses the instantaneous amplitude squared (IAS) extracted from the residual contact-point (CP) responses of a two-axle passing vehicle in the examination. The authors also discussed the applicability of the proposed technique through parametric studies of vehicle speeds and road roughness grades. This novel approach has significant potential to quickly assess the structural health of a large number of bridges using only ordinary two-axle commercial vehicles.

Kövesdi et al. presented a six-month-long structural health monitoring program performed on a 175-year-old historical bridge in Hungary during its reconstruction in "Temporary Structural Health Monitoring of Historical Széchenyi Chain Bridge". In comparison with a proof load test, the collected field data highlight the importance of ambient temperature fluctuations on the structural behavior of this bridge, particularly the rotational capacity of the pins between the chain elements. This information greatly helps designers and construction companies when making decisions during the reconstruction stage of the bridge.

In "Dynamic Testing and Finite Element Model Adjustment of the Ancient Wooden Structure Under Traffic Excitation", Wang et al. conducted an in situ dynamic test to examine the impact of traffic-induced vibrations on an ancient wooden structure. A finite element model was developed, with the modal parameters being calibrated using modal identification techniques based on a traffic-induced response to accurately represent the dynamic characteristics of the actual structure. This study offers valuable insights into the performance of ancient timber structures along traffic routes.

The intersectional relationship, which correlates bridge responses at different locations, is crucial in assessing structural health and identifying potential damages in a bridge structure. In the study by Lu et al., "Physically Guided Estimation of Vehicle Loading-Induced Low-Frequency Bridge Responses with BP-ANN", a physically guided time-independent machine learning approach, the backpropagation artificial neural network (BP-ANN), is proposed to simulate the intersectional relationship for low-frequency bridge responses. This approach mitigates the need to conduct long-term field monitoring to account for the influence of fluctuations in traffic and temperature on the intersectional relationship. Thus, it allows an efficient estimation of low-frequency bridge responses under various conditions, and the convenience of this approach is expected to be greatly appreciated by practicing engineers.

In comparison with the more traditional sensors used in structural health monitoring, ultra-high-frequency RFID (UHF-RFID) wireless tags are easy to install and can be used in large quantities with very low maintenance costs. Therefore, this type of sensor has been widely used in monitoring the response of civil structures. The feasibility of employing this type of sensor to monitor out-of-plane displacements of brick masonry walls has been evaluated by Gregori et al. in "Innovative Use of UHF-RFID Wireless Sensors for Monitoring Cultural Heritage Structures". The findings from this study suggest the potential of applying wireless technology to monitor the health of civil structures.

Among various environmental factors, civil structures are most frequently exposed to the effects of wind. Therefore, an accurate prediction of wind-induced responses is critical to the design and safe performance of structures. In "Static and Dynamic Response Analysis of Flexible Photovoltaic Mounts" by Lou et al., the wind-induced response of flexible photovoltaic (PV) mounting structures is analyzed numerically. The time history of a fluctuating wind load is simulated in MATLAB and imposed on a structural model of the flexible PV supports developed in SAP2000. The static response under extreme conditions and the wind-induced dynamic response are analyzed. Through this analysis, the critical wind speed of flexible PV supports is determined, and measures to improve the wind resistance of this type of structure are proposed.

The structural performance of a long-span cross-rope suspended system with a suspension insulator (CRSSI), in terms of its dynamic characteristics and deformation resulting from a static wind load, is numerically studied by Qin et al. in "Modeling and Loading Effect of Wind on Long-Span Cross-Rope Suspended Overhead Line with Suspension Insulator". The impact of the self-weight of the conductor and insulator on the initial catenary shape of the suspended cable is considered in this study. The results show that the horizontal displacement of the suspension insulator, which increases with wind speed, contributes to the maximum displacement of the long-span CRSSI.

Seismic load is another important type of dynamic excitation for structures. Globally, there are about, on average, 20–25 earthquakes with a magnitude of 7 every year. Earthquakes can cause severe damage to structures, and their significance depends on numerous factors. In addition to the magnitude, the focal depth, the epicentral distance, the characteristics of the structural system, and the soil condition can all affect the seismic response of a structure. For example, structures built on soft soils or near fault lines are more vulnerable to seismic excitations and experience more destructive damage. The seismic response of a four-story frame structure and a sixteen-story frame structure are numerically studied by Bian and Wang in "Study of Structural Seismic Damage Considering Seasonal Frozen Soil–Structure Interaction". The seasonal frozen soil–structure interaction is considered in the ABAQUS models developed for these two frame structures. The results reveal that the soil ambient temperature, which directly affects the soil condition, plays an important role in the seismic-induced response of structures. Compared to when the soil ambient temperature is above the freezing point, a structure would typically experience significantly less damage if the soil ambient temperature is below the freezing point.

Slope instability has become the most common earthquake-induced secondary hazard in many countries in recent years. The impact of landslides is not only extensive but can also be fatal. Therefore, it is imperative to perform an accurate assessment of the dynamic stability of slopes when subjected to seismic load. In the study by Sun et al., "Stability Analysis of Seismic Slope Based on Relative Residual Displacement Increment Method", a novel method to analyze seismic slope stability is proposed, combining the relative residual displacement increment method with the strength reduction method and the dynamic interaction between soil masses. Since an assumption of the sliding surface is not required in this approach, the determination of the slope safety factor involves minimal human influence.

The accurate identification of modal properties is essential for predicting the response of structures under dynamic loads. When developing a finite element model for a frame structure, each member may be discretized into various elements. Further, though the accuracy of the modal analysis results improves with a greater number of elements, the associated computational cost increases accordingly. To address this issue, Urruzola and Garmendia proposed a method to improve the accuracy of the numerically predicted modal frequencies of frame structures by applying a local correction to the kinetic and elastic energy of certain elements, considerably reducing error. These finds are presented in "Improved FEM Natural Frequency Calculation for Structural Frames by Local Correction Procedure". The accuracy and flexibility of this novel approach are demonstrated through numerical examples covering both simple canonical cases and more realistic ones.

Ensuring user comfort is also an essential criterion of structural design. In "Dynamic Assessment of the Structural Behavior of a Pedestrian Bridge Aiming to Characterize and Evaluate Its Comfort Level", El Dahr et al. assessed if the performance of an arch-and-tie pedestrian bridge in Greece meets the comfort criteria stated by EN1990, HIVOSS, and SETRA guidelines. The bridge acceleration responses, which were recorded by a computer-based data acquisition system through the LabVIEW platform and pre-processed by a Butterworth bandpass filter, were used to identify the modal properties of the bridge in terms of the modal frequencies, associated mode shapes, and modal damping ratios. The results indicate that the bridge can satisfy the comfort criteria with the installation of additional dampers.

Dampers are commonly used in structures to enable supplemental energy dissipation and improve their dynamic responses. In "Investigating Large-Scale Tuned Liquid Dampers through Real-Time Hybrid Simulations", Sorkhabi et al. conducted experiments on the effects of tuned liquid dampers (TLDs) on the seismic resistance of buildings through a real-time hybrid simulation, where the resistive force generated by a real TLD is applied to a numerically simulated structural system under seismic excitation. This novel hybrid approach allows the use of a large-scale TLD in physical tests. By numerically varying structural properties during simulation, different scenarios of TLD–structure interactions are examined.

We hope that the papers collected in this Special Issue reflect the latest trends and advancements in the research on structural dynamics and health monitoring and that they are of interest to researchers seeking to develop their professional skills and expertise in these areas. A thorough understanding of structural responses under different types of dynamic excitations and the novel techniques and tools applicable to monitoring structural health is imperative to ensure the safe and reliable performance of structures, which ultimately leads to the design and construction of more resilient and sustainable infrastructure to combat the challenges brought by climate change.

Last but not least, we would like to express our gratitude to the authors for their enthusiasm in sharing their latest research, and to the reviewers for their support and their in-depth and constructive comments, which made the publication of this Special Issue possible. Many thanks to Ms. Marion Ma, the Section Managing Editor, for her continuous assistance in preparing this Special Issue.

**Conflicts of Interest:** The authors declare no conflicts of interest.

**Disclaimer/Publisher's Note:** The statements, opinions and data contained in all publications are solely those of the individual author(s) and contributor(s) and not of MDPI and/or the editor(s). MDPI and/or the editor(s) disclaim responsibility for any injury to people or property resulting from any ideas, methods, instructions or products referred to in the content.

Article

# Dynamic Assessment of the Structural Behavior of a Pedestrian Bridge Aiming to Characterize and Evaluate Its Comfort Level

Reina El Dahr *, Xenofon Lignos, Spyridon Papavieros and Ioannis Vayas

Institute of Steel Structures, National Technical University of Athens, 15772 Athens, Greece; vastahl@central.ntua.gr (I.V.)
* Correspondence: rdahr@mail.ntua.gr

**Abstract:** The assessment of infrastructure integrity is considered paramount to verify its structural health and to build its resilience. In this study, a monitoring strategy, consisting of a pre-developed microcontroller-based data acquisition system (DAQ) hardware and a software program for post processing built on LabVIEW platform, was conducted to assess the structural behavior of an arch-and-tie pedestrian bridge located in Haidari, Greece, following its construction phase. This endeavor aimed to delineate its systemic state and to verify the fulfillment of comfort criteria stated by EN1990, HIVOSS and SETRA guidelines. To this end, four trademark Bridge Diagnostic Inc. (BDI) triaxial accelerometers were meticulously deployed along the bridge expanse to scrutinize the structure's response toward a spectrum of induced perturbations. The established framework effectively compiled the acquired acceleration time domain then employed a Butterworth bandpass filter to derive the bridge eigenfrequencies, eigenmodes, and damping ratios. The resultant findings conclusively indicate that the bridge response towards pedestrian crossing conforms to the established specifications and thus does not necessitate the installation of dampers. The bridge maintains comfortable structural integrity for pedestrian traversal up to an upper frequency limit of 3.67 Hz, substantiating its ability to absorb the dissipated energy generated by pedestrian movement.

**Keywords:** structural health monitoring; bridge assessment; comfort level characterization; damping; eigenfrequency; LabVIEW

## 1. Introduction

In pursuit of meeting architectural requirements, engineers often aim to design elongated-spanned pedestrian bridges, and to adopt lightweight yet high-strength materials [1]. This innovation considerably lowers the eigenfrequency of the footbridge, which in return renders the structure more vulnerable to oscillations, resulting in the discomfort of pedestrians when crossing the bridge [2]. Nonetheless, the amount of reported bridge harm has dramatically escalated, along with increased complaints about the deterioration state, following the expansion of service duration and the high traffic loads bridges are subjected to [3]. In such a situation, it becomes crucial to give priority to any infrastructure for renovation and restoration depending on its assessed health [4].

Ongoing development in bridge design and construction, coupled with advancements in assessment techniques, has highlighted the importance of monitoring its performance from the construction phase through operation and maintenance for safety and comfort characterization [5]. Therefore, assessing a bridge's health has emerged to prevent any adverse event that may befall the structure [6–11]. In their 2001 research, Peeters et al. classified the aspects that could harm a bridge, such as metal corrosion and material aging, resulting in strength loss. Furthermore, any externally induced disturbance has a significant impact on the vibrational evaluation of bridges. Among these, the system can be stimulated by the crowd standing atop the structure, the force of the wind, and the vibrations induced at the base of the structure [12]. Consequently, dynamic assessment is conducted to evaluate vibrational properties intending to certify its design safety, analyze the health state, and detect any harmful deterioration [13–16]. The most crucial vibrational characteristics to assess are eigenfrequencies, eigenmodes, and damping ratios [17,18]. Pirskawetz and Schmidt, in 2023, evaluated the structural response of a prestressed concrete bridge located in Germany after being exposed to acoustic emission through destructive tests to detect wire breakage [19]

As a result, modal analysis is established in assessing the dynamic behavior of structures [20–23]. Thus, operational modal analysis (OMA) is particularly employed in health-monitoring strategies, deemed to evaluate modifications in the framework vibrational measurements [24,25]. Gonzalez et al., in 2023, proposed a power spectral density-based algorithm for bridge monitoring purposes within vehicle measurements. It was able to identify, localize, and assess single cracks on a 15 m span simply supported bridge [26]. In this study, we have adopted an operational modal testing procedure to estimate the dynamic measurements of a pedestrian bridge by inducing perturbations at various positions along the bridge.

The operational lifespan of a pedestrian bridge is intricately tied to the influence of individuals traversing it, mainly the number of people crossing, their activities, and the duration of their presence on the bridge [27], resulting in modifications to its dynamic aspect and modal attributes. Generally, pedestrians exhibit a proclivity for coordinated interactions while crossing a bridge in order not to intersect. Therefore, this human–human interface results in modifying their paths. Accordingly, neighbor pedestrians adjust their walking cadence to harmonize with those around them [28]. Furthermore, the human–structure interface may generate a discomfort for pedestrians when crossing a bridge, since their walking frequencies tend to match with the bridge's motion causing a resonance oscillation state. Dallard et al. referred to this encounter impact as the "lock-in phenomenon" ([29], p. 413).

Pedestrian bridges experience not only vertical vibrations caused by dynamic forces induced by crowd movement, but also significant lateral vibrations, as exemplified by the unexpected lateral oscillations that arose in the London Millennium Footbridge [30]. These movements were triggered by a significant lateral loading effect, a factor that was not initially foreseen during the design phase and had received limited prior investigation.

In the realm of bridge dynamics, evaluating the system response toward an induced stimulation indicates that the bridge oscillation may reach an uncomfortable state for pedestrians, and so it becomes imperative to implement a vibration absorbent framework for the undesirable bridge motion.

Passive damping mechanisms such as tuned mass dampers (TMDs) are adopted on structures that are vulnerable to oscillation, such as pedestrian bridges, stadiums, or high-rise building constructions. When it comes to the advancement of damping systems, bridges, regardless of their specific design, offer a fascinating area of investigation [31]. TMDs have proven valuable not only in the design of new structures, but, also, they are implemented on existing ones. Moreover, they come with a decent maintenance price [32]. Caetano et al. [33,34] conducted a study on the Pedro e Inés bridge in Coimbra, Portugal, focusing on the structure oscillation caused by pedestrians while crossing the bridge. Their research involved extended monitoring to analyze the bridge dynamic behavior and the implementation of tuned mass dampers (TMDs) to mitigate vertical and lateral vibrations.

In this study, a monitoring methodology was conducted, aiming to assess the structural behavior and verify the fulfillment of the comfort criteria of the Haidari pedestrian bridge located in Greece after the completion of its construction.

## 2. Comfort Level of Pedestrian Bridges

In the present work, the emphasis on pedestrian comfort is gaining significant consideration in both the design and functionality evaluations of footbridges. Prioritizing the comfort of individuals when crossing a footbridge is of utmost importance, given the multifaced challenge this issue may present. The comfort of individuals traversing a pedestrian bridge is influenced by a range of subjective factors, among them the ambient noise, traffic volume on the bridge, bridge elevation from the ground, and the aspect of the people crossing themselves. In 2016, Tubino at al. carried out an extensive experimental study on two well-utilized footbridges located Italy. The design objectives were set in accordance with the bridge owner's specifications, focusing on achieving both the average and the ultimate comfort stage [35].

It is widely acknowledged that vibrational acceleration stands as the primary influencing factor affecting pedestrian comfort [36]. In previous investigations, researchers primarily focused on the impact of vibrational magnitude and velocity on experienced comfort [37–39]. Nevertheless, as research has progressed in examining human experiences in their surroundings, there is a consensus among scholars that this comfort is chiefly governed by the dynamic acceleration experienced over time, rather than velocity. In their 2017 study, Dey et al. assessed various design protocols using data obtained from tests conducted on two real-time pedestrian bridges. Their findings indicated that the protocol typically defines comfort thresholds based primarily on acceleration [40].

ISO 2631-1 [41] categorized the pedestrians' comfort limits into six distinct groups aligned with various acceleration amplitudes, and several recent studies have embraced this comfort partition [42]. Similarly, alternative standards, such as the European HIVOSS guideline from 2008 [43] and the French guideline Sétra from 2006 [44], have outlined acceleration associated with specific comfort levels, as highlighted by Van Nimmen et al. in 2014 [45].

This research presents the evaluations of the vibrational performance of the Haidari pedestrian bridge, with the goal of characterizing its structural condition and emphasizing the pedestrian's comfort. This approach is grounded in the correlation between pedestrians' comfort and the highest acceleration experienced on the footbridge.

## 3. Case Study

A monitoring strategy was conducted aiming to assess the structural behavior and the comfort of Haidari pedestrian bridge located in Greece after the completion of construction. The structure is an arch-and-tie bridge with a span length of 44.6 m and width of 2.74 m. Along one side, the arch stands in an eccentrical position connected to six PFEIFER type PV115 wire cables, as shown in Figure 1. The concrete deck is supported by steel girders-cantilevers of variable trapezoidal profile sections which are connected to the arch element. The bridge rests on two pedestals situated atop piles. The measured total dead weight of the bridge is 152 tons.

**Figure 1.** Cross-section of Haidari pedestrian bridge.

Four triaxial BDI accelerometers were strategically placed along the bridge to monitor time-varying oscillations. A predefined sensor placement was suggested in accordance with the areas on the deck expected to experience the most significant disturbances, deemed as the optimal sensor placement. Specifically, two sensors were deployed at the midpoint of the bridge, one on the cantilever section, and one adjacent to the bow. The remaining two sensors were positioned at the quarter-span, near the edge of the cantilever, as illustrated in Figure 2. These sensors recorded accelerations in the vertical (z), longitudinal (x), and transversal (y) directions along the bridge deck. Subsequently, the sensor data were transmitted via wiring to a control unit located outside the bridge structure. The spatial arrangement of these sensors in a top–down view is illustrated in Figure 3. The sensor network was connected to a data acquisition system in order to process and evaluate the recorded vibrational signals collected by the accelerometers.

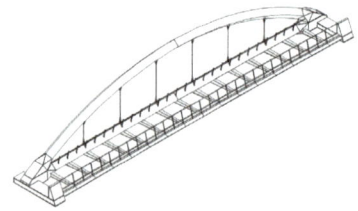

**Figure 2.** Side view of Haidari pedestrian bridge.

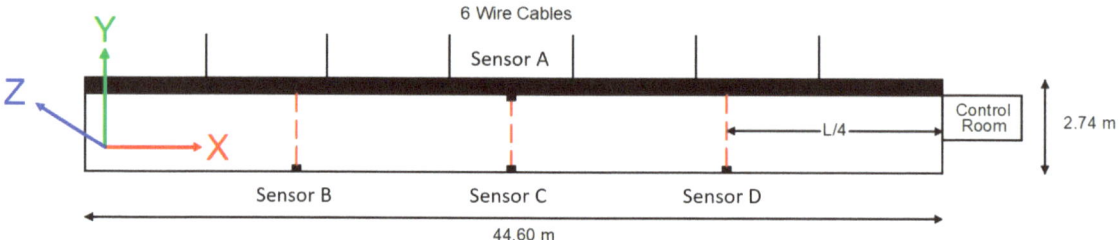

**Figure 3.** Sensor network mounted on Haidari pedestrian bridge.

The adopted DAQ system was designed and validated by El Dahr et al. in 2022 [46]. It is a microcontroller-based, accurate, and low-cost acquisition framework that facilitates the aggregation and analysis of gathered data, relying on a Teensy 4.1 digital microcontroller of a resolution of 32 bits to execute these operations. Along with its PC computer, it was employed to receive the data and calculate the output through a programming software such as MATLAB or LabVIEW.

In this study, the results were computed using a LabVIEW programming platform developed by El Dahr et al. in 2023 [47]. LabVIEW, which stands for Laboratory Virtual Instrument Engineering Workbench, is a graphical user interface-based programming tool predominantly employed for data acquisition and structural assessment. One of the primary advantages of this approach is its well-defined conceptual framework, enabling the calculation of modal properties and reducing computational complexity while facilitating its versatile application in various projects, such as bridges, towers, and tall structures. Furthermore, its network of sensors and topological architecture ensures superior precision in data collection and an optimized strategy for analysis when compared to other data acquisition (DAQ) methodologies.

## 4. Experimental Procedure

The aim of the study was to observe how the system responds to various external disturbances in order to estimate the dynamic characteristics of the bridge under scrutiny, characterizing the comfort level experienced by pedestrians when crossing the bridge. Therefore, the investigations were conducted in two distinct phases.

The first phase was intended to calculate the bridge eigenfrequencies, damping ratios, and eigenmodes. This was achieved through the application of controlled excitations, with a particular focus on inducing vertical and lateral oscillations. These disturbances were initiated by both cases, an individual and a group of people, who, through rhythmical bouncing actions, excited the bridge within its natural frequency spectrum. These jumping events predominantly occurred at positions corresponding to 1/2 and 1/4 of the bridge's length. Rhythmic activities encompassed an impact vertical jump with landing on two feet, and hops from one leg to the other were performed to induce vertical and horizontal oscillations, respectively. The pedestrians complied with the rhythm of a tone generator. The frequency of foot-to-foot jumps was 3.67 Hz, which from preliminary measurements had given the first vertical eigenfrequency of the bridge, with 2.0 Hz corresponding to normal walking. The jumps stopped abruptly after reaching a level of oscillations and the free response of the carrier until rest was measured. The set of Stage 1 tests is presented in Table 1.

**Table 1.** Protocol of imposed stimulations of Phase 1 tests.

| Pedestrian: Mass [Kg] | Position | Type/Frequency |
|---|---|---|
| A: 80.9 Kg<br>B: 94.8 Kg<br>C: 103.6 Kg | 0.5 L<br>0.5 L<br>0.5 L<br>0.25 L<br>0.25 L<br>0.25 L | Impact Jump<br>3.67 Hz foot to foot<br>2 Hz foot to foot<br>Impact Jump<br>3.67 Hz foot to foot<br>2 Hz foot to foot |
| Six Pedestrians: 543.1 Kg | 0.5 L<br>0.5 L<br>0.25 L<br>0.25 L | Impact Jump<br>3.67 Hz foot to foot<br>Impact Jump<br>3.67 Hz foot to foot |

The second phase of testing was aimed at assessing whether the pedestrian bridge conformed to the requisite standards for oscillation comfort during pedestrian transit. Data acquisition involved recording the movements of one pedestrian and a crowd of nine people walking on a predefined path for specific frequencies.

The traffic on the bridge is classified between very light and light according to HIVOSS guidelines [43] and SETRA [44], since the bridge is located in an urban area that can be occasionally loaded, with a pedestrian density of 0.1–0.2 pedestrian/m$^2$.

Three different types of gait characteristics of walking, running, and random walking, where each pedestrian walked at their own pace, were tested for the intentional stimulation of the subject. The recording of accelerations in all crossings started 10 s before the beginning of pedestrian movement on the bridge deck and ended 20 s after they stopped. The set of examined crossings for one pedestrian and for a group of nine pedestrians is given in Table 2.

**Table 2.** Protocol of imposed stimulations of Phase 2 tests.

| Pedestrian: Mass [Kg] | Type/Frequency | Path |
|---|---|---|
| A: 80.9 Kg<br>B: 94.8 Kg<br>C: 103.6 Kg | 2.0 Hz Walk<br>3.67 Hz Walk<br>Random Walk | |
| Nine Pedestrians: 791.2 Kg | 2.0 Hz Walk<br>3.67 Hz Walk<br>Random Walk | |

## 5. Results and Interpretation

### 5.1. Acceleration Calculation

The DAQ system and the BDI accelerometers have a sampling frequency of 200 Hz. Accelerometers along the bridge were recording raw data in response to external disturbances. The LabVIEW code was employed to compute and eliminate the mean value from the recorded acceleration, thereby mitigating the offset inherent in the raw acceleration–time graph. The removal of this offset is crucial to minimize potential sources of error. To derive the corrected acceleration–time domain, the mean value is subtracted from the raw acceleration–time domain. The structure is designed to experience a maximum acceleration of 0.7 m/s$^2$ in the vertical direction and 0.2 m/s$^2$ in the lateral direction.

An evaluation of pedestrian A leaping at the bridge's midpoint is provided in the paragraphs that follow. Figure 4 shows the corrected acceleration time domain collected by accelerometer A recording the structural response toward pedestrian A disturbing the bridge with an impact jump at the mid-length of the bridge. The results are presented in the vertical direction. The mean value was determined to be 9.8049 m/s$^2$ and was subtracted. The highest acceleration recorded was 0.92 m/s$^2$ reported at 8.15 s when the bridge was disturbed. The acceleration is higher than the maximum allowable acceleration in the vertical direction of 0.7 m/s$^2$ that the bridge is originally designed to experience, causing a discomfort feeling for a 1 s period of time.

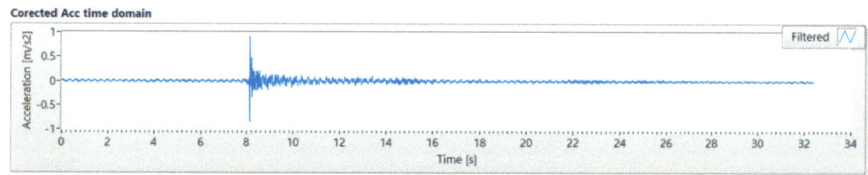

**Figure 4.** Corrected acceleration–time domain of accelerometer A for pedestrian A in vertical direction.

Figure 5 shows the corrected acceleration time domain collected by accelerometer A recording the structural response toward pedestrian A disturbing the bridge with an impact jump at the mid-length of the bridge. The results are presented in the lateral direction. The mean value was determined to be $-0.27864$ m/s$^2$ and was retrieved. The highest acceleration recorded was 0.16 m/s$^2$, reported at 8.15 s when the bridge was disturbed. The acceleration is lower than the maximum allowable acceleration in the lateral direction of 0.2 m/s$^2$, which the bridge is originally designed to experience.

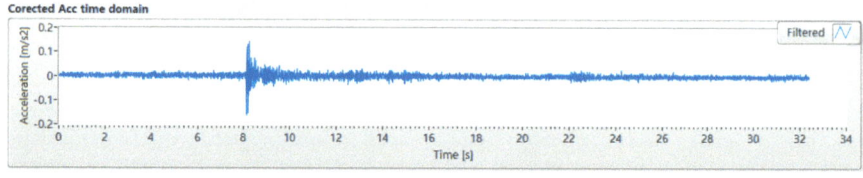

**Figure 5.** Corrected acceleration–time domain of accelerometer A for pedestrian A in lateral direction.

Figure 6 shows the corrected acceleration time domain collected by accelerometer A recording the structural response toward the six pedestrians disturbing the bridge with an impact jump at the mid-length of the bridge. The results are presented in the vertical direction. The highest acceleration recorded was 0.6 m/s$^2$ reported at 13.3 s when the bridge was disturbed. The acceleration is lower than the maximum allowable acceleration in the vertical direction of 0.7 m/s$^2$, which the bridge is originally designed to experience.

Figure 7 shows the corrected acceleration time domain collected by accelerometer A recording the structural response toward the six pedestrians disturbing the bridge with an impact jump at the mid-length of the bridge. The results are presented in the lateral direction. The highest acceleration recorded was 0.25 m/s$^2$ reported at 13.3 s when the bridge was disturbed. The acceleration is higher than the maximum allowable acceleration in the lateral direction of 0.2 m/s$^2$, which the bridge is originally designed to experience, causing a discomfort feeling for a 1 s period of time.

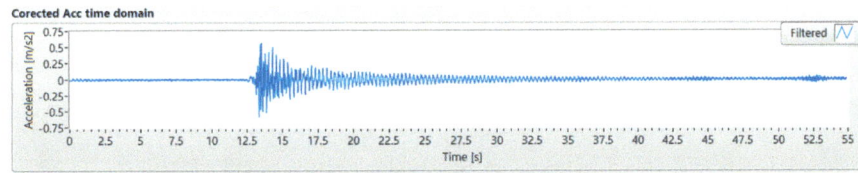

**Figure 6.** Corrected acceleration–time domain of accelerometer A for 6 pedestrians in vertical direction.

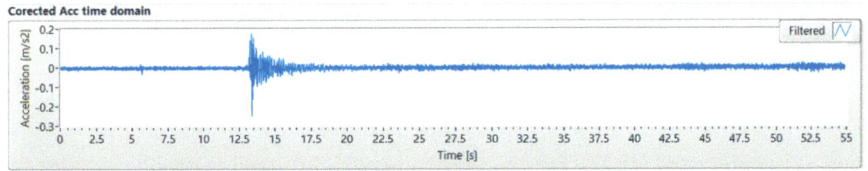

**Figure 7.** Corrected acceleration–time domain of accelerometer A for 6 pedestrians in lateral direction.

### 5.2. Natural Frequencies

Determining the eigenfrequencies of a pedestrian bridge is useful to inspect its sensitivity to oscillations during pedestrian crossing. Indeed, if a structure's eigenfrequencies are close to the eigenfrequencies of pedestrian traffic, there is a risk of resonance. The critical eigenfrequency intervals according to the EN 1990 standard [48] and the SETRA [44] and HIVOSS [43] guidelines are given in Table 3.

**Table 3.** Frequency ranges with resonance risk.

| | Frequency [Hz] | | | | | |
|---|---|---|---|---|---|---|
| | **Vertical Oscillations** | | | **Lateral Oscillations** | | |
| **Coordination Risk** | **EN 1990** | **HIVOSS** | **SETRA** | **EN 1990** | **HIVOSS** | **SETRA** |
| Negligible | >5 | <1.25<br>>4.6 | <1.0<br>>5.0 | >2.5 | <0.5<br>>1.2 | <0.3<br>>2.5 |
| Small | | | 2.6–5.0 | | | 1.3–2.5 |
| Medium | <5 | 1.25–4.6 | 1.0–1.7<br>2.1–2.6 | <2.5 | 0.5–1.2 | 0.3–0.5<br>1.1–1.3 |
| Big | | | 1.7–2.1 | | | 0.5–1.1 |

The eigenfrequencies calculated in the designed phase (with contribution of the pedestrians mass with an estimation of 0.6 pedestrian/m², for testing purposes, considering a pedestrian to be 0.8 kN) are as follows: 3.042 Hz, 7.76 Hz, and 10.28 Hz.

The frequency domain is obtained after performing power spectral density (PSD) function on the corrected acceleration time domain of accelerometer A in the vertical direction. The signal from PSD is evaluated to find the peaks in terms of natural frequencies in (Hz) and their respective power in $\left[\frac{(m/s^2)^2}{Hz}\right]$ (Figure 8). It reports three eigenfrequencies, respectively, at 3.67 Hz, 7.62 Hz, and 10.22 Hz (Figure 9).

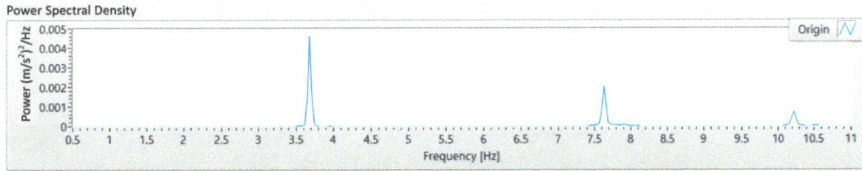

**Figure 8.** Power spectral density of the system eigenfrequency in vertical direction.

| Eigenfrequencies | |
|---|---|
| 3.6742 | 0.0046076 |
| 7.6261 | 0.0020377 |
| 10.218 | 0.00074054 |

**Figure 9.** Power spectral density with numerical inquiry of the system eigenfrequency in vertical direction.

The frequency domain is obtained after performing the power spectral density (PSD) function on the corrected acceleration time domain of accelerometer A in the lateral direction. The signal from PSD is evaluated in Figure 10 and reports three eigenfrequencies, respectively, at 3.67 Hz, 6.24 Hz, and 7.62 Hz (Figure 11).

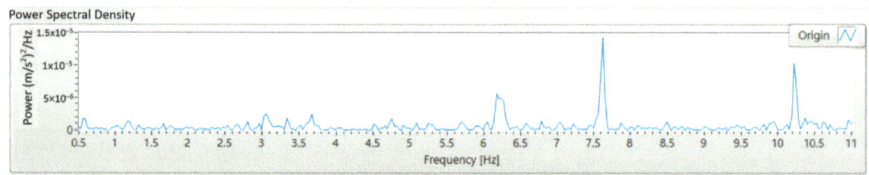

**Figure 10.** Power spectral density of the system eigenfrequency in lateral direction.

| Eigenfrequencies | |
|---|---|
| 6.1839 | 0.0000059215 |
| 7.6223 | 0.000014445 |
| 10.225 | 0.000010649 |

**Figure 11.** Power spectral density with numerical inquiry of the system eigenfrequency in lateral direction.

The eigenfrequencies of the first two eigenmodes in the vertical and transverse directions, as well as their evaluation in terms of resonance risk, are given in Table 4.

**Table 4.** Bridge frequencies and comparison with resonant risk specifications.

| Eigen Frequency | Frequency [Hz] | | Coordination Risk | | | | | |
|---|---|---|---|---|---|---|---|---|
| | Vertical | Lateral | Vertical | | | Lateral | | |
| | | | EN 1990 | HIVOSS | SETRA | EN 1990 | HIVOSS | SETRA |
| 1st | 3.67 | 6.18 | Intermediate | Intermediate | Small | Negligible | Negligible | Negligible |
| 2nd | 7.62 | 7.62 | Negligible | Negligible | Negligible | Negligible | Negligible | Negligible |
| 3rd | 10.22 | 10.22 | Negligible | Negligible | Negligible | Negligible | Negligible | Negligible |

## 5.3. Damping

The damping ratio was determined by LabVIEW through Hilbert transform for the eigenfrequencies of the bridge in both directions. It is estimated to be a maximum of 5% as per the original bridge design.

For the first eigenfrequency, a second-order Butterworth bandpass filter was applied on the corrected acceleration–time domain data of accelerometer A in the vertical direction, with cutoff frequencies between 3.61 and 3.73 Hz. According to the Hilbert transform, the damping ratio is 2.25% (Figure 12).

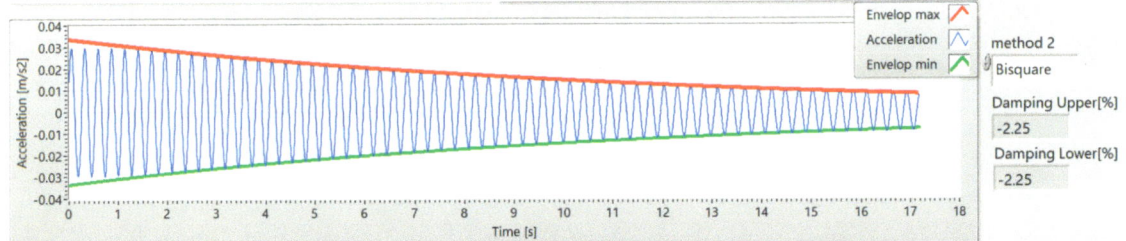

**Figure 12.** LabVIEW graph showing the acceleration–time domain of accelerometer A with envelopes for the first eigenfrequency in the vertical direction calculated by Hilbert transform.

For the second eigenfrequency, a second-order Butterworth bandpass filter was applied on the corrected acceleration–time domain data in the vertical direction, with cutoff frequencies between 7.56 and 7.68 Hz. According to Hilbert transform, the damping ratio is 1.45%. Same for the lateral direction, for the first eigenfrequency, a second-order Butterworth bandpass filter was applied on the corrected acceleration–time domain data, with cutoff frequencies between 6.1 and 6.2 Hz. According to the Hilbert transform, the damping ratio is 1.93%. For the second eigenfrequency in the lateral direction, a second-order Butterworth bandpass filter was applied on the corrected acceleration–time domain data, with cutoff frequencies between 7.56 and 7.69 Hz. According to Hilbert transform, the damping ratio is 1.14%. All four acceleration–time domains with envelopes for both eigenfrequencies in vertical and lateral directions calculated by Hilbert transform showed similar shapes.

Table 5 shows the system damping ratios for both eigenfrequencies in both directions.

**Table 5.** Damping ratios of the first 2 eigenfrequencies.

| Eigenfrequency | Damping Ratio [%] | |
| --- | --- | --- |
| | Vertical Direction | Lateral Direction |
| 1st | 2.25 | 1.93 |
| 2nd | 1.45 | 1.14 |

The calculated damping ratios for the first and second eigenfrequencies in both directions satisfy the specified criteria, as they fall below the maximum allowable damping for which the bridge has been designed.

### 5.4. Eigenmodes

Acceleration is proportional to displacement [49] since a double integration is needed to calculate displacement. Therefore, the mode shapes of the bridge can be pictured by reporting the filtered acceleration for each eigenfrequency.

For the first eigenfrequency, in the vertical direction the three accelerations delineated in blue dots along the bridge length (outlined in white) synchronize, having the same phase at a specific moment with a different altitude. From the reported data of the second eigenfrequency, both accelerometers installed on the quarter edges of the bridge share the same phase, yet the accelerometer mounted on the mid-length of the bridge is shifted by $\pi/2$. The amplitude of the accelerometers indicates the displacement aspect at each sensor location, revealing the two consecutive mode shapes of the bridge (represented in red) in Figures 13 and 14.

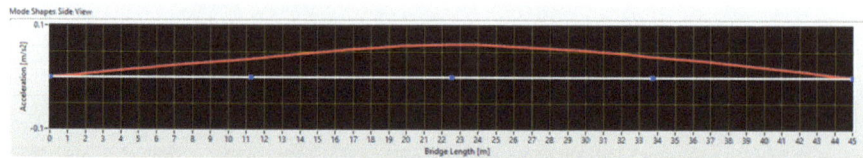

**Figure 13.** Bridge mode shapes in vertical direction for the first eigenfrequency.

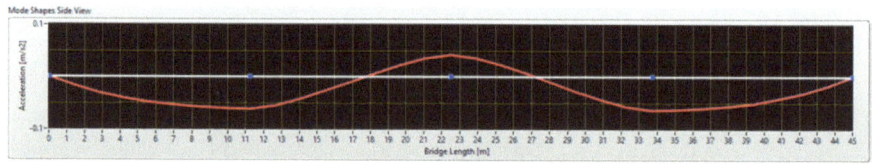

**Figure 14.** Bridge mode shapes in vertical direction for the second eigenfrequency.

Likewise, for the first eigenfrequency in the lateral direction, the three accelerations delineated in blue dots along the bridge length (outlined in white) synchronize, having the same phase at a specific moment with a different altitude. From the reported data of the second eigenfrequency, both accelerometers installed on the quarter edges of the bridge share the same phase, yet the accelerometer mounted on the mid-length of the bridge is shifted by $\pi/2$. The amplitude of the accelerometers indicates the displacement aspect at each sensor location, revealing the two consecutive mode shapes of the bridge (represented in red) in Figures 15 and 16.

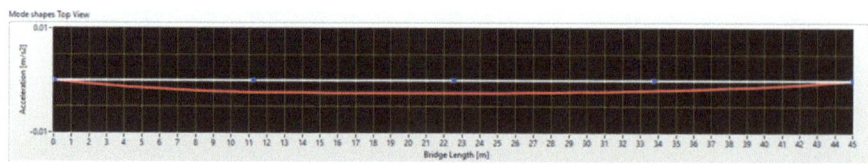

**Figure 15.** Bridge mode shapes in lateral direction for the first eigenfrequency.

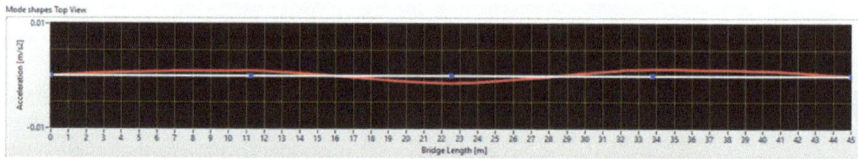

**Figure 16.** Bridge mode shapes in lateral direction for the second eigenfrequency.

In conclusion, it may be said that the analysis of the dynamic behavior of the tested pedestrian bridge after the completion of construction showed three eigenfrequencies of 3.67, 7.62, and 10.22 Hz for the vertical direction. A damping of 2.25% for the first and 1.45% for the second eigenfrequency were found. For the lateral direction, the three detected eigenfrequencies were 6.18, 7.62, and 10.22 Hz. And a damping of 1.93% for the first and 1.14% for the second eigenfrequency were found. For each eigenfrequency, a distinct mode shape was found.

### 5.5. Comfort Level

The second phase referred to finding the comfort levels for one pedestrian and a group of nine people. The activities of pedestrian A (80.9 Kg) and the group of nine pedestrians (791.2 Kg) were recorded when crossing the bridge through a predetermined path for a

2 Hz walk and a 3.67 Hz run and a random walk in both lateral and vertical directions. The comfort feeling was observed in pedestrians for all activities in the lateral and vertical directions. When crossing the bridge at 3.67 Hz, for the activity of one pedestrian, the comfort limits were touching the limit in the vertical direction, as is shown in Figure 17, but they were not surpassed. However, for the lateral direction, the pedestrian did not feel any structural movement causing their discomfort, as shown in Figure 18. Same for the activity of a group of pedestrians, the comfort limits were touching the limit in the vertical direction, as is shown in Figure 19, but they were not surpassed. However, for the lateral direction, the pedestrian did not feel any structural movement causing their discomfort, as shown in Figure 20.

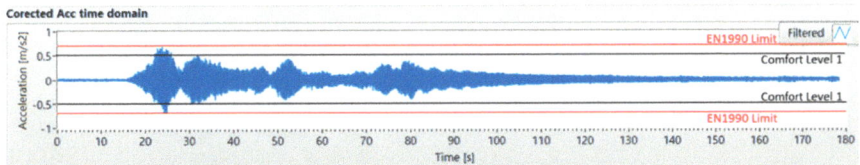

Figure 17. Comfort level for pedestrian A running at 3.67 Hz frequency in vertical direction.

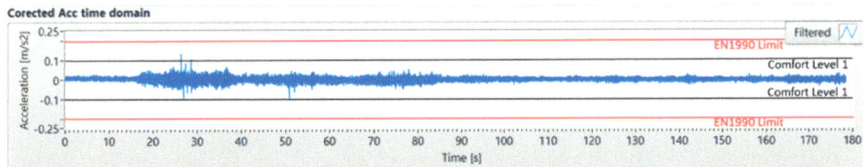

Figure 18. Comfort level for pedestrian A running at 3.67 Hz frequency in lateral direction.

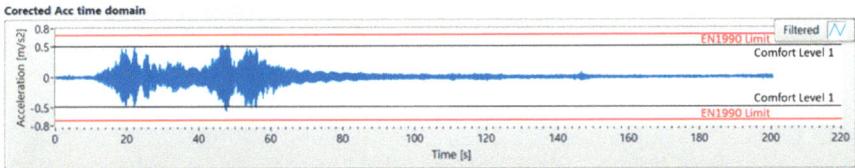

Figure 19. Comfort level of a 9-pedestrian group running at 3.67 Hz frequency in vertical direction.

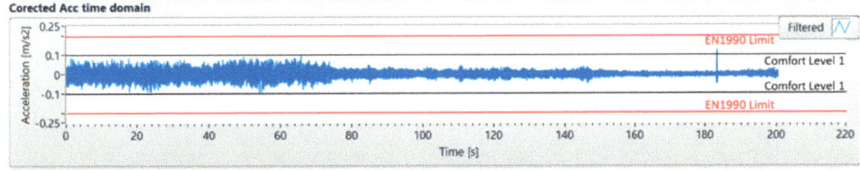

Figure 20. Comfort level of a 9-pedestrian group running at 3.67 Hz frequency in lateral direction.

The comfort standards are outlined in terms of maximum acceleration in EN 1990, A2.4.3.2 [48], and are as follows:
1. For vertical vibrations, 0.7 m/s$^2$.
2. For horizontal vibrations resulting from typical use, 0.2 m/s$^2$.

Comfortability does not have to reduce the bridge safety regulations, since damping calculations indicate and affirm having a safe structure. However, the movement of bridge is due to its capability of absorbing the energy produced by the pedestrian using it.

## 5.6. Spatial Distribution of Maximum Accelerations

A comprehensive investigation of the spatial distribution of peak accelerations along the longitudinal and lateral dimensions of the bridge can be ascertained from the depictions in Figures 21 and 22. These figures illustrate the maximum recorded acceleration values obtained from each sensor (accelerometers A and C at L/2, B at L/4, and D at 3 L/4, where B, C, and D are located at mid-width, and A is located at the cantilever side) during the three different crossings (normal walk at 2 Hz, random walk, and normal run at 3.67 Hz) exerted by pedestrian A and a group consisting of nine pedestrians. It is shown that for the case of pedestrian A, accelerometer C was recording the most intensified response while disturbing the bridge with the three different frequencies in both directions, revealing a symmetric response for sensors at quarter-edges with respect to the sensors at mid-length. Conversely, for the case of the nine pedestrians, it is shown that accelerometers B and D record higher acceleration than accelerometer C, as shown in the results of a random run scenario in the vertical direction. Moreover, the results of only one of the quarter-edge sensors can exceed that of the mid-length, addressing an asymmetric response, as is shown in the result of a random walk scenario in the lateral direction. This is due to unsynchronized footsteps of numerous pedestrians taking more time to adjust their movement with their neighbors while crossing the bridge. Then, the whole crowd readjust their pace to harmonize with the that of the bridge. For both cases of one and nine pedestrians and at any disturbance frequency, accelerometer C always records a higher acceleration intensity than accelerometer A. It is noteworthy that, in the vertical direction, a maximum acceleration of 1.5 m/s$^2$ was reported for both cases of one pedestrian and a crowd.

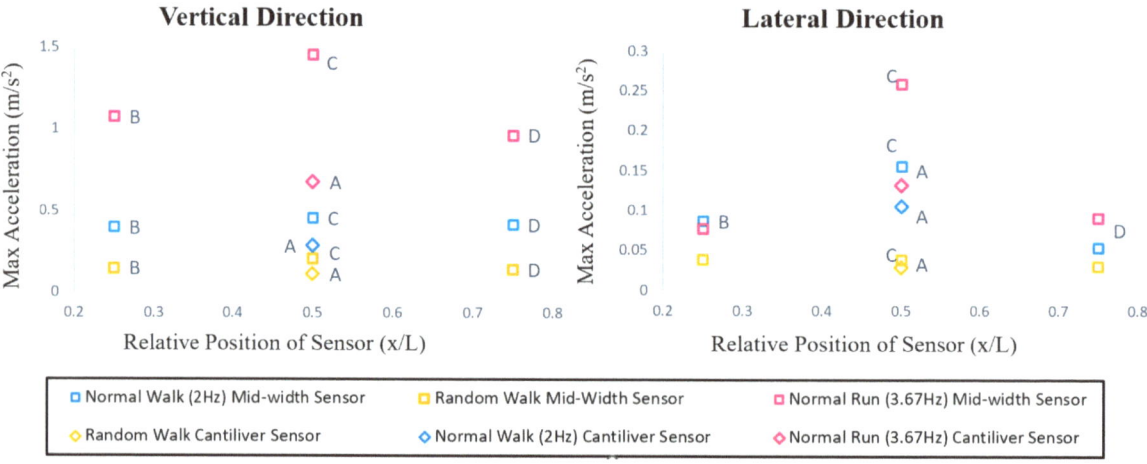

**Figure 21.** Spatial distribution of maximum accelerations as pedestrian A crosses along the bridge length.

## 5.7. Comfort Level Control

The level of comfort is assessed by comparing the maximum recorded accelerations on different crossings with the limits of the regulation and by directly recording the subjective feeling of the test participants.

Table 6 presents the limit values of accelerations as defined by EN 1990–A2 [48], and the SETRA [44] directives based on which level of comfort, in the pedestrian bridge under study, was evaluated.

**Figure 22.** Spatial distribution of maximum accelerations as the 9-pedestrian group crosses along the bridge length.

**Table 6.** Maximum allowable accelerations based on specifications.

| Comfort Level | Degree of Comfort | Acceleration [m/s²] | | | |
|---|---|---|---|---|---|
| | | Vertical Direction | | Lateral Direction | |
| | | EN 1990 | SETRA | EN 1990 | SETRA |
| 1 | Maximum | | <0.5 | | <0.1 |
| 2 | Medium | 0.7 | 0.5–1.0 | 0.2 | 0.1–0.3 |
| 3 | Minimum | | 1.0–2.5 | | 0.3–0.8 |
| 4 | Not acceptable | | >2.5 | | >0.8 |

Figure 23 compares the maximum accelerations recorded by one individual and group pedestrian crossings for each type of walk. The differences in accelerations between people for almost all crossings are evident in both directions. However, there is no apparent ratio between pedestrian weight and deployed acceleration, leading to the conclusion that the amount of acceleration recorded when pedestrians cross depend on other biometric characteristics.

The limit values for accelerations, as defined in the specifications, are also indicated in the same figure. It should be noted that for all passages, the developing accelerations are classified at the maximum comfort level on the basis of specifications in both vertical and lateral directions. The exceptions are the crossings of pedestrian A and the group of nine pedestrians running with a frequency equal to the first vertical frequency of the 3.67 Hz bridge where vertical accelerations are at medium comfort levels.

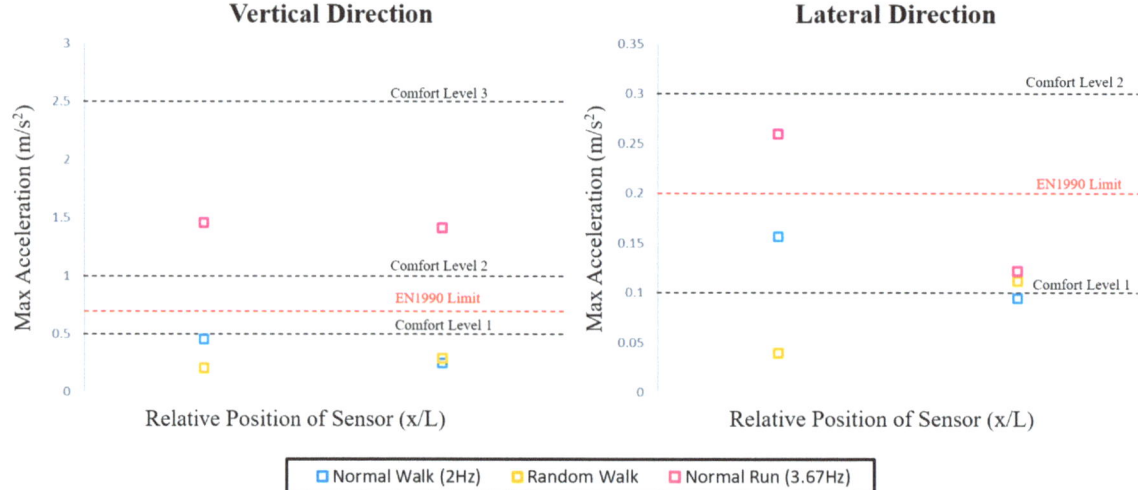

**Figure 23.** Maximum vertical and horizontal accelerations for each type of walking from individual pedestrian and group of 9 pedestrians.

## 6. Conclusions

In conclusion, this paper presented the use of a computer-based data acquisition system and an automated coding software, LabVIEW, for structural health monitoring and system identification of a real-time pedestrian bridge located in Haidari, Greece, after the completion of construction. It calculated its dynamic properties, and characterized its comfort level.

Dynamic properties were found to have three eigenfrequencies of 3.67, 7.62, and 10.22 Hz in the vertical direction, with a damping of 2.25% for the first and 1.45% for the second eigenfrequency. For the lateral direction, the three detected eigenfrequencies were 6.18, 7.62, and 10.22 Hz. And a damping of 1.93% for the first and 1.14% for the second eigenfrequency were found. For each eigenfrequency, a distinct mode shape was found.

As safety was proven, the comfort level was tested as pedestrians crossed according to EN 1990, A.2.4.3.2 [48]. The results demonstrated comfort in crossing the bridge in both directions until a limit of 3.67 Hz running activity was reached, where the bridge absorbed the dissipated energy from the pedestrians by vibrating for seconds to finally restore to its initial posture.

It is concluded that the bridge excitations during pedestrian crossing are within the specifications and do not require the installation of dampers. But it is recommended to avoid malicious use of the bridge.

**Supplementary Materials:** The following supporting information can be downloaded at: https://www.mdpi.com/article/10.3390/buildings13123053/s1.

**Author Contributions:** Conceptualization, R.E.D.; Methodology, R.E.D. and I.V.; Software, R.E.D., X.L. and S.P.; Validation, R.E.D., X.L., I.V. and S.P.; Formal Analysis, R.E.D.; Writing—Original Draft, R.E.D.; Writing—Review and Editing, I.V.; Supervision, I.V. All authors have read and agreed to the published version of the manuscript.

**Funding:** This research received no external funding.

**Data Availability Statement:** The data presented in this study are available in Supplementary Materials.

**Conflicts of Interest:** The authors declare no conflict of interest.

## References

1. Lu, P.; Zhou, Y.; Wu, Y.; Li, D.; Zhou, C. Vibration reduction using tuned mass dampers in composite steel box girder footbridge with self-anchored suspension. *Int. J. Struct. Stab. Dyn.* **2021**, *21*, 2150110. [CrossRef]
2. Caprani, C.C.; Ahmadi, E. Formulation of human–structure interaction system models for vertical vibration. *J. Sound Vib.* **2016**, *377*, 346–367. [CrossRef]
3. Morichika, S.; Sekiya, H.; Zhu, Y.; Hirano, S.; Maruyama, O. Estimation of displacement response in steel plate girder bridge using a single MEMS accelerometer. *IEEE Sens. J.* **2021**, *21*, 8204–8208. [CrossRef]
4. Liu, Y.; Bao, Y. Review of electromagnetic waves-based distance measurement technologies for remote monitoring of civil engineering structures. *Measurement* **2021**, *176*, 109193. [CrossRef]
5. Gao, J.; Li, D.; Feng, Y.; Wan, L.; Wu, G. Application and Research of Health Monitoring System of Xiangshan Port Bridge. In Proceedings of the IOP Conference Series: Earth and Environmental Science, Nanchang, China, 12 April 2021; IOP Publishing: Bristol, UK; Volume 719, p. 032098.
6. Ko, J.M.; Ni, Y.Q. Technology developments in structural health monitoring of large-scale bridges. *Eng. Struct.* **2005**, *27*, 1715–1725. [CrossRef]
7. Li, H.N.; Li, D.S.; Song, G.B. Recent applications of fiber optic sensors to health monitoring in civil engineering. *Eng. Struct.* **2004**, *26*, 1647–1657. [CrossRef]
8. Caicedo, J.M.; Marulanda, J.; Thomson, P.; Dyke, S.J. Monitoring of bridges to detect changes in structural health. In Proceedings of the 2001 American Control Conference, Arlington, VA, USA, 25–27 June 2001; IEEE: Piscataway, NJ, USA; Volume 1 (Cat. No. 01CH37148), pp. 453–458. [CrossRef]
9. Li, Z.X.; Chan, T.H.; Ko, J.M. Fatigue analysis and life prediction of bridges with structural health monitoring data—Part I: Methodology and strategy. *Int. J. Fatigue* **2001**, *23*, 45–53. [CrossRef]
10. Basharat, A.; Catbas, N.; Shah, M. A framework for intelligent sensor network with video camera for structural health monitoring of bridges. In Proceedings of the Third IEEE International Conference on Pervasive Computing and Communications Workshops, Kauai, HI, USA, 8–12 March 2005; IEEE: Piscataway, NJ, USA; pp. 385–389. [CrossRef]
11. Park, K.T.; Kim, S.H.; Park, H.S.; Lee, K.W. The determination of bridge displacement using measured acceleration. *Eng. Struct.* **2005**, *27*, 371–378. [CrossRef]
12. Peeters, B.; Maeck, J.; De Roeck, G. Vibration-based damage detection in civil engineering: Excitation sources and temperature effects. *Smart Mater. Struct.* **2001**, *10*, 518. [CrossRef]
13. Matsuoka, K.; Collina, A.; Somaschini, C.; Sogabe, M. Influence of local deck vibrations on the evaluation of the maximum acceleration of a steel-concrete composite bridge for a high-speed railway. *Eng. Struct.* **2019**, *200*, 109736. [CrossRef]
14. Bačinskas, D.; Kamaitis, Z.; Kilikevičius, A. A sensor instrumentation method for dynamic monitoring of railway bridges. *J. Vibroeng.* **2013**, *15*, 176–184.
15. Brownjohn, J.M.W.; De Stefano, A.; Xu, Y.L.; Wenzel, H.; Aktan, A.E. Vibration-based monitoring of civil infrastructure: Challenges and successes. *J. Civil. Struct. Health Monit.* **2011**, *1*, 79–95. [CrossRef]
16. Xia, H.; Zhang, N.; Gao, R. Experimental analysis of railway bridge under high-speed trains. *J. Sound Vib.* **2005**, *282*, 517–528. [CrossRef]
17. Chaudhari, P.K.; Patel, D.; Patel, V. Theoretical and software-based comparison of cantilever beam: Modal analysis. *Int. J. Innov. Res. Adv. Eng.* **2014**, *1*, 75–79.
18. Xia, Y.; Li, H.; Fan, Z.; Xiao, J. Modal parameter identification based on hilbert vibration decomposition in vibration stability of bridge structures. *Adv. Civ. Eng.* **2021**, *2021*, 6688686. [CrossRef]
19. Pirskawetz, S.M.; Schmidt, S. Detection of wire breaks in prestressed concrete bridges by Acoustic Emission analysis. *Dev. Built Environ.* **2023**, *14*, 100151. [CrossRef]
20. Doebling, S.W.; Farrar, C.R.; Prime, M.B.; Shevitz, D.W. *Damage Identification and Health Monitoring of Structural and Mechanical Systems from Changes in Their Vibration Characteristics: A Literature Review*; USDOE: Washington, DC, USA, 1996. [CrossRef]
21. Gentile, C.; Saisi, A. Ambient vibration testing of historic masonry towers for structural identification and damage assessment. *Constr. Build. Mater.* **2007**, *21*, 1311–1321. [CrossRef]
22. Gentile, C.; Saisi, A.; Cabboi, A. Structural identification of a masonry tower based on operational modal analysis. *Int. J. Archit. Herit.* **2015**, *9*, 98–110. [CrossRef]
23. Foti, D. Non-destructive techniques and monitoring for the evolutive damage detection of an ancient masonry structure. *Key Eng. Mater.* **2015**, *628*, 168–177. [CrossRef]
24. Lacanna, G.; Ripepe, M.; Coli, M.; Genco, R.; Marchetti, E. Full structural dynamic response from ambient vibration of Giotto's bell tower in Firenze (Italy), using modal analysis and seismic interferometry. *NDT E Int.* **2019**, *102*, 9–15. [CrossRef]
25. Bayraktar, A.; Türker, T.; Altunişik, A.C. Experimental frequencies and damping ratios for historical masonry arch bridges. *Constr. Build. Mater.* **2015**, *75*, 234–241. [CrossRef]
26. González, A.; Feng, K.; Casero, M. Effective separation of vehicle, road and bridge information from drive-by acceleration data via the power spectral density resulting from crossings at various speeds. *Dev. Built Environ.* **2023**, *14*, 100162. [CrossRef]
27. Zäll, E.; Andersson, A.; Ülker-Kaustell, M.; Karoumi, R. An efficient approach for considering the effect of human-structure interaction on footbridges. *Procedia Eng.* **2017**, *199*, 2913–2918. [CrossRef]

28. Živanović, S. Modelling human actions on lightweight structures: Experimental and numerical developments. In Proceedings of the MATEC Web of Conferences, Dübendorf (Zürich), Switzerland, 19–21 October 2015; EDP Sciences: Les Ulis, France; Volume 24. [CrossRef]
29. Dallard, P.; Fitzpatrick, T.; Flint, A.; Low, A.; Smith, R.R.; Willford, M.; Roche, M. London Millennium Bridge: Pedestrian-induced lateral vibration. *J. Bridge Eng.* **2001**, *6*, 412–417. [CrossRef]
30. Willford, M. Solving the vibration problems of the London Millennium footbridge. In *Schwingungen in der Baupraxis: 12*; Dresdner Baustatik-Seminar: Dresden, Germany, 2008; pp. 157–179.
31. Wieczorek, N.; Gerasch, W.J.; Rolfes, R.; Kammerer, H. Semiactive friction damper for lightweight pedestrian bridges. *J. Struct. Eng.* **2014**, *140*, 04013102. [CrossRef]
32. Jones, R.T.; Pretlove, A.J. Two case studies in the use of tuned vibration absorbers on foot bridges. *Struct. Engineer. Part B* **1981**, *59*, 27–32. Available online: http://worldcat.org/issn/00392553 (accessed on 16 September 2023).
33. Caetano, E.; Cunha, Á.; Magalhães, F.; Moutinho, C. Studies for controlling human-induced vibration of the Pedro e Inês footbridge, Portugal. Part 1: Assessment of dynamic behaviour. *Eng. Struct.* **2010**, *32*, 1069–1081. [CrossRef]
34. Caetano, E.; Cunha, Á.; Moutinho, C.; Magalhães, F. Studies for controlling human-induced vibration of the Pedro e Inês footbridge, Portugal. Part 2: Implementation of tuned mass dampers. *Eng. Struct.* **2010**, *32*, 1082–1091. [CrossRef]
35. Tubino, F.; Carassale, L.; Piccardo, G. Human-induced vibrations on two lively footbridges in Milan. *J. Bridge Eng.* **2016**, *21*, C4015002. [CrossRef]
36. Feng, P.; Wang, Z.; Jin, F.; Zhu, S. Vibration serviceability assessment of pedestrian bridges based on comfort level. *J. Perform. Constr. Facil.* **2019**, *33*, 04019046. [CrossRef]
37. Wright, D.T.; Green, R. *Human Sensitivity to Vibration*; No. 7; Queen's University: Kingston, ON, Canada, 1959.
38. Smith, J.W. *Vibration of Structures: Applications in Civil Engineering Design*; Chapman & Hall: New York, NY, USA, 1988.
39. Wheeler, J.E. Prediction and control of pedestrian-induced vibration in footbridges. *J. Struct. Div.* **1982**, *108*, 2045–2065. [CrossRef]
40. Dey, P.; Narasimhan, S.; Walbridge, S. Evaluation of design guidelines for the serviceability assessment of aluminum pedestrian bridges. *J. Bridge Eng.* **2017**, *22*, 04016109. [CrossRef]
41. Anon, B. *SS ISO 2631(1)*; Mechanical Vibration and Shock-Evaluation of HUMAN Exposure to Whole-Body Vibration. International Organization for Standardization: Geneva, Switzerland, 1997.
42. Wang, W.; Yan, W.; Deng, L.; Kang, H. Dynamic analysis of a cable-stayed concrete-filled steel tube arch bridge under vehicle loading. *J. Bridge Eng.* **2015**, *20*, 04014082. [CrossRef]
43. Feldman, M. *HiVOSS—Human-Induced Vibrations of Steel Structures-Design of Footbridges: Guideline*; Office for Official Publications of the European Communities: Luxembourg, 2008. Available online: http://www.stb.rwth-aachen.de/projekte/2007/HIVOSS/download.php.ISO (accessed on 20 April 2023).
44. *Sétra—Service D'études sur les Transports, les Routes et Leurs Aménagements*; Assessment of Vibrational Behaviour of Footbridges under Pedestrian Loading; Technical Guide; Sétra: Paris, France, 2006. Available online: https://www.academia.edu/40689257/S%25C3%25A9tra_Footbridges_Assessment_of_vibrational_behaviour_of_footbridges_under_pedestrian_loading (accessed on 20 April 2023).
45. Van Nimmen, K.; Lombaert, G.; De Roeck, G.; Van den Broeck, P. Vibration serviceability of footbridges: Evaluation of the current codes of practice. *Eng. Struct.* **2014**, *59*, 448–461. [CrossRef]
46. El Dahr, R.; Lignos, X.; Papavieros, S.; Vayas, I. Design and Validation of an Accurate Low-Cost Data Acquisition System for Structural Health Monitoring of a Pedestrian Bridge. *J. Civ. Eng. Constr.* **2022**, *11*, 113–126. [CrossRef]
47. El Dahr, R.; Lignos, X.; Papavieros, S.; Vayas, I. Development and Validation of a LabVIEW Automated Software System for Displacement and Dynamic Modal Parameters Analysis Purposes. *Modelling* **2023**, *4*, 189–210. [CrossRef]
48. EN 1990 (English): Eurocode—Basis of Structural Design; Authority: The European Union Per Regulation 305/2011, Directive 98/34/EC, Directive 2004/18/EC. 2002. Available online: https://www.phd.eng.br/wp-content/uploads/2015/12/en.1990.2002.pdf (accessed on 20 April 2023).
49. Hinrichsen, P.F. Acceleration, velocity, and displacement for magnetically damped oscillations. *Phys. Teach.* **2019**, *57*, 250–253. [CrossRef]

**Disclaimer/Publisher's Note:** The statements, opinions and data contained in all publications are solely those of the individual author(s) and contributor(s) and not of MDPI and/or the editor(s). MDPI and/or the editor(s) disclaim responsibility for any injury to people or property resulting from any ideas, methods, instructions or products referred to in the content.

Article

# Temporary Structural Health Monitoring of Historical Széchenyi Chain Bridge

Balázs Kövesdi *, Dénes Kollár and László Dunai

Department of Structural Engineering, Faculty of Civil Engineering, Budapest University of Technology and Economics, Műegyetem rkp. 3, 1111 Budapest, Hungary; kollar.denes@emk.bme.hu (D.K.); dunai.laszlo@emk.bme.hu (L.D.)
* Correspondence: kovesdi.balazs@emk.bme.hu; Tel.: +36-1-463-1726; Fax: +36-1-463-1784

**Abstract:** A temporary monitoring system was installed on the 175-year-old historical Széchenyi Chain Bridge during its reconstruction. The bridge is in the downtown area in the capital city of Hungary and plays a significant role in the city life of Budapest. Six-month-long measurements were conducted during the reconstruction process of the bridge, yielding crucial insights into the structural behaviour of the historical structure. The measurement results were evaluated; the findings encompass the rotation capacity of the pins between the chain elements and the structural response to temperature changes. This information helped the decision-making between 2021 and 2023 by the designers and construction company during the reconstruction. For instance, daily temperature fluctuations resulted in increased bending moments in the chain elements, rising up to 158% compared to the values observed during a proof load test in 2018. Furthermore, the measurements reveal an approximate 42% increase in normal forces compared to the proof load test, which highlights the high sensitivity of chain bridges to temperature fluctuations, where geometric stiffness plays a crucial role. Reconstruction, namely reducing self-weight, notably intensifies the impact on normal forces and bending moments. These outcomes strongly emphasize the dominance of the dead load and self-weight in the case of chain bridges.

**Keywords:** structural health monitoring; historical structures; measurement; chain bridge

**Citation:** Kövesdi, B.; Kollár, D.; Dunai, L. Temporary Structural Health Monitoring of Historical Széchenyi Chain Bridge. *Buildings* **2024**, *14*, 535. https://doi.org/10.3390/buildings14020535

Academic Editors: Shaohong Cheng and Haijun Zhou

Received: 8 January 2024
Revised: 2 February 2024
Accepted: 5 February 2024
Published: 17 February 2024

**Copyright:** © 2024 by the authors. Licensee MDPI, Basel, Switzerland. This article is an open access article distributed under the terms and conditions of the Creative Commons Attribution (CC BY) license (https://creativecommons.org/licenses/by/4.0/).

## 1. Introduction

The historical Széchenyi Chain Bridge is a 175-year-old structure in Budapest, Hungary, which has a vital role in the life of the city. The road bridge spanning the Danube River sees substantial daily vehicular traffic, serving as a major link between Buda and Pest. Its construction began in 1839 and was finished in 1849. It was renowned as the most extensive chain bridge of its era, featuring a maximum mid-span of 202.60 m (Figure 1). Currently, only the Hercílio Luz Bridge in Brazil (339 m) and the Clifton Suspension Bridge in England (214 m) surpass it in terms of span.

Subsequently, the bridge has undergone several renovations. The original bridge was the first permanent bridge in the capital city of Hungary; it operated until 1913. The original structure lacked a stiffening girder, and a lightweight timber deck system was used, resulting in noticeable bridge deck vibrations. Therefore, a new supporting structure was designed, incorporating twenty-five carbon steel chain bars between each node. It resulted in doubling the length of the chain bars and an increased load-bearing capacity compared to the previous structure; thus, the distance between the pins and the suspension bars increased from 1.8 m to 3.6 m. The total mass of the ironwork increased to 5200 tonnes following the introduction of a new truss stiffening girder made of carbon steel, with the ultimate strength ranging between 480 and 560 MPa. Additionally, a reinforced concrete deck was also installed on the superstructure (Figure 2a). The bridge was destroyed in 1945 during World War II. Nevertheless, it was rebuilt without any significant changes to the structural system, and it was re-opened for traffic in 1949.

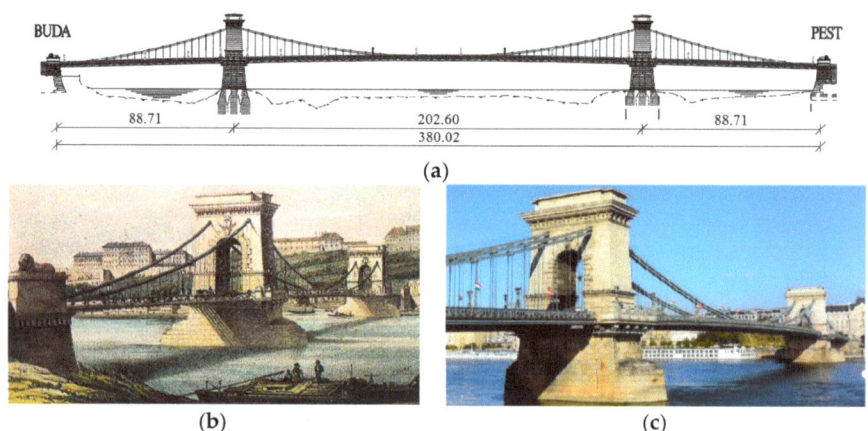

**Figure 1.** Széchenyi Chain Bridge located in Budapest, Hungary. (**a**) Side view of Széchenyi Chain Bridge with the main dimensions (m). (**b**) Original bridge built between 1839 and 1849. (**c**) Novel structure built between 1913 and 1915.

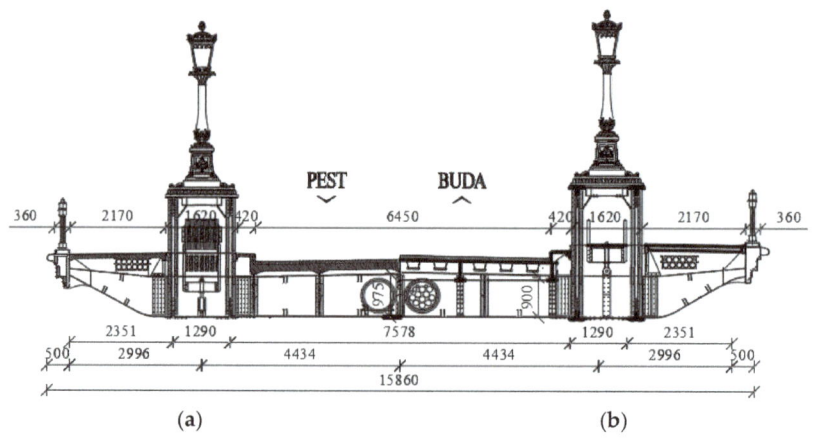

**Figure 2.** Cross section of the bridge (**a**) before and (**b**) after its renewal in 2021–2023, with the main dimensions (mm).

The Budapest University of Technology and Economics, Department of Structural Engineering, conducted extensive investigations focused on the Széchenyi Chain Bridge. Proof load tests of the bridge were performed in 2002 and 2018 to analyse the rotational capacity of the pins of the chain elements. Fixed or partly stuck pins, due to corrosion, cause bending moments within the chain system and, thus, alter the structural behaviour of the bridge. From 1949 to 2021, no significant maintenance or reconstruction work was made on the structure (except for small forms of corrosion protection), despite the chain elements reaching a lifetime of 100 years and the deck system being more than 70 years old. Historical failures of similar bridges underscored the need for a comprehensive assessment. A significant chain bridge failure occurred in the USA in 1967, claiming the lives of 46 individuals [1]. The collapse of the Silver Bridge stemmed from the failure of a single chain element due to a stress corrosion crack resulting in fatigue and eventually a fracture, leading to the complete breakdown of the entire chain system. Consequently, assessing the structural condition of structural elements became a crucial aspect of the historical bridge since it is essential for determining its load-bearing capacity and remaining lifetime. In 2019, noticeable corrosion problems were detected within the deck system, prompting the execution of an in-depth reliability analysis [2] to evaluate the risk of failure of the deck system until reconstruction commenced. On-site corrosion measurements were conducted, leading to the development of a Monte Carlo simulation-based stochastic reliability assessment method with a confidence level corresponding to a 1-year lifetime. The approach employed an advanced finite element model-based resistance calculation (GMNI analysis) alongside a state-of-the-art corrosion model. Based on the numerical simulation results, the bridge deck could have been verified only by a reduction in loading to keep the bridge in operation for one additional year. It was also concluded that the renovation of the historical structure could not be avoided and delayed any longer. During the latest reconstruction phase between 2021 and 2023, the bridge underwent substantial renewal. The aging deck system was substituted with an orthotropic steel deck (Figure 2b). However, the chain elements, steel stiffening girder, and cross-girder system remained unaltered, solely receiving corrosion protection enhancements. Simultaneously, the material loss of the chain bars due to corrosion was estimated by measurements during the reconstruction since it can cause reduced tensile resistance, leading to inappropriate ultimate resistance. Coupled with decreased pin rotational capability, deteriorating chain bars can reduce structural integrity.

The current paper primarily showcases findings from a six-month-long temporary monitoring measurement conducted during the reconstruction process. The evaluated data provide a pivotal understanding of the structural behaviour of the historical structure, including the pin rotational capacity and structural response due to temperature differences. These insights significantly influenced the decisions made by designers and the construction company during the bridge reconstruction. On the other hand, the importance of temporary structural health monitoring is highlighted in the paper as well. The strategy for analysing the structural behaviour of the Széchenyi Chain Bridge and predicting its structural integrity and the performance of the chain elements is the following:

- Evaluating the measurement results of a proof load test, which was carried out in 2018, to conclude whether fixed or partly fixed pins would start rotating due to a live load on the bridge;
- Assessing the temporary measurement results during reconstruction to conclude whether pins would start rotating due to reducing self-weight (dead load), which is mostly dominant for chain bridges.

## 2. Literature Review

The literature review introduces previously published results regarding structural health monitoring (SHM) systems related to bridges. Therefore, the findings presented in this paper can be readily introduced and differentiated.

SHM has been extensively applied across engineering sectors and remains a focal point in structural engineering research. The processing of periodically sampled real-time data in SHM facilitates early defect detection to support decision making on repairs, retrofitting, maintenance strategies, and accurate remaining-life predictions by integrating diverse sensing technologies. Overall, the operational safety of the monitored structures can be upheld. The cost of monitoring and repairs typically outweighs the expenses of a new construction, pressuring authorities to prolong structures' lifespans while ensuring public safety. SHM potentially reduces costs by replacing scheduled maintenance with as-needed maintenance. Integrating SHM even during the design phase of new structures offers opportunities for reduced life-cycle expenses [3,4].

Long-term monitoring systems are currently in operation on bridges; the structural health monitoring of bridges has developed since the early 1990s. Utilizing in situ field experimental techniques aids in comprehending the behaviour and performance of actual, full-scale bridges subject to real loading and environmental conditions. It serves to verify the safety, serviceability, durability, and sustainability of bridges. For instance, Li and Ou [5] and Hovhanessian [6] have already recommended design approaches for SHM systems for bridges.

The characteristics of structures (e.g., modal parameters [7,8]) are influenced by the natural environment (wind, temperature, etc.). Wind is one of the critical loads for long-span cable-stayed bridges and can cause vortex-induced vibrations of decks and cables and rain-wind-induced vibrations of cables. Anemoscopes are widely applied to measure wind velocity. Thermocouples or optical fibre Bragg grating (FBG) temperature sensors are frequently used to measure the temperature of bridges. Degrauwe et al. [9] examined the influence of temperature and its measurement error on natural vibration frequencies. Furthermore, Li et al. [10] applied a nonlinear principle component analysis (NPCA) to remove the influence of temperature and wind. Strain is one of the most important variables for the safety evaluation, fatigue assessment, and validation of models. Strain can be measured using, e.g., a traditional strain gauge, a vibrating-wire strain gauge, or FBG strain sensors [11–13]. Okasha and Frangopol [14] presented a performance-based life-cycle bridge management framework with the integration of SHM, which can be used for the safety evaluation of different types of bridges. Li et al. [15–18] presented a framework for the safety evaluation of bridges based on load-induced or environment-induced strains and deformations. Various new sensing technologies have been developed in the last two decades. Optical fibre and wireless sensing technologies have shown great potential and have been widely used in many SHM systems for bridges [19]. Nevertheless, the application of artificial intelligence is also emerging for evaluating measurement results [3,20].

SHM systems are not only installed on relatively new structures; historical, aging bridges are also involved [21,22]. However, the application of an SHM system during the reconstruction of a historical bridge has not been published yet, according to the authors' knowledge. This is a new application for evaluating structural behaviour using a temporary system and assessing continuous six-month-long measurement data.

## 3. Proof Load Test

### 3.1. Configuration and Measurement Locations

The purpose of the proof load test is to determine the rotation capacity of the pins connecting the chain links based on the determination of the normal stresses resulting from the normal forces and bending moments in the chains by using strain gauges. Based on static calculations using the finite element method, it was found that significant bending in the chain elements can only be generated in the first elements near the pylons (P1–P4) and in the structural bearings at the abutments (H1–H4). Therefore, these areas near the directional changes of the chain system are the focus of the current measurements. For the left pylon, three measurement locations are installed for a detailed analysis, while for the right pylon, only one location is used as a reference. A total of eight different measurement locations are selected, and the global layout is shown in Figure 3. The selection of the measurement locations followed the conditions of the bridge, taking into account the limitations (max. possible channel number) of the measurement system. A total of eight strain gauges are placed on chain elements at each measurement point (notations are shown in Figure 4). Four strain gauges are placed at each measurement location on the extreme fibres of the chain elements. The strain gauges denoted by Hx/1–Hx/8 are placed on the eyebars around the abutment, where the chains have knickpoints. The strain gauges marked by Px/1–Px/8 are placed on the eyebars around the pylons near the breaking point of the chain system (x = 1...4 for the pylon and the abutment). In each analysed cross-section, two strain gauges are placed at the upper and two at the lower extreme fibres to be able to determine the normal force and the in-plane bending moment changes during loading.

Strain measurement is performed using a laptop-controlled HBM MGCplus data acquisition system and HBM CANhead amplifiers. The CANhead amplifiers are connected by high-performance CanBus cables, which transmit the measurement signals via the data acquisition system to a laptop. Uniaxial strain gauges with a nominal resistance of 350 Ω are applied for the short-term measurements. During the static proof load test, continuous measurements are taken for each load case at a sampling rate of 2 Hz. The strain gauges are placed on the structure loaded by self-weight so that the monitoring measurements show the strain changes during the measurement period. The applied strain gauges were temperature-compensated strain gauges made to be installed in steel structures.

**Figure 3.** Measurement locations for proof load test executed in 2018.

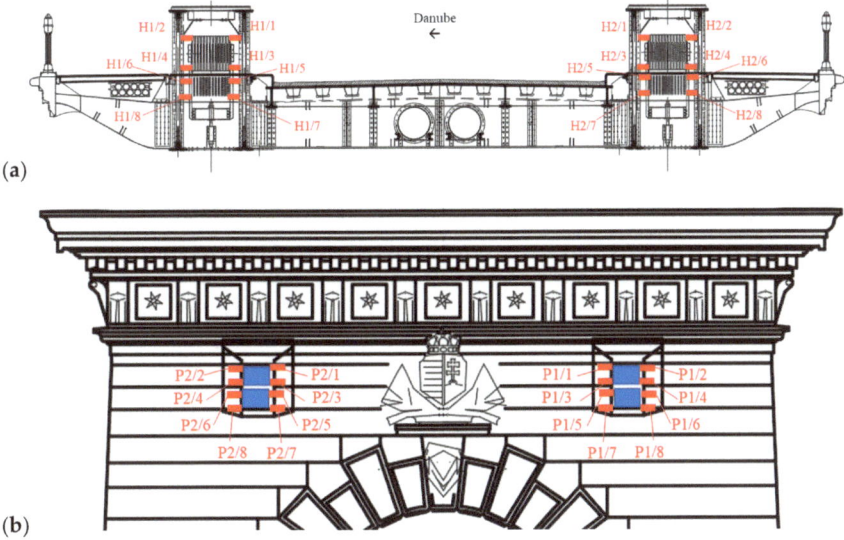

**Figure 4.** Notation of strain gauges (i = 1…8) for proof load test in 2018: (**a**) Hx/i: strain gauges at abutment and (**b**) Px/i: strain gauges at pylon (x = 1…4).

### 3.2. Load Cases

The bridge was loaded with 12 four-axle trucks with an average weight of ~20 t. A total of 13 load cases were examined (load cases with trucks on the inflow side are shown in Figure 5), including unloaded load cases, to determine the effect of temperature change, $\Delta T$, in a several-hour-long proof load test and the possible deterioration of the structure between different loading situations (i.e., to detect plastic strain, if any). The applied load cases were the following:

1. Unloaded bridge;
2. Three trucks in one lane in the middle span of the inflow side;
3. Six trucks in one lane in the middle span of the inflow side;
4. Nine trucks in one lane in the middle span of the inflow side;
5. Twelve trucks in one lane in the middle span of the inflow side;
6. Unloaded bridge (evaluating the effect of $\Delta T$);
7. Six trucks in the middle span of the outflow side;
8. Twelve trucks in the middle span of the outflow side.
9. Unloaded bridge (evaluating the effect of $\Delta T$);

10. Ten trucks, five in each side span, on the inflow side;
11. Unloaded bridge (evaluating the effect of $\Delta T$);
12. Ten trucks, five on each side span, on the outflow side;
13. Unloaded bridge (evaluating the effect of $\Delta T$).

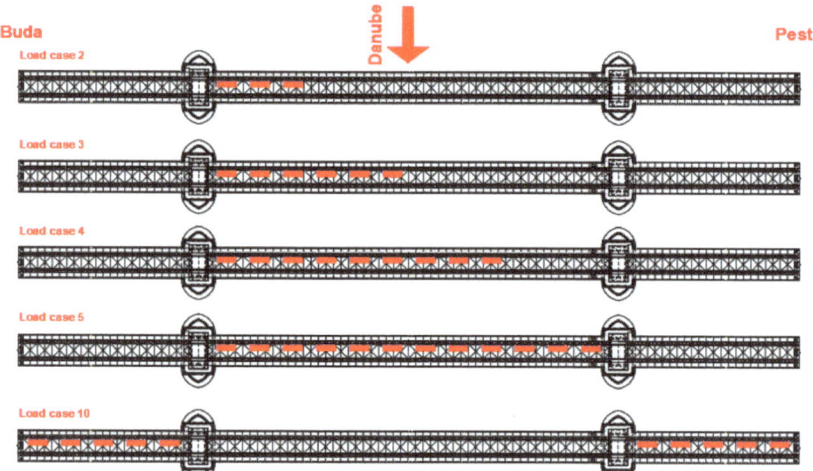

**Figure 5.** Examples of analysed load cases for proof load test in 2018 (trucks are denoted by red rectangles, while flow direction is shown by a red arrow).

### 3.3. Measurement Results

The axial strains due to the vehicle load are determined for all the load cases. Since the strain gauges are installed on the extreme fibres, normal forces and bending moments could be determined and separated by averaging ($\varepsilon_{mean}$) and deriving the average difference between the top and bottom fibres ($\Delta \varepsilon$), respectively. The normal forces are then determined by using $N = \varepsilon_{mean} \times EA$, where $E = 210$ MPa is the Young's modulus and $A = 1274$ cm$^2$ is the cross-sectional area. The bending moments are calculated by $M = 0.5 \Delta \varepsilon \times EW$, where $W = 7749$ cm$^3$ is the elastic cross-sectional modulus. The derived changes in normal forces, $\Delta N$, and bending moments, $\Delta M$, are plotted in Figures 6–8 for the measurement locations at the abutment and pylon.

The peak normal forces at the Pest abutment (Figure 6) ranged between 907 and 972 kN, while on the Buda side, they varied between 927 and 1019 kN. In the side span (Figure 7), the normal force in the chain elements at the pylons varied from 1040 to 1200 kN, with a maximum of 1482 kN (Figure 8) in the mid-span (for comparison purposes, the maximum normal force in the chain elements coming from self-weight is ~11,300 kN). The measurements reveal a significant disparity between the variation in normal forces recorded in the side spans and mid-span, surpassing the variation expected from the change in the chain element direction alone. Consequently, these findings suggest that the structural bearings at the top of the pylons can withstand a portion of the horizontal forces exerted by the applied load.

The measurements reveal significant variations in the maximum bending moment at the abutments, ranging from 248 to 320 kNm for load cases 5 and 8, respectively, and from $-142$ to $-198$ kNm for load cases 10 and 12. Similarly, the maximum bending moment variation in the chain elements near the pylon, specifically at measurement points P1, P2, and P4, oscillated between 107 and 141 kNm for load cases 5 and 8 and $-141$ to $-147$ kNm for load positions 10 and 12. Notably, at the measurement location P3, the pin connection shifted following an approximate 230 kNm bending moment change, resulting in decreased bending. Hence, the measurements indicate that among the eight tested pins, only one displayed the ability to rotate under the applied live load. This observation suggests that the applied live load was insufficient to surpass the friction between the chain elements for the remaining pins, which might be notably increased due to corrosion.

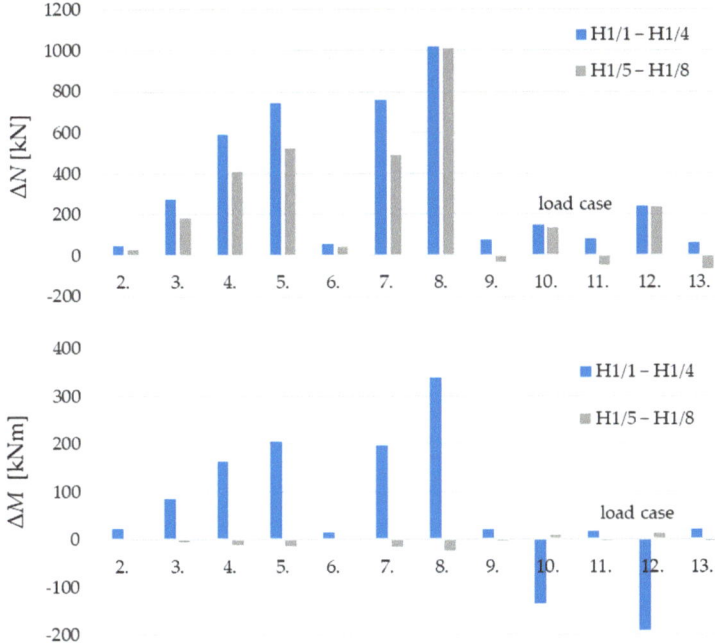

**Figure 6.** Derived measurement results at the abutment for proof load test in 2018.

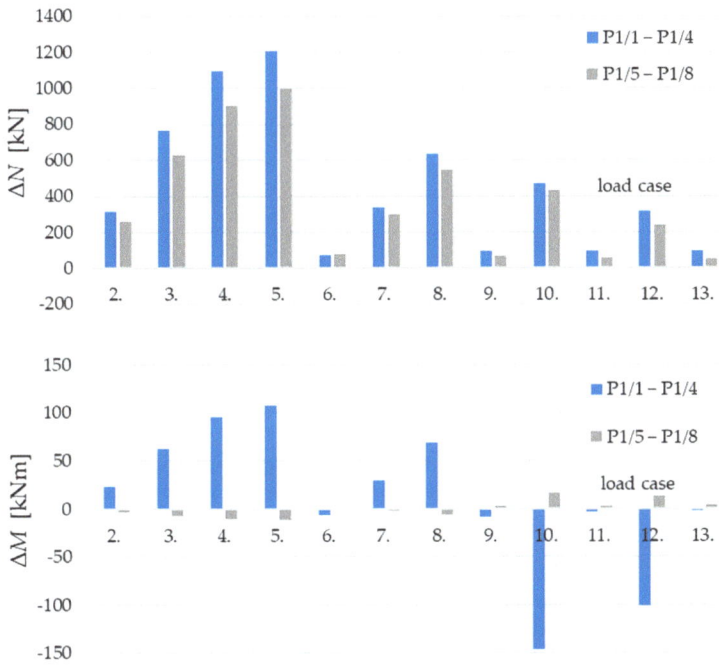

**Figure 7.** Derived measurement results at the pylon (side span) for proof load test in 2018.

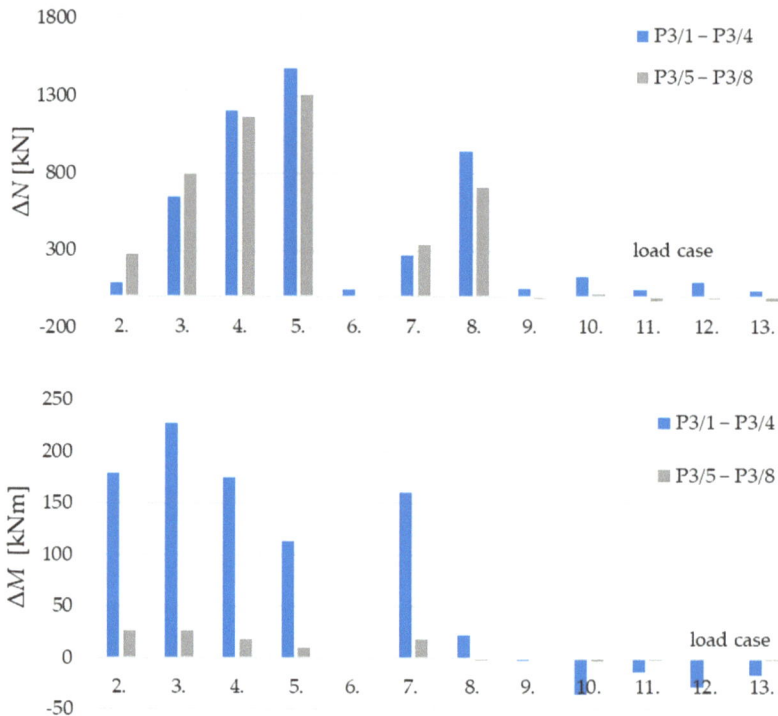

**Figure 8.** Derived measurement results at the pylon (main span) for proof load test in 2018.

Consequently, further measurements were planned to be made during the reconstruction process of the bridge, anticipating larger internal force changes attributed to the alteration in the self-weight of the bridge. These measurements were executed by using a temporary monitoring system.

## 4. Temporary Monitoring System

### 4.1. Configuration and Measurement Locations

The temporary measurement system consists of 80 strain gauges, which were installed on chain elements on both the inflow and outflow sides in order to measure the elongation variation and track the structural behaviour during reconstruction. The data obtained from the measurement system also provide information on the changes in the elongation of the structure due to non-reconstruction loads (e.g., due to temperature changes or other meteorological effects), which can be used to better understand the behaviour of the structure. In addition, the temperatures of the air and the steel structure are recorded as well. Continuously processed data, i.e., 24/7 data acquisition, made it possible to determine intra-day, weekly, and monthly measurement trends and changes between individual reconstruction stages.

The purpose of the measurement is to assess the stress induced on the chain elements under varying loads to infer the rotational capacity of the pins. Eight different locations along the chains are measured. Four measurement sites (H1–H4) are positioned at the bridge abutments on both the inflow and outflow sides, while four other sites (P1–P4) are established at the pylon on the Buda side, similarly to the proof load test, as shown in Figures 3 and 4. Each location undergoes measurements on both the lower and upper chain elements. At the abutments (measurement sites H1–H4), strain gauges are placed at the end of the parallel part of the chain elements (located at 100 mm from the rounding of the pin head in the axial direction, near the directional change at the structural bearing).

Strain gauges are installed on both sides of the chain bars, 20 mm from the lower and upper edges. Accordingly, a total of four strain gauges are used per measurement location at the abutments. This approach allows for the independent determination and comparison of changes in bending moments and normal forces within the chains. The same considerations are made for the strain gauges at the pylon (measurement sites P1–P4), except that additional sensors are installed at the neutral axis of the chain elements. Thus, six sensors are used per measurement location at the pylon, as shown in Figure 9.

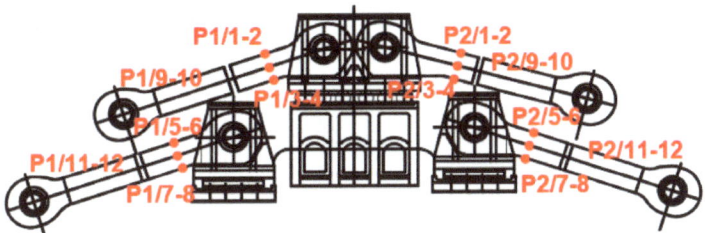

**Figure 9.** Position of strain gauges at the pylon—temporary monitoring system.

HBM PMX data acquisition systems are used for accurate, reliable, and flexible measurements, which are ideally suited to processing large data volumes for long-term multi-channel applications. Temperature-compensated biaxial strain gauges with a nominal resistance of 350 Ω were installed. Measurement and data logging are controlled using CatmanEasy v4.5, the software by HBM. A sampling rate of 1 Hz is applied during data acquisition.

*4.2. Reconstruction Stages*

A detailed organisation plan for the current reconstruction was drawn up. This paper does not describe the entire construction process, but only the stages that are relevant for the measurement evaluation, which are the following:

1. The crane runway is built on the superstructure (15 July 2021);
2. Suspended scaffolding is installed, while the reinforced concrete slab is demolished in the main span (1 August 2021);
3. Old steel stingers are dismantled in the main span, a new orthotropic deck is installed on half of the main span, and suspended scaffolding is installed in the side spans (3 November 2021);
4. The old concrete slab and steel stringers are dismantled from the entire bridge, the new orthotropic deck is installed between the pylons, the sidewalks in the main span are dismantled, and the suspended scaffolding is dismantled (3 January 2022).

For illustration purposes, Figure 10 shows the superstructure of the bridge between Phases 3 and 4. The suspended scaffolding was installed in the side spans, and the old deck system (concrete slab and steel stringers) had already been demolished. From a static point of view, this erection phase gave rise to a dominant loading situation. Thus, the maximum load was applied in the middle span, and the minimum in the side spans. It was expected that this erection phase could make the hinges rotate.

*4.3. Measurement Results*

The strain gauge results are presented in a segmented manner. Firstly, longer-term data series are presented, which aim to offer an overview of the daily cyclical elongation variations triggered by temperature changes and the major construction phases. Initially, observations from measurement site P1, at the pylon, are synthesized. Figure 11a,b showcase the results from strain gauges P1/1–P1/4 (upper chain) and P1/5–P1/8 (lower chain). These graphs highlight substantial intra-day temperature-induced fluctuations, recording a difference of 100–120 μm/m (21–25.2 MPa) between the lower and upper extreme fibres due to temperature shifts, resulting in additional stress on the structure. Meanwhile, Figure 11c illustrates the strain changes of sensors P1/9–P1/12 along the neutral axis. A more notable change is noted from late November to early December 2021, primarily attributable to construction activities involving the construction stages of the deck plate between the pylons and the demolition of the reinforced concrete deck plate and steel stringers in the side spans. The strain gauges located near the upper extreme fibres (P1/1–P1/2 and P1/5–P1/6) experience increased tension, while those near the lower extreme fibres (P1/3–P1/4 and P1/7–P1/8) undergo higher compression. Along the neutral axis (Figure 11c), all sensors indicate a slight increase in tension starting in early December 2021.

**Figure 10.** Superstructure with suspended scaffolding after demolishing old concrete deck.

By averaging and subtracting the measured values from the respective strain gauges, the strain change curves are derived, depicting the effect of normal force, $\Delta\varepsilon_N$, and bending moment changes, $\Delta\varepsilon_M$ (Figure 12). It is evident that the normal forces undergo minimal change, while the bending moment increases significantly in both the upper and lower chains. The measurement charts display continuity, apart from minor fluctuations within a day, suggesting no movement in the chain links during this timeframe.

The evaluation of the measurement results at the test sites also includes separate Sundays (Figure 13), when no construction work occurred, enabling the analysis of solely meteorological influences, primarily temperature changes. On 27 June 2021, variations of 110–125 µm/m were observed in the daily strain near the upper extreme fibre of P1/1 and P1/2 (inflow side, upper chain, Buda side). Correspondingly, lower values, in the range of 80–100 µm/m and 60–65 µm/m, were recorded on 4 July and 11 July 2021, respectively, mainly at P1/2 (south side of the chain). The recorded air temperatures in Budapest ranged from 19 to 31 °C on these days, with a temperature fluctuation of 11–12 °C, although no significant changes in the structural behaviour occurred during this period. The effect of daily temperature fluctuations (heating and cooling) is clearly visible in the measurement results. The variations caused by daily temperature changes are comparable to the strains observed during the proof load test. The maximum measured daily variation in the strain, normal force, and bending moment for the pylon sites are shown in Table 1. In the upper chain elements, the maximum change is 125 µm/m, while it is 140 µm/m for the lower ones in the extreme fibres. In the neutral fibre, the magnitude of the maximum strain variation is 80 µm/m. The results show a quasi-linear strain pattern within the sections. Notably, for sensor sets P1 and P3, larger strains (tension) are observed in the upper fibres compared to the lower ones. Conversely, an inverse pattern is observed for sensor sets P2 and P4. This trend illustrates a linear increase towards the top extreme fibres, influenced by additional moments in the chain links.

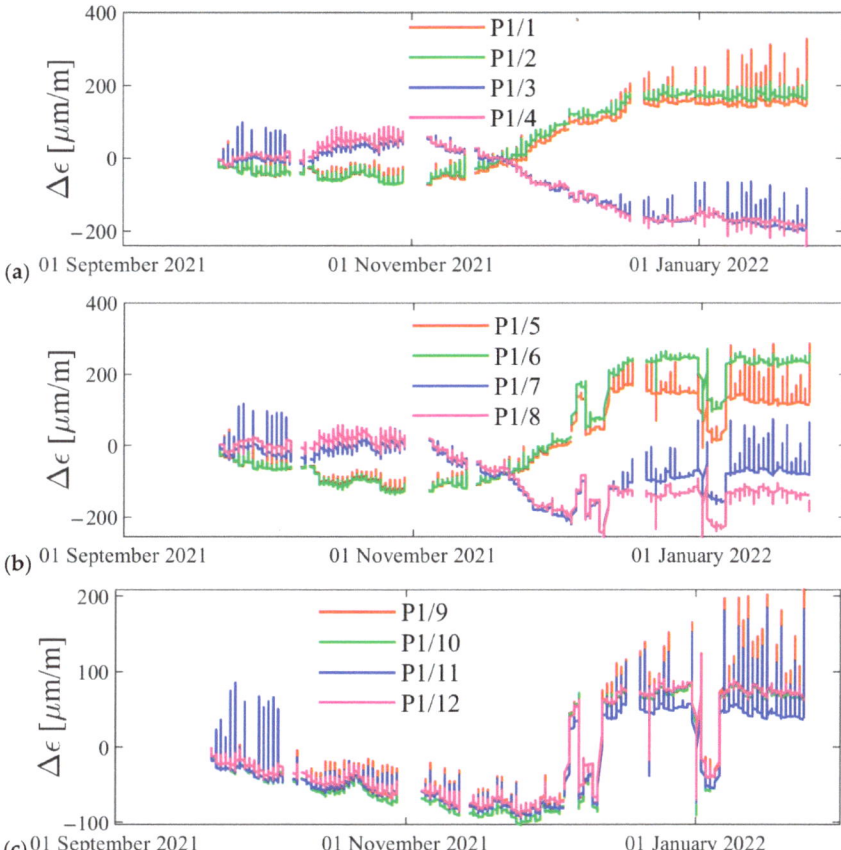

**Figure 11.** Changes in strains in the pylon: (**a**) upper chain, (**b**) lower chain, and (**c**) neutral axis.

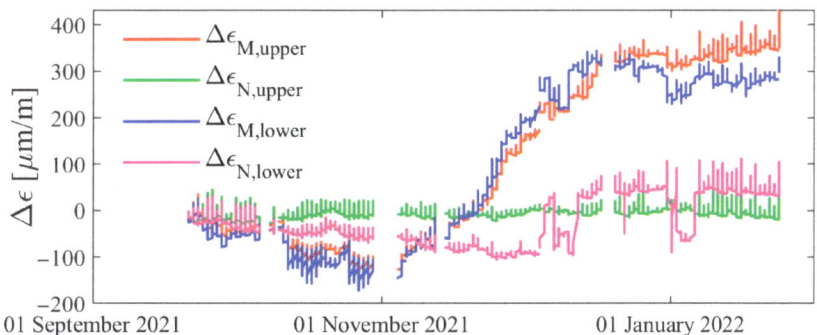

**Figure 12.** Derived strain changes concerning normal force ($\Delta\varepsilon_N$) and bending moment ($\Delta\varepsilon_M$) on the upper and lower chains at measurement location P1.

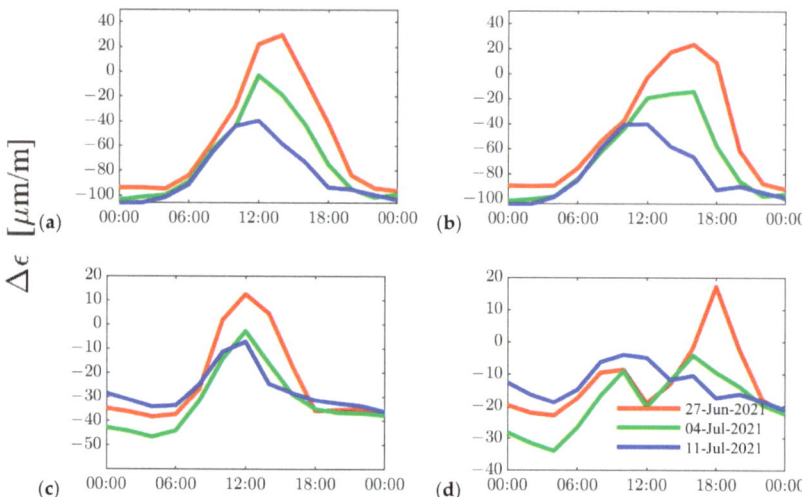

**Figure 13.** Strain changes within a day without construction works on the bridge: (**a**–**d**) P1/1 – P1/4.

**Table 1.** Measured maximum daily strain variations [μm/m].

| Fibre | Chain | P1 | P2 | P3 | P4 |
| --- | --- | --- | --- | --- | --- |
| Top | Upper | 110–125 | 85–110 | 105–120 | 80–105 |
|  | Lower | 100–125 | 110–135 | 100–140 | 95–140 |
| Neutral | Upper | 60–80 | 35–80 | 60–80 | 40–80 |
|  | Lower | 55–70 | 35–80 | 65–85 | 25–80 |
| Bottom | Upper | 40–50 | 85–120 | 45–50 | 115–125 |
|  | Lower | 40–110 | 115–115 | 45–110 | 95–140 |

The maximum normal force and bending moment variations at the pylons (P1–P4) due to the proof load test, reconstruction, and daily temperature fluctuations are derived according to the methodology described in Section 4.3, and the results are summarized in Table 2. The analysis of the data suggests that daily temperature variations could result in additional bending moments of up to 102% (P4, upper chain—141 kNm vs. 285 kNm) compared to the values observed during the proof load test (~80% of the design live load of the bridge)). Furthermore, the normal force measurements even show a 58% higher value (P1, upper chain—1206 kN vs. 1904 kN) than those registered during the load testing. This highlights the high sensitivity of chain bridges to temperature fluctuations, where geometric stiffness plays an important role. The mechanical background of this is that the chain system has a special shape under the self-weight of the structure (causing approximately 12,000 kN tensile normal force), which can change significantly with temperature change. Unlike beam-type bridges, where temperature change does not cause a significant normal force, in chain bridges, the interaction between the chains and the deck system can change because of temperature change. When the temperature increases, the chain will be longer, increasing the clear height of the structure. This effect can lead to a reduction in the normal force in the chain elements, causing a reduction in the geometric stiffness of the system, leading to internal force transfer between the chain and stiffening girders of the deck system. In this case, a larger part of the internal forces are absorbed by the stiffening girders of the bridge deck system. The same effect can also occur in the opposite direction, where a drop in temperature increases the normal force in the chain system, which can be observed between summer and winter.

Table 2. Derived maximum normal force ($\Delta N$) and bending moment ($\Delta M$) variations due to proof load test (PLT), reconstruction (REC), and daily temperature fluctuations ($\Delta T$).

| Chain | Quantity | P1 | | | P2 | | | P3 | | | P4 | | |
|---|---|---|---|---|---|---|---|---|---|---|---|---|---|
| | | PLT | REC | $\Delta T$ | PLT | REC | $\Delta T$ | PLT | REC | $\Delta T$ | PLT | REC | $\Delta T$ |
| Upper | $\Delta N$ [kN] | 1206 | 1517 | 1904 | 1036 | 1682 | 1439 | 1482 | 4568 | 1768 | 1042 | 2379 | 1426 |
| | $\Delta M$ [kNm] | 147 | 702 | 151 | 146 | 359 | 268 | 228 | 457 | 142 | 141 | 366 | 285 |
| Lower | $\Delta N$ [kN] | 998 | 2996 | 1215 | 801 | 2943 | 1134 | 1305 | - | 1316 | 959 | 2565 | 1132 |
| | $\Delta M$ [kNm] | 17 | 560 | 197 | 23 | 263 | 270 | 27 | - | 220 | 21 | 347 | 326 |

The results also show that if the bending moment applied by the live load would cause the pins to rotate, a daily temperature change would also cause them to rotate on a daily basis. However, most of the pins did not rotate during the proof test load, even under the internal forces caused by the temperature change. Both prove that the pins of this historical bridge are stuck and that the static skeleton of the structure can be considered fixed within the static calculations under the live load and meteorological loads.

Furthermore, reconstruction significantly increases the effect on normal forces and bending moments due to reduced self-weight. For instance, the bending moment variation in the upper chain at location P1 increased by approximately 380% (147 kNm vs. 702 kNm). Although the lower chains had relatively small bending moments (<30 kNm) during the proof load test, the normal forces experienced a significant increase, measuring 267% higher at location P2 (801 kN vs. 2943 kN). These results emphasise the dominance of dead load and self-weight in the case of chain bridges. The measurement results also showed that even the most significant bending moment change during the construction could not initiate a rotation of the pins, showing that they are badly corroded and completely stuck.

For easier interpretation and presentation of the results, the cross-sectional resistances of the chains with nominal geometric dimensions are also evaluated for comparison purposes with the measured internal forces. In 2015, at the BME Department of Structural Engineering, a statistical evaluation of previous tensile tests from 1913 and 1948 was carried out, and the characteristic yield strength, $f_{yk}$, was determined. Based on the measured values, the design resistances are calculated by Eurocode 3 formulae, as follows: the pure tensile resistance of a chain using nominal cross-section properties is $N_{Rd} = A \times f_{yk}/\gamma_{M0} = 1274$ cm$^2$ $\times$ 28.1 kN/cm$^2$/1.0 = 35,799 kN, and the bending moment resistance of a cross section is $M_{Rd} = W \times f_{yk}/\gamma_{M0} = 7749$ cm$^3$ $\times$ 28.1 kN/cm$^2$/1.0 = 2177.5 kNm. It can be seen that the largest change in the normal force and bending moment within the chain system resulting from the proof load test, reconstruction, or temperature change reaches only 13% of the tensile resistance and 33% of the bending resistance, respectively.

It is crucial to highlight that chains with fixed pins are subjected to a combination of axial tension and bending moments, compounded by the effects of corrosion on their cross-sectional properties, thereby reducing their overall resistance.

## 5. Summary and Conclusions

This paper presents the results of two temporary measurements carried out on the 175-year-old historic Széchenyi Chain Bridge during its reconstruction process. The major objective of the measurements was to investigate the rotational capacity of the pins between the chain elements (eyebars). This can significantly affect the structural integrity of the bridge, depending on the corrosion state of the chains, and has a clear impact on the further lifetime of the structure, which had to be assessed by the designers.

The first measurement was a proof load test, which aimed to check whether the live load (traffic load) could cause the pins of the bridge to rotate. The second measurement was taken by a six-month temporary monitoring system operating during the reconstruction process, aiming to check the structural behaviour of the bridge over a longer period of time while monitoring the rotation of the pins under temperature changes and during the removal of the old concrete deck, which was replaced by a new orthotropic steel deck system. Based on the on-site measurements, the following conclusions about the bridge behaviour could be drawn:

- All the measured pins are stuck, so no rotations were expected due to the live load (proof test load), temperature change, or the removal of the concrete deck during the bridge reconstruction.
- The internal forces resulting from daily and/or seasonal temperature changes can equal or exceed the magnitude of the internal forces resulting from the design traffic load; the largest normal force and bending moment changes compared to the characteristic resistances from the proof load test are 3% and 10%, respectively, whereas they are 5% and 15%, respectively, for temperature changes.
- The effect of reconstruction was dominant, with the largest normal force and bending moment changes reaching 13% of the tensile resistance and 33% of the bending resistance, respectively, but these significant internal force changes could not cause the pins to rotate.
- Normal stresses due to bending within the chain elements are significant, and therefore, the bending component should always be considered in the static verification of the chain elements.
- Half-a-year-long monitoring of data could significantly contribute to the understanding of the structural behaviour of the Széchenyi Chain Bridge and its specialties, including (i) the error in the pin rotation capacity and (ii) significant internal forces due to temperature change, which were not previously considered significant issues during the design process.
- The change in normal force has a significant effect on the geometric stiffness of the chain system, as shown by the analysis of the monitoring system data. This effect can also be caused by temperature change, which warrants attention from the designers.

**Author Contributions:** Conceptualization, B.K. and L.D.; methodology, B.K. and L.D.; software, D.K..; investigation, B.K. and D.K.; resources, B.K. and L.D.; data curation, D.K.; writing—original draft preparation, D.K.; writing—review and editing, B.K. and L.D.; visualization, D.K.; supervision, B.K. and L.D.; funding acquisition, B.K. All authors have read and agreed to the published version of the manuscript.

**Funding:** This research was funded by the Hungarian Academy of Sciences, grant number MTA-BME Lendület LP2021-06/2021 "Theory of new generation steel bridges".

**Data Availability Statement:** The raw data supporting the conclusions of this article will be made available by the authors on request.

**Acknowledgments:** The authors would like to express special thanks to the designers (Főmterv Co. and MSC Ltd. design offices) of the bridge reconstruction for their cooperation in the expertizing tasks and evaluation of the on-site measurements. Special thanks are also given to Hídépítő Co., who executed the reconstruction work of the bridge, provided the opportunity to execute the on-site measurements, and always offered strong technical support.

**Conflicts of Interest:** The authors declare no conflicts of interest.

# References

1. Åesson, B. *Understanding Bridge Collapses*, 1st ed.; CRC Press: London, UK, 2008.
2. Kövesdi, B.; Kollár, D.; Dunai, L.; Horváth, A. Reliability analysis-based investigation of the historical Széchenyi Chain Bridge deck system. *Results Eng.* **2022**, *15*, 100555. [CrossRef]
3. Neves, A.C.; González, I.; Leander, J.; Karoumi, R. Structural health monitoring of bridges: A model-free ANN-based approach to damage detection. *J. Civ. Struct. Health Monit.* **2017**, *7*, 689–702. [CrossRef]
4. Neves, A.C.; Leander, J.; González, I.; Karoumi, R. An approach to decision-making analysis for implementation of structural health monitoring in bridges. *Struct Control Health Monit.* **2019**, *26*, 1. [CrossRef]
5. Li, H.; Ou, J.P. Design approach of health monitoring system for cable-stayed bridges. In Proceedings of the 2nd International Conference of Structural Health Monitoring for Intelligent Infrastructure, Shenzhen, China, 16–18 November 2005.

6. Hovhanessian, G. Health monitoring of cable stayed structures experience and implementation. In Proceedings of the 24th Conference and Exposition on Structural Dynamics, St. Louis, MO, USA, 30 January–2 February 2006.
7. Dacol, V.; Caetano, E.; Correia, J.R. Modal identification and damping performance of a full-scale GFRP-SFRSCC hybrid footbridge. *Struct. Control Health Monit.* **2022**, *29*, e3137. [CrossRef]
8. Nicoletti, V.; Quarchioni, S.; Tentella, L.; Martini, R.; Gara, F. Experimental Tests and Numerical Analyses for the Dynamic Characterization of a Steel and Wooden Cable-Stayed Footbridge. *Infrastructures* **2023**, *8*, 100. [CrossRef]
9. Degrauwe, D.; De Roeck, G.; Lombaert, G. Uncertainty quantification in the damage assessment of a cable-stayed bridge by means of fuzzy numbers. *Comput. Struct.* **2009**, *87*, 1077–1084. [CrossRef]
10. Li, H.; Li, S.; Ou, J.; Li, H. Modal identification of bridges under varying environmental conditions: Temperature and wind effects. *Struct. Control Health Monit.* **2010**, *17*, 495–512. [CrossRef]
11. Xiao, F.; Hulsey, J.L.; Balasubramanian, R. Fiber optic health monitoring and temperature behavior of bridge in cold region. *Struct. Control Health Monit.* **2017**, *24*, e2020. [CrossRef]
12. Ding, Y.; Xiao, F.; Zhu, W.; Xia, T. Structural health monitoring of the scaffolding dismantling process of a long-span steel box girder viaduct based on BOTDA technology. *Adv. Civ. Eng.* **2019**, *2019*, 5942717. [CrossRef]
13. Xiao, F.; Hulsey, J.L.; Chen, G.S.; Xiang, Y. Optimal static strain sensor placement for truss bridges. *Int. J. Distrib. Sens. Netw.* **2017**, *13*, 1550147717707929. [CrossRef]
14. Okasha, N.M.; Frangopol, D.M. Integration of structural health monitoring in a system performance based life-cycle bridge management framework. *Struct. Infrastruct. Eng.* **2012**, *18*, 316–333. [CrossRef]
15. Li, D.; Hu, Q.; Ou, J. Fatigue damage evolution and monitoring of carbon fiber reinforced polymer bridge cable by acoustic emission technique. *Int. J. Distrib. Sens. Netw.* **2012**, *8*, 282139. [CrossRef]
16. Li, D.; Ou, J.; Lan, C.; Li, H. Monitoring and failure analysis of corroded bridge cables under fatigue loading using acoustic emission sensors. *Sensors* **2012**, *12*, 3901–3915. [CrossRef] [PubMed]
17. Li, H.; Lan, C.M.; Ju, Y.; Li, D.S. Experimental and Numerical Study of the Fatigue Properties of Corroded Parallel Wire Cables. *J. Bridg. Eng.* **2011**, *17*, 211–220. [CrossRef]
18. Li, H.; Li, S.; Ou, J.; Li, H. Reliability assessment of cable-stayed bridges based on structural health monitoring techniques. *Struct. Infrastruct. Eng.* **2012**, *8*, 829–845. [CrossRef]
19. Li, H.; Ou, J. The state of the art in structural health monitoring of cable-stayed bridges. *J. Civ. Struct. Health Monit.* **2016**, *6*, 43–67. [CrossRef]
20. Al-Hijazeen, A.Z.O.; Fawad, M.; Gerges, M.; Koris, K.; Salamak, M. Implementation of digital twin and support vector machine in structural health monitoring of bridges. *Arch. Civ. Eng.* **2023**, *69*, 31–47. [CrossRef]
21. Barros, B.; Conde, B.; Cabaleiro, M.; Riveiro, B. Deterministic and probabilistic-based model updating of aging steel bridges. *Structures* **2023**, *54*, 89–105. [CrossRef]
22. Borlenghi, P.; Gentile, C.; Pirrò, M. Vibration-Based Structural Health Monitoring of a Historic Arch Bridge. In *Proceedings of the Experimental Vibration Analysis for Civil Engineering Structures, EVACES 2023, Milan, Italy, 30 August–1 September 2023*; Lecture Notes in Civil Engineering; Limongelli, M.P., Giordano, P.F., Quqa, S., Gentile, C., Cigada, A., Eds.; Springer: Berlin/Heidelberg, Germany, 2023; Volume 432.

**Disclaimer/Publisher's Note:** The statements, opinions and data contained in all publications are solely those of the individual author(s) and contributor(s) and not of MDPI and/or the editor(s). MDPI and/or the editor(s) disclaim responsibility for any injury to people or property resulting from any ideas, methods, instructions or products referred to in the content.

Article

# Modeling and Loading Effect of Wind on Long-Span Cross-Rope Suspended Overhead Line with Suspension Insulator

Qixin Qin [1], Xi Tu [1,2], Yujing Hu [1,3], Zhisong Wang [1,2,*], Lin Yu [4] and Shengli Hou [4]

1. College of Civil Engineering, Chongqing University, Chongqing 400044, China; tuxi@cqu.edu.cn (X.T.)
2. Key Laboratory of New Technology for Construction of Cities in Mountain Area, Chongqing University, Ministry of Education, Chongqing 400045, China
3. Design Institute of Chongqing Iron & Steel Group Co., Ltd., Chongqing 400084, China
4. Chongqing Haizhuang Wind Power Engineering Technology Co., Ltd., Chongqing 401258, China; hzgcjszx@163.com (S.H.)
* Correspondence: wangzhisong@cqu.edu.cn

**Abstract:** The long-span Cross-Rope Suspended (CRS) system is composed of a transmission line (conductor), a long-span suspension cable, and an insulator. The previously introduced long-span CRS with a Tension Insulator (CRSTI) has shown applicability in mountainous areas. However, the tension insulator divided the suspension cable into several sections, which made the construction of a long-span CRS rather difficult. This paper introduces long-span CRS with a Suspension Insulator (CRSSI), in which the suspension cable was not disconnected, and the conductor was supported by a suspension insulator connected to the suspension cable. For the purposes of assessment, the initial shape of the suspension cable with concentrated loading from the self-gravity of the suspension insulator and the conductors was studied, and practical lengths in construction could be calculated exactly. Secondly, the structural performance of CRSSI, including its dynamic properties and the loading effect of wind, was discussed by means of numerical analysis. Vibration modes of the structure were obtained by FE analysis. Finally, structural deformation under static wind loading was studied. The result of the analysis showed that the stiffness of CRSSI was lower than CRSTI. The first frequency of CRSSI was 6% smaller than CRSTI. Regarding static wind loading, additional displacement of the insulator contributed to the maximum displacement of long-span CRSSI. Apparently, the displacement of the suspension insulator increased with wind speed. Moreover, the number of spans has an insignificant influence on tension force and deformation.

**Keywords:** cross-rope suspension; dynamics; long span; power transmission line; suspension insulator; wind load; finite element analysis; geometric nonlinear

Citation: Qin, Q.; Tu, X.; Hu, Y.; Wang, Z.; Yu, L.; Hou, S. Modeling and Loading Effect of Wind on Long-Span Cross-Rope Suspended Overhead Line with Suspension Insulator. *Buildings* **2024**, *14*, 656. https://doi.org/10.3390/buildings14030656

Academic Editor: Giuseppina Uva

Received: 18 December 2023
Revised: 18 January 2024
Accepted: 1 February 2024
Published: 1 March 2024

**Copyright:** © 2024 by the authors. Licensee MDPI, Basel, Switzerland. This article is an open access article distributed under the terms and conditions of the Creative Commons Attribution (CC BY) license (https://creativecommons.org/licenses/by/4.0/).

## 1. Introduction

Long-span Cross-Rope Suspended (CRS) overhead lines are a type of structure in which the transmission line is supported by a long-span suspension cable. They are suitable in mountainous areas. Compared with conventional CRS, steel pylons are removed, and the span of the cross-rope increases to hundreds of meters. Generally, both ends of the cross-rope, also called a suspension cable, are directly fixed on top of the mountains.

The first long-span CRS structure was reported in Cape Town, South Africa, in 2011: it was called the "invisible tower line", and it provided better protection of the local landscape [1]. Cross-Rope Suspended systems with a Tension Insulator (CRSTI) (Figure 1) are currently the adopted type of CRS. For CRSTI, a Tension Insulator (TI) connects multiple sections of suspension cable and becomes a key member of the structure. Thus, the transmission line is directly supported by a suspension cable. Li [2] established a finite element model for CRSTI, which was used to analyze the dynamic characteristics and study the wind-induced response. The horizontal displacements and tension force of the suspension cables of CRSTI increased with the increase in wind speed. These results provide a basis for the practical engineering design of CRSTI. Tu [3] studied the corresponding vortex-induced vibration and the controlling methods of CRSTI by numerical simulation. However, due to the huge tension force, high tensional mechanical capacity is required for TI, which results in difficulty in construction and relatively poor economic efficiency. Therefore, a new type of CRS system is proposed, which is CRS with a Suspension Insulator (CRSSI) (Figure 2).

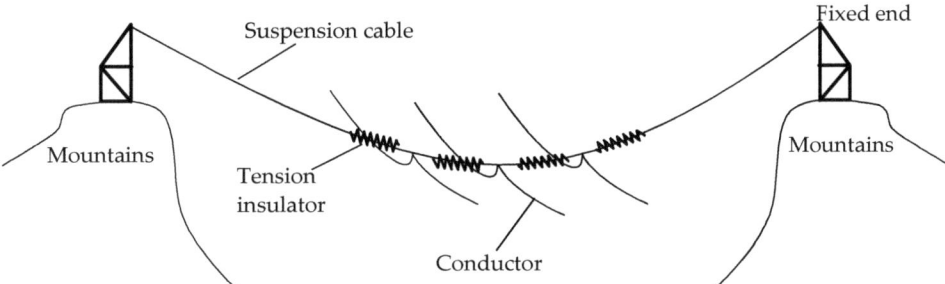

**Figure 1.** Long-span Cross-Rope Suspension overhead transmission line with Tension Insulator.

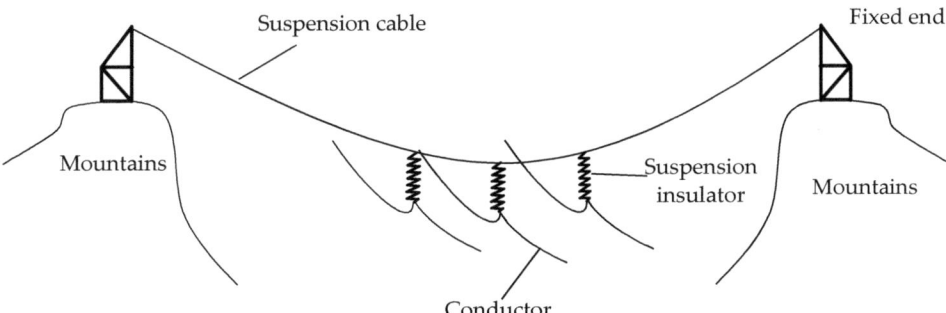

**Figure 2.** Long-span Cross-Rope Suspension overhead transmission line with Suspension Insulator.

For CRSSI, the upper end of the Suspension Insulator (SI) is hung on a suspension cable, and the lower end is connected to the conductor. Thus, the weight load of the transmission line is directly subject to the insulator. The structure for CRSSI is simpler than CRSTI, and construction is easier. Additionally, the investment of CRSSI is less than that of CRSTI. Obviously, the wind-induced response is smaller in CRSTI compared with CRSSI. Simultaneously, the initial configuration of the suspension cable differs from that of CRSTI. Therefore, it is necessary to determine the function of the suspension cable in order to calculate its length accurately during practical construction. To select the appropriate type for CRS construction, a thorough investigation into CRSSI and a comparison between CRSSI and CRSTI were essential.

Currently, the Finite Element Method (FEM) has been widely adopted for analyzing complex flexible structures with large geometric deformations, which is applicable for long-span CRS as well [4]. The basis of the analysis for CRS systems with large spans is the initial shape of the conductors and suspension cables. Based on the traditional shape-finding method for cables, Jia and Liu [5] introduced a method of finding the initial shape of overhead transmission lines. Peyrot [6] proposed a method for structural analysis of cable using nonlinear elastic suspended catenary units and presented the results of static analysis of 500 kV cable tower transmission lines. Nie [7] modeled a guyed tower with different element types based on finite element analysis and compared the influence of different models on the overall response. Kempner [8] studied the dynamic characteristics of a guyed tower and proposed an analysis method for structural modal and vibrations. McClure [9] studied the case of a line section experiencing two tower failures that were caused by conductor breakages during an ice storm and established a macroscopic modeling approach to dynamic analysis. Wang [10] established a finite model for a V-type insulator string under dynamic wind load and compared dynamic and static calculation results. Duan [11] investigated the aerodynamic coefficients of the contact line with two levels of wear under different wind angles by means of the nonlinear finite element model and summarized the effect of a damping dropper. Zhang [12] developed a finite model to estimate the load-bearing capacity of a transmission tower and explained the reason for the failure modes and the difference in buckled members using dynamic analysis and static analysis. Zhang [13] established a design tool with a three-degrees-of-freedom hybrid model that accommodated interactions of vertical, horizontal, and torsional movements. Desai [14] developed a three-node, isoparametric cable element with three translationals and a torsional degree of freedom at each node to obtain the envelope of galloping. Eric [15] explained models for time histories of wind velocities of transient tornadoes and microburst events and performed dynamic structural analysis of the two events.

This type of structure is sensitive to wind load, and the structural displacements caused by wind loads are important to be concerned with [16–18]. For large-span wind-sensitive structures such as cable-supported transmission line systems, vortex-induced vibration caused by uniform flow is the most typical form of vibration and has been the focus of researchers' attention [19]. Jafari [20] summarized different sources of wind-induced cable vibration, consisting of vortex-induced vibration, rain–wind-induced vibration, dry galloping, ice galloping, and wake galloping. Martins [21] investigated the application of optimization techniques to cable-stayed bridges, which showed that bridges with innovative cable arrangements like crossing cables attracted the interest of researchers. Liu [22] summarized the current state of research on pantograph–catenary interaction for high-speed railways and proposed future directions for improving the system to ensure optimal performance at speeds of 400 km/h and above. Yin [23] proposed a filtering method for abnormal working conditions based on density clustering to solve the problem of deviation in the wind vane in wind turbines. Okamura [24] pointed out that the blow-down angle was also important in a wind response analysis of a transmission tower in a mountainous area. For a mountainous area, the combination of wind and ice in extreme conditions has a significant impact on the design load of CRS. Keyhan [25] proposed a new method for determining wind loads on conductors based on fluid–solid coupling analysis. Lalonde [26] carried out a study of Aluminum Conductor Steel Reinforcement (ACSR) under wind-induced loading using the finite element method and compared it with experimental data. Jia [27] compared the fatigue calculation results with those obtained from a linear stochastic dynamic analysis in the frequency domain and certified that wind-induced fatigue calculation procedures were widely adopted in various types of structures. Deng [28] presented a four-span transmission line system subjected to skew incident wind forces on a lattice suspension tower via experimental and numerical approaches. Pombo [29,30] addressed the influence of track and environmental conditions on the pantograph–catenary, and results were obtained for high-speed trains running at 300 km/h in relation to the separation between pantographs. Stickland [31] measured a damped oscillation of a section of the UK East Coast Main Line catenary and increased mechanical damping, which was found to raise the mechanical damping coefficient. Song [32] characterized pointwise stochastics of Contact Wire Irregularity (CWI) and introduced the power spectral density (PSD) function for CWI.

This paper discussed the expression of the initial shape of cable under the action of a single concentrated force. A finite element model was established to analyze the dynamic characteristics of CRSSI. Analysis of static wind loads on the CRSSI was carried out. Furthermore, the response of the static wind load for CRSSI was compared with that of CRSTI, offering a foundational theory for the selection of CRS and practical engineering construction.

## 2. Initial Shape of Cross-Rope under Loading of Conductors

In the CRS system, the initial shape of the cable is meaningful to provide an unstressed length of cable and final shape after construction. As known, the catenary is the initial shape of cable with only self-weight and no additional loading. However, the initial shape of the cable changes when the additional loading of the self-weight for conductor and insulators is considered. In this chapter, the functions of the cable without loading and with additional loading were derived, which is the basis for further FE modeling.

### 2.1. Approximate Equation of Catenary of Suspension Cable

Without additional external vertical loading and considering only self-weight, the catenary is the initial shape of the cable fixed on both ends. For long-span CRS, the height of both ends of the suspension cable varies due to terrain. Therefore, the shape of a cable with unequal altitude and its derivation are studied in this chapter. A catenary with unequal height is shown in Figure 3. In this figure, point A denotes the left end, and point B denotes the right end. A small element of suspension cable composed of two ends of i and j was taken as follows (shown in Figure 4).

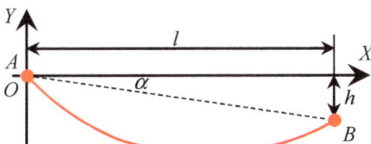

**Figure 3.** Catenary with unequal height at both ends.

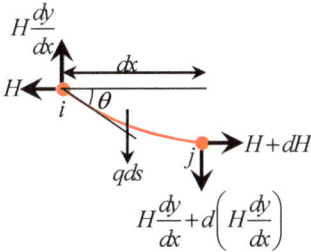

**Figure 4.** Calculation diagram of a catenary with unequal height at both ends.

Both ends of the element were subjected to tension along the tangential direction, which was decomposed into horizontal and vertical directions, respectively. Moreover, the element was subjected to distributed loads caused by its self-weight. The equilibrium equations of the element are as follows:

$$H + dH - H = 0 \tag{1}$$

$$H\frac{dy}{dx} + d\left(H\frac{dy}{dx}\right) - H\frac{dy}{dx} + qds = 0 \tag{2}$$

where $q$ is the mass of the unit length of the cable.

According to Equation (1), the horizontal component of the cable force, $H$, is constant along the cable. According to Equation (2), the differential equation of the cable is rewritten as follows:

$$\frac{d^2y}{dx^2} = -\frac{1}{H}\frac{qds}{dx} \tag{3}$$

The differential formula of arc length gave the following:

$$ds = \sqrt{1 + \left(\frac{dy}{dx}\right)^2} dx \tag{4}$$

Based on Equations (3) and (4), the differential formula of catenary of cable gave

$$\frac{d^2y}{dx^2} = -\frac{q}{H}\sqrt{1 + \left(\frac{dy}{dx}\right)^2} \tag{5}$$

Assuming that the self-weight load $q$ was constant along the cable, parameter $c$ was defined as

$$c = -\frac{q}{H} \tag{6}$$

Substituting $c$ in Equation (6) into Equation (5) and integrating, the expression of cable produced the following:

$$y = \frac{1}{c}\cosh(cx + a) + b \tag{7}$$

Boundary conditions were given:

$$\begin{cases} x = 0, y = 0 \\ x = l, y = h \end{cases} \tag{8}$$

Based on Equations (7) and (8), $a$ and $b$ were solved:

$$a = \operatorname{arcsinh}\left[\frac{hc}{2\sinh\left(\frac{cl}{2}\right)}\right] \tag{9}$$

$$b = -\frac{1}{c}\cosh a \tag{10}$$

The initial shape of the cable considering only self-weight was calculated using the above formula, which served as the initial base for the following analysis.

Also, the sag of the suspension cable was calculated by Equation (11), in which $x$ was half of one span for a conductor.

$$y_{\text{sag}} = \frac{1}{c}\cosh\left(cx_{0.5\text{span}} + a\right) + b \tag{11}$$

## 2.2. Approximate Equations of Suspension Cable under the Action of Single Concentrated Force

In long-span CRSSI, the expression for the cable differed from the above calculation due to the additional loading caused by SI and conductors. For simplification, additional concentrated force was set at the lowest point of the catenary, and the cable was symmetrical in shape. The demonstration of loading on cable is shown in Figure 5, where $m$ denotes the sum of the mass of conductors and the mass of the insulator. In Figure 5, point A denotes the left end, point B denotes the right end, and point C denotes the lowest point.

According to the differential equations of cable mechanics in the above chapter, despite the additional loading from the conductor and the overhanging insulator, the cable between the fixed end and SI kept the original shape of the catenary. Therefore, in order to derive the shape formula of cable considering the concentrated force, half of the mass of conductors and insulator, $m_2$, was transformed into an equivalent cable segment with length $x$, as shown in Figure 6. Point A denotes the fixed end. Point B denotes the lowest end of the cable and the starting point of the equivalent cable. Point C denotes the end of the equivalent cable. The dashed line denotes the symmetric part of the cable from the fixed end, $A(0,0)$, to the hanging point, $B(x_0, y_0)$. The red line segment from B to C denotes the equivalent cable for the mass of conductors and the insulator. Point C denotes the virtual lowest point of the equivalent catenary. Accordingly, A, B, and C were located in the same catenary.

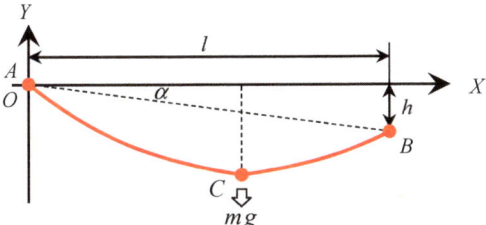

**Figure 5.** Diagram of the force considering the mass of the conductor and the SI.

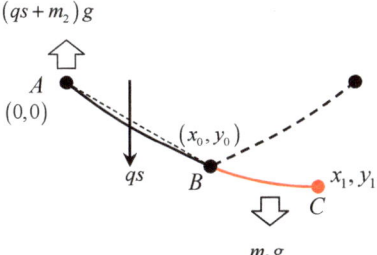

**Figure 6.** Calculation diagram considering the equivalent cable segment.

The base of the differential formula of the arc length is as follows:

$$ds = \sqrt{1 + \left(\frac{dy}{dx}\right)^2} dx \qquad (12)$$

$$s = \int_0^l \sqrt{1 + \left(\frac{dy}{dx}\right)^2} dx \qquad (13)$$

The equivalent length $l_e$ of the virtual suspension cable is given by the mass of the conductors and insulator:

$$l_e = \frac{m_2 g}{q} \qquad (14)$$

Replacing $s$ in Equation (13) with $l_e$ in Equation (14) yields

$$\frac{m_2 g}{q} = \int_{x_0}^{x_1} \sqrt{1 + \left(\frac{dy}{dx}\right)^2} dx \qquad (15)$$

According to the formula of catenary,

$$\frac{dy}{dx} = \sinh(cx + a) \qquad (16)$$

Replacing $dy/dx$ in Equation (15) with Equation (16), the catenary of suspension cable is given as follows:

$$\frac{m_2 g}{q} = \int_{x_0}^{x_1} \sqrt{1 + (\sinh(cx + a))^2} dx \qquad (17)$$

Based on Equations (9) and (17), the coordinate $x_0$ of the equivalent suspension length can be solved. Bringing $x_0$ into Equation (7), $y_0$ is obtained.

According to the geometric relationship,

$$y_f = f(x + x_0) - y_0 \tag{18}$$

Bringing $x_0$ and $y_0$ into Equation (18), the shape of cable under the concentrated force is obtained. The above formula took the lowest point of the catenary as the origin.

### 2.3. Numerical Solution of the Approximate Equations for Cables under the Action of Concentrated Forces

In practical engineering, it is possible to carry out an analysis of the numerical solution of the function using design conditions so that the initial shape and the initial prestress can be defined for construction.

We can assume that the expression of the catenary is as follows:

$$y = a \cosh\left(\frac{x-b}{a}\right) - c \tag{19}$$

where $a$, $b$, and $c$ are unknown parameters for the above equation.

The origin, the lowest point, and the end point of the suspension cable in the practical project were set according to the actual topography. The origin was $A(0,0)$, and the lowest point was $B(x_0, y_0)$. In the above analysis, it was found that the tangent line at the end point C was horizontal, and the mass and length of the equivalent suspension section can be obtained via calculation.

We can bring $A(0,0)$ into Equation (19):

$$c = a \cosh\left(\frac{-b}{a}\right) \tag{20}$$

Replacing $c$ in Equation (19) by Equation (20), the expression was simplified:

$$y = a \cosh\left(\frac{x-b}{a}\right) - a \cosh\left(\frac{-b}{a}\right) \tag{21}$$

We can bring $B(x_0, y_0)$ into Equation (21):

$$0 = a \cosh\left(\frac{x_0 - b}{a}\right) - a \cosh\left(\frac{-b}{a}\right) - y_0 \tag{22}$$

According to Equation (22), $a$ and $b$ were solved by a calculation process. First, the initial values of $a$, $b$ were selected and were brought into Equation (23):

$$\Delta_b = y_0 - \left(a \cosh\left(\frac{x_0 - b}{a}\right) - a \cosh\left(\frac{-b}{a}\right)\right) \tag{23}$$

If $\Delta_b = 0$, the value of $b$ is satisfied. For simplification, the thresholding value for $\Delta_b$ was given:

$$-0.001 < \Delta_b < 0.001 \tag{24}$$

If Equation (24) was satisfied, the value of $b$ was satisfied. If not, the value of $b$ was changed to recalculate. This process continued until the best value of $b$ was determined. The function of the cable was given by $a$ and $b$.

The calculation of the length of the arc was given:

$$s = \int_{x_0}^{x_1} \sqrt{1 + y'^2}\, dx \tag{25}$$

According to Equation (25), the length of the suspension cable from B to C can be calculated by Equation (25), where C is a random point in the suspension cable. The length

$l_{bc}$ from B to C can be compared with the equivalent section length $l_e$, which was defined as Equation (14). As per the analysis above, it was accurate when $l_{bc} = l_e$. For simplification, the thresholding number for $l_{bc}$ was given as follows:

$$-0.001 < \frac{l_{bc} - l_e}{l_{bc}} < 0.001 \qquad (26)$$

If Equation (26) was satisfied, point C was determined. If not, another point was selected to recalculate until Equation (26) was satisfied. As analyzed above, $y'_c = 0$. $y'_c$ can be given based on the coordinate of C and Equation (16). The thresholding number for $y'_c$ was given as follows:

$$-0.001 < y'_c < 0.001 \qquad (27)$$

The values of $a$ and $b$ met the requirements when Equation (27) was satisfied. If not, the value of $a$ and $b$ were changed to recalculate. This process was continued until the function of the suspension cable was determined. The process diagram is shown in Figure 7. The length of section AB of the cable can be calculated according to the determined formula and Equation (25); that is, the actual length of the project after the function was determined.

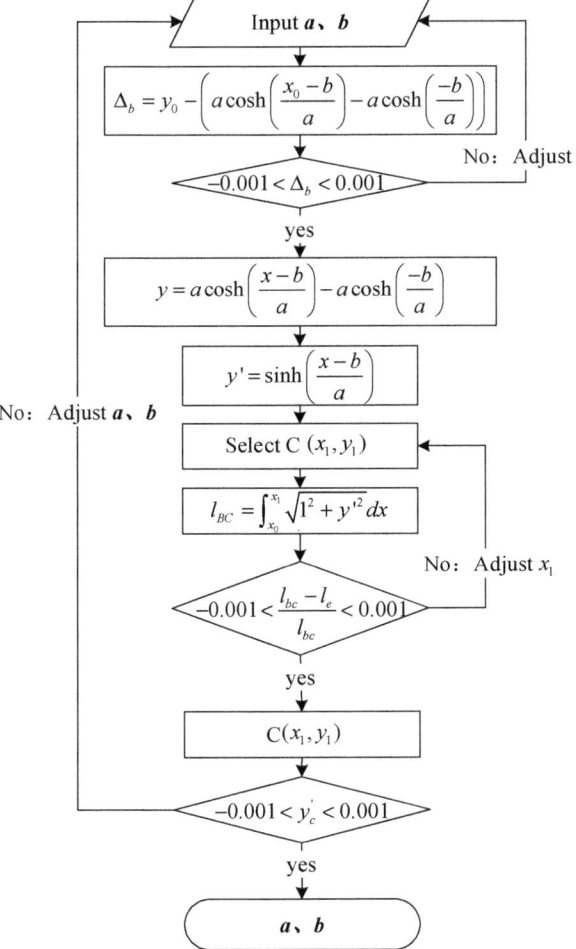

**Figure 7.** Calculation process of parameters $a$ and $b$ with regard to the function of suspension cable.

Based on an example, the numerical simulation process is demonstrated below.

According to the actual engineering design parameters, the overall span of the suspension cable was 1000 m, and the lowest point of the design was 110 m. The coordinates of point $A$ were $(0,0)$, and the coordinates of point $B$ were $(500, -110)$, which is shown in Figure 8. The length of the equivalent section of insulators and conductors was $l_e = 2175$ m. For point $B$, the coordinate was $(500, -110)$, which meant the span of the suspension cable was 1000 m, and the lowest of the suspension cable was $-110$ m. The numerical simulation showed that the requirements were satisfied when $a = 9900$ and $b = 2603.5$. A diagram of the numerical simulation example is shown in Figure 9. Thus, it was calculated that $x_1 = 2655$.

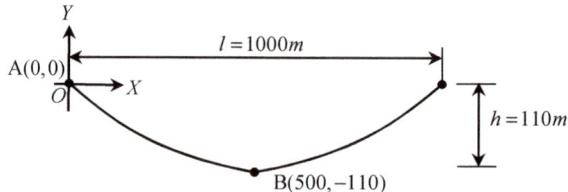

**Figure 8.** Dimension of long-span CRS.

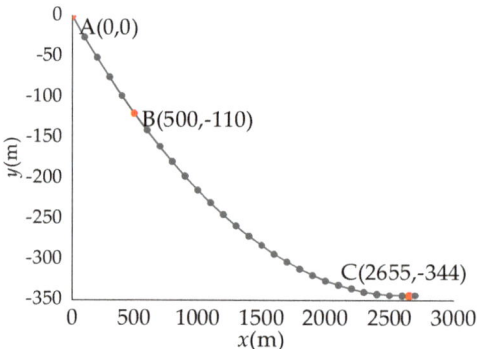

**Figure 9.** Diagram of solution for numerical simulation example.

In this case, the function was

$$y = 9900\cosh\left(\frac{x - 2603.5}{9900}\right) - 9900\cosh\left(\frac{-2603.5}{9900}\right) = 9900\cosh\left(\frac{x - 2603.5}{9900}\right) - 1024.3 \tag{28}$$

The actual length of the suspension cable, which was also the length of section $AB$, was as follows:

$$L = \int_0^{500} 9900\cosh\left(\frac{x - 2603.5}{9900}\right) - 1024.3 = 513.21 \,(\text{m}) \tag{29}$$

## 3. Dynamic Properties Determined by Numerical Analysis

### 3.1. FE Modeling

The CRS system is a flexible transmission line structural system, and wind-induced structural vibration is critical to its structural safety. The CRS system was composed of cables, which were characterized by small stiffness and large deformation. In practical engineering, the CRS system is mostly used in mountainous areas, where the wind field condition is complex. Due to significant flexibility, there is a huge impact on the structure induced by a complex wind field. Therefore, in the structural simulation analysis of the CRS system, a reasonable finite element model was indispensable for evaluating its structural performance. For the finite element model, the geometric nonlinearity, which was suitable for a CRS system with significant flexibility, was considered. Also, the finite element model can be used for static analysis while considering static wind load.

As described above, the CRS system was composed of suspension cables, conductors, insulators, and anchorages, while guyed masts and towers were removed. According to the parameters for practical engineering and function analyzed above, coordinates for a suspension cable and conductor were calculated. For the conductor, the initial shape was catenary. For the suspension cable, the initial shape was the approximate equations of suspension cable under the action of a single concentrated force. The suspension cable that hung the suspension insulator was anchored on both ends. The upper end of the insulator was connected to the suspension cable, and the lower end was connected to the conductor. For the conductor, one end was connected to the suspension cable, while another end was anchored. Details on the FE model are given in Figure 10. For a complex flexible structural system, the convergence problem was critical when considering geometrical nonlinearity. This paper adopted an assembly modeling approach. Using this approach, separate analyses of the CRS of the deformed shape and loading states were conducted and finally assembled. All members were modeled by a two-node link element type in three-dimensional space, which meant only tensile force and strain were considered for each element, and the bending and torsion stiffness were ignored [3]. The multiple spans of CRSSI were also modeled and analyzed while considering application to different topographies. The FE model for a multi-span CRSSI is shown in Figure 11.

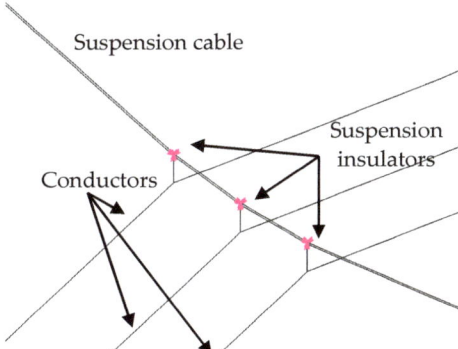

**Figure 10.** Detail of FE model of long-span CRSSI.

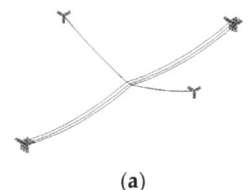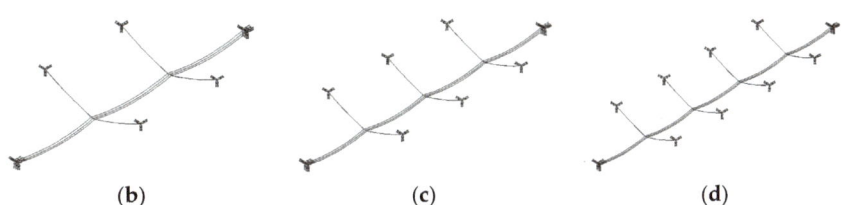

**Figure 11.** FE models of long-span CRSSI with multiple spans of conductors: (**a**) 2 spans, (**b**) 3 spans, (**c**) 4 spans, (**d**) 5 spans.

### 3.2. Dynamic Behavior of CRS

#### 3.2.1. Vibration Modes and Natural Frequencies of Long-Span CRSSI

Firstly, a two-span CRS system was analyzed for modal analysis. The purpose of the modal analysis was to determine the inherent frequency and vibration pattern of the CRS so as to obtained the vibration characteristics. The modal analyses conducted are shown in Figure 12.

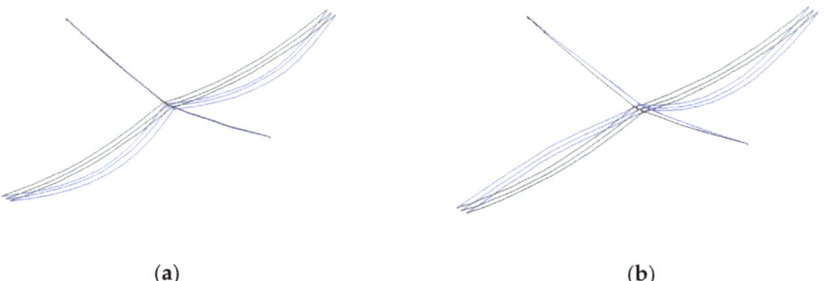

(a)                    (b)

**Figure 12.** Modal analysis of 2-span CRS system (Black: undeformed, Blue: deformed); (**a**) 1st symmetric lateral bending (0.0790 Hz); (**b**) 1st asymmetric vertical bending (0.0813 Hz).

Different numbers of spans were set for the modal analysis of the CRS system. It showed that the frequencies of the same modal for the CRS system were different when considering different numbers of spans. Therefore, the same mode of vibration of the CRS system with different spans should be compared. According to modal calculation results, the frequency of the same mode of vibration decreased as the number of spans increased, as shown in Table 1. The calculated results were plotted on a line graph, as shown in Figure 13. The modes of vibration are shown in Figures 14 and 15. Also, the order of the mode of vibration appearing at different spans was different. At two and three spans, the modes of vibration appeared in the order of the first symmetric lateral bending and the first asymmetric vertical bending. At four and five spans, the orders were the first asymmetric vertical bending and the first symmetric lateral bending. Also, the frequency of the mode of vibration decreased more at the first asymmetric vertical bending. Therefore, it was advised that number of spans selected should be lower than three.

**Table 1.** Frequency of long-span CRS system at different spans.

| Spans | 1st Symmetric Lateral Bending (Hz) | 1st Asymmetric Vertical Bending (Hz) |
| --- | --- | --- |
| 2 | 0.0790 | 0.0813 |
| 3 | 0.0776 | 0.0780 |
| 4 | 0.0771 | 0.0746 |
| 5 | 0.0768 | 0.0715 |

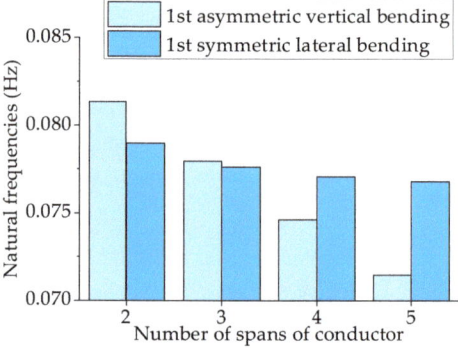

**Figure 13.** Influence of number of spans on natural frequency.

**Figure 14.** The 1st symmetric lateral bending (Black: undeformed, Blue: deformed): (**a**) 2 spans, (**b**) 3 spans, (**c**) 4 spans, (**d**) 5 spans.

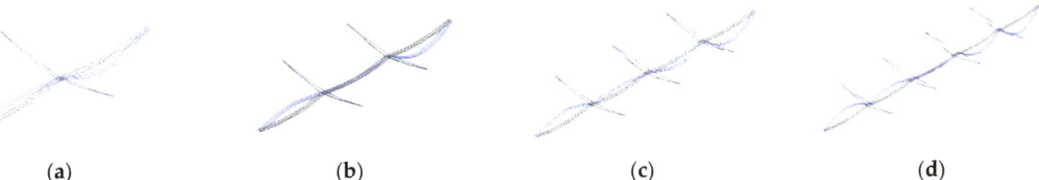

**Figure 15.** The 1st asymmetric vertical bending (Black: undeformed, Blue: deformed): (**a**) 2 spans, (**b**) 3 spans, (**c**) 4 spans, (**d**) 5 spans.

3.2.2. Influence of Insulator Structural Parameters on the Dynamic Characteristics of the CRSSI

The type of insulator and the corresponding parameters were different for multiple applications. In the study of dynamic characteristics, the length of insulators should be concerned. Different lengths of the insulators were modified, and the corresponding dynamic characteristics of the CRS system were studied. For insulators, the length of composite insulators used in fouled areas was longer. In areas with hard pollution, the number of pieces of composite insulators was higher, and the total insulator length was 15 m [33]. This chapter focused on the influence of insulator parameters on the dynamic characteristics of the CRS system by modifying the length of the insulator.

Different lengths of SI were set up for the modal analysis of the CRS system. It can be summarized from the calculation results that the natural frequency of the CRS system decreased as the insulator length increased. The reason was that the increment in the length of the SI decreased the stiffness of the structure. Also, with the increase in the number of spans, the impact of the length of the SI on the natural frequency of the structure decreased. The change in the length of the insulator had a small effect on the modal and frequency of the first asymmetric vertical bending but a large influence on the frequency of the first symmetric lateral bending. The calculated results were plotted on a line graph, as shown in Figure 16. For CRSSI, the decrease in the length of the insulator can reduce the natural frequency. For the transmission tower, when the length of the insulator was too small, the conductor and suspension cable were close to each other, which may lead to a danger of discharge. Therefore, an appropriate and safe insulator length should be selected in practical projects when construction.

3.2.3. Comparison of CRSSI and CRSTI

For a CRS system, there are two main types, CRSSI and CRSTI. In order to compare the dynamic characteristics of the two systems, FE models were established. The dynamic characteristics were calculated and summarized for both systems.

FE models were established to calculate the frequency of CRSTI, and a comparison was made between the natural frequency of the same mode of vibration of CRSSI and CRSTI. The natural frequency of each mode of vibration is shown in Table 2. The calculated results were plotted on a line graph, as shown in Figure 17. For the first symmetric lateral bending, the natural frequency of CRSTI was higher than CRSSI in the two spans. The opposite was true when the number of spans was higher than two. For asymmetric vertical bending, the natural frequency of CRSTI was lower than CRSSI. According to the results, an increase in the number of spans caused a decrease in the stiffness of the structure, which led to a decrease in the natural frequency. The decrease in structural stiffness was not linear. As the number of spans increases, the reduction in structural stiffness decreases with an increase in span. Compared with CRSSI, the decrease in stiffness for CRSTI was more pronounced with an increase in the number of spans. This indicated that CRSTI was more sensitive to the number of spans. In the case of CRSSI, the crossing of conductors at lower frequencies led to structural damage or short circuits in the transmission line, resulting in economic losses. Therefore, in practical construction, the selection of an appropriate system should align with diverse requirements related to topography and engineering considerations.

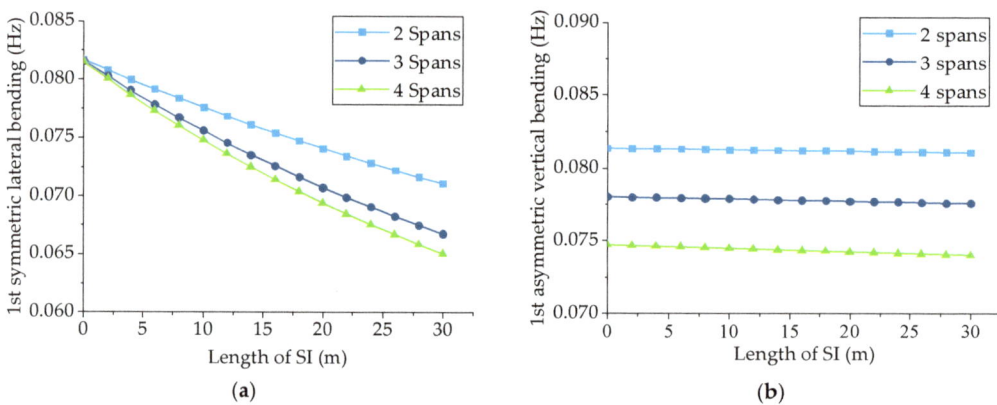

**Figure 16.** Influence of insulator length on the natural frequency: (**a**) 1st symmetric lateral bending; (**b**) 1st asymmetric vertical bending.

**Table 2.** Comparison of natural frequency between the CRSSI and the CRSTI.

| Spans | 1st Symmetric Lateral Bending (Hz) | | | 1st Asymmetric Vertical Bending (Hz) | | |
|---|---|---|---|---|---|---|
| | CRSTI | CRSSI (SI: 6.42 m) | CRSSI (SI: 12 m) | CRSTI | CRSSI (SI: 6.42 m) | CRSSI (SI: 12 m) |
| 2 | 0.0818 | 0.0790 | 0.0768 | 0.0653 | 0.0813 | 0.0812 |
| 3 | 0.0689 | 0.0776 | 0.0746 | 0.0585 | 0.0780 | 0.0779 |
| 4 | 0.0650 | 0.0771 | 0.0736 | 0.0540 | 0.0746 | 0.0744 |

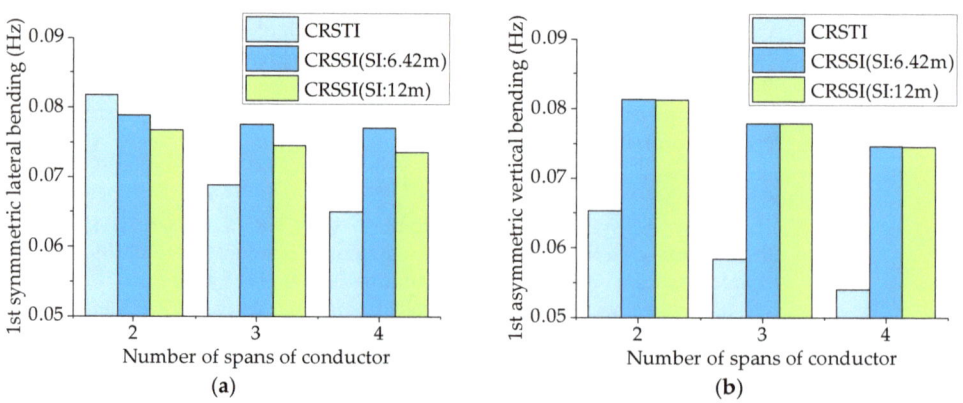

**Figure 17.** Comparison of natural frequency between CRSSI and CRSTI: (**a**) 1st symmetric lateral bending; (**b**) 1st asymmetric vertical bending.

## 4. Study on Static Wind Load Response for CRSSI

### 4.1. Calculation of Wind Load

CRS systems with insulators were mainly applied in mountainous areas. The wind load was one of the main external loads that the structure was subjected to. The CRS system with insulator was a wind-sensitive structure. To ensure security, a structural analysis of wind load should be carried out. This chapter focused on the calculation and analysis of the internal force of the suspension cable and the lateral displacement of the conductor for the CRSSI.

Wind loads were considered static wind loads for convenience. According to the wind profile, the average speed of wind in different altitudes was calculated by

$$\bar{v}(z) = \bar{v}_b \left(\frac{z}{z_b}\right)^\alpha \tag{30}$$

where $\bar{v}(z)$ is the average speed of winds in target altitude (m/s), $\bar{v}_b$ is the standard speed of wind (m/s), $z$ is the target altitude (m), and $z_b$ is the standard target altitude (m). $\alpha$ is the ground roughness exponent. Static wind loads can be calculated from a combination of air density, wind speed, windward area, and drag coefficient [34].

It was clear that the windward area was proportional to the wind load. Therefore, the most adverse condition for wind direction was perpendicular to conductors or suspension cables. Wind speeds were calculated for conditions from 0 m/s to 25 m/s. Figure 18 shows a diagram of the structure under wind load.

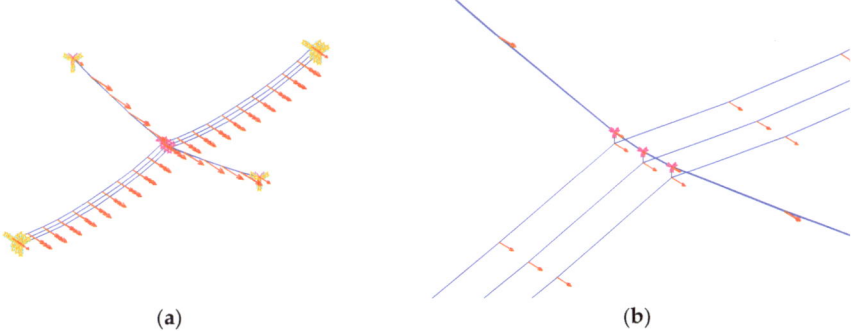

**Figure 18.** Diagram of wind loading on FE model of 2-span long-span CRS: (**a**) Fully loaded model; (**b**) Detail of loaded model.

### 4.2. Response of Wind Load

As described above, the major concern in static wind load conditions was the internal force and horizontal deformation of the structure. Typical deformation of the long-span CRS under static wind load is shown in Figure 19.

A static wind load was applied to obtain the horizontal displacement of CRSSI. The horizontal displacement of CRSSI was calculated. The length of the suspension insulator was 6.42 m. The displacement of CRSSI was composed of displacement for the insulator, suspension cable, and conductor. In order to analyze the increment in displacement, the displacement of the insulator, suspension cable, and conductor was also calculated. A diagram of different displacements of CRSSI is shown in Figure 20. Moreover, the same calculations were used for CRSSI, in which the length of SI was 0 m in comparison.

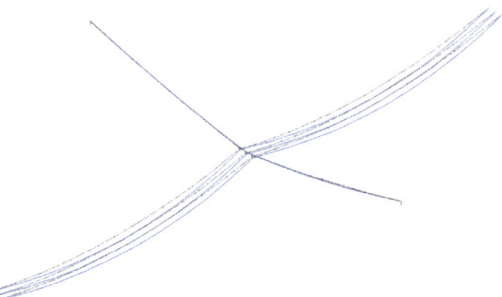

**Figure 19.** Unscaled deformation of cable-supported structures due to static wind load (Dotted: undeformed, Solid: deformed).

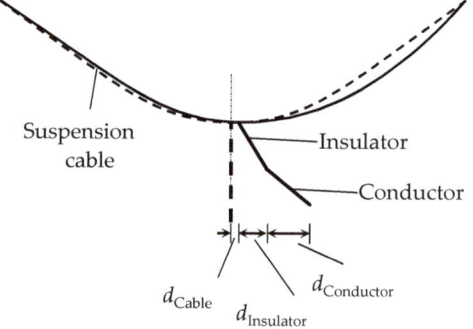

**Figure 20.** Diagram of displacement of suspension cable of long-span CRSSI (Dotted: undeformed, Solid: deformed, SI = 6.42 m).

As analyzed above, $d_{\text{Sum}}$ was calculated:

$$d_{\text{Sum}} = d_{\text{Cable}} + d_{\text{Insulator}} + d_{\text{Conductor}} \tag{31}$$

where $d_{\text{Cable}}$ is the displacement of the conductor, $d_{\text{Conductor}}$ is the placement of the conductor, and $d_{\text{Insulator}}$ is the displacement of the insulator. Here, the length of the SI was 6.42 m.

When the length of the SI was 0 m, the displacement of the insulator was 0 m; a diagram of each displacement is shown in Figure 21. As analyzed above, $d'_{\text{Sum}}$ was calculated as follows:

$$d'_{\text{Sum}} = d'_{\text{Cable}} + d'_{\text{Conductor}} \tag{32}$$

where $d'_{\text{Cable}}$ is the displacement of the conductor, and $d'_{\text{Conductor}}$ is the placement of the conductor. Here, the length of the SI was 0 m.

In Table 3, $d_{\text{Cable}}$ is approximately equal to $d'_{\text{Cable}}$, which means the displacement of the suspension cable had a small influence on the increment in displacement. On the contrary, the displacement of the insulator could not be ignored. To analyze the reason for the increment in displacement, $\Delta_d$ was calculated:

$$\Delta_d = d_{\text{Sum}} - d'_{\text{Sum}} \tag{33}$$

where $d_{\text{Sum}}$ is the horizontal displacement for SI = 6.42 m, and $d'_{\text{Sum}}$ is the horizontal displacement for SI = 0 m.

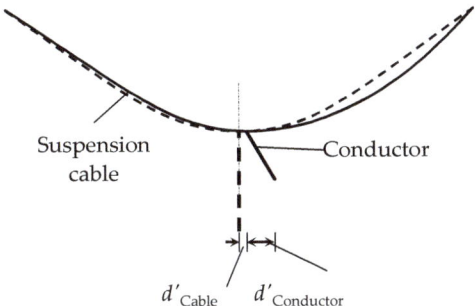

**Figure 21.** Diagram of displacement of suspension cable of long-span CRSSI (Dotted: undeformed, Solid: deformed, SI = 0 m).

**Table 3.** Comparison of displacement for SI with length of 6.42 m and length of 0 m.

| Wind Speed (m/s) | SI = 6.42 m | | | | SI = 0 m | | | $\Delta_d$ |
|---|---|---|---|---|---|---|---|---|
| | $d_{Sum}$ | $d_{Cable}$ | $d_{Insulator}$ | $d_{Conductor}$ | $d'_{Sum}$ | $d'_{Cable}$ | $d'_{Conductor}$ | |
| 0  | 0.00  | 0.00 | 0.00 | 0.00  | 0.00  | 0.00 | 0.00  | 0.00 |
| 5  | 0.93  | 0.01 | 0.12 | 0.80  | 0.87  | 0.01 | 0.86  | 0.06 |
| 10 | 3.73  | 0.05 | 0.46 | 3.22  | 3.50  | 0.05 | 3.45  | 0.23 |
| 15 | 8.20  | 0.11 | 1.01 | 7.08  | 7.68  | 0.11 | 7.57  | 0.52 |
| 20 | 14.20 | 0.20 | 1.75 | 12.25 | 13.29 | 0.20 | 13.09 | 0.91 |
| 25 | 21.00 | 0.30 | 2.60 | 18.10 | 19.70 | 0.30 | 19.40 | 1.30 |

$d_{Sum}$, $d'_{Sum}$, $\Delta_d$, and $d_{Insulator}$ were plotted as a line graph in Figure 22. $\Delta_d$ was approximately half of $d_{Insulator}$. The reason for this was that maximum horizontal displacement for the conductor was at the midpoint of the conductor. The increase in $d_{Insulator}$ increased the displacement of one end for the conductor, while the other end of the conductor did not change. Thus, based on conditions of geometry, the increment of $d_{Conductor}$ was approximately half of $d_{Insulator}$. So, $\Delta_d$ was approximately half of $d_{Insulator}$. The larger $d_{Insulator}$ resulted in a larger $d_{Conductor}$, and the horizonal displacement of the CRS system increased. In summary, a longer SI resulted in lower frequency and greater displacement, while a shorter SI posed a risk of discharge and made construction more challenging. Consequently, the length of the SI must be constrained within reasonable limits.

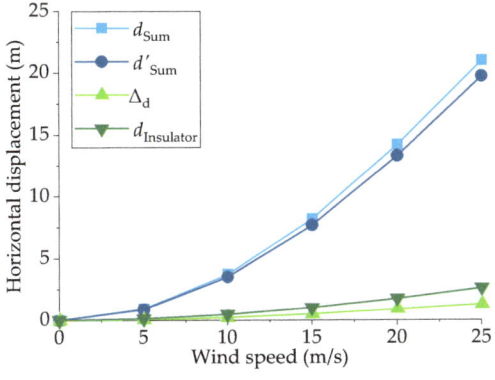

**Figure 22.** Influence of wind speed on maximum horizontal displacement of conductor.

A static wind load was applied to obtain the horizontal displacement of CRSTI, and a comparison between CRSTI and CRSSI was made. The displacements of the conductor under different wind speeds for the two systems are shown in Figure 23. It was summarized that horizontal displacements of the conductor were increased with the increase in wind speed in the two systems. Further, the horizontal displacement of CRSSI was higher than that of CRSTI. The reason for this was that under the same condition of wind speed, for CRSSI, the wind load acted not only on the conductor and the cable but also on the insulator. The increment in the displacement caused by the insulator needed to be considered, which led to the displacement of CRSSI being higher. In practical application, an excessive lateral displacement led to a distance between the conductor and the cable that fell below the safe space, posing a risk to the integrity of the transmission structure.

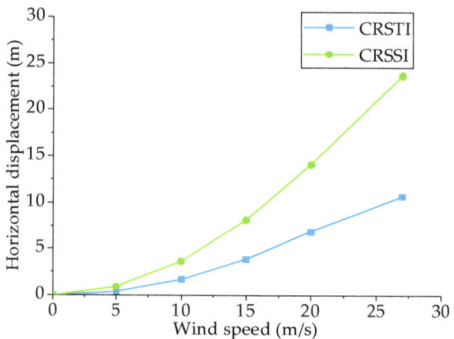

**Figure 23.** Influence of wind speed on tensile force of suspension cable.

Different numbers of spans were used to study their influence on the tension force of the suspension cable and horizontal displacement. The results are shown in Figure 24. As shown in Figure 24, the increase in the spans had no effect on the tensile force of the suspension cable and the horizontal displacement of the conductor. The same calculation was used for CRSTI, and the results are shown in Figure 25. The calculation results were similar for both systems, and the number of spans had no effect on the two systems. In the case of horizontal displacement, an increase in spans not only raised the wind load on the structure but also added weight to the entire system. As a result, the incremental increase in horizontal displacement could be disregarded for both structures. Regarding tension force, the conductors were connected to insulators or suspension cables, and an increase in span had no influence on the individual conductor, resulting in the constancy of tensile force on both structures.

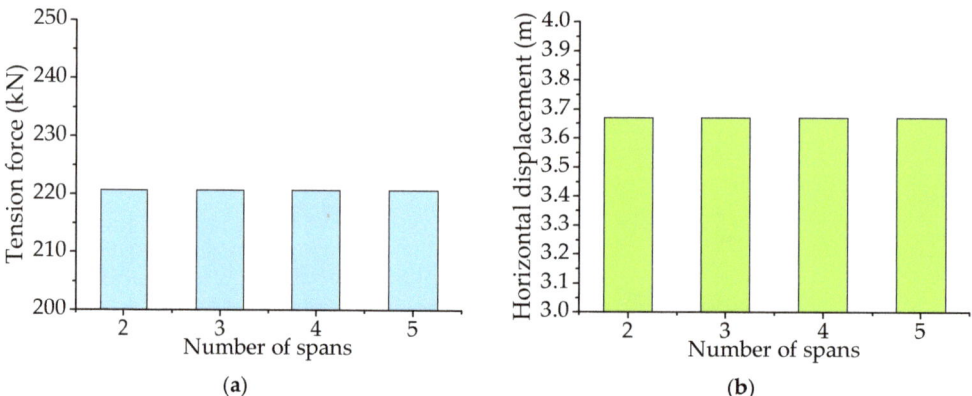

**Figure 24.** Influence of number of spans of conductor on CRSSI: (**a**) tensile force of suspension cable (**b**) horizontal displacement (wind speed = 10 m/s).

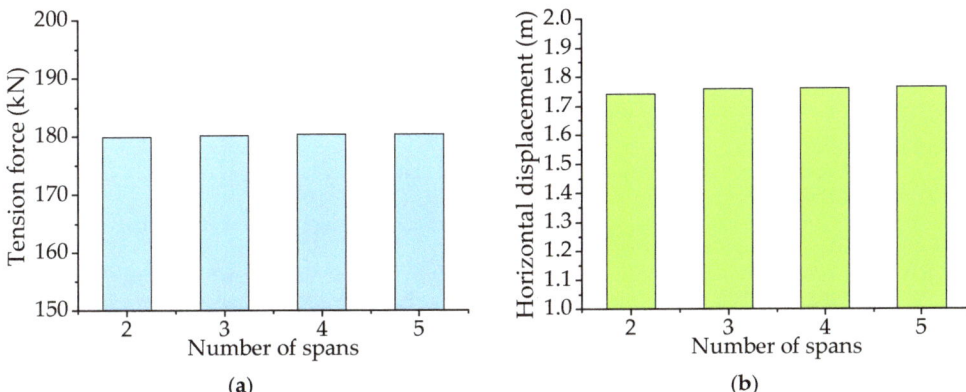

**Figure 25.** Influence of number of spans of conductor for CRSTI: (**a**) tensile force of suspension cable (**b**) horizontal displacement (wind speed = 10 m/s).

## 5. Conclusions

This paper presents a study of a theoretical modeling approach and FE analysis for long-span CRS with a suspension insulator. The following conclusions were drawn:

- The formula for cables of a long-span CRS system with an insulator and a process of numerical solution were given. Based on classic expression of catenary, the approximate formula of suspension cable under the action of a single concentrated force was derived. A process for numerical solution was given and demonstrated. The presented discussion about the expression of cable was proved to be meaningful for further modeling in FEA. The function of suspension cables and conductors deduced in this paper was applicable to calculate the non-tensional length before construction.
- With an FE model, dynamic properties of a long-span CRS with a suspension insulator were analyzed. The natural frequency of CRSSI decreased with the increase in the number of spans and the length of the SI. Moreover, comparisons between CRSSI and CRSTI were made. With regard to the vibration mode of the first symmetric lateral bending, the natural frequency of CRSTI was higher than that of CRSSI in the two spans. The opposite was true when the number of spans was higher than two. With regard to the mode of vibration of the first asymmetric vertical bending, the natural frequency of CRSTI was lower than that of CRSSI.
- The loading effect of static wind on long-span CRS with a suspension insulator was calculated by means of FEA. Increasing wind speed resulted in an increase in horizontal displacement of the conductor for CRSSI. The number of spans had less influence on the tension of the suspension cable and the horizontal displacement of the conductor. With the same conditions of wind speed, the horizontal displacement of CRSSI was higher than CRSTI.

**Author Contributions:** Conceptualization, X.T.; Methodology, Q.Q., X.T. and L.Y.; Software, Q.Q., Z.W. and S.H.; Validation, Y.H. and Z.W.; Investigation, S.H.; Resources, L.Y. All authors have read and agreed to the published version of the manuscript.

**Funding:** The research reported in this paper was conducted with the support of the National Natural Science Foundation of China (Project No. 52178455).

**Data Availability Statement:** All data are summarized in the tables.

**Conflicts of Interest:** Author Yujing Hu was employed by the company Design Institute of Chongqing Iron & Steel Group Co., Ltd. Authors Lin Yu and Shengli Hou were employed by the company Chongqing Haizhuang Wind Power Engineering Technology Co., Ltd. The remaining authors declare

## References

1. Burger, B.A.; Serrano, J.D.; Marais, P.; Jacobs, B. Construction of overhead lines in environmentally sensitive areas. *Transm. Distrib.* **2011**, *3*, 36–43.
2. Li, Z.; Hu, Y.; Tu, X. Wind-Induced Response and Its Controlling of Long-Span Cross-Rope Suspension Transmission Line. *Appl. Sci.* **2022**, *12*, 1488. [CrossRef]
3. Tu, X.; Wu, Y.; Li, Z.; Wang, Z. Vortex induced vibration and its controlling of long span Cross-Rope Suspension transmission line with tension insulator. *Struct. Eng. Mech.* **2021**, *78*, 87–102.
4. Toklu, Y.C.; Bekdaş, G.; Temur, R. Analysis of cable structures through energy minimization. *Struct. Eng. Mech.* **2017**, *62*, 749–758.
5. Jia, Y.; Liu, R. Form-Finding System for Overhead Transmission Line Based on ANSYS. *Energy Procedia* **2012**, *17*, 975–982.
6. Peyrot, A.H.; Lee, J.W.; Jensen, H.G.; Osteraas, J.D. Application of Cable Elements Concept to a Transmission Line with Cross Rope Suspension Structures. *IEEE Trans. Power Appar. Syst.* **1981**, *7*, 3254–3262. [CrossRef]
7. Nie, X.; Yan, Z.; Shi, J.; You, Y. The Refined Simulation and Model Analysis of the Suspension Cable Guyed Tower. *J. Shanghai Jiaotong Univ.* **2019**, *53*, 1066–1073.
8. Kempner, L., Jr.; Smith, S. Cross-rope Transmission tower-line dynamic analysis. *J. Struct. Eng. ASCE* **1984**, *110*, 1321–1335. [CrossRef]
9. McClure, G.; Lapointe, M. Modeling the structural dynamic response of overhead transmission lines. *Comput. Struct.* **2003**, *81*, 825–834. [CrossRef]
10. Wang, J.; Zhu, S.; Peng, B.; Duan, S.; Li, P. (Eds.) Static and dynamic mechanical characteristic comparison research of v-type insulator string under gale condition. In *IOP Conference Series: Earth and Environmental Science*; IOP Publishing: Bristol, UK, 2017.
11. Duan, F.; Song, Y.; Gao, S.; Liu, Y.; Chu, W.; Lu, X.; Liu, Z. Study on aerodynamic instability and galloping response of rail overhead contact line based on wind tunnel tests. *IEEE Trans. Veh. Technol.* **2023**, *72*, 7211–7220. [CrossRef]
12. Zhang, J.; Xie, Q. Failure analysis of transmission tower subjected to strong wind load. *J. Constr. Steel Res.* **2019**, *160*, 271–279. [CrossRef]
13. Zhang, Q.; Popplewell, N.; Shah, A. Galloping of bundle conductor. *J. Sound Vib.* **2000**, *234*, 115–134. [CrossRef]
14. Desai, Y.; Yu, P.; Popplewell, N.; Shah, A. Finite element modelling of transmission line galloping. *Comput. Struct.* **1995**, *57*, 407–420. [CrossRef]
15. Savory, E.; Parke, G.A.; Zeinoddini, M.; Toy, N.; Disney, P. Modelling of tornado and microburst-induced wind loading and failure of a lattice transmission tower. *Eng. Struct.* **2001**, *23*, 365–375. [CrossRef]
16. Song, Y.; Zhang, M.; Øiseth, O.; Rønnquist, A. Wind deflection analysis of railway catenary under crosswind based on nonlinear finite element model and wind tunnel test. *Mech. Mach. Theory* **2022**, *168*, 104608. [CrossRef]
17. Chen, T.; Huang, Y.-C.; Xu, Z.-W.; Chen, J.C.Y. Wind vibration control of stay cables using an evolutionary algorithm. *Wind Struct.* **2021**, *32*, 71–80.
18. Li, H.N.; Tang, S.Y.; Yi, T.H. Wind-rain-induced vibration test and analytical method of high-voltage transmission tower. *Struct. Eng. Mech.* **2013**, *48*, 435–453. [CrossRef]
19. Vecchiarelli, J. *Aeolian Vibration of a Conductor with a Stockbridge-Type Damper*; University of Toronto: Toronto, ON, Canada, 1997.
20. Jafari, M.; Hou, F.; Abdelkefi, A. Wind-induced vibration of structural cables. *Nonlinear Dyn.* **2020**, *100*, 351–421. [CrossRef]
21. Martins, A.M.; Simões, L.M.; Negrão, J.H. Optimization of cable-stayed bridges: A literature survey. *Adv. Eng. Softw.* **2020**, *149*, 102829. [CrossRef]
22. Liu, Z.; Song, Y.; Gao, S.; Wang, H. Review of Perspectives on Pantograph-Catenary Interaction Research for High-Speed Railways Operating at 400 km/h and above. *IEEE Trans. Transp. Electrif.* **2023**. [CrossRef]
23. Yin, X.; Shi, Y.; Xu, X.; Duan, Y.; Jia, Y.; Chen, G.; Zhang, X.; Yin, F. (Eds.) Research on Wind Deviation Detection Based on DENCLUE Abnormal Working Condition Filtering. In *IOP Conference Series: Earth and Environmental Science*; IOP Publishing: Bristol, UK, 2020.
24. Okamura, T.; Ohkuma, T.; Hongo, E.; Okada, H. Wind response analysis of a transmission tower in a mountainous area. *J. Wind Eng. Ind. Aerodyn.* **2003**, *91*, 53–63. [CrossRef]
25. Keyhan, H.; McClure, G.; Habashi, W.G. Dynamic analysis of an overhead transmission line subject to gusty wind loading predicted by wind–conductor interaction. *Comput. Struct.* **2013**, *122*, 135–144. [CrossRef]
26. Lalonde, S.; Guilbault, R.; Langlois, S. Modeling multilayered wire strands, a strategy based on 3D finite element beam-to-beam contacts—Part II: Application to wind-induced vibration and fatigue analysis of overhead conductors. *Int. J. Mech. Sci.* **2017**, *126*, 297–307. [CrossRef]
27. Jia, J. (Ed.) Wind induced dynamic response and fatigue assessment—Nonlinear time domain versus linear stochastic analysis. In *Structures*; Elsevier: Amsterdam, The Netherlands, 2021.
28. Deng, H.; Xu, H.; Duan, C.; Jin, X.; Wang, Z. Experimental and numerical study on the responses of a transmission tower to skew incident winds. *J. Wind Eng. Ind. Aerodyn.* **2016**, *157*, 171–188. [CrossRef]
29. Pombo, J.; Ambrósio, J. Environmental and track perturbations on multiple pantograph interaction with catenaries in high-speed trains. *Comput. Struct.* **2013**, *124*, 88–101. [CrossRef]

30. Pombo, J.; Ambrósio, J.; Pereira, M.; Rauter, F.; Collina, A.; Facchinetti, A. Influence of the aerodynamic forces on the pantograph–catenary system for high-speed trains. *Veh. Syst. Dyn.* **2009**, *47*, 1327–1347. [CrossRef]
31. Stickland, M.; Scanlon, T.; Craighead, I.; Fernandez, J. An investigation into the mechanical damping characteristics of catenary contact wires and their effect on aerodynamic galloping instability. *Proc. Inst. Mech. Eng. Part F J. Rail Rapid Transit.* **2003**, *217*, 63–71. [CrossRef]
32. Song, Y.; Liu, Z.; Rønnquist, A.; Nåvik, P.; Liu, Z. Contact wire irregularity stochastics and effect on high-speed railway pantograph–catenary interactions. *IEEE Trans. Instrum. Meas.* **2020**, *69*, 8196–8206. [CrossRef]
33. Xu, J. Wet Snow Flashover Characteristics of 500-kV AC Insulator Strings with Different Arrangements. *Appl. Sci.* **2019**, *9*, 930. [CrossRef]
34. Yan, Z.; Li, Z.; Savory, E.; Lin, W.E. Galloping of a single iced conductor based on curved-beam theory. *J. Wind Eng. Ind. Aerodyn.* **2013**, *123*, 77–87. [CrossRef]

**Disclaimer/Publisher's Note:** The statements, opinions and data contained in all publications are solely those of the individual author(s) and contributor(s) and not of MDPI and/or the editor(s). MDPI and/or the editor(s) disclaim responsibility for any injury to people or property resulting from any ideas, methods, instructions or products referred to in the content.

*Article*

# Innovative Use of UHF-RFID Wireless Sensors for Monitoring Cultural Heritage Structures

**Amedeo Gregori [1], Chiara Castoro [1,*], Micaela Mercuri [1], Antonio Di Natale [2] and Emidio Di Giampaolo [2]**

[1] Department of Civil, Building-Architectural and Environmental Engineering, University of L'Aquila, Piazzale Ernesto Pontieri, Monteluco di Roio, 67100 L'Aquila, Italy; amedeo.gregori@univaq.it (A.G.); micaelamercuri2029@u.northwestern.edu (M.M.)

[2] Department of Industrial and Information Engineering and Economics, University of L'Aquila, Piazzale Ernesto Pontieri, Monteluco di Roio, 67100 L'Aquila, Italy; antonio.dinatale-univaq@outlook.com (A.D.N.); emidio.digiampaolo@univaq.it (E.D.G.)

* Correspondence: chiara.castoro@libero.it

**Citation:** Gregori, A.; Castoro, C.; Mercuri, M.; Di Natale, A.; Di Giampaolo, E. Innovative Use of UHF-RFID Wireless Sensors for Monitoring Cultural Heritage Structures. *Buildings* **2024**, *14*, 1155. https://doi.org/10.3390/buildings14041155

Academic Editors: Shaohong Cheng and Haijun Zhou

Received: 25 March 2024
Revised: 11 April 2024
Accepted: 15 April 2024
Published: 19 April 2024

Copyright: © 2024 by the authors. Licensee MDPI, Basel, Switzerland. This article is an open access article distributed under the terms and conditions of the Creative Commons Attribution (CC BY) license (https://creativecommons.org/licenses/by/4.0/).

**Abstract:** This paper reports a novel investigation in applying commercial Ultra High-Frequency RFID tags (UHF-RFID tags), which are widely used in logistics as sensing elements in civil engineering structures, particularly for monitoring out-of-plane displacements of brick masonry walls. Both laboratory tests and in situ experimental tests assessed the feasibility of the proposed application. Laboratory tests showed a very satisfactory response while the in situ experiments showed a weaker response. Nevertheless, the potential reliability of the proposed technique can be stated. The authors traced back the causes of the performance decrease to environmental interference, mainly due to the extensive presence of a rigid steel frame surrounding the out-of-plane loaded panels. Measurements of displacements, in fact, are obtained indirectly from the phase of UHF-RFID signals that strongly suffer from multipath generated by metallic surfaces. Despite some limitations, the proposed measurement technique permits a reliable and sustainable approach to the monitoring of structures. The use of commercial UHF-RFID wireless tags, in fact, assures easy and fast installation operations and assures the possibility of placing a large number of sensors over the structure with very low maintenance costs with respect to the more traditional monitoring techniques. Moreover, using very thin and small commercial UHR-RFID tags on cultural heritage structures can represent an opportunity for sustainable long-time monitoring with reduced costs. Overall, the results of this study are sufficiently satisfactory to be considered as the opening of new possible scenarios in wireless structural monitoring in the civil engineering field. The authors propose as future work to use UHF-RFID tags for the real-time monitoring of an existing masonry facade that, not being characterized by the presence of a steel frame, can potentially assure an adequate response and properly transmit the electromagnetic signal.

**Keywords:** damage detection; structural monitoring; wireless sensors; UHF-RFID tags; masonry structures; out of plane behavior; experimental data

## 1. Introduction

Structural damage identification is a topic of paramount importance among researchers, engineering practitioners and a large variety of stakeholders [1–6]. In fact, the quantification of the wellness state of the built environment is the first fundamental step, necessary to individuate sustainable and optimized strategies leading to repair interventions [7] of degraded structures or their demolition and future reconstruction [8]. The future of Structural Health Monitoring (SHM) is to resort to an intelligent way of monitoring systems, aiming to analyze both features and damage of infrastructures [9], or the structural behavior of historical buildings subjected to seismic loads and fatigue effects [10], as well as the material aging of quasibrittle materials that are part of our everyday life [11–17].

Song et al. [18] investigated the boundaries of SHM for civil structures discussing different topics such as data processing algorithms to detect damage, modeling, simulation, sensor development, materials studies, state-of-the-art reviews, and case studies. Different methods and approaches have been investigated by researchers for the SHM of civil structures, in particular bridges. Real-time kinematic global positioning system (GPS) continuous health monitoring using relative deformations was carried out on a long-span Zhujiang Huangpu Bridge by Kaloop and Kim [19]. Guzman-Acevedo et al. [20] investigated the application of GPS receivers, accelerometers, and smartphones, integrating a smart sensor for the SHM of a bridge.

To monitor the health status of buildings, Qingkai Kong et al. [21] used sensors inside smartphones to demonstrate their potential usage as a way to monitor displacements of small local earthquakes. Sivasuriyan et al. [22], instead, investigated the real-time monitoring and response of a building using advanced sensor technology.

Among all the available monitoring systems, wireless methodologies are increasingly used and developed [23–28]. Wireless sensor networks (WSNs), in fact, permit more easy and fast installation operations, especially for measurement points difficult to access. Other advantages typical of the mentioned wireless techniques are related to the possibility of placing a large number of sensors over the structure, and therefore obtaining a distributed assessment of the structural condition, as both the devices and the maintenance costs are very low with respect to the more traditional monitoring techniques [29]. One of the most important features of the wireless technique is related to the possibility of monitoring structures belonging to the historical, cultural, and architectural heritage, which manifested collapse or extensive damage phenomenon during the last earthquakes [30–32]. Regardless of this potentiality, researchers have still not extensively applied wireless monitoring systems to the cultural heritage structures and this will be the aim of our proposed study. The latest research investigates antennas operating at microwave frequency as wireless sensing units [33–38]. The antenna is itself the sensor so that these devices have a long lifetime with almost negligible maintenance since do not have batteries and, because of the very low cost they can be deployed over wide structures or embedded inside them. Some devices are based on Radio Frequency Identification (RFID) technology, they load the antenna with a microchip that performs the modulation of the back-scattered signal and gives a unique identification, the antenna typically is stuck on the structure to be monitored. Forces acting on the structure cause small changes in the shape of the antenna that shift its resonance frequency. That shift can be wirelessly detected and is an indirect measurement of the effects of the forces acting on the structure [39–45].

Among the actions to which cultural heritage structures and in particular masonry structures can be subjected, the monitoring of out-of-plane actions deserves particular attention. Under seismic excitation, masonry walls go under out-of-plane and in-plane actions (at the same time) [46]. Out-of-plane collapse of peripheral walls occurs at lower seismic intensities than in-plane ones so it is the most recurrent damage observed in post-earthquake investigations [47]. Also, the heterogeneous nature of the masonry [48], composing a large part of the world cultural patrimony, makes the constituent material strongly anisotropic [49] and, therefore, the necessity of placing over the structure a large number of sensors, can be easily accomplished through the newly proposed technique of RFID wireless sensors. The out-of-plane displacement of the walls represents a much more insidious and dangerous kinematic mechanism than the collapse of the walls due to in-plane actions and requires generally more demanding equipment and measurement systems to install and use for monitoring over time. For the measurement of the out-of-plane displacements of the walls [50], optical wireless techniques can be used through the use of prisms fixed on the surfaces observed by theodolites or surveys with laser scanners. In the first case, the number of points monitored is generally limited by the cost of the prisms and the survey operations; in the second case, the management of the point clouds generated by the laser scanner and the cost of this equipment make the technique possible only for very particular applications (monuments of great value, absolute displacements easily recognizable for the entire structure rather than for its individual parts). The accuracy of these techniques is also extremely variable, rarely in the order of a mm, more commonly in the order of a few mm, depending on the distance of the instrument (theodolite or laser scanner) from the structure. The use of terrestrial photogrammetry also represents an alternative, characterized by accuracy of mm but also by high costs and reduced applicability for widespread and rapid surveys. More recently, the use of drones has simplified the execution of photogrammetric surveys of an architectural type and also of detail, although with an accuracy that is not adequate for the purposes of precision structural monitoring.

In recent years, many authors investigated the use of UHF-RFID sensors [51–53]. Erman et al. [54] provided a complete review of the UHF-RFID tags based on operating frequencies, performance, size, cost, and compatibility with the targeted applications. The study by Liu et al. [45] provides a systematic comprehensive review of a suite of RFID strain sensing technology that has been developed in recent years within the context of structural health monitoring. The design and application of various kinds of RFID strain sensors in SHM are presented including Ultra High-Frequency RFID strain sensing technology. The interest in using this type of tag in civil applications has encouraged the development of our work.

In this study, we investigate commercial UHF-RFID tags as displacement sensors to be employed in civil engineering applications, particularly for monitoring historical structures belonging to the cultural heritage. In particular, this study provides the testing of the newly proposed RFID tags against a set of experimental data related to the out-of-plane behavior of masonry brick walls.

The innovative measurement technique proposed in this study permits a more sustainable and precise approach to the monitoring of structures. The use of wireless tags assures easy and fast installation operations, especially for measurement points difficult to access, and the possibility of placing a large number of sensors over the structure with very low maintenance costs with respect to the more traditional monitoring techniques. Moreover, on cultural heritage structures, it is not actually always possible to install a large number of sensors due to their large size and expensive cost and, in this sense, using very thin and small commercial UHR-RFID wireless tags for monitoring both cultural heritage structures and civil structures in general, represent a sustainable aim of the proposed study.

## 2. The RFID Technology

Generally and commercially, the RFID technology permits, automatically, the identification and/or the storage of data relating to objects [55–57] since it is based on the storage capacity of information regarding the object to which electronic labels (tags or transponders) are coupled. These tags are remotely interrogated by devices called readers. Over the years, RFID technology has developed and has been used in many sectors: industrial, automotive, medical, e-Government (see passports, identity cards, etc.), transport, and other uses. This technology allows the development of a reliable system of interconnected objects that collects and processes data in a single large global network (i.e., the Internet of Things). Given its versatility, it is considered a general-purpose technology.

An RFID system mainly is composed of four main parts:

1. A tag, which is composed of an antenna and an integrated circuit (IC) that has simple memory and simple control logic functions and is packaged as a plastic or paper label. The tag is powered up by other elements of the system through an electric or magnetic field, then it is able to transmit the information that contains. Reading and writing are allowed in handling such information in the tag memory, which stores a unique identification code.
2. The battery-less microchip inside the tag receives power through electromagnetic waves that are collected by the antenna of the RFID tag, then it allows the sending and receiving of the data contained in the memory by modulating the field back-scattered by the antenna.

3. The reader, the device used to interrogate tags also reads and filters the information back-scattered from the tags. Readers can include their own antenna in an integrated structure or can use a distinct antenna.
4. The management system (server, host computer) acts as an information interface between the reader and the network. It allows us to obtain all the available information associated with tagged objects, the identification codes of each tag, and to manage the whole system for the purposes of the use case.

Figure 1 is represented by an RFID system with its components.

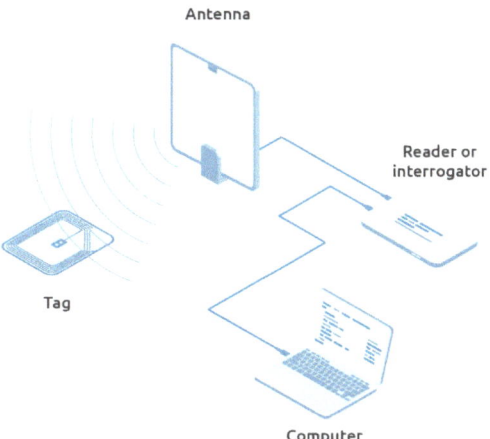

**Figure 1.** Example of an RFID reading system and its components: Tag, Antenna, Reader, Computer.

Tags are classified into three main groups: Passive, Active, Semi-Active, or Semi-Passive. Moreover, they can vary in size, shape, material, and operating frequency.

In this study, we make use of passive UHF-RFID tags, they do not have a battery but they take energy from the electromagnetic signal sent by the antenna of the reader.

In the far-field region, the interaction of the components is dominated by the electromagnetic field created by the antenna. The RFID tag resonates with the frequency of the electromagnetic field and the current generated activates the chip. The UHF class of tags operates at 867/868 MHz with distances up to thirty meters.

In this research, we used "LabId UH105" RFID commercial tags to check the displacements of two brick walls 1 m wide and 2.70 m high that underwent out-of-plane forces provided by a concentrated load acting along the middle of each wall. The application of this type of sensor in civil engineering can be considered an innovation for this kind of research since no literature reports similar applications. Experimental tests were first conducted in a controlled environment (the laboratory room) to study the feasibility of the method, and subsequently conducted on-site.

## 3. Experimental Investigation of the Application of the UHF-RFID Tags for Structural Monitoring

The commercial UH105 passive transponder made by LAB-ID have been used (Figure 2). The dimension of each tag is 17.85 × 90.85 mm$^2$ and it consists of a polyester (PET) substrate (38 µm thick), an aluminum dipole antenna (9 µm thick), and an EPC Class 1 Gen2 Impinj Monza 5 chip operating in the 840 MHz–960 MHz band, linked to the terminals of the antenna. Thanks to the good radiative properties, and specifically to the insensitivity with respect to the orientation in the space in which it is positioned, these tags can be detected at a great distance and it is suitable in situations in which there is a great number of tags, like in logistics.

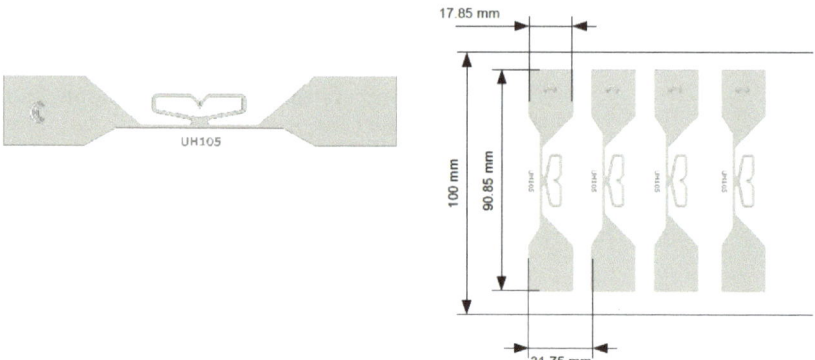

**Figure 2.** A detail of the commercial UH105 passive tag.

Table 1 and Figure 3 report the main features of the UH105 tag.

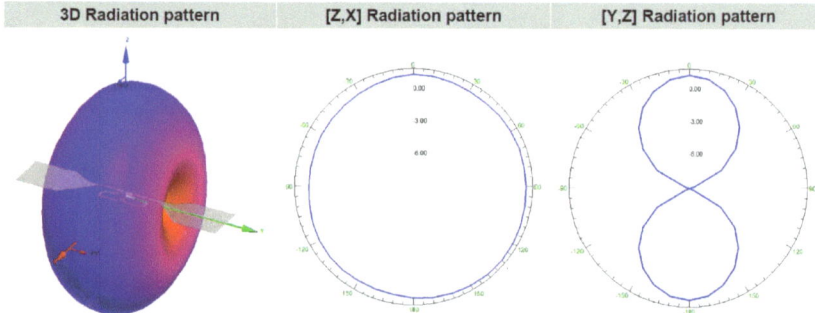

**Figure 3.** Radiation pattern of the commercial UH105 passive tag.

**Table 1.** Characteristics of the tag UH105.

| Composition | Material | Thickness [μm] |
|---|---|---|
| Top | Aluminum | $9 \pm 5\%$ |
| Support | Polyester PET | $38 \pm 5\%$ |
| Tag | Operating frequency<br>840–960 MHz | Operating temperature<br>−40 °C to +85 °C |

*3.1. Laboratory Tests: Monitoring the Tags Displacements under Out-of-Plane Action*

For assessing the feasibility and reliability of UHF RFID tags in monitoring out-of-plane displacements, two experimental tests were carried out in a laboratory environment.

In order to compare secondarily the laboratory results and the in situ experimental results, the same configuration of tag position, measurement distances, and spaces were designed and applied to the in situ experimental set-up of each test, so that laboratory and in situ tests would have the same boundary conditions, except for the environment.

The first laboratory test set-up was composed of six tags positioned following a 3 × 2 grid. Each tag was identified by an ID number, so they were identified as Tag 2.2, Tag 1.5, Tag 1.1, Tag 1.3, Tag 2.1, and Tag 1.4.

The authors decided to position the tags on a polystyrene panel since polystyrene results "transparent" to the electromagnetic waves so it does not influence the back-scattered signal. The position of the tags is shown in Figure 4. The reader's antenna was placed in front of the polystyrene panel, with a distance greater than 60 cm. The center of the reader's antenna (represented as a projection by a violet dot in Figure 4) appears on the panel at

3 cm (approximately) below the central row of the tags. The operating frequency is 867 MHz while the radiated power was set at 20 dBm since it was sufficient for a correct reading of each tag. A micro-metric screw was applied to the panel in order to move it orthogonal to its plane for simulating forces that cause out-of-plane displacements. The displacements were performed by moving the panel at steps of 5 mm, reaching 60 mm of distance from the starting position.

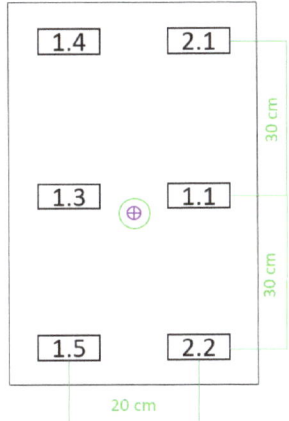

**Figure 4.** Scheme of the experimental set-up of the 1st laboratory test.

A second laboratory experimental test was performed, with a similar set-up. The tags chosen for the 2nd experimental test were: Tag 2.4, Tag 2.2, Tag 2.1, Tag 1.4, Tag 2.3, and Tag 1.2.

Only a few tags were chosen for both laboratory tests in order to not overlook any anomalies related to the specific characteristics of a given tag.

The tags were positioned on a polystyrene panel, as represented in Figure 5. The reader's antenna was placed in front of the panel, at 62 cm of distance. In this case, the projection of the center of the reader's antenna on the panel (dot in violet in Figure 5) results at 15 cm from the center of Tag 2.1 and 10 cm from the center of Tag 1.4. The panel was subjected to the same out-of-plane displacements of the 1st test (orthogonal to the panel) with steps of 5 mm, by the use of a micrometric screw, reaching 70 mm of maximum distance compared with the starting 0 position. In this case, the radiated power was set at 24 dBm, which ensured a correct reading of each tag. The test set-up is shown in Figure 6.

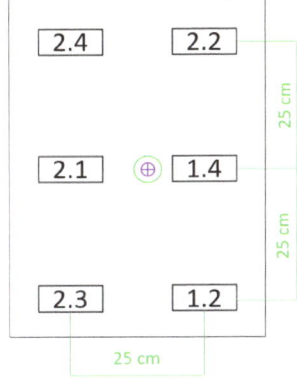

**Figure 5.** Scheme of the experimental set-up of the 2nd laboratory test.

**Figure 6.** 2nd laboratory campaign: experimental set-up.

*3.2. Results of the Laboratory Experimental Tests*

In both laboratory tests, the measurement system recorded the displacement at each step (each 5 mm). The quantities useful to determine the displacement are the phase and RSSI ("Received Signal Strength Indicator") of the signal backscattered by tags and received by the reader. The results of the displacement measurements are reported for each tag, determining the mobile mean and standard deviation of the phase, for each step of measurement. The RSSI is also reported. Values around $-52$ dBm shows a good signal's quality.

3.2.1. Results of the 1st Laboratory Test

In Figure 7, Figure 8, Figure 9, Figure 10, Figure 11, and Figure 12, the results of the acquisition systems of Tag 2.2, Tag 1.5, Tag 1.1, Tag 1.3, Tag 2.1, and Tag 1.4 are reported, respectively. The values of the mean and standard deviation of the phase recorded at each step of measurement, and RSSI values, are reported for each Tag.

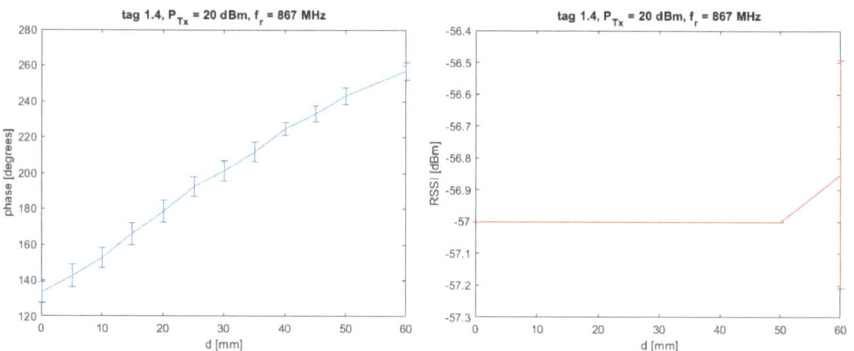

**Figure 7.** 1st laboratory test: mean and standard deviation of phase (**left side**) and RSSI (**right side**) recorded for each step of measurement of Tag 1.4.

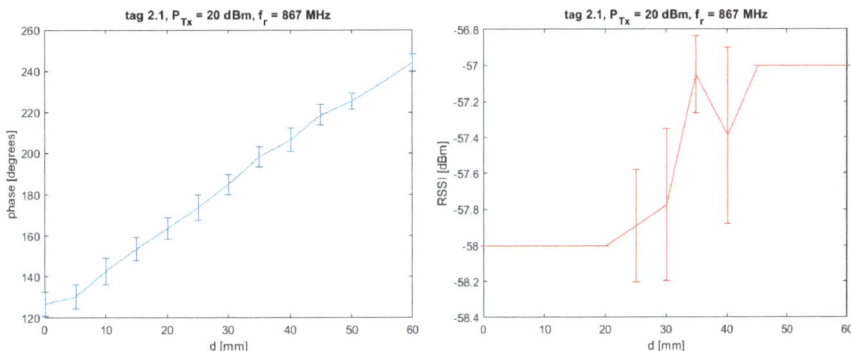

**Figure 8.** 1st laboratory test: mean and standard deviation of phase (**left side**) and RSSI (**right side**) recorded for each step of measurement of Tag 2.1.

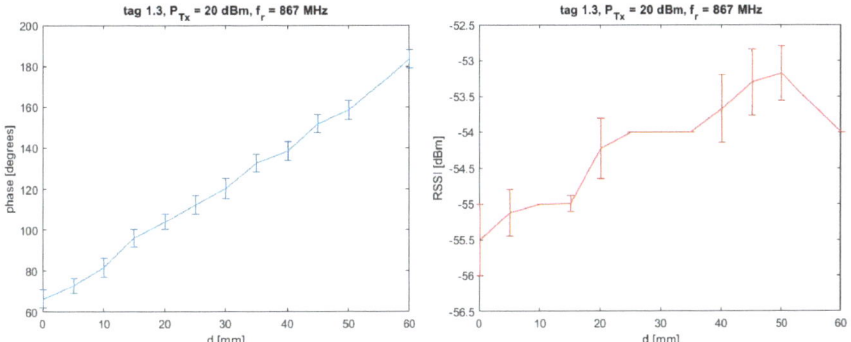

**Figure 9.** 1st laboratory test: mean and standard deviation of phase (**left side**) and RSSI (**right side**) recorded for each step of measurement of Tag 1.3.

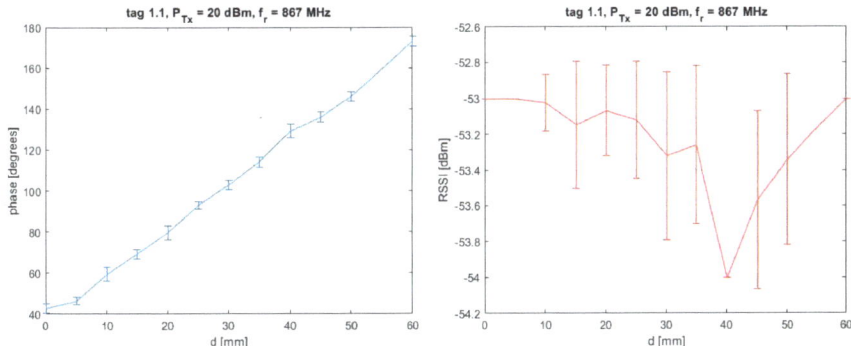

**Figure 10.** 1st laboratory test: mean and standard deviation of phase (**left side**) and RSSI (**right side**) recorded for each step of measurement of Tag 1.1.

Evidently, the values of phase change pass from 0 mm to 60 mm. In detail, values of phase are increasing passing from one measurement step to the successive (from Figures 7–12). This demonstrates that tags are sensitive to the displacements imposed on the panel. For Tags 1.4, 1.5, and 2.2, the RSSI values are quite constant (meaning stale communication), while for the other tags, RSSI values show very small fluctuations, which are acceptable.

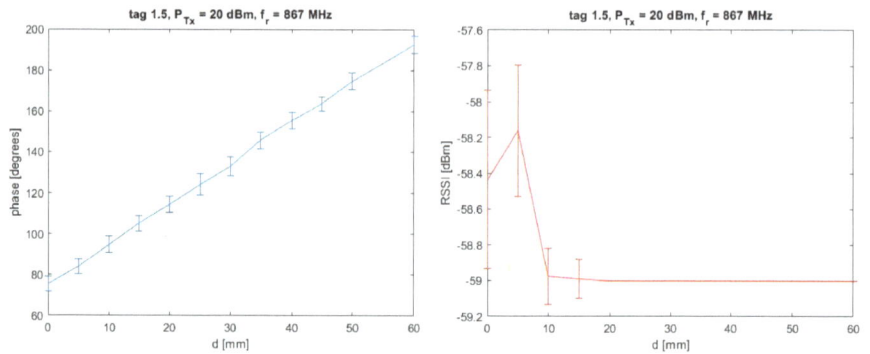

**Figure 11.** 1st laboratory test: mean and standard deviation of phase (**left side**) and RSSI (**right side**) recorded for each step of measurement of Tag 1.5.

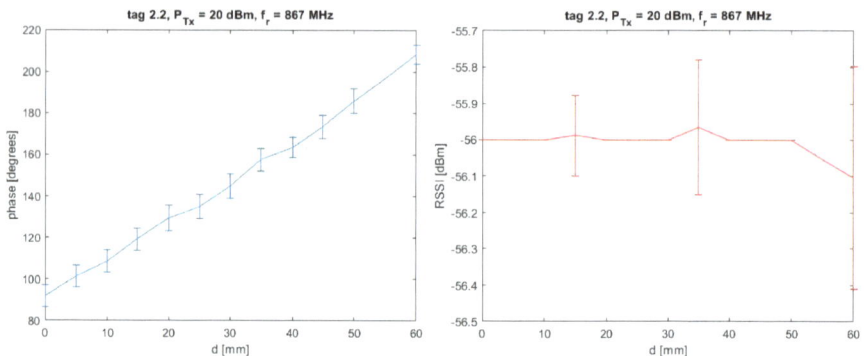

**Figure 12.** 1st laboratory test: mean and standard deviation of phase (**left side**) and RSSI (**right side**) recorded for each step of measurement of Tag 2.2.

In Figure 13, a flowchart illustrating the methodology used to obtain the results is represented.

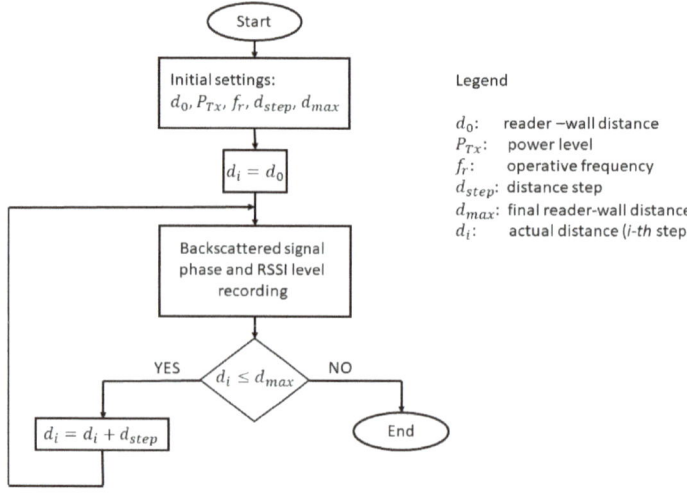

**Figure 13.** Flowchart of the methodology used to obtain the results.

The assessment of the feasibility of this new wireless monitoring system can be achieved by converting the phase difference between two consecutive measurement steps into distance difference (which should be related to the imposed displacement) by using the following equation:

$$d - d_0 = \frac{(f - f_0) \cdot \lambda}{4 \cdot 180} \quad (1)$$

where $f - f_0$ is the difference in phase between a specific step of measurement and the previous step, and $\lambda$ is the wavelength of the electromagnetic signal that is 0.346 m in this specific case.

From Equation (1), we determine the difference in distance $d - d_0$ that occurs when the panel or the tag moves from one position to another.

This distance measured by the tags does not correspond to the displacement we are interested in knowing, i.e., the measured distance concerns the slant path between the reader's and tag's antenna while we are interested in the movement (out-of-plane) along the direction orthogonal to the plane on which the tag is placed. For this reason, the out-of-plane displacement was calculated geometrically projecting the measured slant path onto the orthogonal direction by exploiting the knowledge of measurement set-up.

In order to assess the feasibility of the proposed technique we compare the results of the displacements measured by the tags with the actual displacements imposed (indicated as "displacement reference" in the following graphs).

For faster comprehension, the comparison of displacements has been shown according to the position of the tags (see Figure 4).

Figure 14 shows the displacements measured by Tag 2.1 and 1.4, compared to the displacements imposed on the panel. Figure 15 shows the displacements measured by Tags 1.1 and 1.3 and Figure 16 shows the displacements of Tags 2.2 and 1.5.

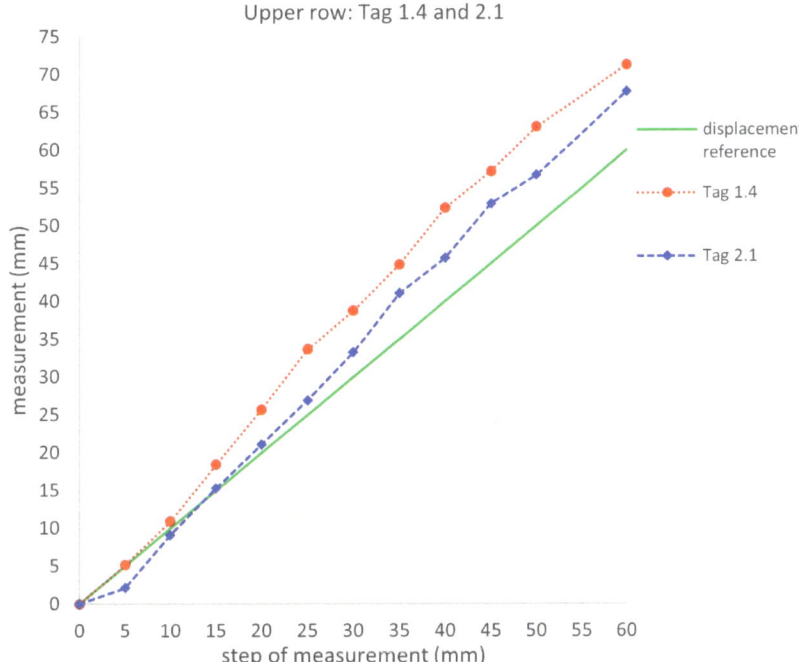

**Figure 14.** 1st laboratory test: Upper row Tag 1.4 and 2.1. Comparison between the displacements measured using tags and that imposed on the panel (displacement reference).

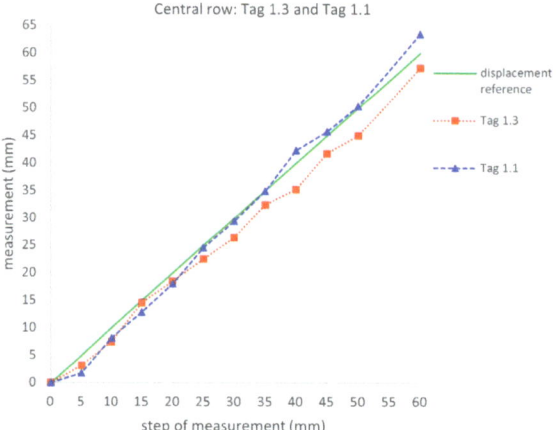

**Figure 15.** First laboratory test: Central row Tag 1.3 and 1.1. Comparison between the displacements measured using tags and that imposed on the panel (displacement reference).

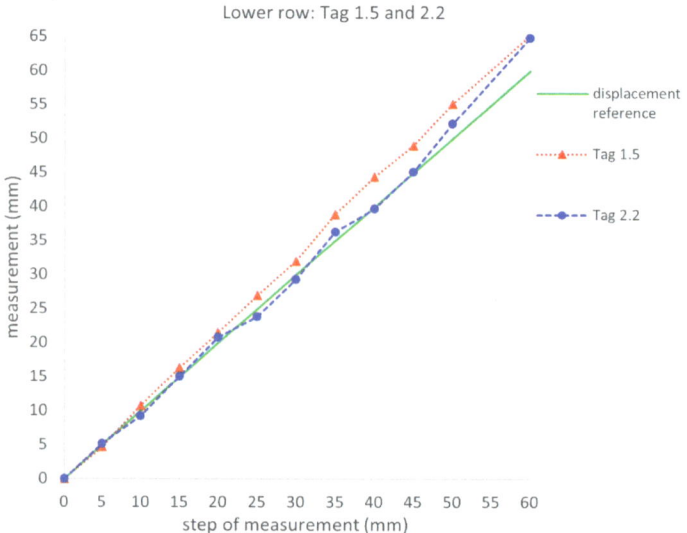

**Figure 16.** First laboratory test: Lower row Tag 1.5 and 2.2. Comparison between the displacements measured using tags and that imposed on the panel (displacement reference).

All the tags show almost matching displacements, as can be seen from the graphs. Considering the standard deviations of the values calculated using the phase measurements and the intrinsic measurement errors of the reader itself, this represents a surprising result.

It should be considered that, generally, RFID tags are influenced by metals since the electromagnetic waves are strongly scattered by metallic objects. Specifically, tags reflect part of the electromagnetic power received from the reader, this phenomenon is known as "back-scattering". Metal objects around the tag can modify or screen the signals exchanged with the reader, it is undesired in our experiments since it corrupts the expected results as shown later on. For this reason, experiments were performed initially in a laboratory room where no metals or other obstacles were detected.

In this experiment, a higher error is observed for the upper row tags, in particular for Tag 1.4.

The cause of higher error is supposed to be the larger distance of the reader's antenna from the corresponding tags with respect to central and lower row tags (see Figure 4). Tags in fact are placed on a rigid panel that translates rigidly so that their out-of-plane movement should be the same. Hence, the resulting discrepancies could be due to the environment since Tag 1.4 is located close to a plasterboard wall of the laboratory. We suppose that the metallic frame of the plasterboard wall has affected the signal, modifying the tag's response. Tags 1.5 and 1.3 (see Figure 6) also have a distance from the plasterboard wall as that of tag 1.4 but their response is better, they probably suffer less from the frame of the wall.

3.2.2. Results of the 2nd Laboratory Test

In this second test, the same Tags 2.1, 1.4, and 2.2 were used together with new Tags 2.4, 2.3, and 1.2.

In Figure 17, Figure 18, Figure 19, Figure 20, Figure 21, and Figure 22 the results of the acquisition systems of the Tag 2.4, Tag 2.2, Tag 2.1, Tag 1.4, Tag 2.3, and Tag 1.2 are reported, respectively. The values of mean and standard deviation of the phase recorded for each step of measurement, and RSSI values, are reported for each Tag.

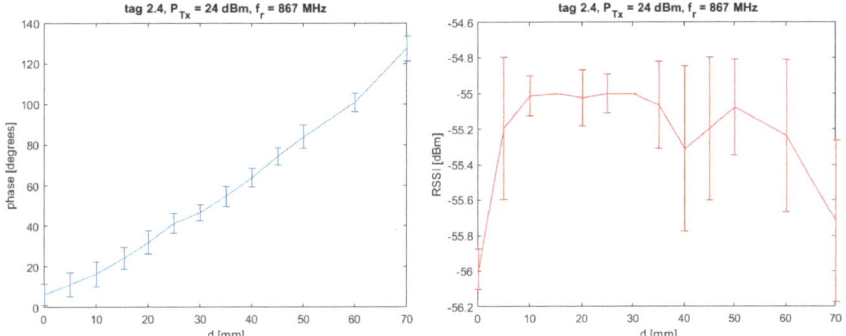

**Figure 17.** 2nd laboratory test: mean and standard deviation of phase (**left side**) and RSSI (**right side**) recorded for each step of measurement for Tag 2.4.

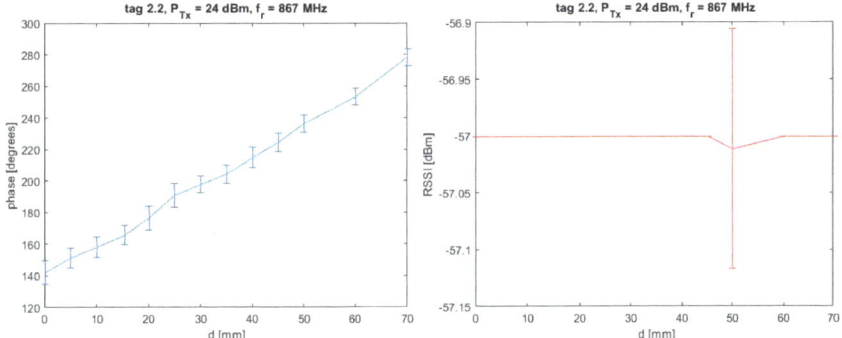

**Figure 18.** 2nd laboratory test: mean and standard deviation of phase (**left side**) and RSSI (**right side**) recorded for each step of measurement for Tag 2.2.

As can be observed from the graphs, the values of the phase increase for increasing displacement: from the starting point (0 mm) to the final point (70 mm) (see from Figures 17–22). The RSSI values are acceptable. They are constant for Tags 2.1 and 2.2, and present small fluctuations for the other tags.

To assess also, in this case, the feasibility of the proposed wireless monitoring system (and so consider it definitely feasible), the phase differences have been converted into distance differences by using Equation (1) and the displacements of the tags in the out-of-plane direction have been geometrically calculated by a 3D modeling.

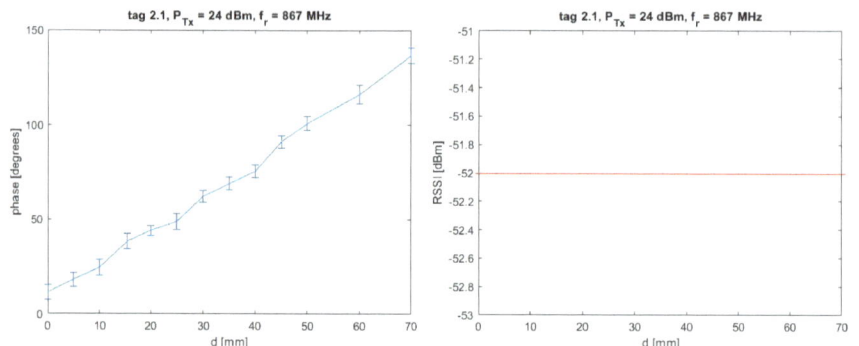

**Figure 19.** 2ond laboratory test: mean and standard deviation of phase (**left side**) and RSSI (**right side**) recorded for each step of measurement for Tag 2.1.

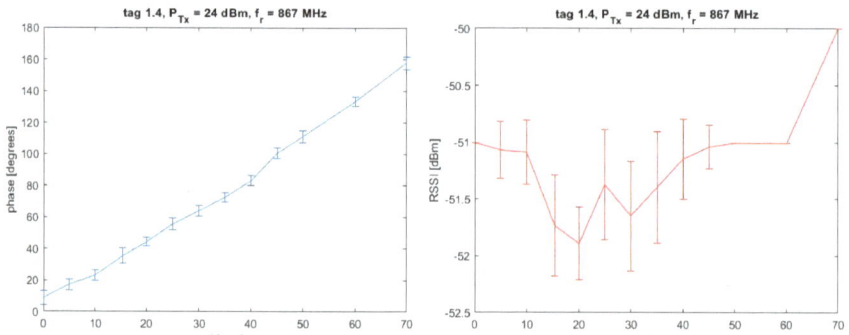

**Figure 20.** 2ond laboratory test: mean and standard deviation of phase (**left side**) and RSSI (**right side**) recorded for each step of measurement for Tag 1.4.

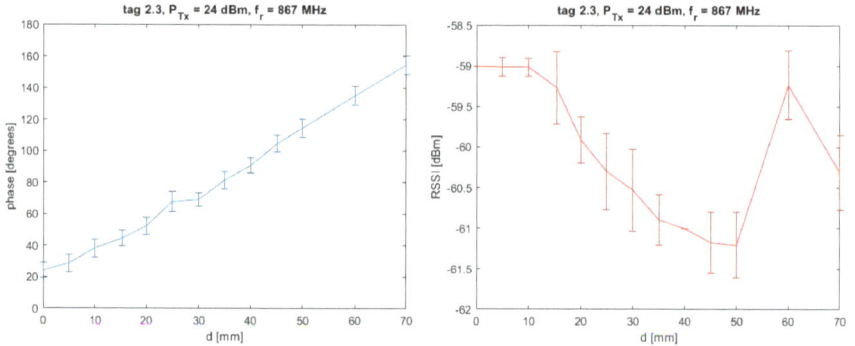

**Figure 21.** 2ond laboratory test: mean and standard deviation of phase (**left side**) and RSSI (**right side**) recorded for each step of measurement for Tag 2.3.

Similarly to the previous test, we compare the results of the displacement measured by the tags with the displacements imposed using the micro-screw (indicated as "displacement reference" in the following graphs).

Similarly to the previous test, we compare the results of the displacement measured by the tags with the displacements imposed using the micro-screw (indicated as "displacement reference" in the following graphs).

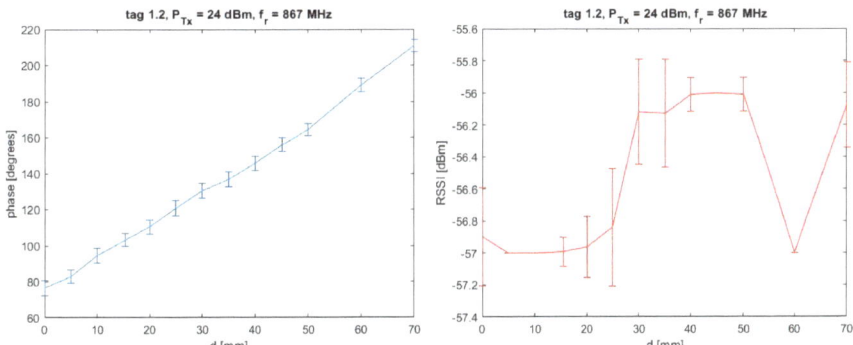

**Figure 22.** 2nd laboratory test: mean and standard deviation of phase (**left side**) and RSSI (**right side**) recorded for each step of measurement for Tag 1.2.

The comparison of displacements has been shown according to the tag's position (see Figure 5).

Figure 23 shows the displacements measured by Tag 2.2 and 2.4 compared with the displacements imposed. Figure 24 shows the displacements measured by Tag 1.4 and 2.1 and Figure 25 shows the displacements of Tag 1.2 and 2.3.

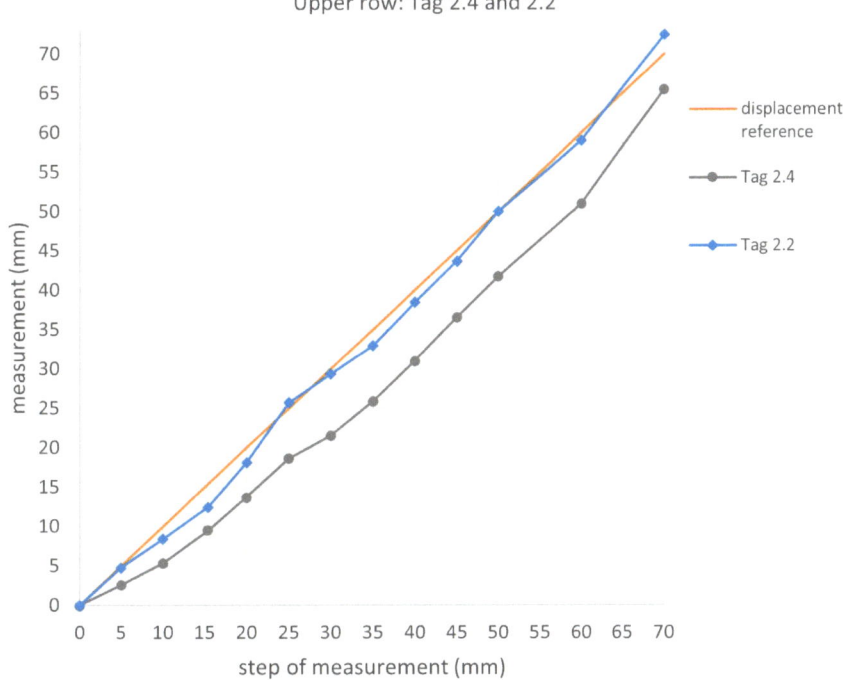

**Figure 23.** 2nd laboratory test: Upper row Tag 2.4 and 2.2. Comparison of displacements detected by the tags with that imposed on the panel (displacement reference).

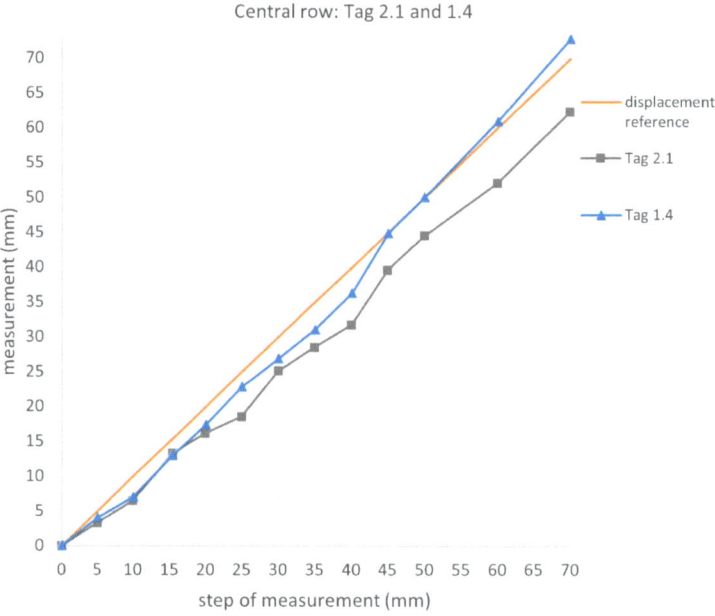

**Figure 24.** 2nd laboratory test: Central row Tag 2.1 and 1.4. Comparison of displacements detected by the tags with that imposed on the panel (displacement reference).

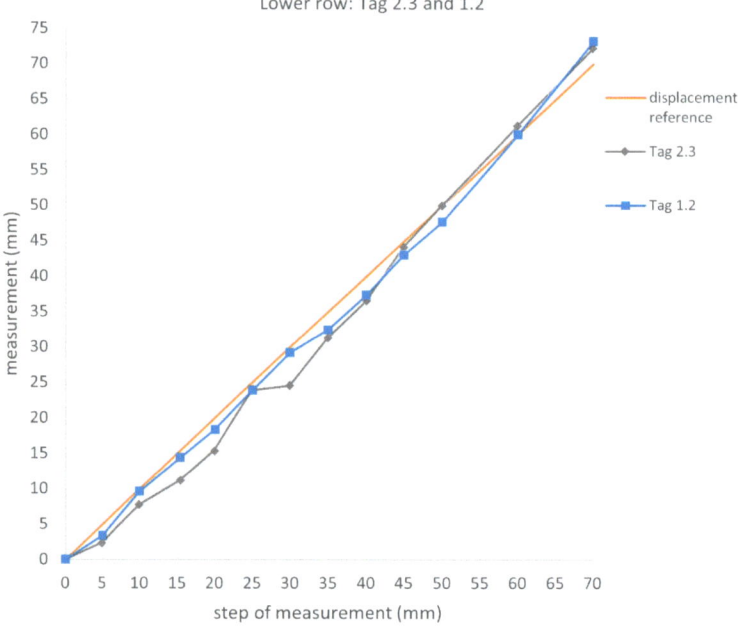

**Figure 25.** 2nd laboratory test: Lower row Tag 2.3 and 1.2. Comparison of displacements detected by the tags with that imposed on the panel (displacement reference).

As can be seen from the graphs, the tags all show quite matching displacements. More in-depth, we can observe that the tags that are positioned to the right (Tag 2.2, Tag 1.4, and

Tag 1.2) are those that better match the real displacements. Actually, these tags detected the displacements almost perfectly. This could be due to the nearer presence of the antenna (see the projection of the center in Figure 5). The tags positioned to the left are those that present higher errors, except for Tag 1.2. It can be supposed that the reduced response of these tags is due to their position, which is more distant from the antenna, together with the influence of the plasterboard wall.

Overall, it can be observed that:

- The displacements detected by the tags quite perfectly match the displacements imposed;
- The altered response of some tags is due to interference in the environment and also to the more distant position of the tags in relation to the reader's antenna;
- Measurements are intrinsically affected by the built-in errors of the reader and by the errors that occur during the processing of the data received specifically the standard deviations of the phase's values).

For example, if we consider Tag 1.4, which has been used in both laboratory tests, in the 1st test the response of the tag is not so good because it is positioned at a greater distance from the center of the antenna (upper row) and it is near the plasterboard wall (left side). In the 2nd test, instead, the same tag is positioned in the central row (nearer the antenna) and on the right side (more distant from the plasterboard wall) and the response of the tag is very satisfactory.

We can conclude that the operation of the t in a laboratory environment is very satisfactory; thus, the innovative utilization of wireless UHF-RFID tags with the purpose of monitoring out-of-plane displacements results in being feasible and quite reliable.

Considering these results, two experimental campaigns have been performed also in situ and are described in the next section.

### 3.3. In Situ Experiments: Monitoring the Out-of-Plane Displacements of the Tags on Brick Walls

The wireless UH105 tags were used to monitor the displacements of two brick walls 1 m wide and 2.70 m high. The walls were both realized and tested on a building site. Each wall underwent an out-of-plane action caused by a concentrated load applied along the middle axis of the wall. In the set-up, each wall had a fixed constraint disposed along the entire lower side on the ground and a hinge constraint at the upper side that was anchored to the metal frame.

On the first wall, the tag's position followed the same $3 \times 2$ grid used in the 1st laboratory test, in order to compare the results at the same geometric conditions. The reader's antenna was placed at 1.27 m from the ground. The wall was 0.60 m distant from the center of the antenna. A power of 20 dBm was used for the wireless acquisition of data. The experimental set-up is reported in Figure 26.

For the 2nd wall, the same tags of the 2nd laboratory test were used. Tags were placed in a $3 \times 2$ grid pattern preserving the same set-up and distances. The antenna was placed at 0.62 m from the wall and at 1.35 m from ground, while the radiated power to interrogate the tags was 24 dBm. The schemes of the set-ups are shown in Figure 27.

The tags were placed on polystyrene spacers 5 cm thick in order to mitigate the electromagnetic interaction of the tag with the materials constituting the wall.

In correspondence with the expected maximum displacement (coinciding with the half of each wall and the central tags position), a wired displacement transducer was placed in order to assess the measurement. In particular, the displacement transducer was placed at a distance of 20 cm from the left-side Tag.

Compared to laboratory tests, in this case, the walls are not expected to translate rigidly since they are constrained. Consequently, the walls are subjected to deformations and the tags cannot have the same displacements as in the laboratory tests. The recording of measurements were made at each step of measurement (5 mm).

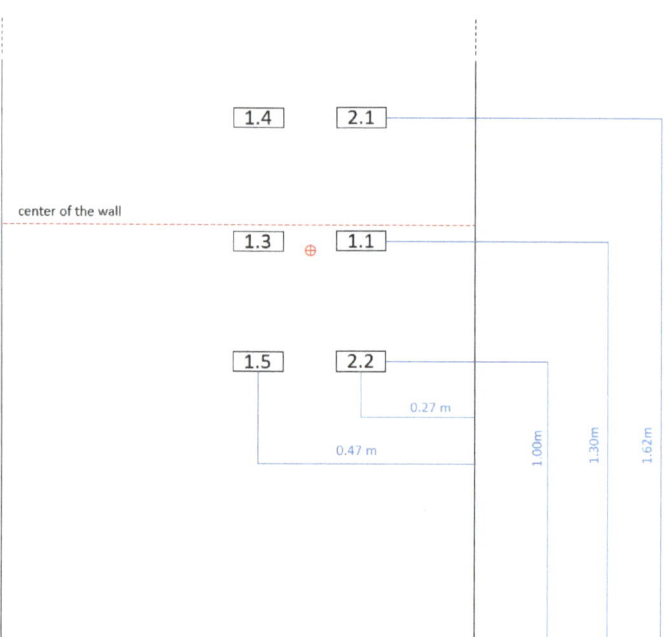

**Figure 26.** Scheme of the in-situ experimental set-up of the first wall.

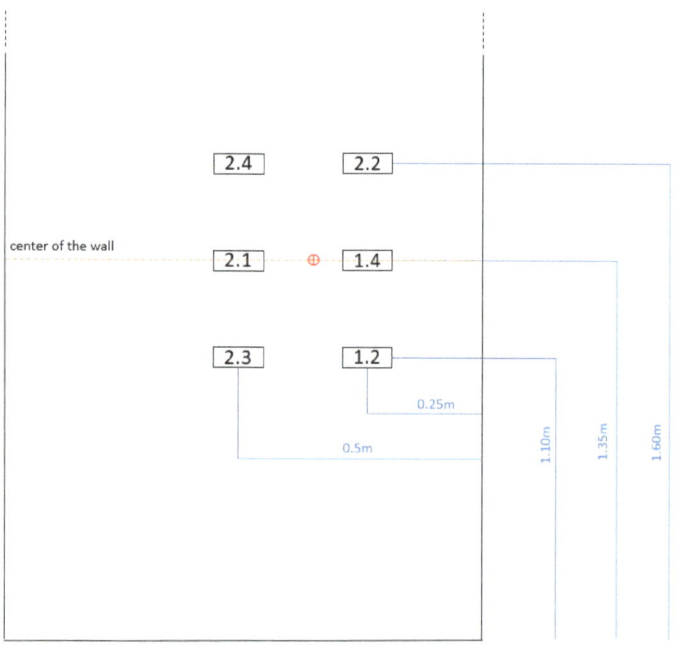

**Figure 27.** Scheme of the in-situ experimental set-up of the second wall.

Figure 28(1) shows the set-up for the experimental test on the 1st wall. Figure 28(2) shows a detail of the tags with the deformation and cracks that appear on the wall as the displacement increases. The complete deformation and final maximum displacement are shown in Figure 28(3).

The set-up for the experimental test on the 2nd wall is shown instead in Figure 29(1) and in Figure 28(2) with a detail of the deformation and cracks.

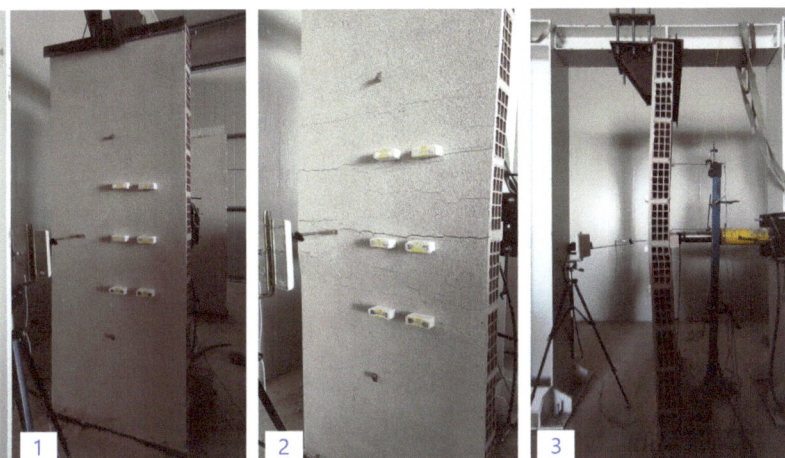

**Figure 28.** In situ experimental test conducted on the 1st wall: (**1**) Set-up; (**2**) first deformations and cracks; (**3**) Maximum deformation reached at 60 mm of displacement.

**Figure 29.** In situ experimental test conducted on the 2nd wall: (**1**) Set-up; (**2**) Complete deformation of the wall in correspondence of the final displacement of 70 mm.

## 4. Results of the In Situ Experimental Tests

*4.1. Test on the 1st Wall: Comparison between Wireless Tags Displacements and Displacements of the Wired Transducer*

The results of the measurement acquisitions of the Tag 2.1, Tag 1.4, Tag 1.1, Tag 1.3, Tag 2.2, Tag 1.5 positioned on the 1st wall are reported in Figure 30, Figure 31, Figure 32, Figure 33, Figure 34, and Figure 35, respectively. The values of mean and standard deviation of the recorded phase for each step of measurement, and RSSI values, are reported for each tag. The variation of results mainly depends on signal-to-noise ratio, i.e., if the strength of the signal is weak the reader feels the effect of the noise more than in the case the signal is strong. Even the noise can be variable since it is a superimposition of Gaussian noise and multipath (or interference), while the former depends mainly on the quality of the used equipment the latter depends on variable environmental conditions.

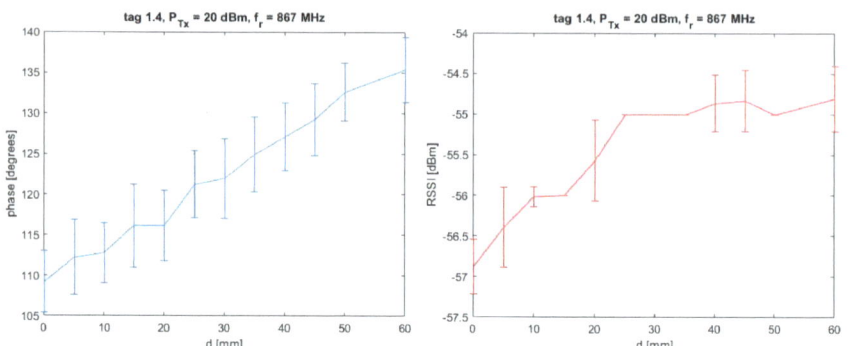

**Figure 30.** In situ experimental test on the 1st wall: mean and standard deviation of phase (**left side**) and RSSI (**right side**) recorded for each step of measurement of Tag 1.4.

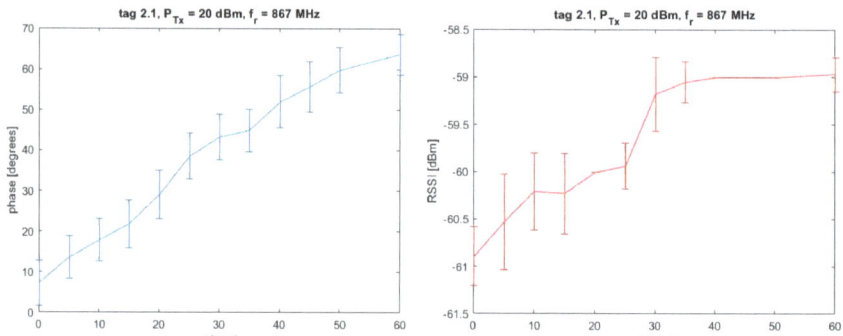

**Figure 31.** In situ experimental test on the 1st wall: mean and standard deviation of phase (**left side**) and RSSI (**right side**) recorded for each step of measurement of Tag 2.1.

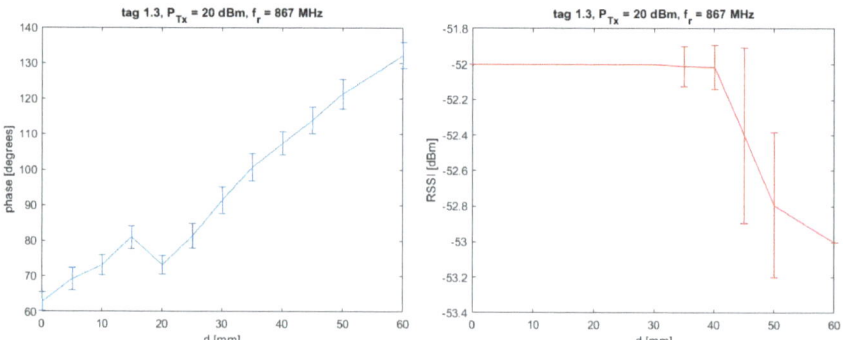

**Figure 32.** In situ experimental test on the 1st wall: mean and standard deviation of phase (**left side**) and RSSI (**right side**) recorded for each step of measurement of Tag 1.3.

As can be observed from the graphs, the values of the phase are increasing at each measurement step, from 0 mm to the maximum displacement of 60 mm (see from Figures 30–35). The tags demonstrate a sensitive response to the displacements. The RSSI values are acceptable, quite constant for tags 1.1, 1.3, and 2.2, and with very small fluctuations for the other tags.

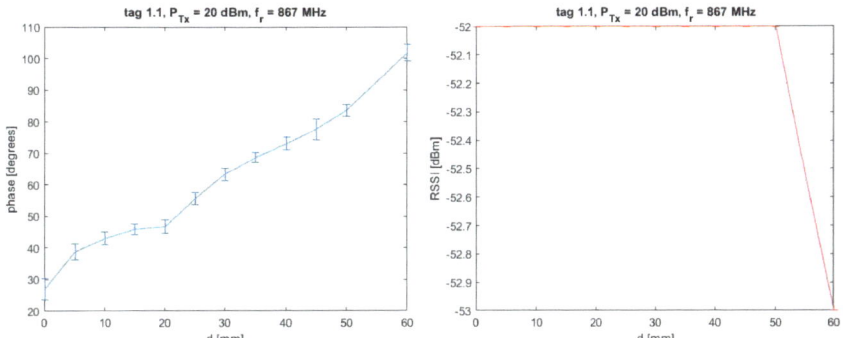

**Figure 33.** In situ experimental test on the 1st wall: mean and standard deviation of phase (**left side**) and RSSI (**right side**) recorded for each step of measurement of Tag 1.1.

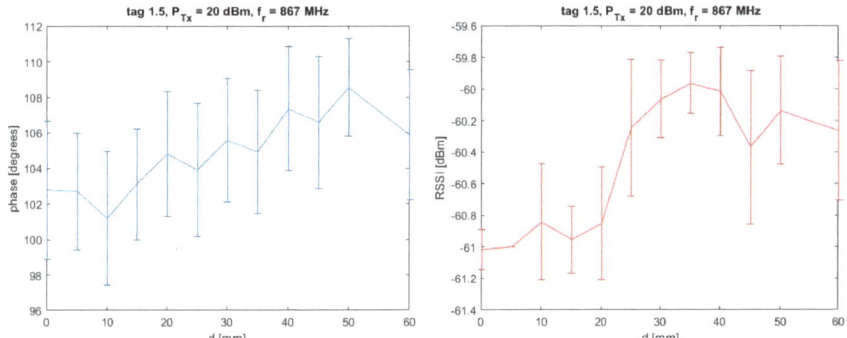

**Figure 34.** In situ experimental test on the 1st wall: mean and standard deviation of phase (**left side**) and RSSI (**right side**) recorded for each step of measurement of Tag 1.5.

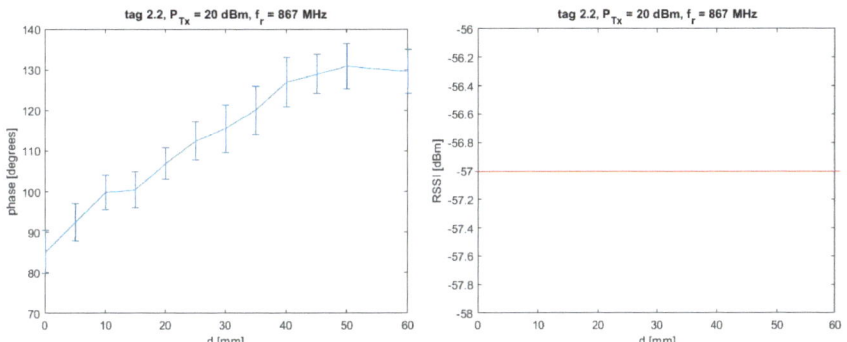

**Figure 35.** In situ experimental test on the 1st wall: mean and standard deviation of phase (**left side**) and RSSI (**right side**) recorded for each step of measurement of Tag 2.2.

The detected phase differences have been converted into distance differences by using Equation (1).

The following graphs compare the displacements of the tags in the out-of-plane direction and the displacements detected by the wired transducer.

It should be pointed out that the deformation of the wall was not uniform over its surface since the wall is constrained and the deformation is caused by a load cell that imposes forces along the center of the wall pressing in the out-of-plane direction. For this reason, the measurements to consider as reference for the tags positioned up and below the middle of the wall were calculated considering a theoretic model in which the wall was simplified as a beam constrained with fixed and hinge joints on which a concentrated load is applied in the middle.

For each tag (see Figure 26), the displacement results were plotted for comparison with those calculated for the reference wired transducer.

The displacements detected by Tag 2.1 and 1.4 are reported in Figure 36 compared with the calculated displacements detected by the wired transducer (plotted as displacement reference). Similarly, the displacements detected by Tags 1.1 and 1.3 are reported in Figure 37 and the displacements of Tags 2.2 and 1.5 are reported in Figure 38.

Observing the graphs in Figures 36–38, it can be stated that the displacements detected by the tags in the in situ test on the 1st wall are lower than those recorded simultaneously by the wired transducer. Some hypotheses can be advanced to explain this phenomenon.

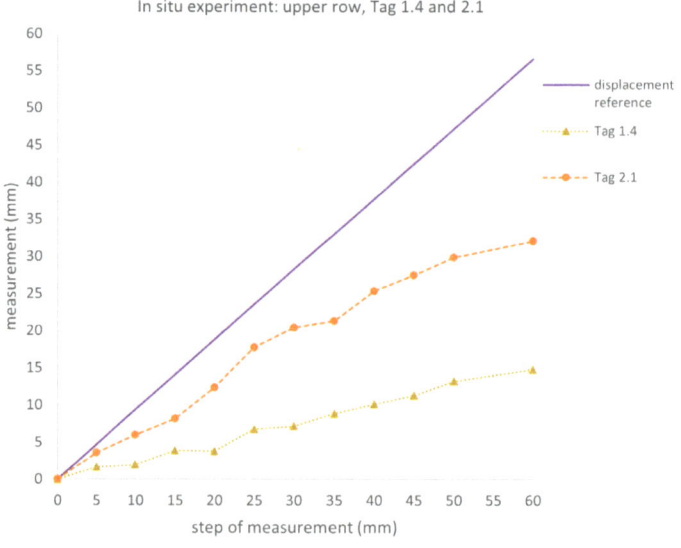

**Figure 36.** In situ experimental test on the 1st wall: the displacements detected by Tags 2.1 and 1.4 are compared with the calculated displacements of the wired transducer.

The laboratory tests demonstrated that the t performed very well and since the power of the acquisition system and the layout of the tags have remained the same for the in situ test, the causes of the response defects should be investigated in the environmental conditions of the experimental set-up.

To perform the in-situ test, a steel frame was positioned to mount the load cell and constrain the wall. In addition, the steel frame was necessarily located near the metal walls of the building, creating of course a disadvantage. In fact, the large presence of metal negatively affected the performance of the tags, giving smaller displacements compared with the actual ones.

Tags 1.5, 1.3, and 1.4, which were placed on the left side, showed smaller displacements compared to Tags 2.2, 1.1, and 2.1, which were placed on the right side of the grid. The cause could be the presence of the metal wall, as shown in Figure 28, which interfered with the transmission of the signal, modifying the phases and so the distances and displacements, despite being about 140 cm away from the tags.

The central Tags 1.1 and 1.3 showed the best response among all the tags because they were positioned nearer to the antenna.

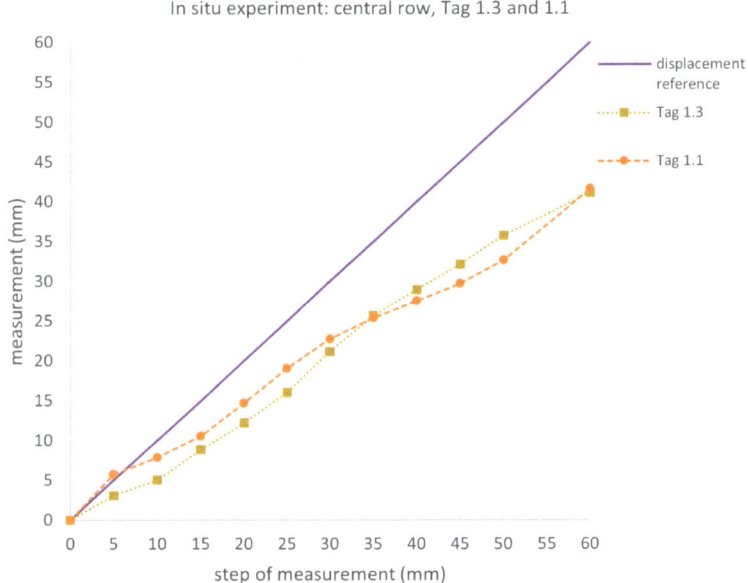

**Figure 37.** In situ experimental test on the 1st wall: the displacements detected by Tags 1.1 and 1.3 are compared with the calculated displacements of the wired transducer.

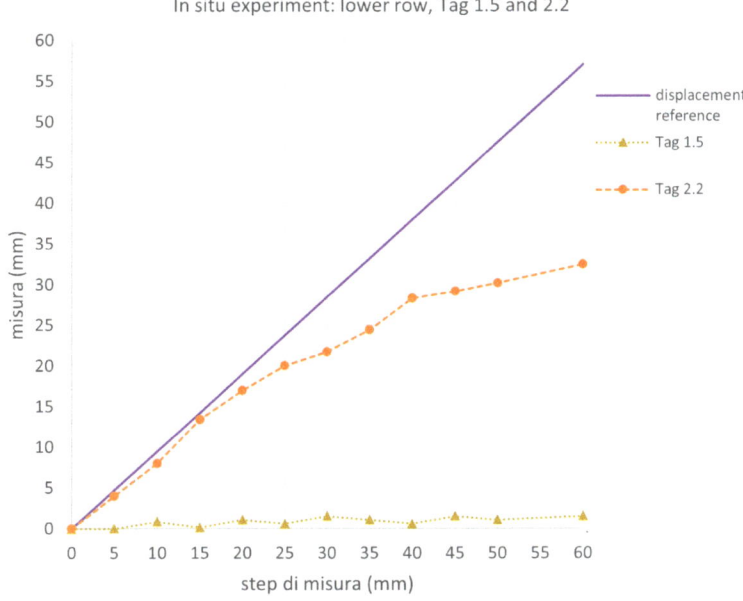

**Figure 38.** In situ experimental test on the 1st wall: the displacements detected by Tags 2.2 and 1.5 are compared with the calculated displacements of the wired transducer.

## 4.2. Test on the 2nd Wall: Comparison between Wireless Tags Displacements and Displacements of the Wired Transducer

In regards to the test performed on the 2nd wall, the results of the signal acquisition of Tag 2.4, Tag 2.2, Tag 2.1, Tag 1.4, Tag 2.3, and Tag 1.2 are reported in Figure 39, Figure 40, Figure 41, Figure 42, Figure 43, and Figure 44, respectively. The values of the mean and standard deviation of the recorded phase for each step of measurement, and RSSI values, are reported for each tag.

As can be observed from the graphs, the values of the phase are increasing at each measurement step, from 0 mm to the maximum displacement of 70 mm (see from Figures 39–44). Also, in this case, the t is sensitive to the displacements that occur on the wall.

The distance differences have been calculated according to Equation (1).

The displacements of the tags in the out-of-plane direction, have been geometrically calculated as for the previous tests. The following graphs compare the displacements of the tags in the out-of-plane direction and the displacements detected by the transducer. Also, in this case, the measurements to consider as reference for the tags positioned up and below the middle of the wall were calculated considering a theoretic model, and were plotted together with the results of the tags as reference for comparison.

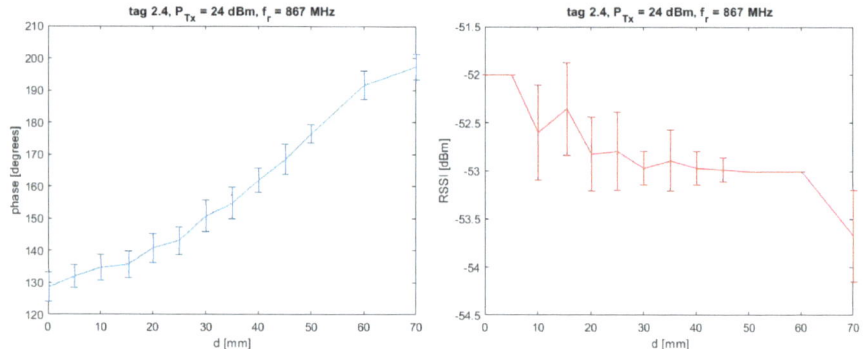

**Figure 39.** In situ experimental test on the 2nd wall: mean and standard deviation of phase (**left side**) and RSSI (**right side**) recorded for each step of measurement of Tag 2.4.

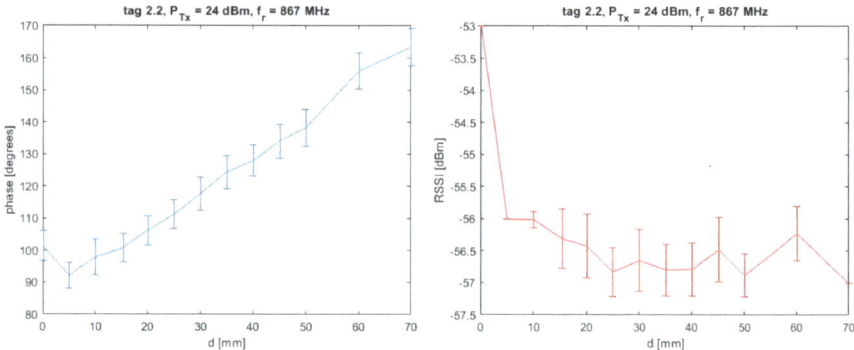

**Figure 40.** In situ experimental test on the 2nd wall: mean and standard deviation of phase (**left side**) and RSSI (**right side**) recorded for each step of measurement of Tag 2.2.

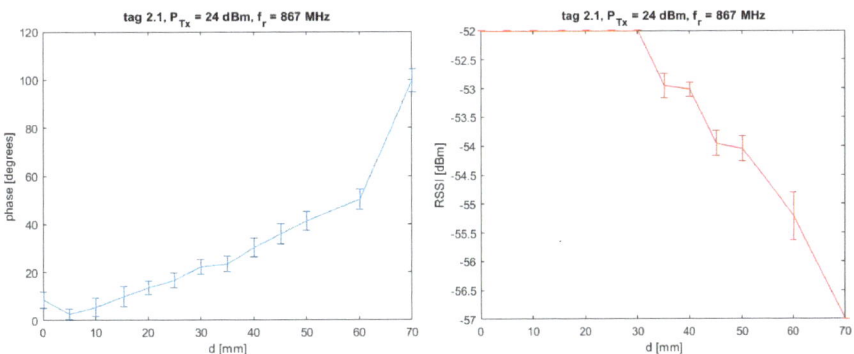

**Figure 41.** In situ experimental test on the 2nd wall: mean and standard deviation of phase (**left side**) and RSSI (**right side**) recorded for each step of measurement of Tag 2.1.

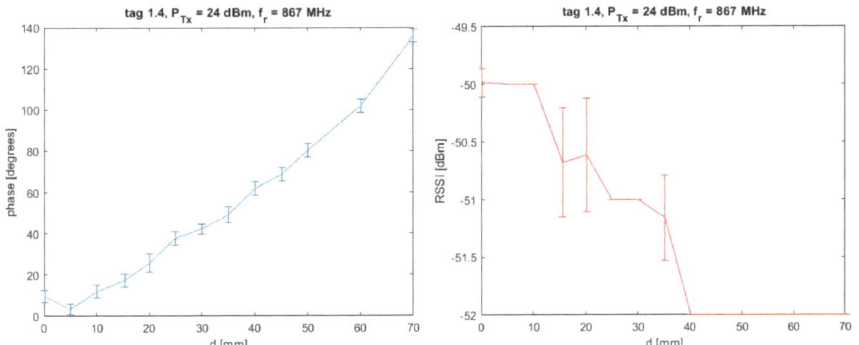

**Figure 42.** In situ experimental test on the 2nd wall: mean and standard deviation of phase (**left side**) and RSSI (**right side**) recorded for each step of measurement of Tag 1.4.

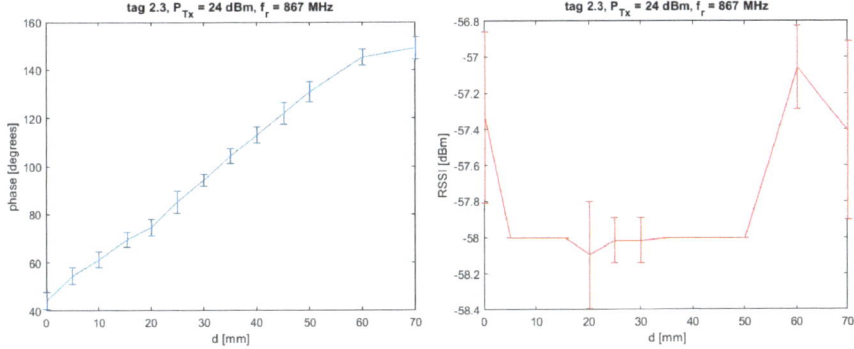

**Figure 43.** In situ experimental test on the 2nd wall: mean and standard deviation of phase (**left side**) and RSSI (**right side**) recorded for each step of measurement of Tag 2.3.

The displacements detected by Tag 2.4 and 2.2 are reported in Figure 45 compared with the calculated displacements of the wired transducer (plotted as displacement reference). The displacements detected by central row Tags 2.1 and 1.4 are reported in Figure 46 and the displacements of the lower row Tags 2.3 and 1.2 are reported in Figure 47.

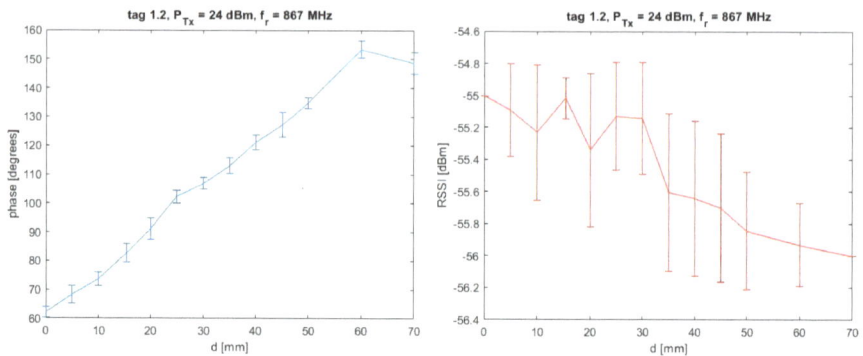

**Figure 44.** In situ experimental test on the 2nd wall: mean and standard deviation of phase (**left side**) and RSSI (**right side**) recorded for each step of measurement of Tag 1.2.

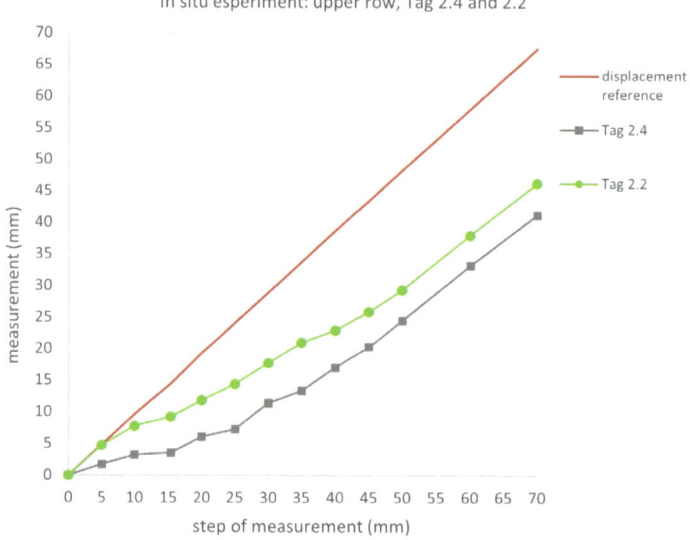

**Figure 45.** In situ experimental test on the 2nd wall: the displacements detected by the upper row Tags 2.4 and 2.2 are compared to the calculated displacements detected by the wired transducer.

As shown in the graphs of Figures 45–47, the displacements detected by the t in the in situ test are lower than those recorded simultaneously by the wired transducer. Substantially, the same hypotheses made for the test on the 1st wall can be advanced.

Since the power of the acquisition system and the layout of the tags have remained the same for the in situ test, (compared to the laboratory test with the same tags), the causes of a lower response are due to the environmental conditions of the experimental set-up.

The steel frame used to mount the load cell and constrain the wall and the metal walls of the building, all contribute to negatively affect the performance of the tags, giving smaller displacements compared to the actual ones.

In particular, the tags that were placed on the left side (Tag 2.4 and 2.1) showed smaller displacements, except for Tag 2.3.

Tag 2.3 in fact is the only Tag that correctly matches the actual displacements.

The tags positioned on the right side are less affected by the presence of the metal, in particular Tag 1.4 and 1.2.

In this test, it is observed a generally better response for the lower row t. It is not easy to establish the causes, but it is supposed that the environment and its interference are crucial in determining a good response.

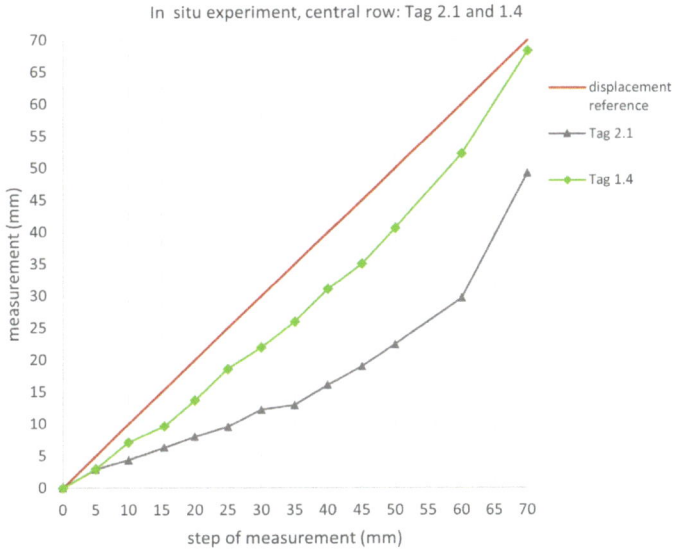

**Figure 46.** In situ experimental test on the 2nd wall: the displacements detected by Tags 2.1 and 1.4 are compared with the calculated displacements of the wired transducer.

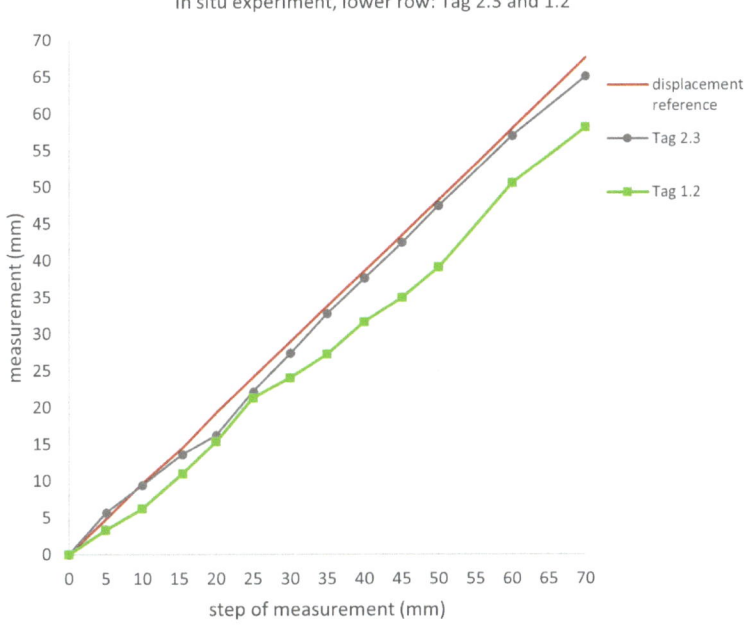

**Figure 47.** In situ experimental test on the 2nd wall: the displacements detected by Tags 2.3 and 1.2 are compared with the calculated displacements of the wired transducer.

## 5. Conclusions

The use of commercial passive UHF-RFID tags in the field of civil engineering for monitoring out-of-plane displacements of brick walls has been investigated and discussed. The novelty of this research concerns the application of commercial tags as simple movement sensors. In particular, we used LabID UH105 passive tags, which are tags that are created and used in logistics, etc. The feasibility of the utilization of the tags in the proposed way was assessed by means of laboratory and in situ tests. The set-ups of the in situ tests were organized taking into account the same distances and spaces used in the laboratory tests, in order to compare the results with the same layout conditions, apart from environmental conditions.

Some conclusions can be drawn:

- The response of the t in the laboratory environment was demonstrated to be very satisfactory, proving that the new application of wireless RFID tags for the monitoring of out-of-plane displacements is feasible and potentially very reliable.
- A weaker response of some t can be attributed to the intrinsic measurement errors of the reader itself and the errors in processing the received data (standard deviations of the calculated mean values of the phases) and to environmental interference together with the position of the tags with respect to the antenna.
- In situ experiments showed a weaker response of the t which registered displacements lower than those recorded by the wired transducer used as reference. The high presence of metal in the environment affected negatively the transmission of the electromagnetic signals, modifying the phases and consequently the indirect measurements of displacements. Unluckily, the position of the experimental set-ups necessarily near a metal wall of the building site contributed to negatively affecting the displacement results and the set-ups required steel frames to constrain the single walls and to fix the load cell.
- Technology limits related to environmental interference can be overcome in future research by using commercial UHF-RFID tags for the real-time monitoring of an existing masonry facade that does not need a steel frame and can potentially respond adequately and properly transmit the electromagnetic signal.

In conclusion, it can be stated that the application of commercial UHF-RFID devices in the civil engineering field is promising and opens up new scenarios for sustainable, wireless, non-invasive, low-cost, and widespread remote monitoring of structures. Despite some technology limits that can be overcome, the results are very satisfactory. In fact, the use of this new measurement technology allows the advantage of sustainable remote and widespread monitoring.

**Author Contributions:** Conceptualization, A.G., C.C. and E.D.G.; methodology, A.G., C.C., A.D.N., M.M. and E.D.G.; software, C.C. and A.D.N.; validation, C.C.; formal analysis, C.C. and A.D.N.; resources, A.G.; data curation, C.C. and A.D.N.; writing—original draft preparation, C.C.; writing—review and editing, C.C., A.D.N. and M.M.; supervision, A.G. and E.D.G. All authors have read and agreed to the published version of the manuscript.

**Funding:** This research received no external funding.

**Data Availability Statement:** Data is contained within the article.

**Conflicts of Interest:** The authors declare no conflicts of interest.

## Abbreviations

The following abbreviations are used in this manuscript:

| | |
|---|---|
| UHF-RFID | Ultra High-Frequency - Radio Frequency Identification |
| SHM | Structural Health Monitoring |
| WSNs | Wireless Sensor Networks |

| | | |
|---|---|---|
| IC | | Integrated Circuit |
| PET | | Polyethylene terephthalate (polyester) |
| EPC | | Electronic Product Code |
| RSSI | | Received Signal Strength Indicator |

## References

1. Stepinski, T.; Uhl, T.; Staszewski, W. *Advanced Structural Damage Detection: From Theory to Engineering Applications*; John Wiley & Sons, Inc.: Hoboken, NJ, USA, 2013. [CrossRef]
2. Gomes, G.F.; Mendéz, Y.A.D.; Alexandrino, P.d.S.L.; da Cunha, S.S., Jr.; Ancelotti, A.C., Jr. The use of intelligent computational tools for damage detection and identification with an emphasis on composites—A review. *Compos. Struct.* **2018**, *196*, 44–54. [CrossRef]
3. dos Santos, J.A.; Maia, N.; Soares, C.M.; Soares, C.M. Structural damage identification: A survey. *Trends Comput. Struct. Technol.* **2008**, *1*, 1–24. [CrossRef]
4. Kong, X.; Cai, C.S.; Hu, J. The state-of-the-art on framework of vibration-based structural damage identification for decision making. *Appl. Sci.* **2017**, *7*, 497. [CrossRef]
5. Li, Y. Hypersensitivity of strain-based indicators for structural damage identification: A review. *Mech. Syst. Signal Process.* **2010**, *24*, 653–664. [CrossRef]
6. Wang, S.; Xu, M. Modal strain energy-based structural damage identification: A review and comparative study. *Struct. Eng. Int.* **2019**, *29*, 234–248. [CrossRef]
7. Alba-Rodríguez, M.D.; Martínez-Rocamora, A.; González-Vallejo, P.; Ferreira-Sánchez, A.; Marrero, M. Building rehabilitation versus demolition and new construction: Economic and environmental assessment. *Environ. Impact Assess. Rev.* **2017**, *66*, 115–126. [CrossRef]
8. Munarim, U.; Ghisi, E. Environmental feasibility of heritage buildings rehabilitation. *Renew. Sustain. Energy Rev.* **2016**, *58*, 235–249. [CrossRef]
9. Hodge, V.J.; O'Keefe, S.; Weeks, M.; Moulds, A. Wireless sensor networks for condition monitoring in the railway industry: A survey. *IEEE Trans. Intell. Transp. Syst.* **2014**, *16*, 1088–1106. [CrossRef]
10. Zhang, R.; Wood, J.; Young, C.; Taylor, A.; Balint, D.; Charalambides, M. A numerical investigation of interfacial and channelling crack growth rates under low-cycle fatigue in bi-layer materials relevant to cultural heritage. *J. Cult. Herit.* **2021**, *49*, 70–78. [CrossRef]
11. Li, H.N.; Ren, L.; Jia, Z.G.; Yi, T.H.; Li, D.S. State-of-the-art in structural health monitoring of large and complex civil infrastructures. *J. Civ. Struct. Health Monit.* **2016**, *6*, 3–16. [CrossRef]
12. Seo, J.; Hu, J.W.; Lee, J. Summary Review of Structural Health Monitoring Applications for Highway Bridges. *J. Perform. Constr. Facil.* **2016**, *30*, 824. [CrossRef]
13. Kulkarni, S.S.; Achenbach, J.D. Structural health monitoring and damage prognosis in fatigue. *Struct. Health Monit.* **2008**, *7*, 37–49. [CrossRef]
14. Dissanayake, P.; Karunananda, P. Reliability Index for Structural Health Monitoring of Aging Bridges. *Struct. Health Monit.* **2008**, *7*, 175–183. [CrossRef]
15. Rivard, P.; Ballivy, G.; Gravel, C.; Saint-Pierre, F. Monitoring of an hydraulic structure affected by ASR: A case study. *Cem. Concr. Res.* **2010**, *40*, 676–680. [CrossRef]
16. Anas, S.; Alam, M.; Shariq, M. Damage response of conventionally reinforced two-way spanning concrete slab under eccentric impacting drop weight loading. *Def. Technol.* **2023**, *19*, 12–34. [CrossRef]
17. Anas, S.; Alam, M.; Umair, M. Experimental and numerical investigations on performance of reinforced concrete slabs under explosive-induced air-blast loading: A state-of-the-art review. *Structures* **2021**, *31*, 428–461. [CrossRef]
18. Song, G.; Wang, C.; Wang, B. Structural Health Monitoring (SHM) of Civil Structures. *Appl. Sci.* **2017**, *7*, 789. [CrossRef]
19. Kaloop, M.R.; Kim, D. GPS-structural health monitoring of a long span bridge using neural network adaptive filter. *Surv. Rev.* **2014**, *46*, 7–14. [CrossRef]
20. Guzman-Acevedo, G.M.; Vazquez-Becerra, G.E.; Millan-Almaraz, J.R.; Rodriguez-Lozoya, H.E.; Reyes-Salazar, A.; Gaxiola-Camacho, J.R.; Martinez-Felix, C.A. GPS, Accelerometer, and Smartphone Fused Smart Sensor for SHM on Real-Scale Bridges. *Adv. Civ. Eng.* **2019**, *2019*, 15. [CrossRef]
21. Kong, Q.; Allen, R.M.; Kohler, M.D.; Heaton, T.H.; Bunn, J. Structural Health Monitoring of Buildings Using Smartphone Sensors. *Seismol. Res. Lett.* **2018**, *89*, 594–602. [CrossRef]
22. Sivasuriyan, A.; Vijayan, D.S.; Górski, W.; Wodzyński, Ł.; Vaverková, M.D.; Koda, E. Practical Implementation of Structural Health Monitoring in Multi-Story Buildings. *Buildings* **2021**, *11*, 263. [CrossRef]
23. Lynch, J.P. An overview of wireless structural health monitoring for civil structures. *Philos. Trans. R. Soc. Math. Phys. Eng. Sci.* **2007**, *365*, 345–372. [CrossRef] [PubMed]
24. Lynch, J.P.; Loh, K.J. A summary review of wireless sensors and sensor networks for structural health monitoring. *Shock Vib. Dig.* **2006**, *38*, 91–130. [CrossRef]
25. Abdulkarem, M.; Samsudin, K.; Rokhani, F.Z.; A Rasid, M.F. Wireless sensor network for structural health monitoring: A contemporary review of technologies, challenges, and future direction. *Struct. Health Monit.* **2020**, *19*, 693–735. [CrossRef]

26. Sofi, A.; Regita, J.J.; Rane, B.; Lau, H.H. Structural health monitoring using wireless smart sensor network—An overview. *Mech. Syst. Signal Process.* **2022**, *163*, 108113. [CrossRef]
27. Huang, J.; He, L.; Xue, J.; Zhou, S.; Briseghella, B.; Castoro, C.; Aloisio, A.; Marano, G. Dynamic assessment of a stress-ribbon CFST arch bridge with SHM and NDE. In *Life-Cycle of Structures and Infrastructure Systems*; CRC Press: Boca Raton, FL, USA, 2023; pp. 2762–2769.
28. He, L.; Castoro, C.; Aloisio, A.; Zhang, Z.; Marano, G.C.; Gregori, A.; Deng, C.; Briseghella, B. Dynamic assessment, FE modelling and parametric updating of a butterfly-arch stress-ribbon pedestrian bridge. *Struct. Infrastruct. Eng.* **2022**, *18*, 1064–1075. [CrossRef]
29. Aygün, B.; Cagri Gungor, V. Wireless sensor networks for structure health monitoring: recent advances and future research directions. *Sens. Rev.* **2011**, *31*, 261–276. [CrossRef]
30. Ramos, L.F.; Aguilar, R.; Lourenço, P.B.; Moreira, S. Dynamic structural health monitoring of Saint Torcato church. *Mech. Syst. Signal Process.* **2013**, *35*, 1–15. [CrossRef]
31. Pallarés, F.J.; Betti, M.; Bartoli, G.; Pallarés, L. Structural health monitoring (SHM) and Nondestructive testing (NDT) of slender masonry structures: A practical review. *Constr. Build. Mater.* **2021**, *297*, 123768. [CrossRef]
32. Barsocchi, P.; Bartoli, G.; Betti, M.; Girardi, M.; Mammolito, S.; Pellegrini, D.; Zini, G. Wireless Sensor Networks for Continuous Structural Health Monitoring of Historic Masonry Towers. *Int. J. Archit. Herit.* **2020**, *15*, 22–44. [CrossRef]
33. Roy, S.; Jandhyala, V.; Smith, J.R.; Wetherall, D.J.; Otis, B.P.; Chakraborty, R.; Buettner, M.; Yeager, D.J.; Ko, Y.C.; Sample, A.P. RFID: From supply chains to sensor nets. *Proc. IEEE* **2010**, *98*, 1583–1592. [CrossRef]
34. Caizzone, S.; DiGiampaolo, E.; Marrocco, G. Wireless crack monitoring by stationary phase measurements from coupled RFID tags. *IEEE Trans. Antennas Propag.* **2014**, *62*, 6412–6419. [CrossRef]
35. Caizzone, S.; DiGiampaolo, E. Wireless passive RFID crack width sensor for structural health monitoring. *IEEE Sens. J.* **2015**, *15*, 6767–6774. [CrossRef]
36. Caizzone, S.; DiGiampaolo, E.; Marrocco, G. Constrained pole-zero synthesis of phase-oriented RFID sensor antennas. *IEEE Trans. Antennas Propag.* **2015**, *64*, 496–503. [CrossRef]
37. DiNatale, A.; DiCarlofelice, A.; DiGiampaolo, E. A Crack Mouth Opening Displacement Gauge Made with Passive UHF RFID Technology. *IEEE Sens. J.* **2022**, *22*, 174–181. [CrossRef]
38. Paggi, C.; Occhiuzzi, C.; Marrocco, G. Sub-millimeter displacement sensing by passive UHF RFID antennas. *IEEE Trans. Antennas Propag.* **2013**, *62*, 905–912. [CrossRef]
39. DiGiampaolo, E.; DiCarlofelice, A.; Gregori, A. An RFID-Enabled Wireless Strain Gauge Sensor for Static and Dynamic Structural Monitoring. *IEEE Sens. J.* **2017**, *17*, 286–294. [CrossRef]
40. Martínez-Martínez, J.J.; Herraiz-Martínez, F.J.; Galindo-Romera, G. A Contactless RFID System Based on Chipless MIW Tags. *IEEE Trans. Antennas Propag.* **2018**, *66*, 5064–5071. [CrossRef]
41. Jayawardana, D.; Liyanapathirana, R.; Zhu, X. RFID-Based Wireless Multi-Sensory System for Simultaneous Dynamic Acceleration and Strain Measurements of Civil Infrastructure. *IEEE Sens. J.* **2019**, *19*, 12389–12397. [CrossRef]
42. Wang, Q.; Zhang, C.; Ma, Z.; Jiao, G.; Jiang, X.; Ni, Y.; Wang, Y.; Du, Y.; Qu, G.; Huang, J. Towards long-transmission-distance and semi-active wireless strain sensing enabled by dual-interrogation-mode RFID technology. *Struct. Control. Health Monit.* **2022**, *29*. [CrossRef]
43. Gregori, A.; DiGiampaolo, E.; DiCarlofelice, A.; Castoro, C. Presenting a New Wireless Strain Method for Structural Monitoring: Experimental Validation. *J. Sensors* **2019**, *2019*, 5370838. [CrossRef]
44. Gregori, A.; Castoro, C.; DiNatale, A.; Mercuri, M.; DiGiampaolo, E. Using commercial UHF-RFID wireless tags to detect structural damage. *Procedia Struct. Integr.* **2023**, *44*, 1586–1593. [CrossRef]
45. Liu, G.; Wang, Q.A.; Jiao, G.; Dang, P.; Nie, G.; Liu, Z.; Sun, J. Review of Wireless RFID Strain Sensing Technology in Structural Health Monitoring. *Sensors* **2023**, *23*, 6925. [CrossRef] [PubMed]
46. Mercuri, M.; Pathirage, M.; Gregori, A.; Cusatis, G. Computational modeling of the out-of-plane behavior of unreinforced irregular masonry. *Eng. Struct.* **2020**, *223*, 111181. [CrossRef]
47. Mercuri, M.; Pathirage, M.; Gregori, A.; Cusatis, G. On the collapse of the masonry Medici tower: An integrated discrete-analytical approach. *Struct. Eng. Rev.* **2021**, *246*, 113046. [CrossRef]
48. Cecchi, A.; Sab, K. Out of plane model for heterogeneous periodic materials: the case of masonry. *Eur. J. -Mech.-A/Solids* **2002**, *21*, 715–746. [CrossRef]
49. Smilović Zulim, M.; Radnić, J. Anisotropy Effect of Masonry on the Behaviour and Bearing Capacity of Masonry Walls. *Adv. Mater. Sci. Eng.* **2020**, *2020*, 5676901. [CrossRef]
50. Dominici, D.; Galeota, D.; Gregori, A.; Rosciano, E.; Alicandro, M.; Elaiopoulos, M. Integrating geomatics and structural investigation in post-earthquake monitoring of ancient monumental Buildings. *J. Appl. Geod.* **2014**, *8*, 141–154. [CrossRef]
51. Li, X.; Gao, G.; Zhu, H.; Li, Q.; Zhang, N.; Qi, Z. UHF RFID tag antenna based on the DLS-EBG structure for metallic objects. *IET Microwaves Antennas Propag.* **2020**, *14*, 567–572. [CrossRef]
52. Moraru, A.; Ursachi, C.; Helerea, E. A New Washable UHF RFID Tag: Design, Fabrication, and Assessment. *Sensors* **2020**, *20*, 3451. [CrossRef]
53. Wang, P.; Dong, L.; Wang, H.; Li, G.; Di, Y.; Xie, X.; Huang, D. Passive Wireless Dual-Tag UHF RFID Sensor System for Surface Crack Monitoring. *Sensors* **2021**, *21*, 882. [CrossRef] [PubMed]

54. Erman, F.; Koziel, S.; Leifsson, L. Broadband/Dual-Band Metal-Mountable UHF RFID Tag Antennas: A Systematic Review, Taxonomy Analysis, Standards of Seamless RFID System Operation, Supporting IoT Implementations, Recommendations, and Future Directions. *IEEE Internet Things J.* **2023**, *10*, 14780–14797. [CrossRef]
55. Zhu, X.; Mukhopadhyay, S.K.; Kurata, H. A review of RFID technology and its managerial applications in different industries. *J. Eng. Technol. Manag.* **2012**, *29*, 152–167. [CrossRef]
56. Nambiar, A.N. RFID technology: A review of its applications. In Proceedings of the World Congress on Engineering and Computer Science, San Francisco, CA, USA, 20–22 October 2009; International Association of Engineers: Hong Kong, China, 2009; Volume 2, pp. 20–22.
57. Kumar, P.; Reinitz, H.; Simunovic, J.; Sandeep, K.; Franzon, P. Overview of RFID technology and its applications in the food industry. *J. Food Sci.* **2009**, *74*, R101–R106. [CrossRef]

**Disclaimer/Publisher's Note:** The statements, opinions and data contained in all publications are solely those of the individual author(s) and contributor(s) and not of MDPI and/or the editor(s). MDPI and/or the editor(s) disclaim responsibility for any injury to people or property resulting from any ideas, methods, instructions or products referred to in the content.

Article

# Improved FEM Natural Frequency Calculation for Structural Frames by Local Correction Procedure

Javier Urruzola and Iñaki Garmendia *

Mechanical Engineering Department, Engineering School of Gipuzkoa, University of the Basque Country UPV/EHU, Plaza de Europa, 1, E-20018 Donostia-San Sebastián, Spain; javier.urruzola@ehu.eus
* Correspondence: inaki.garmendia@ehu.es

**Abstract:** The accurate calculation of natural frequencies is important for vibration and earthquake analyses of structural frames. For this purpose, it is necessary to discretize each beam or column of the frame into one or more smaller elements. The required number of elements per member increases when the frame's modal shapes have wavelengths similar to the beam lengths. This paper presents a method that reduces the number of elements needed for a precise calculation. This is achieved by implementing a straightforward local correction to the kinetic and elastic energy of certain elements, resulting in a substantial decrease in error. The validity of this method is demonstrated through a range of examples, from simple canonical cases to more realistic ones. Additionally, the paper discusses the unique features of this method and examines its relationship with other approaches.

**Keywords:** structure; frame; mechanical; vibration; natural frequency; finite element; beam; column

Citation: Urruzola, J.; Garmendia, I. Improved FEM Natural Frequency Calculation for Structural Frames by Local Correction Procedure. *Buildings* **2024**, *14*, 1195. https://doi.org/10.3390/buildings14051195

Academic Editors: Shaohong Cheng and Haijun Zhou

Received: 18 March 2024
Revised: 12 April 2024
Accepted: 14 April 2024
Published: 23 April 2024

Copyright: © 2024 by the authors. Licensee MDPI, Basel, Switzerland. This article is an open access article distributed under the terms and conditions of the Creative Commons Attribution (CC BY) license (https://creativecommons.org/licenses/by/4.0/).

## 1. Introduction

Modal analysis and natural frequency calculation by the FEM are very valuable tools to study the dynamic behavior of building structures [1]. For example, the Spanish Structural Code [2], the Eurocode [3] and the American Code ASCE [4,5] accept their validity for seismic analysis and wind load induced vibration analysis. Therefore, the most popular structural analysis programs such as ETABS, Robot or Staad implement these numerical techniques.

Frames are usually modelled using one element per member (beam or column), which is accurate enough for linear structural analysis, but it falls short for vibration eigenvalue problems [6,7] because of the inadequacy of polynomials to represent localized modal shapes. Therefore, the need arises to develop methods to perform modal analysis in a more accurate way with the least numerical cost and implementation effort. Consequently, several approaches have been proposed in the scientific literature to estimate the incurred error and possibly reduce it, including correction formulas, the superconvergent patch recovery technique (SPR), the hierarchical FEM (HFEM), the smoothed FEM (SFEM), the mass-redistributed FEM (MRFEM) and the use of various higher-order beam finite elements.

Correction formulas were applied by Xie and Steven [8] to improve the accuracy of the FEM calculation of natural frequencies in beam/column elements. Their approach stems from a previous study by Mackie [9] on the topic of numerical dispersion error reduction. A similar technique [10] can be applied to linear structural buckling critical load calculations. Their method can also be applied to structural frames by means of a weighted average of single beam/column correction terms.

FEM error estimates [11,12] deal with the problem of numerical inaccuracy induced by the discretization of the continuum of differential equations. They are more detailed than convergence graphs and can be used to refine the mesh where necessary to achieve a certain level of precision. Residual-based estimators measure the error on the exact differential equations [11] while recovery-based estimators build a better approximation of the displacement or stress field [13–15] that can be used to obtain a more precise value of the natural frequencies.

The superpatch recovery technique (SPR) [16] uses a patch of neighboring elements to adjust a higher order polynomial to approximate the stress in a finite element using the element values as well as those in the conveniently weighted patch. It originates [14,17] from the idea of fitting an improved stress distribution field to a set of so-called super-convergent points, when they exist, where stresses are calculated with a higher accuracy. Wiberg et al. [18] fitted the polynomial to displacements instead of stresses (SPRD) in order to improve the calculated value of natural frequencies, which depend not only on the displacement derivatives, but also on the displacements themselves.

The smoothed finite element method (SFEM) [19] uses a gradient smoothing technique to reduce the overstiffening of the FEM. This method is based on the G space theory [20] that makes it possible to use discontinuous shape functions in the element formulation while maintaining stability and convergence to the exact solution. The node-based smoothed finite element method (NS-FEM) [21] improves accuracy and gives an upper bound of the elastic energy, whereas the edge-based smoothed finite element method (ES-FEM) [22] provides a lower bound.

The hierarchical FEM [23] employs nested polynomial shape functions of different orders to increase the accuracy of the elements when necessary. Therefore, it can be used for error estimation and adaptative mesh refinement. Early application of the method to dynamic analysis focused on Bernoulli–Euler beams [24]. More recently, the method has been applied to various types of beams such as Timoshenko beams [25], three-dimensional sandwich beams [26], etc.

Modifying the element mass matrix is another strategy to improve natural frequency calculations. Fried and Chavez [27] used a weighted average of the consistent matrix and the lumped matrix to model strings and membranes. A more economical alternative was developed by Fried and Leong [28] using the consistent matrix for the modal shape calculation and a weighted mass matrix for a Rayleigh quotient correction. Li and He [29] changed the location of the Gaussian points used to integrate the element mass matrix. Their approach stems from previous work in acoustics by Gudatti [30].

Higher-order Euler–Bernoulli elements [31] and the Timoshenko element [32–34] provide improved accuracy due to the better representation of displacements. This leads to a reduction in the number of elements required to calculate natural frequencies. However, their implementation is more complex, and the resulting equations have more unknown variables and will be worse conditioned [35]. Thin-walled beams [36] also require enriched sets of modelling variables because of their complex geometrical and deformation patterns.

The present paper shows a new method for improving the accuracy of the calculation of the natural frequencies of structural frames when beams and columns are modelled with a small number of elements (possibly one or two). Sway frames can often be analyzed accurately with one element per member but non sway ones usually require a finer mesh or a higher precision technique like ours. The algorithm proceeds in two stages. In the first stage, a coarse solution is calculated whereas in the second one, local corrections are added at a finer level. If necessary, some elements are subdivided if the local correction excessively distorts the modal shape.

Concerning the novelty of this work, the authors recently wrote a closely related paper [37] about calculating the critical buckling loads of structural frames using one element per member. This latest work presents some fundamentally novel developments. First, preventing structural buckling requires knowing just the lowest critical load, but in order to model structural dynamics accurately, multiple natural frequencies are needed and the algorithm has to be modified accordingly. Second, the interplay between multiple frequencies coupled with the limited accuracy of individual elements leads to using two subelements instead of four. Third, because of the same reasons, some members will have to be modelled with more than one element per member according to a novel specific element distortion criterion that we will later introduce. Lastly, the derivation of the equations and algorithms has been optimized for clarity, ease of implementation and performance.

The subsequent sections of this paper are outlined next. First, natural frequency calculations are carried out for five fundamental cases of one-bar (beam/column) structural elements with the aim of assessing the error associated with coarse meshes and the problems arising from multiple modal interplay. Second, the vibration modes of these bars are modified by a local correction procedure and the elements are subdivided in two according to a distortion criterion. Third, the method is extended to structural frames made up of more than one bar. Next, the devised algorithms are validated using 2D and 3D cases representative of realistic building structures taken from [10,37]. Finally, the results, discussion and conclusions are presented.

## 2. Natural Frequency Analysis of Some Fundamental Cases Using One Element Per Bar

We have selected a set of fundamental cases [38] (see Figure 1) to test our method against the standard FEM. Various support conditions such as clamped (C), pinned (P) and free (F) are considered. We have added the case of the second mode of the pinned–pinned beam (PP2) because it will help us better explain the algorithm.

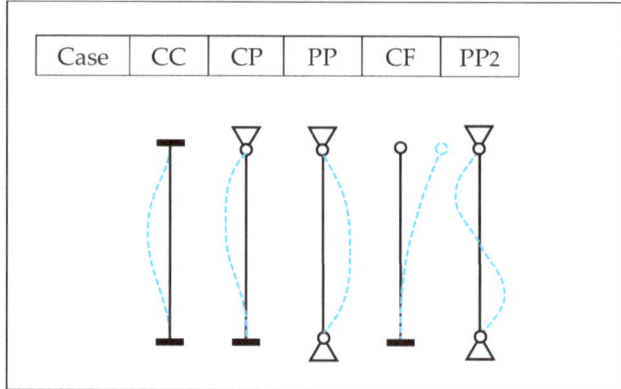

**Figure 1.** Five fundamental beam vibration cases.

Natural frequencies of a structural frame can be calculated by the FEM as the solution of the eigenvalue problem

$$\left(K - \omega^2 M\right)\phi = 0 \qquad (1)$$

where $K$ and $M$ are the stiffness and mass matrices, $\omega$ is any natural frequency and $\phi$ is its corresponding modal shape.

Table 1 shows the accuracy of the FEM calculation with $N_{el}$ cubic elements. The relative errors using a single element are excessive in all cases except CF. Errors larger than 1% are considered excessive from a structural engineering point of view [37].

**Table 1.** Relative error [1] in natural frequency computation for some fundamental cases.

| Nel [2] | CC | CP | PP | CF | PP2 |
|---|---|---|---|---|---|
| 1 | - | 32.92% | 10.99% | 0.48% | 27.14% |
| 2 | 1.62% | 0.93% | 0.39% | 0.05% | 10.98% |
| 3 | 0.41% | 0.20% | 0.08% | 0.01% | 1.17% |
| 4 | 0.13% | 0.06% | 0.03% | 0.00% | 0.38% |

[1] Relative error refers to "nearly exact" values calculated with Abaqus and Nel = 10. [2] Nel: number of elements in the discretization.

Looking at Figure 1 and by analogy with the column buckling problem, we can interpret that a single element is not accurate enough to model more than a quarter of a sinusoidal deformation wavelength. We will see how to reduce these errors in the next section.

## 3. Corrected Calculation of Natural Frequencies in Some Fundamental Cases Using One Element Per Bar

In this section, we will improve the quality of the displacements inside the structural element in two ways: (1) we will use an auxiliary discretization of the bar elements (see Figure 2) with two subelements and three nodes (1–3) to obtain a local correction of the coarse mesh solution and (2) we will split some elements in half when necessary (adaptive mesh refinement). This approximation results in acceptable errors near those obtained in Table 1 with four elements.

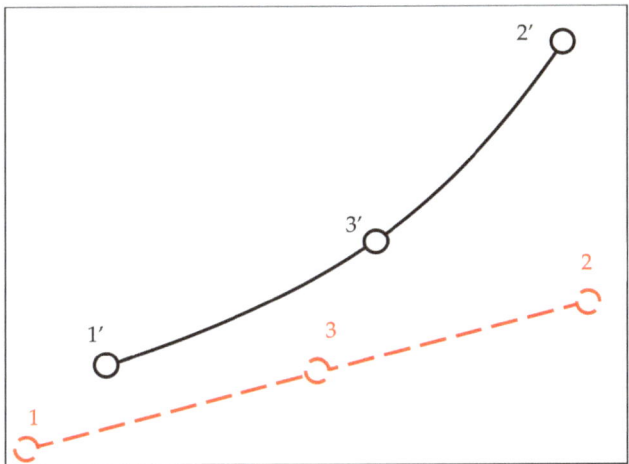

**Figure 2.** Bar element "global" displacement $u^g$ (from 1–3 to 1'–3').

In our previous work on buckling [37] we used an auxiliary discretization of four subelements instead of two, but we will see that this approach is not possible when calculating multiple eigenvalues (or multiple frequencies) because of the override problem that is later explained.

We express the nodal displacements $u_r$ (r: 1–3) as the sum of a "global" term derived from the coarse solution and a "local" correction term.

The global displacement $u^g$ (see Figure 2) results from a static analysis in which we fix the external displacements $u_1^g$ and $u_2^g$ and obtain the value of the internal nodal displacement $u_3^g$ by condensation [7].

The nodal displacements of the element nodes in the local reference frame of the bar, $u_1^l$ and $u_2^l$, can be expressed as

$$u_1^l = \phi_1 \eta \quad u_2^l = \phi_2 \eta \tag{2}$$

where $\phi_1$ and $\phi_2$ are the coarse modal shapes at nodes 1 and 2 expressed in the local reference frame and $\eta$ is a modal amplitude variable.

In order to find the inner nodal displacement $u_3^l$ we will need the element stiffness matrix. Assuming a uniform beam, each subelement (1-3 and 3-2) will have the same stiffness and mass matrices, $K_S$ and $M_S$, which we can express in terms of their nodal submatrices:

$$K_S = \begin{bmatrix} K_{AA} & K_{AB} \\ K_{BA} & K_{BB} \end{bmatrix} \quad M_S = \begin{bmatrix} M_{AA} & M_{AB} \\ M_{BA} & M_{BB} \end{bmatrix} \tag{3}$$

Assembling these subelement matrices, we obtain the stiffness and mass matrices of the refined element, $K_r$ and $M_r$:

$$K_r = \begin{bmatrix} K_{AA} & 0 & K_{AB} \\ 0 & K_{BB} & K_{BA} \\ K_{BA} & K_{AB} & K_{AA} + K_{BB} \end{bmatrix} \quad M_r = \begin{bmatrix} M_{AA} & 0 & M_{AB} \\ 0 & M_{BB} & M_{BA} \\ M_{BA} & M_{AB} & M_{AA} + M_{BB} \end{bmatrix} \quad (4)$$

Therefore, the sought internal displacement results in

$$u_3^l = (K_{AA} + K_{BB})^{-1}(K_{BA} u_1^l + K_{AB} u_2^l) = \phi_3 \eta \quad (5)$$

where we define $\phi_3$ as

$$\phi_3 = (K_{AA} + K_{BB})^{-1}(K_{BA} \phi_1 + K_{AB} \phi_2) \quad (6)$$

The local displacement term $\Delta u^l$ (see Figure 3), increases the internal node displacement ($\Delta u_3^l$) without modifying the external nodal displacements (for economy of notation, we group nodal rotations and displacements in one term).

$$\Delta u^l = \begin{Bmatrix} 0 \\ 0 \\ \Delta u_3^l \end{Bmatrix} \quad (7)$$

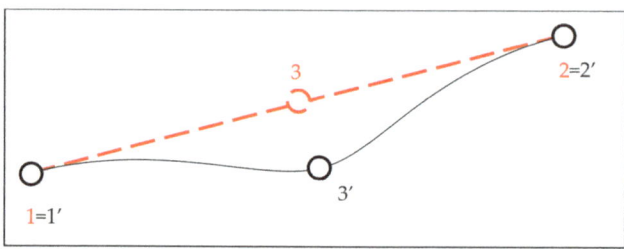

**Figure 3.** Element incremental local displacements $\Delta u^l$ (from 1–3 to 1'–3').

Figure 4 shows the total nodal displacement of the refined element $u_r$ resulting from both the global and the local term.

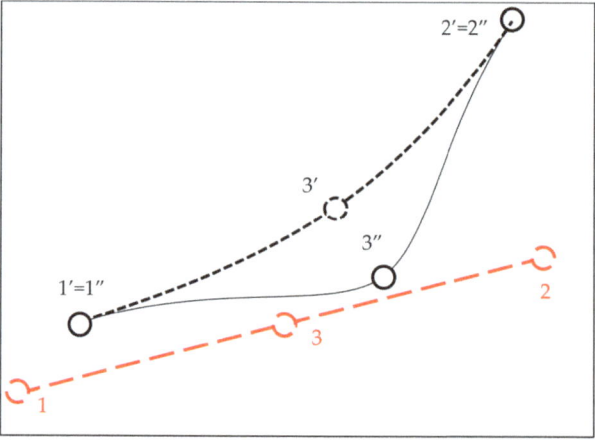

**Figure 4.** Refined element total displacements $u_r$ (global from 1–3 to 1'3' and local from 1'–3' to 1''–3'').

Now, we define the refined element nodal displacements $u_r$ as a function of the modal coordinate $\eta$ and the internal incremental displacement $\Delta u_3^l$ using a projection matrix $P$

$$u_r = \begin{bmatrix} \phi_1 & 0 \\ \phi_2 & 0 \\ \phi_3 & I \end{bmatrix} \begin{Bmatrix} \eta \\ \Delta u_3^l \end{Bmatrix} = P \begin{Bmatrix} \eta \\ \Delta u_3^l \end{Bmatrix} \qquad (8)$$

where $I$ is the identity matrix. As a result, we can obtain a corrected natural frequency $\omega_p$ by solving the projected eigenvalue problem

$$P^T K_r P \phi_p = \omega_p^2 P^T M_r P \phi_p \qquad (9)$$

We summarize the procedure to calculate the corrected natural frequency in Algorithm 1.

**Algorithm 1.** Correction of the natural frequency of a one-element bar

Evaluate $K_r$ and $M_r$ as 2-subelement refinements of $K_e$ and $M_e$ using Equation (3)
Evaluate the projection matrix P with Equation (8)
Calculate $\omega_p$ as the lowest natural frequency in Equation (9)

After the correction process the errors in natural frequencies change as shown in Table 2.

**Table 2.** Relative error in corrected natural frequency calculation (Nel = 1).

| Nel | CC    | CP    | PP    | CF    | PP2    |
|-----|-------|-------|-------|-------|--------|
| 1   | 1.61% | 0.93% | 0.39% | 0.05% | 42.42% |

Looking at these results, we can see that correcting the one element per member model in the CC and PP2 cases does not reduce the error up to a level that is acceptable in engineering. We can understand what is happening if we study what we will designate as the distortion factor: the maximum change in V or T after applying the correction (see Table 3), where V and T are the stiffness and mass quadratic forms, respectively.

**Table 3.** Distortion factor (maximum percentage change in V or T) after correction (Nel = 1).

| Nel | CC | CP      | PP     | CF    | PP2                  |
|-----|----|---------|--------|-------|----------------------|
| 1   | -% | 211.33% | 49.66% | 1.73% | $1.4 \times 10^{29}$% |

What we can see here is that the local correction has largely distorted V and/or T in both cases (most notably for PP2).

First, we will study the cause for the most troubling case, PP2. We can see a graphical depiction of its distortion with altered scales in Figure 5. The softer CC mode (K = 22.4) has almost completely overridden the stiffer PP2 mode (K = 39.5) thereby suppressing an existing mode and replacing it with a rough duplicate of a previously calculated one (CC).

Second, we turn our attention to the origin of the slightly unacceptable error of the CC case. We can attribute it to the fact that the correction process can never surpass the accuracy of doubling the element at the coarse level.

In order to solve both problems, we propose splitting elements in half when the distortion factor (from now on called $\gamma$) surpasses the 100% threshold. The PP2 spurious modal override problem will be solved because the half element corrections cannot roughly represent the CC mode in isolation. In turn, the CC slightly unacceptable error will be reduced because of the superior quality of the refined coarse mesh.

It Is clear now that using a four subelement discretization for local element correction is not acceptable because it will be plagued by the override problem in the same way as the two-subelement one.

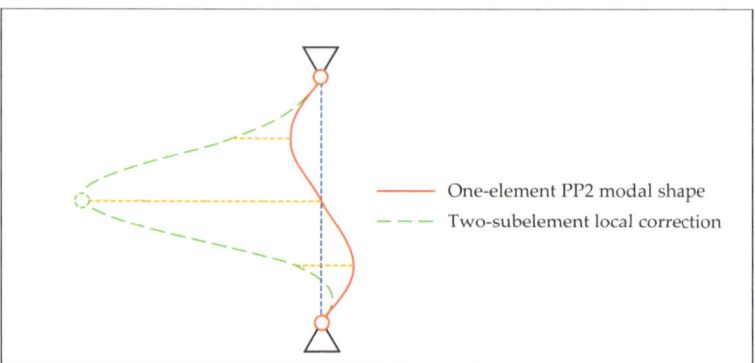

**Figure 5.** Locally corrected PP2 modal shape using one element and two subelements.

Therefore, we will allow one or two elements per member at the coarse level and two subelements at the local level, which allows for a total of four subelements per member, roughly equivalent to what we did for buckling in [37].

In the next section, we extend this correction/refinement process to general structural frames made up of multiple bars and one or two elements per bar.

## 4. Correction of Natural Frequencies for Multiple-Element Structures

Similarly to what we did in [37], we are going to generalize the procedure for single elements based on four main ideas:

1. The local element corrections can be combined additively into an overall modal correction.
2. When calculating local corrections for an element, the rest of the structure can be sufficiently represented by the frame modal shape $\phi$ and an amplitude variable $\eta$.
3. The corrected natural frequency for the whole frame can be calculated using Rayleigh's quotient with the corrected modal shape.
4. Local corrections for different natural frequencies can be calculated in isolation from each other once the distortion factor has been introduced to solve the override problem.

Let us examine how the whole procedure would work for our most problematic case, PP2. Figure 6 shows the modal shape of the PP2 case beam discretized at the coarse level with two elements per member. In order to improve the quality of the modal shape, we will fix the end nodal displacements of each coarse element and subsequently correct its inner displacements, and, as a result, we will obtain the corrected vibration shape in the same figure.

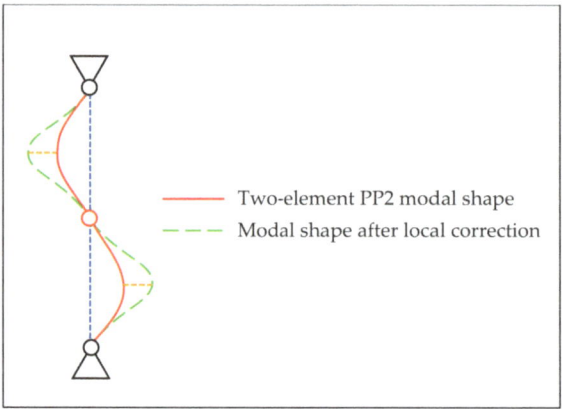

**Figure 6.** PP2 modal shape using two elements after local correction.

The local corrections for each element will be calculated separately (as shown in Figure 7). For this purpose, we maintain all the elements in the frame mesh except the one to be corrected, which is replaced with two subelements (see Figure 7).

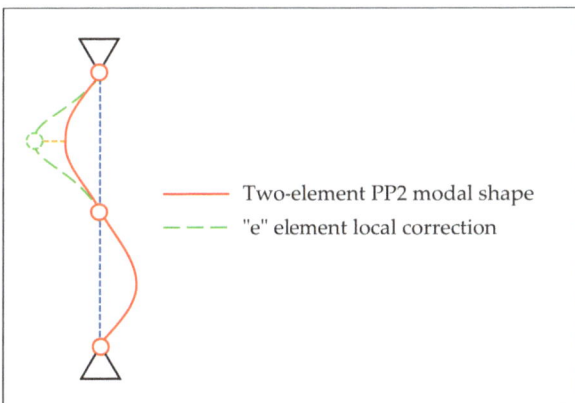

**Figure 7.** Structural discretization used to correct the upper part of two-element PP2 modal shape.

The local modal shape correction is the solution of a projected eigenvalue problem that is derived below.

The structure stiffness quadratic form calculated with the coarse mesh can be expressed as:

$$V = u^T K u \tag{10}$$

where $u$ and $K$ are the nodal displacement vector and stiffness matrix of the frame.

We can modify $V$ by replacing element e contribution with its refined counterpart

$$V = u^T K u - u_e^T K_e u_e + u_r^T K_r u_r \tag{11}$$

where $u_e$ and $K_e$ are the nodal displacement vector and stiffness matrix of element e, while $u_r$ and $K_r$ are their refined versions (using two subelements and three nodes) calculated in the local reference frame of the element.

Next, the nodal displacements can be expressed as a function of the modal coordinate $\eta$ and the incremental inner nodal displacement of the element being corrected $\Delta u_3^l$, similarly to what we did for a single-element bar in Equation (8).

$$u = \phi \eta \tag{12}$$

$$u_e = \phi_e \eta \tag{13}$$

$$u_r = \begin{Bmatrix} \phi_1 \eta \\ \phi_2 \eta \\ \phi_3 \eta + \Delta u_3^l \end{Bmatrix} \tag{14}$$

and the same operations can be performed on the mass quadratic form:

$$T = u^T M u - u_e^T M_e u_e + u_r^T M_r u_r \tag{15}$$

As a result, we obtain a projected eigenvalue problem whose solution contains the local modal shape correction:

$$K_p \phi_p = \omega_p^2 M_p \phi_p \tag{16}$$

where
$$K_p = \begin{bmatrix} V - V_e + V_r & 0 \\ 0 & K_{AA} + K_{BB} \end{bmatrix} \quad (17)$$

$$M_p = \begin{bmatrix} T - T_e + T_r & \phi_1^T M_{AB} + \phi_2^T M_{BA} + \phi_3^T (M_{AA} + M_{BB}) \\ \text{symmetric} & M_{AA} + M_{BB} \end{bmatrix} \quad (18)$$

$$\phi_r = \begin{Bmatrix} \phi_1 \\ \phi_2 \\ \phi_3 \end{Bmatrix} \quad (19)$$

$$V_r = \phi_1^T K_{AA} \phi_1 + \phi_2^T K_{BB} \phi_2 + \phi_1^T K_{AB} \phi_3 + \phi_3^T K_{AB} \phi_2 \quad (20)$$

$$T_r = \phi_1^T M_{AA} \phi_1 + \phi_2^T M_{BB} \phi_2 + \phi_3^T (M_{AA} + M_{BB}) \phi_3 + 2\phi_1^T M_{AB} \phi_3 + 2\phi_3^T M_{AB} \phi_2 \quad (21)$$

We can partition the projected mode in terms of its modal amplitude part $\phi_{p0}$ and its internal correction $\phi_{p3}$

$$\phi_{pe} = \begin{Bmatrix} \phi_{p0} \\ \phi_{p3} \end{Bmatrix} \quad (22)$$

and dividing the right-hand side by $\phi_{p0}$, we generate a projected mode

$$\phi_p^* = \begin{Bmatrix} 1 \\ \frac{\phi_{p3}}{\phi_{p0}} \end{Bmatrix} \quad (23)$$

which represents the sum of the overall modal shape $\phi$ plus the local internal correction term $\Delta \phi_{c3}$

$$\Delta \phi_{c3} = \frac{\phi_{p3}}{\phi_{p0}} \quad (24)$$

and this modal shape can be used to calculate the corrected mass and stiffness quadratic forms of the element.

$$V_{ce} = V_r + \Delta \phi_{c3}^T (K_{AA} + K_{BB}) \Delta \phi_{c3} \quad (25)$$

$$T_{ce} = T_r + 2\Delta \phi_{c3}^T (M_{BA} \phi_1 + M_{AB} \phi_2) + \Delta \phi_{c3}^T (M_{AA} + M_{BB})(2\phi_3 + \Delta \phi_{c3}) \quad (26)$$

We show in Algorithm 2 the complete procedure for computing $V_{ce}$ and $T_{ce}$.

**Algorithm 2.** Computation of the corrected quadratic forms of an element $V_{ce}$ and $T_{ce}$

Overall frame inputs: $\phi^T K \phi$, $\phi^T M \phi$
Frame element inputs: $\phi_e^T K_e \phi_e$, $\phi_e^T M_e \phi_e$, $\phi_e$
Subelement inputs: $K_{AA}$, $K_{AB}$, $K_{BB}$, $M_{AA}$, $M_{AB}$, $M_{BB}$
Evaluate $K_r$ and $M_r$ as 2-subelement refinements of $K_e$ and $M_e$ using Equation (3)
Convert $\phi_e$ to local element coordinates by the following operations:
$\phi_1 = R_e^T \phi_{e1}$ $\phi_2 = R_e^T \phi_{e2}$ ($R_e$: element rotation matrix)
Calculate $\phi_3$, $\phi_r$ in Equations (6) and (19)
Calculate $K_p$, $M_p$ in Equations (17) and (18)
Obtain $\phi_p$ as the first eigenvector of Equation (16)
Evaluate $V_{ce}$, $T_{ce}$ by applying Equations (24)–(26)

The element-corrected quadratic forms of the whole structure can be collected in Rayleigh's quotient to obtain an improved value of the structure's natural frequency $\omega_c$

$$\omega_c^2 = \frac{\sum_e V_{ce}}{\sum_e T_{ce}} \quad (27)$$

The complete procedure to calculate N natural frequencies is given in Algorithm 3.

It should be pointed out that the denominators of the distortion factor $\gamma_e$ have been modified to cope with the possibility of elements with very small $V_e$ or $T_e$, which would lead to near division by zero. Therefore, one hundredth of the frame $V$ or $T$ is distributed equally among all elements when measuring relative change, while the other 99% comes from the element itself.

---

**Algorithm 3.** Computation of N corrected natural frequencies of whole frame

Receive as inputs frame magnitudes $K, M, \phi_j, \omega_j, j = 1..N$
For all elements, receive as inputs one-element magnitudes $K_e, M_e, \phi_e$
For $j = 1..N$
   $V = \phi_j^T K \phi_j, T = \phi_j^T M \phi_j, \omega = \omega_j$
   For e = 1.. number of elements
      $V_e = \phi_e^T K_e \phi_e, T_e = \phi_e^T M_e \phi_e$
      Calculate $V_{ce}, T_{ce}$ with Algorithm 2
   End
   Calculate $\omega_c^2$ with Equation (27)
   Calculate element distortion factor:
      $\gamma_e = 100 \cdot \max(|V_{ce} - V_e|/(0.01V/Nel + 0.99V_e), |T_{ce} - T_e|/(0.01T/Nel + 0.99T_e))$
End
If $\gamma_e > 100\%$ in an element, split it in half and repeat

---

Now we can preliminarily assess the merits of these algorithms by recalculating the natural frequencies of the fundamental cases discussed before. The associated relative errors and distortion factors are given in Tables 4 and 5 respectively.

**Table 4.** Relative error in corrected natural frequency calculation with one and two elements per member.

| Nel | CC | CP | PP | CF | PP2 |
| --- | --- | --- | --- | --- | --- |
| 1 | 1.61% | 0.93% | 0.39% | 0.05% | 42.42% |
| 2 | 0.13% | 0.06% | 0.03% | 0.00% | 0.47% |

**Table 5.** Maximum percentage change in $V_e$ or $T_e$ with one and two elements per member after applying the proposed correction.

| Nel | CC | CP | PP | CF | PP2 |
| --- | --- | --- | --- | --- | --- |
| 1 | -% | 211.33% | 49.66% | 1.73% | $1.4 \times 10^{29}$% |
| 2 | 6.28% | 2.57% | 1.49% | 0.09% | 55.81% |

We can observe that after doubling the number of elements, the error becomes acceptable for all cases and the distortion factor falls to an acceptable value of 56%.

The algorithm admits further tweaks to reduce calculation time as follows:

- Axial displacements can be eliminated from the correction procedure on account of their higher stiffness [37].
- In most cases $V_r - V_e = 0$ exactly or approximately and needs not be calculated.
- $\phi_3(\phi_1, \phi_2)$ can often be calculated explicitly as a linear expression, and consequently, Equation (6) is unnecessary.
- Equations (17), (18), (25) and (26) can be easily programmed with scalar operations in terms of their constituent parts thereby avoiding matrix/vector operations.
- Using all of the above, the main component of the computational cost is the solution of the local eigenvalue problem which can be obtained with a few iterations of the power method.

## 5. Results

Our proposed novel algorithm has been coded into a custom MATLAB R2021b 2D and 3D vibration program. The program has been validated against Abaqus for some of the 2D and 3D cases presented below. Errors in natural frequency computations are measured against "near exact" values obtained when discretizing each structural member with ten elements. As shown below, the standard FEM with one or two elements per member calculated with Abaqus (or our code validated with Abaqus) gives errors that are 10 times larger or more.

### 5.1. 2D Building Portal Frame

This test case taken from [37] is shown in Figure 8. The first modal shape ϕ1 (red dashed lines) is superimposed on the undeformed geometry (continuous black lines). The second and third modal shapes (ϕ2 and ϕ3) are shown on the right in smaller sizes.

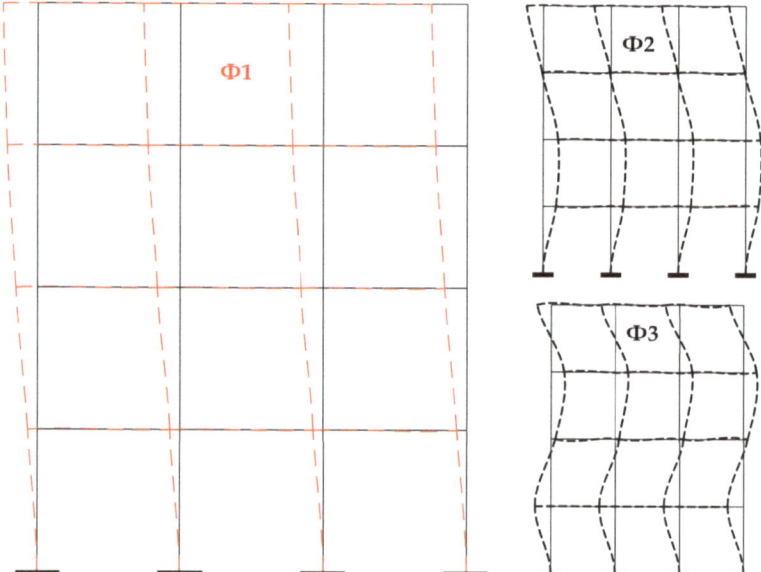

**Figure 8.** 2D sway portal: first three modal shapes with one element per member.

Numerical results are shown in Table 6 with one element per structural member for the first four natural frequencies. The relative error of the corrected calculation is more than five times smaller than the non-corrected one. The one-element calculation without correction gives a low error as happens with sway structures because modal wavelengths are distributed over several elements. Distortion factors lie below 7% and therefore do not surpass our 100% threshold value that would require splitting highly distorted elements in half.

**Table 6.** Corrected calculation statistics (2D sway portal frame with 1 element/member).

| Mode # | Exact [1] $\omega$ (rad/s) | 1-Elem. [2] $\omega$ (rad/s) | Relative [3] Error (%) | Corrected $\omega$ (rad/s) [4] | Relative [5] Error (%) | Distortion Factor $\gamma$ (%) | Distorted Elements # |
|---|---|---|---|---|---|---|---|
| 1 | 34.88  | 34.89  | 0.02 | 34.88  | 0.00 | 1.14 | 0 |
| 2 | 110.12 | 110.28 | 0.14 | 110.13 | 0.01 | 6.11 | 0 |
| 3 | 195.67 | 196.28 | 0.31 | 195.73 | 0.03 | 4.27 | 0 |
| 4 | 277.60 | 278.38 | 0.28 | 277.75 | 0.05 | 6.46 | 0 |

[1] "Exact" value of $\omega$ calculated with Abaqus and Nel = 10. [2] Value of $\omega$ calculated with Abaqus and Nel = 1.
[3] Relative error of the 1-element calculation [4] Value of $\omega$ after applying our correction to the 1-element value.
[5] Relative error of the corrected value.

Next, the calculation is repeated with diagonal bracing added to each floor, restricting horizontal displacement and minimizing the side-sway frame effect as shown in Figure 9. The statistics of the corrected calculation are shown in Table 7, modelling bars with one element. The relative error is reduced significantly in all modes except the third. Our distortion criterion detects the problem since all distortion factors lie above 100% by a very wide margin. As expected, the one-element discretization leads to large errors for a non-sway structure with highly localized vibration shapes from the second mode on.

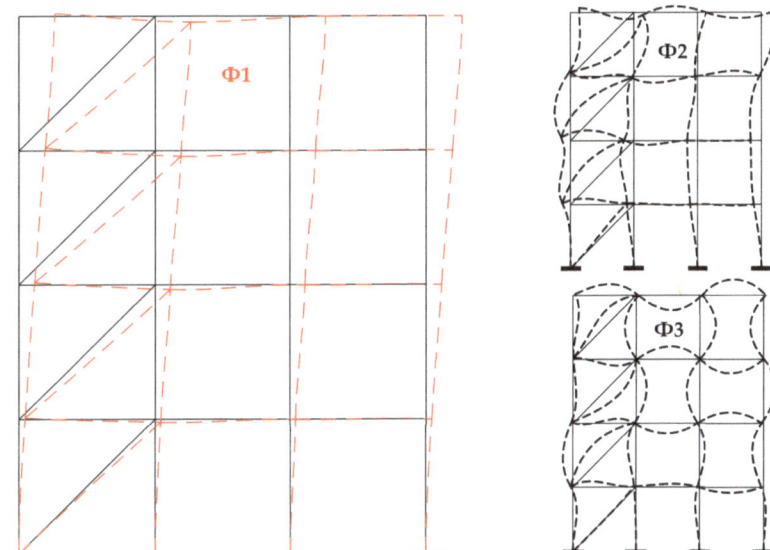

**Figure 9.** 2D framed portal frame: first three modal shapes with one element per member.

**Table 7.** Corrected calculation statistics (2D braced portal frame with 1 element/member).

| Mode # | Exact $\omega$ (rad/s) | 1-Elem. $\Omega$ (rad/s) | Relative Error (%) | Corrected $\omega$ (rad/s) | Relative Error (%) | Distortion Factor $\gamma$ (%) | Distorted Elements # |
|---|---|---|---|---|---|---|---|
| 1 | 161.75 | 162.68 | 0.57 | 161.81 | 0.04 | 125 | 1 |
| 2 | 438.18 | 551.89 | 25.95 | 471.27 | 7.55 | 2854 | 7 |
| 3 | 447.47 | 579.72 | 29.56 | 575.00 | 28.50 | $1.3 \times 10^8$ | 4 |
| 4 | 473.87 | 631.82 | 33.33 | 516.46 | 8.99 | 14,137 | 5 |

According to our distortion criterion, we should subdivide the 7 distorted elements from mode 3 onwards. However, for easiness of implementation we only split the four diagonals and that was enough to reduce the error to very low values (see Table 8). We inspect the second and third mode with subdivided diagonals in Figure 10 and we can see that those modes are highly localized in the diagonal bars. We can interpret that the one-element correction does not decrease error well in Table 7 because it replaces the second and third mode with local vibrations inside the bars, which is easily detected by our distortion factor.

Table 8. Corrected calculation statistics (2D braced portal frame with 2 elems./member diagonals).

| Mode # | Exact ω (rad/s) | 1/2-Elem. ω (rad/s) | Relative Error | Corrected ω (rad/s) | Relat. Error | Distortion Factor γ | Distorted Elements # |
| --- | --- | --- | --- | --- | --- | --- | --- |
| 1 | 161.75 | 162.25 | 0.31% | 161.78 | 0.02% | 122% | 1 |
| 2 | 438.18 | 446.60 | 1.92% | 438.83 | 0.15% | 145% | 2 |
| 3 | 447.47 | 456.15 | 1.94% | 448.13 | 0.15% | 63% | 0 |
| 4 | 473.87 | 482.68 | 1.86% | 474.53 | 0.14% | 364% | 1 |

Therefore, whenever the local correction can produce an inner vibration softer than the coarse mesh mode, it will distort all the modes from that frequency onwards. That is one of the reasons why we chose a two element submodel instead of a four element one like in our previous buckling study [37] because this problem does not appear when only the lowest eigenvalue is required.

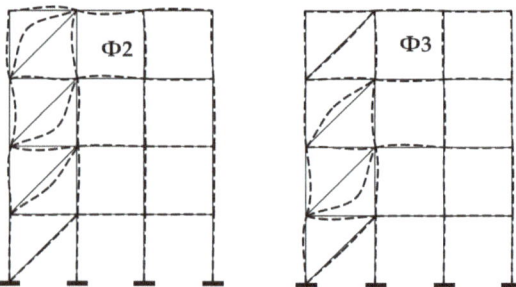

Figure 10. 2D braced portal frame: 2nd and 3rd modal shapes with one element per member except diagonals (two).

### 5.2. 3D Stand Structure

This test case taken from [8] and fully defined in [37] is shown in Figure 11. This is not a typical portal frame structure, which confirms the validity of our approach for generic structural types.

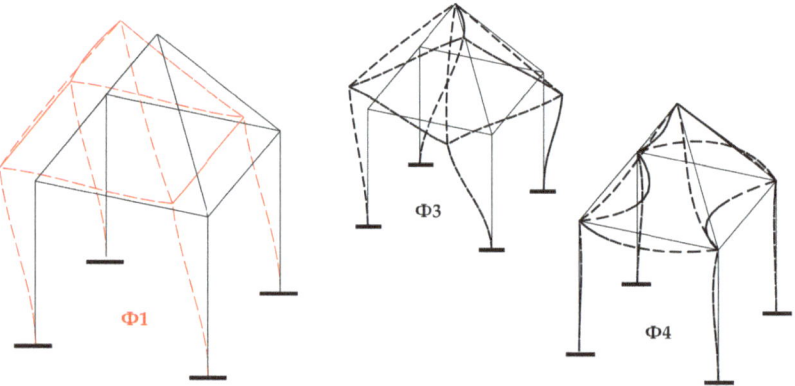

Figure 11. 3D stand frame modal shapes 1, 3 and 4.

The first modal shape φ1 (red dashed lines) is superimposed on the undeformed geometry (continuous black lines). The second shape is very similar to the first one (also a translation of the roof but in a perpendicular direction). The third and fourth shapes (φ3 and φ4) are shown on the right in smaller sizes.

Numerical results are shown in Table 9 with one element per member. A relative error decrease exceeding a factor of 11 is obtained in all cases. The single-element-per-member discretization is quite accurate except for the 4th mode, which shows a distortion factor slightly larger than 100% and should therefore be split in half. Modes 1 to 3 can be considered sway modes (two translations and one rotation of the roof), whereas mode 4 almost keeps the beam ends in their original positions.

**Table 9.** Corrected calculation statistics (3D stand with 1 elem./member).

| Mode # | Exact [1] $\omega$ (rad/s) | 1-Elem. $\omega$ (rad/s) | Relative Error (%) | Corrected $\omega$ (rad/s) | Relative Error (%) | Distortion Factor $\gamma$ (%) | Distorted Elements # |
|---|---|---|---|---|---|---|---|
| 1 | 97.41 | 97.59 | 0.19 | 97.42 | 0.01 | 3.48 | 0 |
| 2 | 97.41 | 97.59 | 0.19 | 97.42 | 0.01 | 3.52 | 0 |
| 3 | 140.11 | 140.45 | 0.24 | 140.14 | 0.02 | 6.40 | 0 |
| 4 | 580.82 | 672.56 | 15.79 | 583.93 | 1.38 | 101.45 | 4 |

[1] "Exact" value calculated with Abaqus and Nel = 10.

### 5.3. 3D Building Structure

This test case taken from [37] is shown in Figure 12. The 1st and 12th modal shapes, (red dashed lines) are superimposed on the undeformed geometry (continuous black lines).

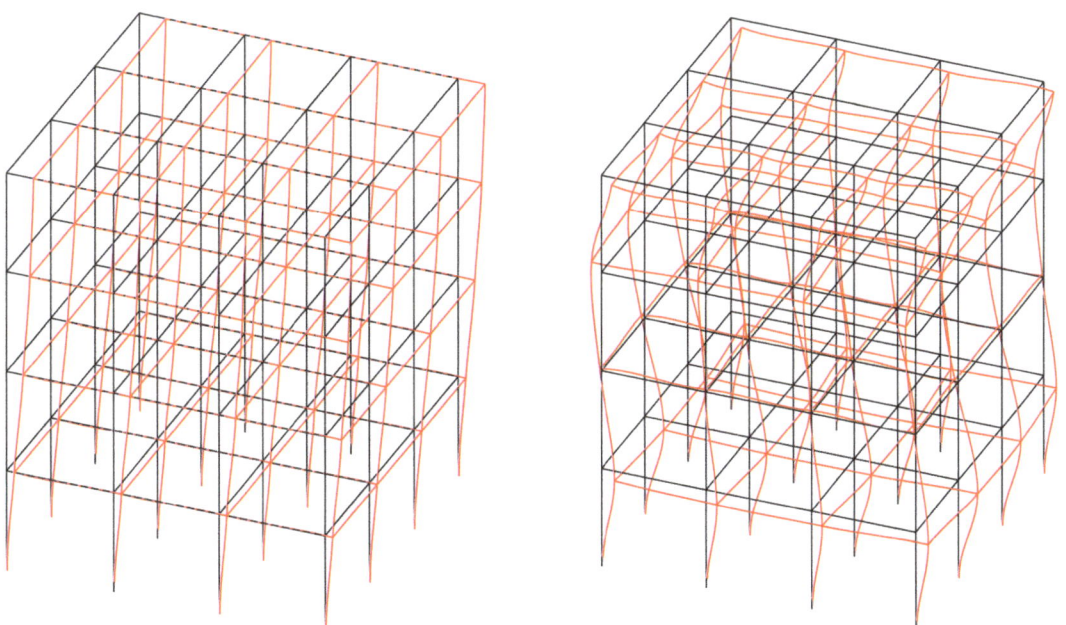

**Figure 12.** 3D sway 160-bar building structure 1st (**left**) and 12th (**right**) modal shapes.

Numerical results are shown in Table 10 for the first 12 modes (the number of floor translational and rotational movements). Although the frame is unbraced and thus does not localize vibration shapes, leading to quite accurate results with a one-element calculation, the relative error is still reduced by a factor greater than 10.

Table 10. Corrected calculation statistics (3D sway building structure with 1 elem./member).

| Mode # | Exact ω (rad/s) | 1-Elem. ω (rad/s) | Relative Error (%) | Corrected ω (rad/s) | Relative Error (%) | Distortion Factor γ (%) | Distorted Elements # |
|---|---|---|---|---|---|---|---|
| 1 | 28.51 | 28.51 | 0.01 | 28.51 | 0.00 | 8.20 | 0 |
| 2 | 28.51 | 28.51 | 0.01 | 28.51 | 0.00 | 8.20 | 0 |
| 3 | 31.81 | 31.82 | 0.02 | 31.81 | 0.00 | 2.01 | 0 |
| 4 | 89.08 | 89.20 | 0.14 | 89.09 | 0.01 | 67.43 | 0 |
| 5 | 89.08 | 89.20 | 0.14 | 89.09 | 0.01 | 64.86 | 0 |
| 6 | 91.72 | 91.85 | 0.14 | 91.73 | 0.01 | 50.67 | 0 |
| 7 | 98.90 | 99.05 | 0.15 | 98.91 | 0.01 | 4.79 | 0 |
| 8 | 129.38 | 129.72 | 0.26 | 129.41 | 0.02 | 11.55 | 0 |
| 9 | 137.88 | 138.27 | 0.29 | 137.91 | 0.02 | 56.25 | 0 |
| 10 | 137.88 | 138.27 | 0.29 | 137.91 | 0.02 | 55.71 | 0 |
| 11 | 155.42 | 156.00 | 0.38 | 155.46 | 0.03 | 189.21 | 4 |
| 12 | 155.42 | 156.00 | 0.38 | 155.46 | 0.03 | 99.61 | 0 |

Figure 13 displays the same calculation after adding diagonal bracing bars. These bars help keep the structure from swaying side to side horizontally.

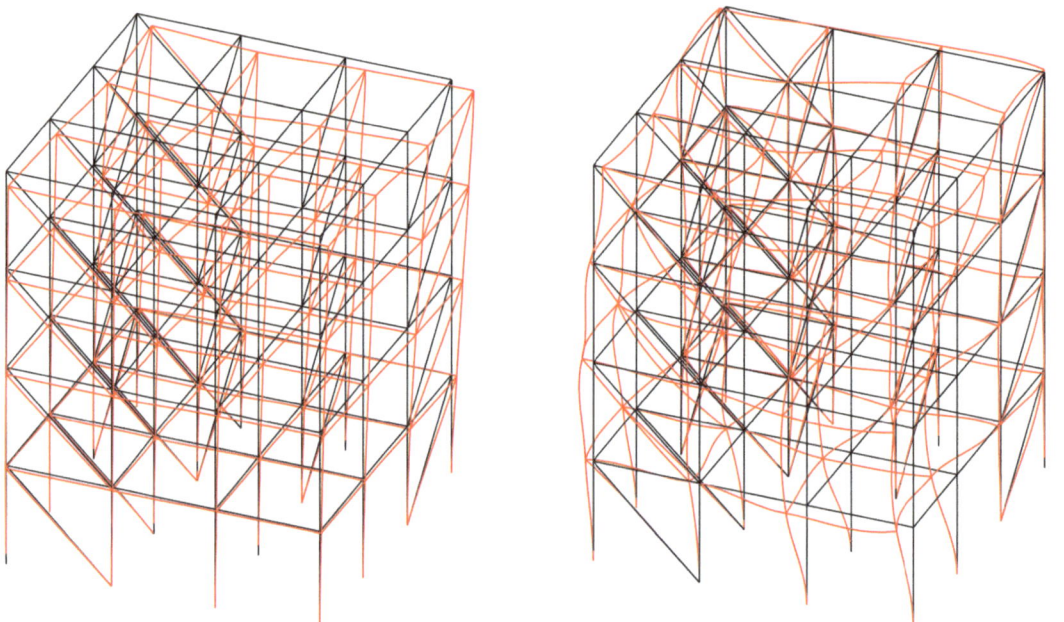

**Figure 13.** 3D braced building structure 1st and 12th modal shapes with one element per member.

Numerical results are shown in Table 11 with one element per member. The relative error is largely decreased by the correction except for the last four modes, when distortion factors reach high values. Errors are higher in this case because of the bracing preventing large amplitude sway modes.

Table 11. Corrected calculation statistics (3D braced building structure with 1 elem./member).

| Mode # | Exact ω (rad/s) | 1-Elem. ω (rad/s) | Relative Error (%) | Corrected ω (rad/s) | Relative Error (%) | Distortion Factor γ (%) | Distorted Elements # |
|---|---|---|---|---|---|---|---|
| 1 | 124.49 | 125.17 | 0.54 | 124.54 | 0.04 | 47.18 | 0 |
| 2 | 126.75 | 127.42 | 0.53 | 126.79 | 0.04 | 59.22 | 0 |
| 3 | 146.27 | 147.08 | 0.55 | 146.33 | 0.04 | 80.42 | 0 |
| 4 | 151.65 | 152.58 | 0.61 | 151.71 | 0.04 | 76.67 | 0 |
| 5 | 184.03 | 185.26 | 0.67 | 184.13 | 0.06 | 182.87 | 1 |
| 6 | 212.50 | 214.77 | 1.07 | 212.67 | 0.08 | 185.24 | 6 |
| 7 | 245.42 | 248.36 | 1.20 | 245.69 | 0.11 | 273.57 | 13 |
| 8 | 276.69 | 281.67 | 1.80 | 277.20 | 0.18 | 729.64 | 18 |
| 9 | 366.95 | 402.78 | 9.77 | 372.53 | 1.52 | 1907.05 | 41 |
| 10 | 384.71 | 434.85 | 13.03 | 396.66 | 3.11 | 2970.10 | 51 |
| 11 | 392.67 | 454.37 | 15.72 | 423.86 | 7.94 | 1200.18 | 35 |
| 12 | 403.95 | 467.65 | 15.77 | 433.75 | 7.38 | 2018.34 | 42 |

Numerical results are shown in Table 12 with two elements per member, even though according to our criterion only 42 out of the 160 bars would need two elements. By applying the correction, we reduce the relative error to a very good level of just 0.06%. It is worth noting that a two-element model of the structure with our correction could be an interesting alternative because of the low errors and distortion factors of the elements, which would make further subdivision unnecessary.

Table 12. Corrected calculation statistics (3D braced building structure with 2 elems./member).

| Mode # | Exact ω (rad/s) | 2-Elem. ω (rad/s) | Relative Error (%) | Corrected ω (rad/s) | Relative Error (%) | Distortion Factor γ (%) | Distorted Elements # |
|---|---|---|---|---|---|---|---|
| 1 | 124.49 | 124.54 | 0.03 | 124.50 | 0.00 | 2.35 | 0 |
| 2 | 126.75 | 126.79 | 0.03 | 126.75 | 0.00 | 4.65 | 0 |
| 3 | 146.27 | 146.33 | 0.04 | 146.28 | 0.00 | 3.94 | 0 |
| 4 | 151.65 | 151.71 | 0.04 | 151.66 | 0.00 | 4.33 | 0 |
| 5 | 184.03 | 184.13 | 0.05 | 184.04 | 0.00 | 6.87 | 0 |
| 6 | 212.50 | 212.66 | 0.08 | 212.52 | 0.01 | 4.66 | 0 |
| 7 | 245.42 | 245.67 | 0.10 | 245.44 | 0.01 | 7.20 | 0 |
| 8 | 276.69 | 277.13 | 0.16 | 276.73 | 0.01 | 17.03 | 0 |
| 9 | 366.95 | 368.89 | 0.53 | 367.08 | 0.04 | 9.62 | 0 |
| 10 | 384.71 | 387.27 | 0.67 | 384.89 | 0.05 | 16.12 | 0 |
| 11 | 392.67 | 395.59 | 0.74 | 392.87 | 0.05 | 3.82 | 0 |
| 12 | 403.95 | 407.28 | 0.82 | 404.18 | 0.06 | 4.83 | 0 |

After examining the results, we can conclude that our models achieve the same level of accuracy as Abaqus standard FEM models with twice as many bars (on the condition that distortion factors lie below 100%), therefore they can work with stiffness and mass matrices twice smaller. In addition, we have attained calculation times 15% smaller measuring the main components of required processing power, i.e., the whole frame eigenvalue problem and the local beam eigenvalue problems.

## 6. Discussion

The method by Xie and Steven [10] provides local natural frequency updates for single bars rather than local modal shape corrections, which leads to using a weighted criterion with a weaker physical foundation than Rayleigh's quotient. In addition, structural members are discretized with four or five elements while in our case one or two (in a few bars) elements are needed.

The SPRD technique by Wiberg et al. [18] bears some similarities with our approach. It relies on a polynomial fitting to the existing mode at some superconvergent points while our procedure completely updates the mode at inner points without being constrained by the coarse calculation on the inside. Plus, the whole structure rather than a single element and its neighboring patch participates in the adjustment by means of the coarse modal amplitude η. It can also be noted that SPR techniques use an external patch of elements while our method relies on an inner set of refined elements.

Gradient smoothing methods such as [19] also rely on neighboring elements to improve the quality of the solution but they do it before solving the system of equations of the whole structure, thereby increasing connectivity and the enhanced element matrix computation time. In addition, there is no straightforward way of applying the smoothing concept to beam elements of different sections and orientations sharing a node.

Modified stiffness and mass matrices [29], while improving the accuracy of dynamic analysis, are limited by the fact that they do not depend on the natural frequency being studied (like in the case of dynamic stiffness methods) or on the actual modal shape, as happens in our method.

Higher-order finite elements [31–34] provide better accuracy but are more complex to implement, have to solve larger systems of equations and lead to worse conditioned matrices. In contrast, our method works well with the standard finite element method and could work with higher-order finite elements as well to improve their accuracy. As for thin-walled beams [36], they require higher-order models in order to represent complex deformation patterns, but they are fully compatible with our correction algorithm.

The hierarchical FEM [23–25] relies on error estimators to refine the structural mesh and improve accuracy. In contrast, our correction does not need a full reanalysis to increase precision but an array of concurrent element-centered corrections. If necessary, the distortion factor indicates what bars require two elements instead of one. Like the higher-order elements discussed above, hierarchical elements of higher order can be used for the corrections instead of our two-subelement set.

As mentioned in the introduction, the authors recently wrote a closely related paper [37] about calculating the critical buckling loads of structural frames using one element per member. For this purpose, a local correction procedure was applied using four subelements. This latest work presents some fundamental differences. First, preventing structural buckling requires knowing just the lowest critical load, but in order to model structural dynamics accurately, multiple natural frequencies are needed. Second, the interplay between multiple frequencies coupled with the limited accuracy of individual elements makes it necessary to use two subelements instead of four. Third, because of the smaller number of subelements involved in the local corrections, some members have to be split into half beams according to a novel element distortion criterion which measures the relative change in kinetic and elastic energy caused by the correction of modal shapes.

As far as the efficiency of our method is concerned, most of what was stated in [37] remains applicable: the algorithm's greatest source of efficiency comes from its fully parallelizable nature and the local eigenvalue problems can be solved with minimal computational resources by the power method. In addition, after shrinking the submodel to two elements, all the matrices that appear in the local eigenvalue problem can be easily programmed with scalar operators and functions, thereby reducing the cost to solving the eigenvalue problem.

Our technique can be applied to enhance the standard FEM analysis of any structure made up of beam/column elements. The structure could also contain shell, plate or lumped elements but the gain in accuracy would only occur for the bar elements. Our approach can be used to calculate natural frequencies with errors acceptable in engineering (below 1%) using one or two elements per member or to increase the accuracy of a calculation with any number of elements per member. Therefore, our approach offers the potential for a reduction in memory requirements and calculation speed when compared with the standard FEM at the cost of some additional coding. In order to fully exploit the advantages of the algorithm, it is advisable to distribute the correction calculations to the GPU.

Concerning future research developments based on the present work, we have selected a few areas of interest. First, there is always a significant discrepancy between numerical vibrational properties and experimental measurements [39,40] because of approximate modelling, nonlinearities, temperature effects, etc., which could be addressed advantageously with the proposed numerical technique or an enhanced version of it. Likewise, in the field of health structural monitoring, there is also the need to deal with discrepancies caused by structural failure or deterioration, and to diagnose their nature and location [41,42]. However, the present study is only concerned with numerical efficiency and has no direct application in these areas in its present form.

## 7. Conclusions

A new method for improving the accuracy of the standard FEM natural frequency calculation of structural frames made up of beam/column elements has been presented. The algorithms are based on previous work by the authors on structural frame buckling, but significant novel modifications have been made to improve efficiency and ease implementation, and to account for the challenges of calculating several eigenvalues instead of the lowest one. The fully parallel nature of the method makes it very convenient to take advantage of the current trend towards GPU-based architectures. For this purpose, the main calculation cost driver is a small individual nodal centered eigenvalue problem solvable with a few power iterations.

Structural members are modelled with one or two elements following a novel subdivision criterion based on the degree of distortion caused by the correction of the original modal shape. As a result, enough accuracy for engineering applications is achieved with a modest increase in computation time and storage requirements. The approach is very flexible and can accommodate different beam types, higher-order models and finer meshes and target precision levels, even though it has been demonstrated with simple cubic elements. Algorithm inputs are readily available data on FEM codes such as frame and element stiffness and mass matrices, rotations and modal shapes that can be processed with scalar functions and operators before the local eigensolver correction step.

**Author Contributions:** Conceptualization, J.U.: methodology, J.U.; software, J.U.; validation, J.U. and I.G.; writing, J.U. and I.G. All authors have read and agreed to the published version of the manuscript.

**Funding:** This research received no external funding.

**Data Availability Statement:** The original contributions presented in the study are included in the article. Further inquiries can be directed to the corresponding author.

**Conflicts of Interest:** The authors declare no conflict of interest.

## References

1. Chopra, A.K. *Dynamics of Structures: Theory and Applications to Earthquake Engineering*, 6th ed.; Pearson: London, UK, 2023.
2. *Spanish Structural Code (Código Estructural)*; Spanish Ministry of Transport, Mobility and the Urban Agenda (Ministerio de Transportes, Movilidad y Agenda Urbana): Madrid, Spain, 2021.
3. EN1993-1-1; Eurocode 3: Design of Steel Structures. European Committee for Standardization: Brussels, Belgium, 2005.
4. Staff, American Society of Civil Engineers (ASCE). *Minimum Design Loads for Buildings and Other Structures*, 3rd ed.; American Society of Civil Engineers: Reston, VA, USA, 2013.
5. Biswas, P.; Peronto, J. *Design and Performance of Tall Buildings for Wind*, 1st ed.; American Society of Civil Engineers (ASCE): Reston, VA, USA, 2020.
6. Petyt, M. *Introduction to Finite Element Vibration Analysis*, 2nd ed.; Cambridge University Press: Cambridge, UK, 2015.
7. Zienkiewicz, O.C.; Taylor, R.L.; Zhu, J.Z. *The Finite Element Method: Its Basis and Fundamentals*; Butterworth-Heinemann: Cambridge, UK, 2013; Volume 3.
8. Xie, Y.M.; Steven, G.P. Improving finite element predictions of buckling loads of beams and frames. *Comput. Struct.* **1994**, *52*, 381–385. [CrossRef]
9. Mackie, R.I. Improving finite element predictions of modes of vibration. *Int. J. Numer. Methods Eng.* **1992**, *33*, 333–344. [CrossRef]
10. Xie, Y.M.; Steven, G.P. Explicit formulas for correcting finite-element predictions of natural frequencies. *Commun. Numer. Methods Eng.* **1993**, *9*, 671–680. [CrossRef]
11. Babuška, I.; Rheinboldt, W.C. A-posteriori error estimates for the finite element method. *Int. J. Numer. Methods Eng.* **1978**, *12*, 1597–1615. [CrossRef]

12. Babuška, I. *Accuracy Estimates and Adaptive Refinements in Finite Element Computations*; Wiley: Chichester, UK, 1986.
13. Zienkiewicz, O.C.; Zhu, J.Z. The superconvergent patch recovery (SPR) and adaptive finite element refinement. *Comput. Methods Appl. Mech. Eng.* **1992**, *101*, 207–224. [CrossRef]
14. Boroomand, B.; Zienkiewicz, O.C. Recovery by equilibrium in patches (REP). *Int. J. Numer. Methods Eng.* **1997**, *40*, 137–164. [CrossRef]
15. Sun, H.; Yuan, S. An improved local error estimate in adaptive finite element analysis based on element energy projection technique. *Eng. Comput.* **2023**, *40*, 246–264. [CrossRef]
16. Wiberg, N.-E.; Abdulwahab, F.; Ziukas, S. Improved element stresses for node and element patches using superconvergent patch recovery. *Commun. Numer. Methods Eng.* **1995**, *11*, 619–627. [CrossRef]
17. Wiberg, N.; Abdulwahab, F. Patch recovery based on superconvergent derivatives and equilibrium. *Int. J. Numer. Methods Eng.* **1993**, *36*, 2703–2724. [CrossRef]
18. Wiberg, N.; Bausys, R.; Hager, P. Improved eigenfrequencies and eigenmodes in free vibration analysis. *Comput. Struct.* **1999**, *73*, 79–89. [CrossRef]
19. Liu, G.R. A generalized gradient smoothing technique and the smoothed bilinear form for Galerkin formulation of a wide class of computational methods. *Int. J. Comput. Methods* **2008**, *5*, 199–236. [CrossRef]
20. Liu, G.R. On G space theory. *Int. J. Comput. Methods* **2009**, *6*, 257–289. [CrossRef]
21. Liu, G.R.; Nguyen-Thoi, T.; Nguyen-Xuan, H.; Lam, K.Y. A node-based smoothed finite element method (NS-FEM) for upper bound solutions to solid mechanics problems. *Comput. Struct.* **2009**, *87*, 14–26. [CrossRef]
22. Liu, G.R.; Nguyen-Thoi, T.; Lam, K.Y. An edge-based smoothed finite element method (ES-FEM) for static, free and forced vibration analyses of solids. *J. Sound Vib.* **2009**, *320*, 1100–1130. [CrossRef]
23. Zienkiewicz, O.C.; De, S.R.; Gago, J.P.; Kelly, D.W. The hierarchical concept in finite element analysis. *Comput. Struct.* **1983**, *16*, 53–65. [CrossRef]
24. Ganesan, N.; Engels, R.C. Hierarchical Bernoulli-Euler beam finite elements. *Comput. Struct.* **1992**, *43*, 297–304. [CrossRef]
25. Tai, C.-Y.; Chan, Y.J. A hierarchic high-order Timoshenko beam finite element. *Comput. Struct.* **2016**, *165*, 48–58. [CrossRef]
26. Hui, Y.; Giunta, G.; Belouettar, S.; Huang, Q.; Hu, H.; Carrera, E. A free vibration analysis of three-dimensional sandwich beams using hierarchical one-dimensional finite elements. *Compos. Part B Eng.* **2017**, *110*, 7–19. [CrossRef]
27. Fried, I.; Chavez, M. Superaccurate finite element eigenvalue computation. *J. Sound Vib.* **2004**, *275*, 415–422. [CrossRef]
28. Fried, I.; Leong, K. Superaccurate finite element eigenvalues via a Rayleigh quotient correction. *J. Sound Vib.* **2005**, *288*, 375–386. [CrossRef]
29. Li, E.; He, Z.C. Development of a perfect match system in the improvement of eigenfrequencies of free vibration. *Appl. Math. Model.* **2017**, *44*, 614–639. [CrossRef]
30. Guddati, M.N.; Yue, B. Modified integration rules for reducing dispersion error in finite element methods. *Comput. Methods Appl. Mech. Eng.* **2004**, *193*, 275–287. [CrossRef]
31. Shang, H.Y.; Machado, R.D.; Abdalla Filho, J.E. Dynamic analysis of Euler–Bernoulli beam problems using the Generalized Finite Element Method. *Comput. Struct.* **2016**, *173*, 109–122. [CrossRef]
32. Hsu, Y.S. Enriched finite element methods for Timoshenko beam free vibration analysis. *Appl. Math. Model.* **2016**, *40*, 7012–7033.
33. Cornaggia, R.; Darrigrand, E.; Le Marrec, L.; Mahé, F. Enriched finite elements and local rescaling for vibrations of axially inhomogeneous Timoshenko beams. *J. Sound Vib.* **2020**, *474*, 115228. [CrossRef]
34. Necib, B.; Sun, C.T. Analysis of truss beams using a high order Timoshenko beam finite element. *J. Sound Vib.* **1989**, *130*, 149–159. [CrossRef]
35. Wang, T.; Mikkola, A.; Matikainen, M.K. An Overview of Higher-Order Beam Elements Based on the Absolute Nodal Coordinate Formulation. *J. Comput. Nonlinear Dynam.* **2022**, *17*, 091001. [CrossRef]
36. Nguyen, T.; Nguyen, N.; Lee, J.; Nguyen, Q. Vibration analysis of thin-walled functionally graded sandwich beams with non-uniform polygonal cross-sections. *Compos. Struct.* **2021**, *278*, 114723. [CrossRef]
37. Urruzola, J.; Garmendia, I. Calculation of Linear Buckling Load for Frames Modeled with One-Finite-Element Beams and Columns. *Computation* **2023**, *11*, 109. [CrossRef]
38. Meirovitch, L. *Fundamentals of Vibrations*; McGraw-Hill: New York, NY, USA, 2001.
39. Luo, J.; Huang, M.; Lei, Y. Temperature Effect on Vibration Properties and Vibration-Based Damage Identification of Bridge Structures: A Literature Review. *Buildings* **2022**, *12*, 1209. [CrossRef]
40. Huang, M.; Zhang, J.; Hu, J.; Ye, Z.; Deng, Z.; Wan, N. Nonlinear modeling of temperature-induced bearing displacement of long-span single-pier rigid frame bridge based on DCNN-LSTM. *Case Stud. Therm. Eng.* **2024**, *53*, 103897. [CrossRef]
41. Deng, Z.; Huang, M.; Wan, N.; Zhang, J. The Current Development of Structural Health Monitoring for Bridges: A Review. *Buildings* **2023**, *13*, 1360. [CrossRef]
42. Huang, M.; Ling, Z.; Sun, C.; Lei, Y.; Xiang, C.; Wan, Z.; Gu, J. Two-stage damage identification for bridge bearings based on sailfish optimization and element relative modal strain energy. *Struct. Eng. Mech. Int. J.* **2023**, *86*, 715–730.

**Disclaimer/Publisher's Note:** The statements, opinions and data contained in all publications are solely those of the individual author(s) and contributor(s) and not of MDPI and/or the editor(s). MDPI and/or the editor(s) disclaim responsibility for any injury to people or property resulting from any ideas, methods, instructions or products referred to in the content.

Article

# Stability Analysis of Seismic Slope Based on Relative Residual Displacement Increment Method

Weijian Sun [1,2], Guoxin Wang [1,2,*] and Juntao Ma [3]

[1] State Key Laboratory of Coastal and Offshore Engineering, Dalian University of Technology, No. 2 Linggong Road, Dalian 116024, China; swjian@mail.dlut.edu.cn
[2] Institute of Earthquake Engineering, Faculty of Infrastructure Engineering, Dalian University of Technology, No. 2 Linggong Road, Dalian 116024, China
[3] Department of Material and Structure, Changjiang River Scientific Research Institute, Wuhan 430010, China; majuntao@mail.crsri.cn
* Correspondence: gxwang@dlut.edu.cn

**Abstract:** The seismic stability analysis of a slope is a complex process influenced by earthquake action characteristics and soil mechanical properties. This paper presents a novel seismic slope stability analysis method using the relative residual displacement increment method in combination with the strength reduction method (SRM) and the actual deformation characteristics of the slope. By calculating the relative displacement of the key point inside the landslide mass and the reference point outside the landslide mass after each reduction, the safety factor of the slope is determined by the strength reduction factor (SRF) corresponding to the maximum absolute value of the relative residual displacement increment that appears after a continuous plastic penetration zone. The method eliminates interference caused by significant displacement fluctuations of key points under earthquake action and reduces the subjective error that can occur when manually identifying displacement mutation points. The proposed method is validated by dynamic calculations of homogeneous and layered soil slopes and compared with three other criteria: applicability, accuracy, and stability.

**Keywords:** seismic slope stability; safety factor; relative residual displacement increment method

---

**Citation:** Sun, W.; Wang, G.; Ma, J. Stability Analysis of Seismic Slope Based on Relative Residual Displacement Increment Method. *Buildings* **2024**, *14*, 1211. https://doi.org/10.3390/buildings14051211

Academic Editor: Jingzhong Tong

Received: 13 March 2024
Revised: 16 April 2024
Accepted: 22 April 2024
Published: 24 April 2024

**Copyright:** © 2024 by the authors. Licensee MDPI, Basel, Switzerland. This article is an open access article distributed under the terms and conditions of the Creative Commons Attribution (CC BY) license (https://creativecommons.org/licenses/by/4.0/).

## 1. Introduction

In recent years, with the frequent occurrence of seismic events, slope instability induced by earthquake action has become the most common secondary hazard in many countries [1]. For example, the Wenchuan earthquake in 2008 triggered more than 15,000 landslides caused by the main shock and aftershocks [2,3]. Therefore, evaluating the dynamic stability of slopes under earthquake action has important theoretical and engineering significance for seismic fortification.

Dynamic slope stability analysis is an important research topic in geotechnical engineering involving multiple fields such as slope engineering, geotechnical mechanics, and earthquake engineering [4]. Currently, the assessment of slope stability subjected to earthquake action is typically classified into three main categories [5]: (1) pseudo-static method [6], (2) permanent-displacement analysis [7], and (3) stress-deformation analysis [8]. These three methods each possess their own set of advantages and disadvantages. In addition, with the continuous development of computer technology, machine learning and artificial intelligence are widely applied in various fields [9,10]. The research on various machine learning-based techniques to predict the safety factor of slopes has attracted widespread attention from researchers [11]. Optimized design of landslides can be achieved through various efficient algorithms [12,13]. The pseudo-static method simplifies earthquake action as a constant inertial force acting on the center of gravity of the slope in the direction of instability [14–19]. The pseudo-static method is a widely used seismic slope stability analysis technique due to its clear physical concept and simple calculation.

However, it has notable shortcomings, as it can not accurately capture the ground motion and dynamic characteristics of the slope material, nor can it account for the dynamic interactions between the soil and structures. The permanent displacement method, also known as the Newmark analysis, bridges the gap between the simplistic pseudo-static analysis and the more complex stress-deformation analysis. This approach estimates slope stability by calculating the permanent displacement of slopes. However, this method falls short in assessing the potential for slope instability under dynamic conditions, especially in complex geological settings. Stress-deformation analysis [20–25] mainly includes the finite element method (FEM), finite difference method (FDM), and discrete element method (DEM). These methods can accurately describe the stress-deformation behavior of slope materials under earthquake action and simulate the damage process of slopes [26,27]. The stress-deformation analysis has made significant advancements in calculating the safety factor of a slope under earthquake conditions, but it currently has limitations in computing only the displacement, stress, and plastic zone of the slope. Despite these advancements, the calculation of the safety factor for slopes remains a challenge, and there is no well-established method for achieving this goal. As a result, many researchers have resorted to using the strength reduction method for calculating the stability of earthquake slopes, which involves selecting an appropriate instability criterion to compute the slope's safety factor [28–30].

There are three main criteria for calculating slope stability under complete earthquake action based on the strength reduction finite difference method [31–35].

(1) The slope stability can be evaluated based on the actual deformation characteristics of the slope, such as the characteristic point displacement catastrophe method (referred to as Criterion I). During an earthquake, the load continuously changes with time; therefore, the sudden change in displacement at a particular moment alone cannot be used as the criterion for slope instability. However, once the seismic activity has ceased, the slope's final displacement changes abruptly, which can be used as an indicator of slope instability;

(2) The stability of a slope can be assessed by examining its stress state (referred to as Criterion II), including the presence of a continuous plastic penetration zone;

(3) The slope stability can be judged according to whether the numerical iteration converges (referred to as Criterion III). Under the earthquake action, when the slope is in a stable state, the displacement trend at the end of the period of the key point displacement time-history curve is convergent, and the displacement on the time-history curve will not change with time in the end. When the slope is in an unstable state, the displacement trend at the end of the period is divergent, and the displacement on the time-history curve increases with time. Therefore, slope instability can be judged if the displacement on the time-history curve diverges and the calculation does not converge at the same time.

Based on the above three criteria, the safety factors of homogeneous soil slopes and layered soil slopes under earthquake action were calculated. By comparing and analyzing their respective advantages and disadvantages, a novel approach is proposed based on the first type of criteria, which incorporates the evolution law of the actual landslide at different stages, termed the relative residual displacement increment method. After each reduction, the relative displacements between the key points inside the landslide mass and the reference points outside the landslide mass are calculated. The safety factor of the slope is determined by taking the strength reduction factor (SRF) corresponding to the maximum value of the relative residual displacement increment that appears first after a continuous plastic penetration zone. The method eliminates interference caused by significant displacement fluctuations of key points under earthquake action and reduces the subjective error that can occur when manually identifying displacement mutation points. This method has been verified to be more applicable, accurate, and stable than the other three criteria.

## 2. Strength Reduction Dynamic Stability Evaluation Method

### 2.1. Principle of Strength Reduction Dynamic Analysis Method

When an earthquake occurs, the slope is subjected to earthquake action while in a static state. The strength reduction method is used to perform a static analysis, followed by a dynamic analysis with the application of earthquake loads to analyze the slope's stability. The strength reduction factor (SRF), which is the safety factor of the slope, is calculated by continuously reducing the strength until the slope reaches the critical equilibrium state. The initial SRF is generally assumed to be a reasonably low value, and the final SRF is treated as the slope's safety factor while continuously adjusting SRF until slope failure occurs [36]. The calculation formulas are as follows:

$$c' = \frac{c}{SRF} \tag{1}$$

$$\varphi' = \tan^{-1}\left(\frac{\tan \varphi}{SRF}\right) \tag{2}$$

$$\sigma^{t'} = \frac{\sigma^t}{SRF} \tag{3}$$

where $\varphi$ is the effective friction angle, $c$ is the effective cohesion, and $\sigma^t$ is the tensile strength of the soil.

### 2.2. Principle of Relative Residual Displacement Increment Method

Evaluating the stability of a slope using the strength reduction method requires determining the critical state of the slope, but different criteria may result in varying safety factor calculations. Due to the complexity of analyzing slope stability under earthquake action, a commonly used approach is calculating safety factors based on three criteria and then comprehensively evaluating dynamic stability. Nevertheless, no widely accepted and effective single method for determining seismic slope stability is currently available. Based on the analysis and comparison of relevant research results and the accumulation of long-term work experience, the authors believe that the displacement catastrophe criterion has a clear physical meaning, relatively reliable identification results, and wide application, but there are still applicability problems in specific applications. If the displacement catastrophe point identification method can be improved, its operability and application value in landslide identification will be further improved. Based on the first kind of criteria combined with the evolution law of the actual landslide at different stages, the relative residual displacement increment method is proposed in this paper. As shown in Figure 1, during the development and evolution of the Xintan landslide, according to the cumulative displacement-time curve, it can be divided into four stages: initial deformation, uniform deformation, accelerated deformation, and sharp deformation [37,38]. When the slope is destroyed, it is in the stage of sharp deformation (May to June 1985). Under the action of seismic load, when the slope is unstable, it is in the stage of rapid deformation, and the deformation rate of the landslide mass reaches the maximum value. Therefore, the relative residual displacement increment method (Criterion IV) is proposed to evaluate the seismic stability of the slope. Because the seismic load changes with time, the displacement after the completion of the seismic action can be used as the final displacement of the slope. The curve of the relative displacement-reduction coefficient can be obtained by calculating the relative displacement between the key points inside the landslide mass and the reference points outside the landslide mass. On this basis, the safety factor of the slope is determined by taking the SRF corresponding to the maximum value of the relative residual displacement increment that appears first after a continuous plastic penetration zone.

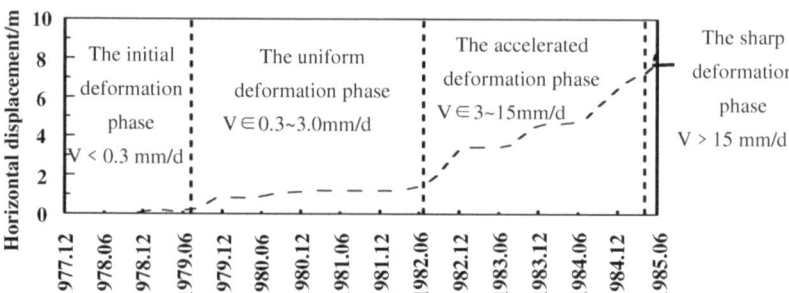

**Figure 1.** The displacement-time curve of the Xintan landslide.

Figure 2 displays the selection of the top point of the landslide body as the key point $K$ and the outer point of the landslide body as the reference point $O$. The calculation of the relative displacement of the slope without reduction is as follows:

$$D_{R0} = D_K - D_O \tag{4}$$

where $D_K$ represents the displacement of a key point located within the landslide mass, $D_O$ represents the displacement of the reference point located outside the landslide.

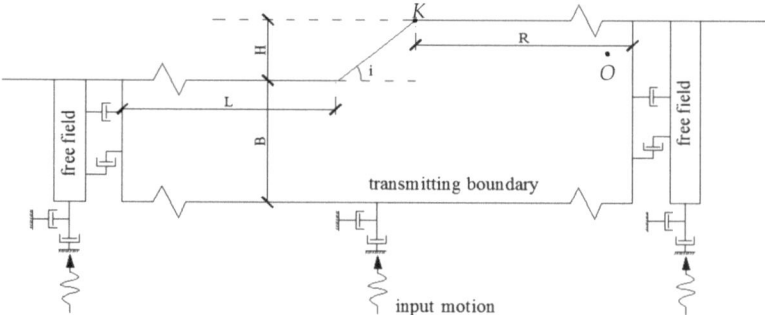

**Figure 2.** Schematic view of the 2D slope model.

The relative residual displacement of the slope after reduction is as follows:

$$D_{SRF} = D_{Ri} - D_{R0} \tag{5}$$

where $D_{Ri}$ represents the relative displacement of the slope after the reduction.

The maximum absolute value of the relative residual displacement increment of the slope is as follows:

$$\Delta D_{SRF} = |D_{SRF+1} - D_{SRF}|_{\max} \tag{6}$$

## 3. Numerical Analysis

### 3.1. 2D Slope Model

This paper uses the finite difference software FLAC 7.0 [39] to calculate the slope stability under an earthquake. The slope model is shown in Figure 2. Both sides of the slope model are free boundaries, which can reduce the reflection of the wavelet. The bottom adopts a viscous boundary, which can absorb the energy of the reflected wave.

### 3.2. Input Ground Motion

Four near-field seismic records are selected as input ground motions for slope dynamic analysis. The seismic records are obtained from the PEER NGA-West2; the detailed information is shown in Table 1. Due to the numerical analysis only considering ground motion frequencies ranging from 0–10 Hz, a low-pass filter with a cutoff frequency of 10 Hz is applied to the acceleration time history. The amplitude of the filtered acceleration is then modulated by 0.1 g. The acceleration time-history curve is shown in Figure 3. Since the bottom boundary is viscous in FLAC, seismic wave input is applied to the bottom boundary in the form of shear stress time history. The finite rigidity of the underlying bedrock is idealized, considering an elastic half-space [40]. The acceleration time history after amplitude modulation is converted into velocity time history $v(t)$, and then the velocity time history is converted into shear stress $\sigma_s(t)$. The calculation formula is as follows [41]:

$$\sigma_S(t) = -2(\rho V_S)v(t) \tag{7}$$

where $\rho$ and vs. represent the medium density and the shear wave velocity, respectively.

Table 1. Information of the selected seismic records.

| No. | Earthquake | Date | $M_W$ | $R_{jb}$ (km) | Station | $V_{S30}$ (m/s) |
|---|---|---|---|---|---|---|
| 1 | Northridge | 17 January 1994 | 6.7 | 23.1 | Vasquez Rocks Park | 996.4 |
| 2 | San Francisco | 22 March 1957 | 5.3 | 9.74 | Golden Gate Park | 874.72 |
| 3 | Whittier Narrows | 1 October 1987 | 6 | 6.78 | Pasadena—CIT Kresge Lab | 969.1 |
| 4 | Whittier Narrows-1 | 1 October 1987 | 6 | 47.25 | Vasquez Rocks Park | 996.4 |

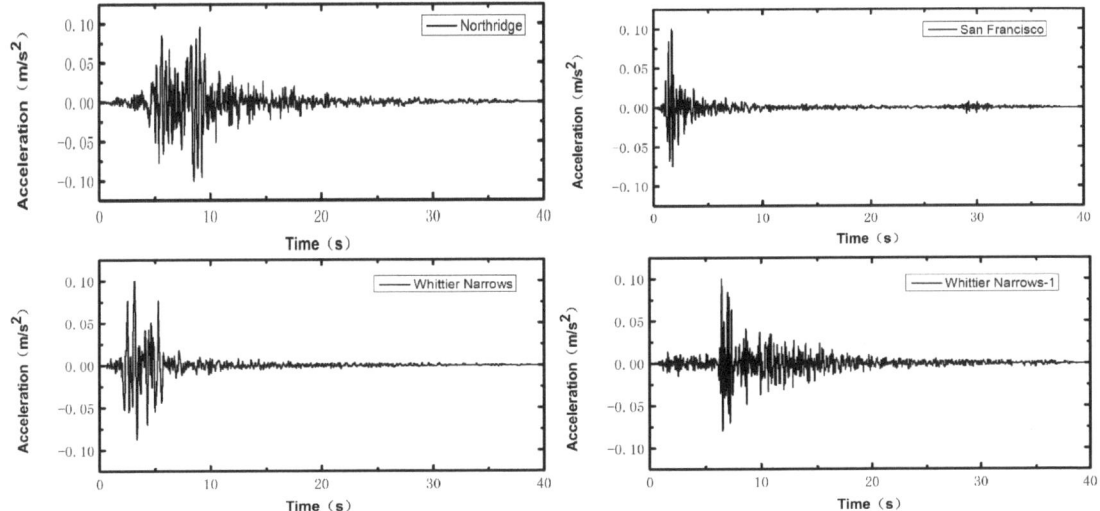

Figure 3. Acceleration time histories of the input motions.

### 3.3. Homogeneous Soil Slope

The homogeneous slope soil mass is an ideal elastic-plastic material conforming to the Mohr–Coulomb yield criterion. The top of the slope is 40 m from the right boundary, the toe of the slope is 40 m from the left boundary, the slope height is 20 m, the slope angle is 45°, and the total thickness of the slope is 40 m. Its material parameters are shown in Table 2 [42].

Table 2. Material parameters.

| $c$ (KPa) | $\psi$ (°) | $\gamma$ (kN/m³) | $G$ (MPa) | $K$ (MPa) | $Rm$ (MPa) |
|---|---|---|---|---|---|
| 40 | 30 | 22 | 30 | 60 | 0.004 |

Where $c$ is the effective cohesion, $\psi$ is the effective friction angle, $\gamma$ is the bulk density, $G$ is the shear modulus, $K$ is the bulk modulus, $Rm$ is the tensile strength.

In the calculation of homogeneous slope, Rayleigh damping is used to simulate the energy dissipation in the dynamic response. The damping matrix $C$ is described as follows [43,44]:

$$C = \alpha M + \beta K \qquad (8)$$

where $M$ and $K$ represent the mass and stiffness matrices, respectively, $\alpha$ and $\beta$ represent the corresponding scale factor.

According to the suggestion of Kwok et al. [45], two control frequencies are selected respectively: the first-order natural vibration frequency $f_1$ of the slope model and five times the first-order natural vibration frequency ($f_2 = 5f_1$). The calculation formulas of $\alpha$ and $\beta$ are as follows:

$$\alpha = \frac{2\xi}{\omega_1+\omega_2}\omega_1\omega_2$$
$$\beta = \frac{2\xi}{\omega_1+\omega_2} \qquad (9)$$

where $\xi$ represents the target damping ratio (5%), $\omega_1$ and $\omega_2$ represent the circular frequency corresponding to $f_1$ and $f_2$, respectively.

In FLAC, the setting of Rayleigh damping needs to input the minimum value of damping ratio $\xi_{\min}$ and corresponding frequency $f_{\min}$, the calculation formula is as follows:

$$\xi_{\min} = \sqrt{\alpha \cdot \beta}$$
$$f_{\min} = \frac{1}{2\pi}\sqrt{\frac{\alpha}{\beta}} \qquad (10)$$

Four seismic waves are input, respectively, and the stability of the homogeneous soil slope under the earthquake action is evaluated by calculating safety factors based on the criterion proposed in this paper and three other types of criteria.

Using the characteristic point displacement catastrophe as the criterion (Criterion I), as depicted in Figures 4 and 5, there are two curves: the vertex displacement-reduction factor curve (Criterion $I_1$) and the relative displacement-reduction factor curve (Criterion $I_2$). In contrast, Figure 4b,d demonstrate that significant fluctuations in the displacement curve can make it challenging to precisely determine the displacement mutation point. To mitigate the impact of curve fluctuation on the reduction factor, the relative displacement curve is used to identify the displacement catastrophe point. Figure 5b,d indicate a reduction in the fluctuation of the relative displacement curve; however, some artificial discrimination errors may still occur.

The penetration zone is taken as the criterion (Criterion II), and the complete penetration zone formed by shear strain increment is taken as the criterion of slope instability. As shown in Figure 6, under this slope model, taking the input Northridge seismic wave as an example, when the reduction factors are 1.24, 1.26, 1.28, and 1.30, the complete through the zone is formed. However, when a continuous plastic penetration zone occurs, the slope does not necessarily break down immediately. Therefore, slope instability cannot be determined by a continuous plastic penetration zone alone.

The iterative non-convergence is used as the criterion (Criterion III), and the criterion for slope instability is based on whether the final displacement diverges after the earthquake. The displacement time history curve is depicted in Figure 7, where Figure 7a,c show that the curve diverges at SRF values of 1.27 and 1.26, respectively. The slope is damaged at this time, leading to a safety factor of 1.26 and 1.25, respectively. In Figure 7b, although the displacement time history curve divergence is indistinguishable, there is a sudden change in displacement. Figure 7d displays a clear displacement time history curve divergence, but its displacement does not change abruptly. Consequently, relying on this criterion to determine slope failure can lead to discrimination errors and failures.

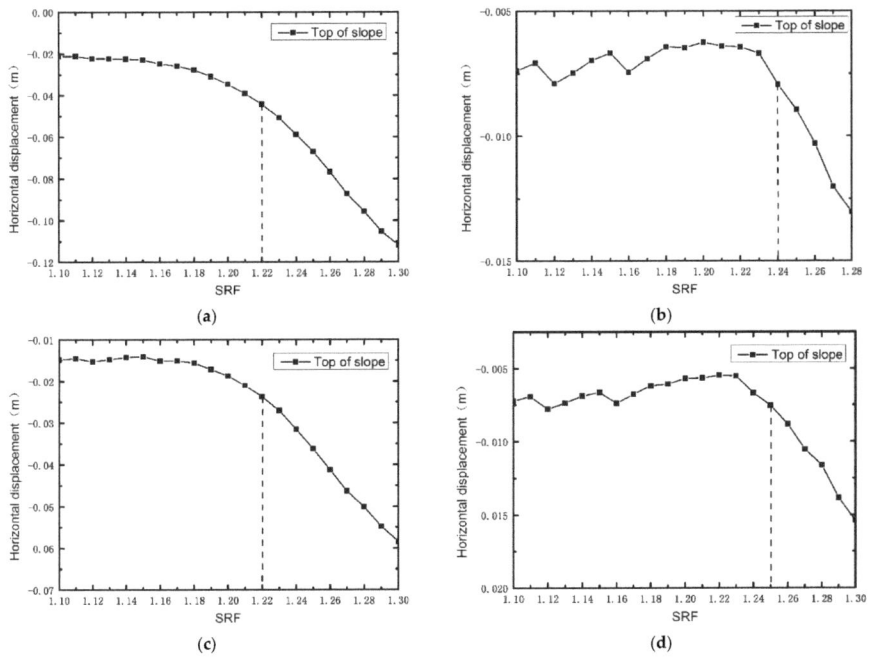

**Figure 4.** The displacement-SRF curves. (**a**) Northridge (SRF = 1.22), (**b**) San Francisco (SRF = 1.24), (**c**) Whittier Narrows (SRF = 1.22), (**d**) Whittier Narrows-1 (SRF = 1.25).

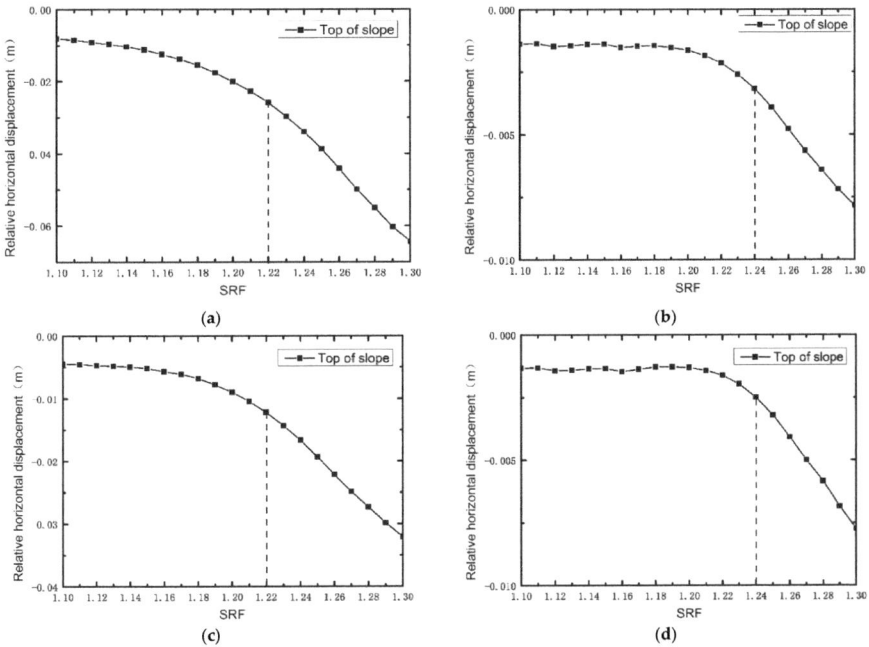

**Figure 5.** The relative displacement-SRF curves. (**a**) Northridge (SRF = 1.22), (**b**) San Francisco (SRF = 1.24), (**c**) Whittier Narrows (SRF = 1.22), (**d**) Whittier Narrows-1 (SRF = 1.24).

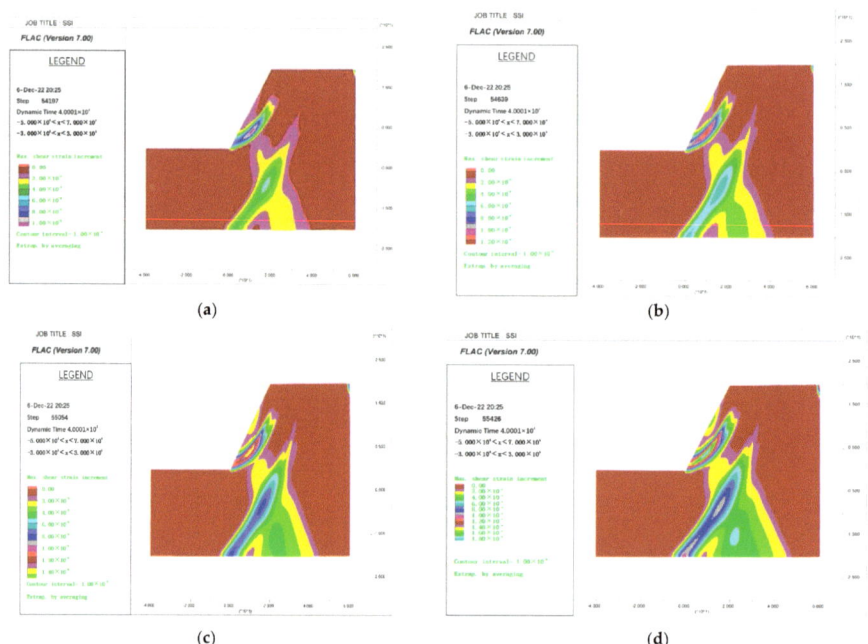

**Figure 6.** Shear strain increment penetration zone (Northridge) (m). (**a**) SRF = 1.24, (**b**) SRF = 1.26, (**c**) SRF = 1.28, (**d**) SRF = 1.30.

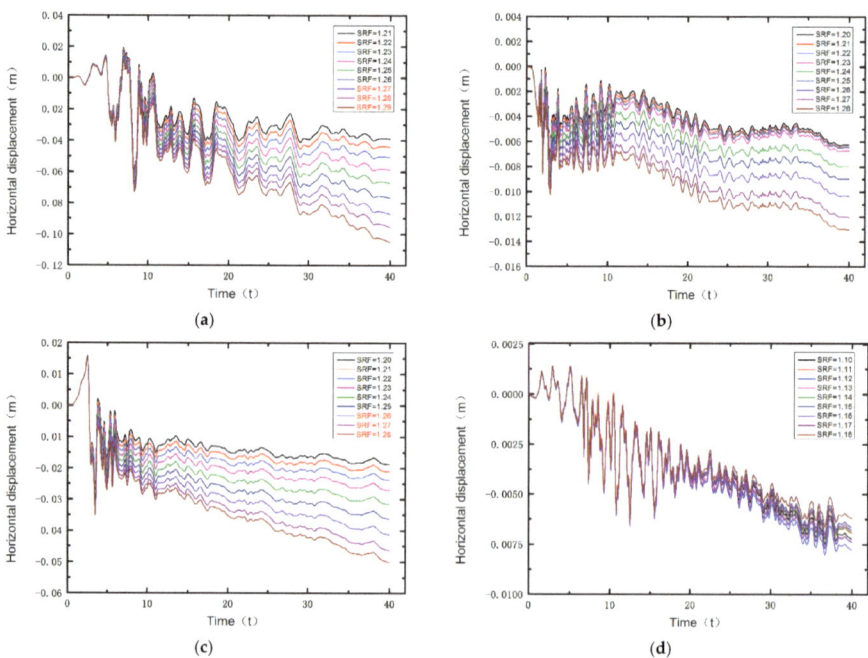

**Figure 7.** Displacement non-convergence. (**a**) Northridge (SRF = 1.26), (**b**) San Francisco, (**c**) Whittier Narrows (SRF = 1.25), (**d**) Whittier Narrows-1.

The paper compares and analyzes the advantages and disadvantages of three criteria. Based on the first criterion and taking into account the evolution law of different stages of actual landslides, this paper proposes an improved method for identifying displacement catastrophe points called the relative residual displacement increment method (Criterion IV). The reduction factor corresponding to the maximum value of the relative residual displacement increment for the first time after the sudden change of displacement is the safety factor of the slope. The relative residual displacement increment is shown in Figure 8. Figure 8 shows that after a continuous plastic penetration zone, the SRF corresponding to the maximum relative residual displacement increment for the first time are 1.26, 1.26, 1.25, and 1.26, respectively.

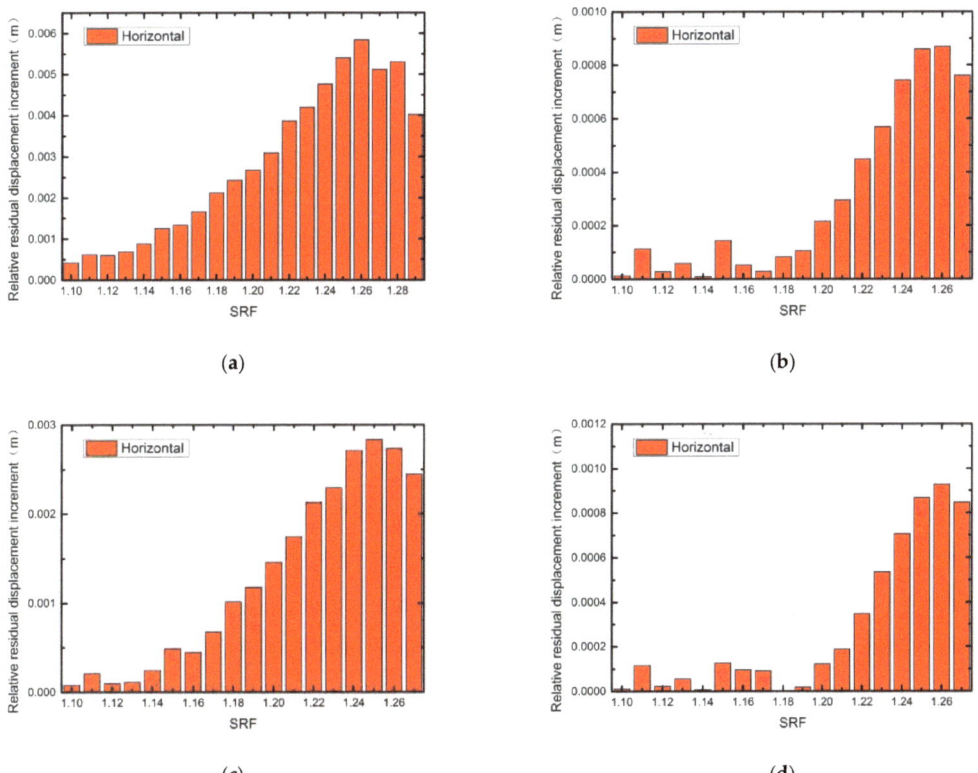

**Figure 8.** Relative residual displacement increment and strength reduction factor histogram. (**a**) Northridge (SRF = 1.26), (**b**) San Francisco (SRF = 1.26), (**c**) Whittier Narrows (SRF = 1.25), (**d**) Whittier Narrows-1 (SRF = 1.26).

The safety factors of slope under seismic action calculated by different criteria are shown in Table 3. Compared with other criteria, the maximum error between this method and other criteria is 0.033, and the minimum error is only 0.008, indicating that the calculation results of this method agree well with those of other criteria. Thus, this method's accuracy, applicability, and stability are verified.

Table 3. Safety factor of homogeneous slopes calculated by different criteria under seismic action.

| Slope Failure Criteria | Safety Factors under Different Earthquakes | | | |
|---|---|---|---|---|
| | Northridge | San Francisco | Whittier Narrows | Whittier Narrows-1 |
| Criterion $I_1$ | 1.22 | 1.24 | 1.22 | 1.25 |
| Criterion $I_2$ | 1.22 | 1.24 | 1.22 | 1.24 |
| Criterion II | 1.23 | 1.24 | 1.23 | 1.24 |
| Criterion III | 1.27 | - | 1.26 | - |
| Criterion IV | 1.26 | 1.26 | 1.25 | 1.26 |
| Error$((IV - I_1)/I_1)$ | 0.033 | 0.016 | 0.025 | 0.008 |
| Error$((IV - I_2)/I_2)$ | 0.033 | 0.016 | 0.025 | 0.016 |
| Error$((IV - II)/II)$ | 0.024 | 0.016 | 0.016 | 0.016 |
| Error$((IV - III)/III)$ | −0.008 | - | −0.008 | - |

*3.4. Layered Soil Slope*

The layered slope soil mass is an ideal elastic-plastic material conforming to the Mohr–Coulomb yield criterion. The top of the slope is 160 m from the right boundary, the toe of the slope is 160 m from the left boundary, the total length of the slope is 340 m, the slope height is 20 m, the slope angle is 45°, and the total thickness of the slope is 100 m. The slope model is shown in Figure 9, and its material parameters are shown in Table 4.

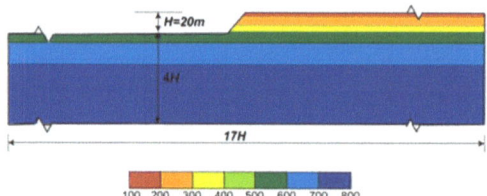

**Figure 9.** Distribution of shear-wave velocity in the 2D slope model (m/s).

**Table 4.** Material parameters.

| No. | Material | Thickness (m) | $V_S$ (m/s) | $\gamma$ (kN/m3) | $\nu$ | Constitutive Law | $\psi$ (°) | c (KPa) |
|---|---|---|---|---|---|---|---|---|
| 1 | Silty clay | 3 | 176.8 | 18.7 | 0.3 | Mohr–Coulomb | 25 | 35 |
| 2 | clay | 8 | 220.3 | 20 | 0.3 | Mohr–Coulomb | 25 | 40 |
| 3 | clay | 6 | 326.6 | 21 | 0.3 | Mohr–Coulomb | 30 | 42 |
| 4 | Clayey sandy gravel | 10 | 512.2 | 21.6 | 0.3 | Mohr–Coulomb | 31 | 30 |
| 5 | Clayey sandy gravel | 20 | 693.1 | 22 | 0.3 | Mohr–Coulomb | 31 | 20 |
| 6 | Bedrock | 53 | 774.2 | 22 | 0.3 | Elastic | | |

In the seismic calculation of layered slopes, hysteretic damping is used for nonlinear elastoplastic analysis [46]. The G/G0-γc and D-γc curves of two types of soil (Clay soil and gravel soil) in the slope model are shown in Figure 10, respectively. The curve for clay soil (1–3 layers) is calculated according to the empirical model proposed by Darendeli [47]. The G/G0-γc and D-γc relationships of gravel soil (4–5 layers) are based on the empirical curves proposed by Rollins et al. [48]. For the bedrock layer, Rayleigh damping is used.

Using the characteristic point displacement catastrophe as the criterion (Criterion I), as depicted in Figure 11, there are two curves: the vertex displacement-reduction factor curve (Criterion $I_1$) and the relative displacement-reduction factor curve (Criterion $I_2$). The displacement curve exhibits significant fluctuations in this example, which can lead to errors when identifying displacement catastrophe points. However, using the maximum value of the relative displacement increment as a criterion can mitigate the impact of these fluctuations and reduce the error.

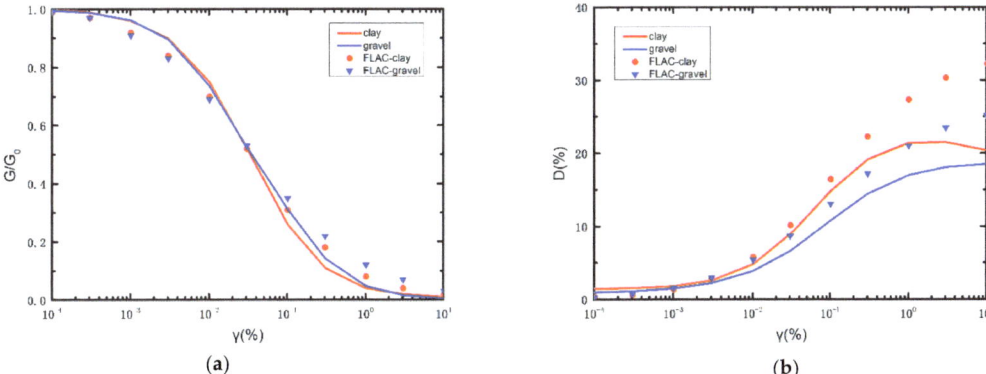

**Figure 10.** Normalized (**a**) shear modulus (G/G0-γ) and (**b**) damping ratio (D-γ) curves for all the soil types used in the numerical analysis. The corresponding relationships obtained using hysteretic damping in FLAC are also shown.

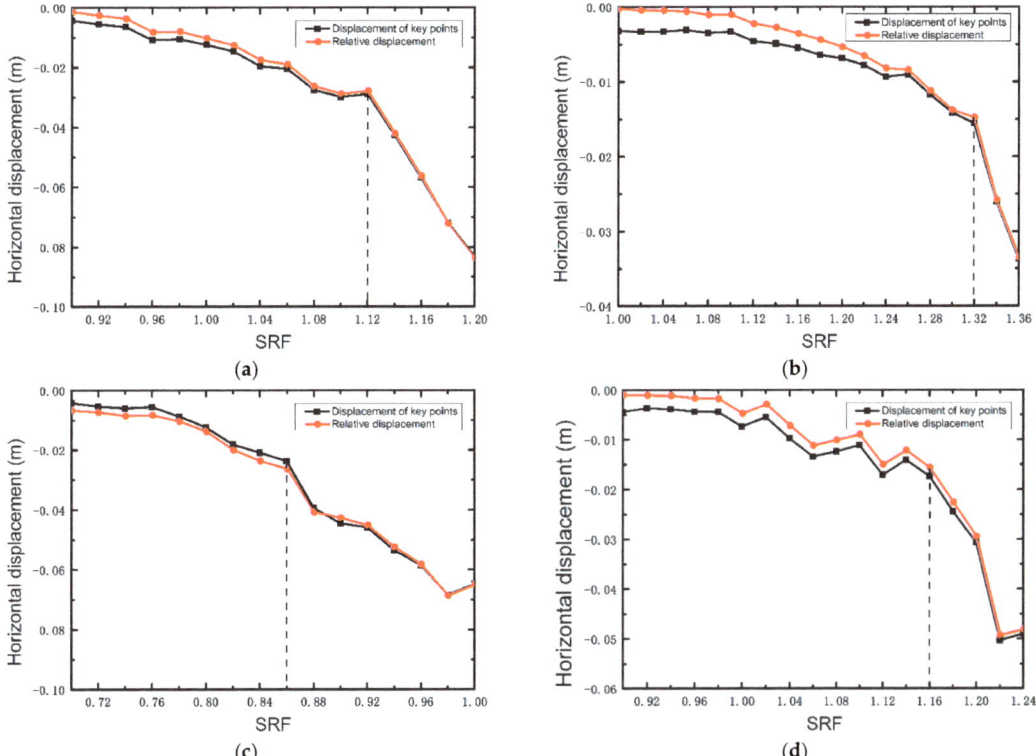

**Figure 11.** The displacement-SRF curves. (**a**) Northridge (SRF = 1.12), (**b**) San Francisco (SRF = 1.32), (**c**) Whittier Narrows (SRF = 0.86), (**d**) Whittier Narrows-1 (SRF = 1.16).

The penetration zone is taken as the criterion (Criterion II), and the complete penetration zone formed by shear strain increment is taken as the criterion of slope instability. As shown in Figure 12, a complete penetration zone can be formed under this slope model. However, slope instability cannot be determined by a continuous plastic penetration zone alone.

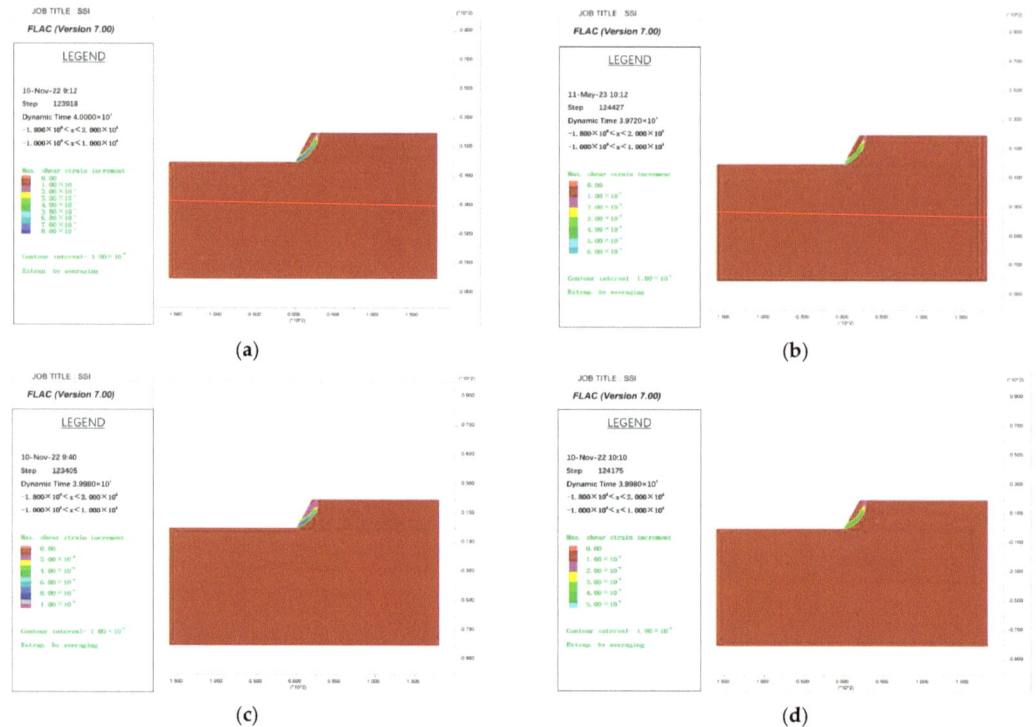

**Figure 12.** Shear strain increment penetration zone (m). (**a**) Northridge (SRF = 1.14), (**b**) San Francisco (SRF = 1.34), (**c**) Whittier Narrows (SRF = 0.94), (**d**) Whittier Narrows-1 (SRF = 1.20).

The iterative non-convergence is used as the criterion (Criterion III), and the criterion for slope instability is based on whether the final displacement diverges after the earthquake. The displacement time history curve is shown in Figure 13. After the completion of the earthquake action, its final displacement is in the horizontal state, and the displacement is not obviously divergent. Therefore, slope failure cannot be identified by this criterion.

The maximum value of the relative residual displacement increment is taken as the criterion (Criterion IV) to calculate the safety factor of the slope. The relative residual displacement increment is shown in Figure 14. From Figure 14, it can be seen that after a continuous plastic penetration zone, the SRF corresponding to the maximum relative residual displacement increment for the first time are 1.16, 1.32, 0.92, and 1.20, respectively. The safety factors under seismic action of a slope calculated by different criteria are shown in Table 5. This method's accuracy, applicability, and stability are once again verified as the maximum error between this method and other criteria is only 0.070, and the minimum error is 0, indicating a high degree of agreement between the present results and those obtained by other criteria.

Table 5. Safety factor of layered soil slopes calculated by different criteria under seismic action.

| Slope Failure Criteria | Safety Factors under Different Earthquakes | | | |
|---|---|---|---|---|
| | Northridge | San Francisco | Whittier Narrows | Whittier Narrows-1 |
| Criterion $I_1$ | 1.12 | 1.32 | 0.86 | 1.16 |
| Criterion $I_2$ | 1.12 | 1.32 | 0.86 | 1.16 |
| Criterion II | 1.12 | 1.32 | 0.92 | 1.18 |
| Criterion III | | | - | |
| Criterion IV | 1.16 | 1.32 | 0.92 | 1.20 |
| Error$((IV - I_1)/I_1)$ | 0.036 | 0.000 | 0.070 | 0.034 |
| Error$((IV - I_2)/I_2)$ | 0.036 | 0.000 | 0.070 | 0.034 |
| Error$((IV - II)/II)$ | 0.036 | 0.000 | 0.000 | 0.017 |
| Error$((IV - III)/III)$ | | | - | |

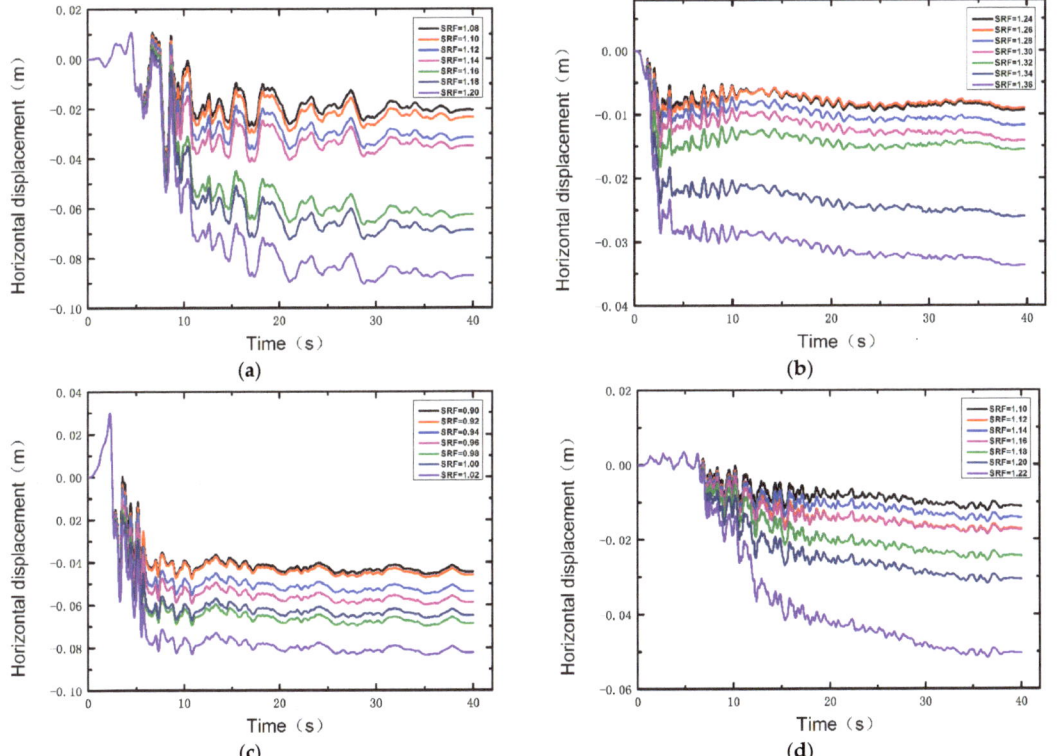

Figure 13. Displacement non-convergence. (a) Northridge, (b) San Francisco, (c) Whittier Narrows, (d) Whittier Narrows-1.

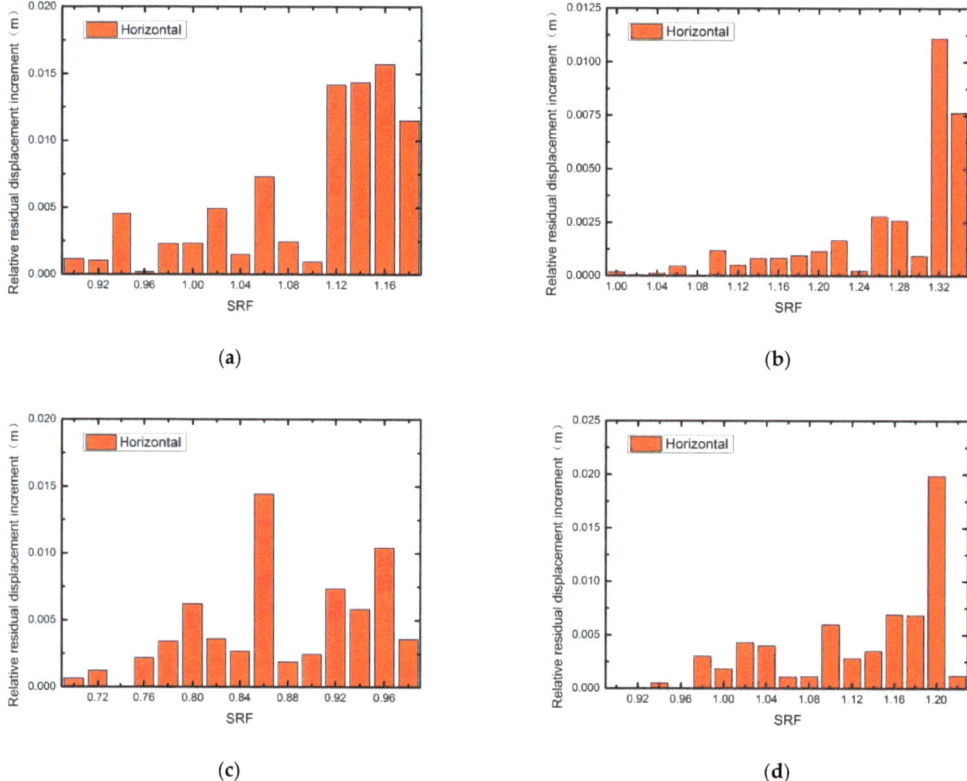

**Figure 14.** Relative residual displacement increment and strength reduction factor histogram. (**a**) Northridge (SRF = 1.16), (**b**) San Francisco (SRF = 1.32), (**c**) Whittier Narrows (SRF = 0.92), (**d**) Whittier Narrows-1 (SRF = 1.20).

## 4. Results and Discussion

This paper employs three types of criteria to compute safety factors for both homogeneous and layered soil slopes when subjected to earthquake action. A comparison and analysis of the benefits and drawbacks of different methods are presented. By conducting a comparative analysis of safety factors, this method's applicability, accuracy, and stability are verified.

The relative displacement of homogeneous slope changes smoothly with the reduction factor under seismic action, while the change of vertex displacement with the reduction factor fluctuates greatly. Due to the interaction between soil layers, layered soil's relative displacement and key point displacement have large fluctuations. The safety factors calculated by Criterion $I_1$ and Criterion $I_2$ for homogeneous soil and layered soil are basically the same. Due to the large fluctuation of displacement, Criterion $I_1$ will produce certain judgment errors when judging the sudden change of displacement. Criterion I1 and Criterion I2 can produce a certain degree of human error when judging the displacement catastrophe points. The safety factor of a slope is determined using Criterion II; when a continuous plastic penetration zone occurs, the slope does not necessarily break down immediately. Therefore, slope instability cannot be determined by a continuous plastic penetration zone alone. Criterion III is used to calculate the safety factor of slopes, but it cannot be used for layered soil slopes that exhibit non-divergent displacement after an earthquake. To summarize, obtaining the safety factor of a slope under earthquake action requires considering all three criteria mentioned above.

Based on the first kind of criterion, this paper improves the method of judging the displacement catastrophe points, and the relative residual displacement increment method (Criterion IV) is proposed. The slope safety factors are calculated for homogeneous and layered soil slopes under seismic action. In a homogeneous soil slope, the maximum error between the safety factor calculated by this method and that calculated by other criteria is 0.033, and the minimum error is only 0.008. In layered soil slope, the maximum error between the safety factor calculated by this method and that calculated by other criteria is 0.070, and the minimum error is only 0. Through the seismic calculation of homogeneous and layered soil slopes and the comparison with the other three types of criteria, the applicability, accuracy, and stability of the method in this paper are verified. This article's method can accurately describe the stress-deformation behavior of slope materials under earthquake action and simulate the damage process of slopes. At the same time, the method in this paper also reflects the influence of different ground motions on slope stability under the same acceleration.

## 5. Conclusions

The strength reduction dynamic analysis method exhibits great potential for application in the stability analysis of earthquake slopes. This comprehensive dynamic analysis method does not require pre-assumption of the sliding surface, which minimizes the influence of human factors on the safety factor. By utilizing actual seismic waves as input and considering the dynamic interaction between soil masses, the stability of the slope under earthquake action can be directly evaluated. An essential aspect of calculating the earthquake slope safety factor through the strength reduction dynamic analysis method is the reasonable selection of instability criteria. This paper proposes an earthquake slope stability analysis method based on the relative residual displacement increment method. This method combines the first criterion type with the slope's actual deformation characteristics. By calculating the relative displacement of the key point inside the landslide mass and the reference point outside the landslide mass after each reduction, the safety factor of the slope is determined by calculating the strength reduction factor corresponding to the maximum value of the relative residual displacement increment, which first appears after a continuous plastic penetration zone. We perform earthquake calculations of homogeneous and layered soil slopes and compare our proposed method with three other criteria. Based on the results, we draw the following conclusions:

(1) Criterion $I_1$ considers the sudden change in key point displacement as the instability criterion by comparing and analyzing three different criteria. When the seismic force acts, the displacement of key points fluctuates significantly, which can interfere with the identification of displacement catastrophe points. Using the sudden change in relative displacement as a criterion (Criterion $I_2$) can somewhat reduce the interference caused by displacement fluctuations. However, Criterion $I_2$ may still lead to some human error when identifying displacement catastrophe points. While Criteria II and III can be used to assess slope instability, they may not provide the slope safety factor in some cases. Therefore, a comprehensive consideration of all three criteria is necessary to obtain an accurate safety factor for earthquake slope stability calculations;

(2) By comparing and analyzing this method with three other criteria, the strength reduction factor corresponding to the maximum value of the relative residual displacement increment, which appears after an abrupt change in displacement, is used as the safety factor for the slope. This improves the method of identifying displacement catastrophe points, avoids errors caused by displacement fluctuations, and reduces human error in judging displacement catastrophe points. As a result, the displacement catastrophe criterion's accuracy, stability, and applicability are enhanced.

**Author Contributions:** Conceptualization, W.S.; Methodology, W.S.; Formal analysis, W.S.; Investigation, J.M.; Writing—original draft, W.S.; Writing—review & editing, G.W.; Supervision, G.W. All authors have read and agreed to the published version of the manuscript.

**Funding:** This research was sponsored by the National Key R&D Program of China (Grant No. 2018YFD1100405).

**Data Availability Statement:** The original contributions presented in the study are included in the article, further inquiries can be directed to the corresponding authors.

**Conflicts of Interest:** The authors declare no conflicts of interest.

## References

1. Wu, M.T.; Liu, F.C.; Yang, J. Seismic response of stratified rock slopes due to incident P and SV waves using a semi-analytical approach. *Eng. Geol.* 2022, prepublish. [CrossRef]
2. Yin, Y.P.; Wang, F.W.; Sun, P. Landslide hazards triggered by the 2008 Wenchuan earthquake, Sichuan, China. *Landslides* **2009**, *6*, 139–151. [CrossRef]
3. Tang, C.; Zhu, J.; Qi, X.; Ding, J. Landslides induced by the Wenchuan earthquake and the subsequent strong rainfall event: A case study in the Beichuan area of China. *Eng. Geol.* **2011**, *122*, 22–23. [CrossRef]
4. Li, S.; Kang, L.M.; Yu, B.; Li, J.; Feng, L.; Zhang, S.; Zhu, W.; Yao, X. Dynamic reliability analysis of bedding rock slopes under earthquake actions. *Build. Struct.* **2021**, *51*, 1679–1683. (In Chinese)
5. Jibson, R.W. Methods for assessing the stability of slopes during earthquakes—A retrospective. *Eng. Geol.* **2011**, *122*, 43–50. [CrossRef]
6. Terzhagi, K. *Mechanism of Landslides Application of Geology to Engineering Practice (Berkey Volume)*; Geological Society of America: New York, NY, USA, 1950. [CrossRef]
7. Newmark, N.M. Effects of earthquakes on dams and embankments. *Geotechnique* **1965**, *15*, 139–160. [CrossRef]
8. Clough, R.W.; Chopra, A.K. Earthquake stress analysis in earth dams. *ASCE J. Eng. Mech. Div.* **1966**, *92*, 197–211. [CrossRef]
9. Groumpos, P.P. A Critical Historic Overview of Artificial Intelligence: Issues, Challenges, Opportunities, and Threats. *Artif. Intell. Appl.* **2023**, *1*, 197–213. [CrossRef]
10. Alkhaled, L.; Khamis, T. Supportive Environment for Better Data Management Stage in the Cycle of ML Process. *Artif. Intell. Appl.* **2023**, *2*, 1–8. [CrossRef]
11. Bui, D.T.; Moayedi, H.; Gör, M.; Jaafari, A.; Foong, L.K. Predicting slope stability failure through machine learning paradigms. *ISPRS Int. J. Geo-Inf.* **2019**, *8*, 395. [CrossRef]
12. Gheisari, M.; Ebrahimzadeh, F.; Rahimi, M.; Moazzamigodarzi, M.; Liu, Y.; Pramanik, P.K.D.; Heravi, M.A.; Mehbodniya, A.; Ghaderzadeh, M.; Feylizadeh, M.R.; et al. Deep learning: Applications, architectures, models, tools, and frameworks: A comprehensive survey. *CAAI Trans. Intell. Technol.* **2023**, *8*, 581–606. [CrossRef]
13. Fan, Q.Q.; Jiang, M.; Huang, W.T.; Jiang, Q. Considering spatiotemporal evolutionary information in dynamic multi-objective optimisation. *CAAI Trans. Intell. Technol.* **2023**, 1–21. [CrossRef]
14. Leshchinsky, D.; San, K.C. Pseudo-static seismic stability of slopes: Design charts. *J. Geotech. Eng.* **1994**, *120*, 1514–1532. [CrossRef]
15. Ausilio, E.; Conte, E.; Dente, G. Seismic stability analysis of reinforced slopes. *Soil Dyn. Earthq. Eng.* **2000**, *19*, 159–172. [CrossRef]
16. Luan, M.T.; Li, Z.; Fan, Q.L. Analysis and evaluation of pseudo-static seismic stability and seism-induced sliding movement of earth-rock dams. *Rock Soil Mech.* **2007**, *28*, 224–230. (In Chinese)
17. Zhao, L.H.; Li, L.; Yang, F.; Dan, H.C.; Liu, X. Dynamic stability pseudo-static analysis of reinforcement soil slopes. *Chin. J. Rock Mech. Eng.* **2009**, *28*, 1904–1917. (In Chinese)
18. Deng, D.P.; Li, L. Pseudo-static stability analysis of slope under earthquake based on a new method of searching for sliding surface. *Chin. J. Rock Mech. Eng.* **2012**, *31*, 86–98. (In Chinese)
19. Qin, C.B.; Chian, S.C. Kinematic analysis of seismic slope stability with a discretisation technique and pseudo-dynamic approach: A new perspective. *Geotechnique* **2018**, *68*, 492–503. [CrossRef]
20. Courant, R. Variational methods for the solution of problems of equilibrium and vibrations. *Bull. Am. Math. Soc.* **1943**, *49*, 1–23. [CrossRef]
21. Clough, R.W. The finite element method in plane stress analysis. In Proceedings of the 2nd Conference on Electronic Computation, Pittsburgh, PA, USA, 8–9 September 1960; American Society of Civil Engineers, Structural Division: Pittsburgh, PA, USA, 1960.
22. Seed, H.B.; Lee, K.L.; Idriss, I.M.; Makdisi, F. *Analysis of the Slides in the San Fernando Dams during the Earthquake of Feb. 9, 1971*; Report No. EERC 73-2; University of California: Berkeley, CA, USA, 1973. [CrossRef]
23. Prevost, J.H. *DYNAFLOW: A Nonlinear Transient Finite Element Analysis Program*; Technical Report; Department of Civil Engineering and Operations Research, Princeton University: Princeton, NJ, USA, 1981.
24. Griffiths, D.V.; Prevost, J.H. Two- and three-dimensional dynamic finite element analyses of the Long Valley Dam. *Geotechnique* **1988**, *38*, 367–388. [CrossRef]
25. Elgamal, A.M.; Scott, R.F.; Succarieh, M.F.; Yan, L. La Villita dam response during five earthquakes including permanent deformation. *J. Geotech. Eng.* **1990**, *116*, 1443–1462. [CrossRef]
26. Zhou, J.W.; Cui, P.; Yang, X.G. Dynamic process analysis for the initiation and movement of the Donghekou landslide-debris flow triggered by the Wenchuan earthquake. *J. Asian Earth Sci.* **2013**, *76*, 70–84. [CrossRef]
27. Luo, J.; Pei, X.J.; Evans, S.G.; Huang, R. Mechanics of the earthquake induced Hongshiyan landslide in the 2014 Mw 6.2 Ludian earthquake, Yunnan, China. *Eng. Geol.* **2019**, *251*, 197–213. [CrossRef]

28. Dawson, E.M.; Roth, W.H.; Drescher, A. Slope stability analysis by strength reduction. *Geotechnique* **1999**, *49*, 835–840. [CrossRef]
29. Zheng, Y.R.; Zhao, S.Y.; Zheng, L.Y. Slope stability analysis by strength reduction FEM. *Eng. Sci.* **2002**, *4*, 57–61+78. (In Chinese)
30. Dai, M.L.; Li, T.C. Analysis of dynamic stability safety evaluation for complex rock slope by strength reduction numerical method. *Chin. J. Rock Mech. Eng.* **2007**, *192*, 2749–2754. (In Chinese)
31. Liu, K.Q.; Liu, H.Y. Stability Analysis of Soil-rock Mixture Slope under Earthquake. *J. Disaster Prev. Mitig. Eng.* **2022**, *42*, 224–230. [CrossRef]
32. Li, D.J.; Zhang, J.Y.; Lian, Y.W.; Tang, W. Dynamic Stability Analysis of Slope Under the Impact Load of Large Diameter Punched Cast-in-Place Pile. *Int. J. Geosynth. Ground Eng.* **2023**, *9*, 29. [CrossRef]
33. Ge, X.R.; Ren, J.X.; Li, C.G.; Zheng, H. 3D-FE analysis of deep sliding stability of #3 dam foundation of left power house of the Three Gorges Project. *Chin. J. Geotech. Eng.* **2003**, *25*, 389–394. (In Chinese)
34. Zheng, Y.R.; Ye, H.L.; Huang, R.Q. Analysis and discussion of failure mechanism and fracture surface of slope under earthquake. *Chin. J. Rock Mech. Eng.* **2009**, *28*, 1714–1723. (In Chinese)
35. Li, H.B.; Xiao, K.Q.; Liu, Y.Q. Factor of safety analysis of bedding rock slope under seismic load. *Chin. J. Rock Mech. Eng.* **2007**, *191*, 2385–2394. (In Chinese)
36. Wu, X.Y.; Liu, Q.; Cang, J.Y. The Sensitivity and Reliability Analysis of Slope Stability Based on Strength Reduction FEM. *Appl. Mech. Mater.* **2013**, *353–356*, 491–494. [CrossRef]
37. Li, C.; Zhu, J.B.; Wang, B.; Jiang, Y.; Liu, X.; Zeng, P. Critical deformation velocity of landslides in different deformation phases. *Chin. J. Rock Mech. Eng.* **2016**, *35*, 1407–1414. (In Chinese)
38. Sun, W.J.; Wang, G.X.; Zhang, L.L. Slope stability analysis by strength reduction method based on average residual displacement increment criterion. *Bull. Eng. Geol. Environ.* **2021**, *80*, 4367–4378. [CrossRef]
39. Itasca Consulting Group Inc. *Itasca FLAC 7.0: Fast Lagrangian Analysis of Continua. User's Guide*; Itasca Consulting Group Inc.: Minneapolis, MN, USA, 2011; Available online: www.itascacg.com (accessed on 12 March 2024).
40. Karafagka, S.; Fotopoulou, S.; Karatzetzou, A.; Kroupi, G.; Pitilakis, K. Seismic performance and vulnerability of gravity quay wall in sites susceptible to liquefaction. *Acta Geotech.* **2023**, *18*, 2733–2754. [CrossRef]
41. Joyner, W.B.; Chen, A.T.F. Calculation of nonlinear ground response in earthquakes. *Bull. Seismol. Soc. Am.* **1975**, *65*, 1315–1336. [CrossRef]
42. Li, J. Study on Determination and Application of Slope Safety Factor under Seismic Action. Master's Thesis, Chongqing Jiaotong University, Chongqing, China, 2011. (In Chinese).
43. Bouckovalas, G.D.; Papadimitriou, A.G. Numerical evaluation of slope topography effects on seismic ground motion. *Soil Dyn. Earthq. Eng.* **2005**, *25*, 547–558. [CrossRef]
44. Zhang, Z.Z.; Fleurisson, J.A.; Pellet, F. The effects of slope topography on acceleration amplification and interaction between slope topography and seismic input motion. *Soil Dyn. Earthq. Eng.* **2018**, *113*, 420–431. [CrossRef]
45. Kwok, A.O.L.; Stewart, J.P.; Hashash, Y.M.A.; Matasovic, N.; Pyke, R.; Wang, Z.; Yang, Z. Use of exact solutions of wave propagation problems to guide lmplementation of Nonlinear seismic ground response analysis procedures. *J. Geotech. Geoenviron. Eng.* **2007**, *133*, 1385–1398. [CrossRef]
46. Ding, Y.; Wang, G.X.; Yang, F.J. Parametric investigation on the effect of near-surface soil properties on the topographic amplification of ground motions. *Eng. Geol.* **2020**, *273*, 105687. [CrossRef]
47. Darendeli, M.B. *Development of a New Family of Normalized Modulus Reduction and Material Damping Curves*; University of Texas at Austin: Austin, TX, USA, 2001.
48. Rollins, K.M.; Evans, M.D.; Diehl, N.B.; William, D.D., III. Shear modulus and damping relationships for gravels. *J. Geotech. Geoenviron. Eng.* **1998**, *124*, 396–405. [CrossRef]

**Disclaimer/Publisher's Note:** The statements, opinions and data contained in all publications are solely those of the individual author(s) and contributor(s) and not of MDPI and/or the editor(s). MDPI and/or the editor(s) disclaim responsibility for any injury to people or property resulting from any ideas, methods, instructions or products referred to in the content.

Article

# Theoretical and Experimental Investigations of Identifying Bridge Damage Using Instantaneous Amplitude Squared Extracted from Vibration Responses of a Two-Axle Passing Vehicle

Siying Liu, Zunian Zhou, Yujie Zhang, Zhuo Sun, Jiangdong Deng * and Junyong Zhou *

School of Civil Engineering, Guangzhou University, Guangzhou 510006, China; 32116160055@e.gzhu.edu.cn (S.L.)
* Correspondence: jddeng@gzhu.edu.cn (J.D.); jyzhou@gzhu.edu.cn (J.Z.)

**Abstract:** Identifying bridge damage using a movable test vehicle is highly regarded for its mobility, cost-effectiveness, and broad monitoring coverage. Previous studies have shown that the residual contact-point (CP) response between connected vehicles is free of the impact of vehicle self-vibrations and road roughness, making it particularly suitable for the indirect extraction of bridge modal properties. However, most experimental campaigns regarding contact-point (CP) responses focus on a single-axle testing vehicle within a non-moving state. This study aims to theoretically and experimentally identify bridge damage using the instantaneous amplitude squared (IAS) extracted from the residual CP response of a two-axle passing vehicle. First, the closed-form solution of the residual CP acceleration was derived for a two-axle vehicle interacting with a simply supported beam. The IAS index was constructed from the driving frequency of the residual CP acceleration. Then, numerical investigations using finite element simulation were conducted to validate using the IAS index for indirect bridge damage identification. The application scope of the approach under various vehicle speeds and road roughness grades was examined. Finally, a laboratory vehicle–bridge interaction system was tested to validate the approach. Numerical studies demonstrated that bridge damage could be directly determined by observing the IAS abnormalities, which were baseline-free. The IAS from the residual CP response outperformed the IAS from CP responses in identifying bridge damage. However, it was better to use the IAS when the vehicle speed was no greater than 2 m/s and the grade of the road surface roughness was not high. Laboratory tests showed that it was possible to identify bridge damage using the IAS extracted from the residual CP acceleration under perfect road surfaces. However, it fell short under rough road surfaces. Hence, further experiments are required to fully examine the capacity of the IAS for bridge damage identification in practical applications.

**Keywords:** bridge; damage detection; vehicle scanning method; two-axle vehicle; experiment; instantaneous amplitude squared; finite element simulation; structural health monitoring

**Citation:** Liu, S.; Zhou, Z.; Zhang, Y.; Sun, Z.; Deng, J.; Zhou, J. Theoretical and Experimental Investigations of Identifying Bridge Damage Using Instantaneous Amplitude Squared Extracted from Vibration Responses of a Two-Axle Passing Vehicle. *Buildings* **2024**, *14*, 1428. https://doi.org/10.3390/buildings14051428

Academic Editor: Humberto Varum

Received: 1 April 2024
Revised: 5 May 2024
Accepted: 14 May 2024
Published: 15 May 2024

**Copyright:** © 2024 by the authors. Licensee MDPI, Basel, Switzerland. This article is an open access article distributed under the terms and conditions of the Creative Commons Attribution (CC BY) license (https://creativecommons.org/licenses/by/4.0/).

## 1. Introduction

Bridges, serving as vital infrastructural components enabling the traversal of terrain barriers, play a significant role in promoting regional economic development and facilitating social communication. However, bridges worldwide are aging, and the identification of damage in bridges has become a prominent focus in the field of structural health monitoring (SHM) [1,2]. Among all SHM methods, vibration-based methods constitute the primary research avenue for the identification of damage in bridges [3,4]. Traditional vibration monitoring involves placing sensors and data acquisition systems directly on the bridge to measure its dynamic responses. Subsequently, the vibrational signals are processed to facilitate the detection, localization, and quantification of bridge damage [1–4]. Given the extensive number of bridges and the limited lifespan of sensors, traditional direct vibration monitoring proves to be both costly and impractical for the health monitoring of a large bridge inventory. Hence, there is a continuous demand for more convenient and rapid structural health monitoring (SHM) methods for the health monitoring of existing bridge stocks.

Recently, a novel SHM paradigm involving the collection of vibration responses from passing vehicles to indirectly monitor bridges has been developing rapidly. This SHM paradigm is known as the vehicle scanning method (VSM), indirect monitoring, drive-by monitoring, vehicle-assisted method, or mobile sensing [5–7]. It is based on the vehicle–bridge interaction (VBI) mechanism wherein the bridge's vibrations are transmitted to the passing vehicle, and processing the vibrational signal of the passing vehicle can identify the dynamic properties of the bridge. The VSM offers exceptional mobility, cost-effectiveness, and extensive detection coverage and eliminates the need for traffic disruptions, which is particularly suitable for assessing the health condition of numerous bridges. The initial VSM concept was proposed and validated in 2004 [8], but it has experienced significant development over the past five years [5–7]. This progress includes a substantial body of theoretical studies, numerical investigations, laboratory tests, and field measurements, covering the indirect measurements of bridge frequencies, mode shapes, damping ratios, road roughness, and damage. The identification of bridge frequencies using the VSM has been well-validated both in theory and experiments, and it has also found successful applications in engineering [9–14]. However, the application of the VSM in identifying bridge modal shapes and damage is primarily limited to theoretical investigations [15–18]. More recently, some laboratory tests on scaled VBI systems have attempted to fill this gap for validating the VSM in identifying bridge mode shapes and damage, but they are often conducted under ideal conditions [19–22]. The significant challenge in identifying bridge modal properties using the VSM arises from extracting weak bridge vibrational signals from vehicle responses amid the pollution caused by vehicle-induced vibrations and road surface roughness.

To mitigate the impact of vehicle vibrations, various filtering techniques have been employed to attenuate interference, including band-pass filters, variational modal decomposition, and particle filters [22]. However, these filtering processes strongly rely on the expertise of the signal processor, posing a risk of inadvertently filtering out the vibrational signals of the bridge. Some studies have introduced a tuned mass damper with its frequency tuned to the vehicle frequency to suppress vehicle self-vibrations, thereby mitigating the overall impact of vehicle-induced vibrations [23]. Moreover, design strategies involving specialized test vehicles with frequencies significantly isolated from vehicle frequencies through the use of large-axle stiffnesses have been proposed. These strategies have successfully enhanced the identification of bridge vibration signals from vehicle responses [24,25]. More recently, a novel approach to utilizing vehicle–bridge contact-point (CP) responses for extracting bridge dynamic properties has been introduced [26]. This strategy is advantageous because CP responses are inherently free from vehicle self-vibrations. To reduce the negative impact of road roughness, different strategies have been proposed, including using ongoing traffic, on-bridge shakers, and non-moving test vehicles [5,7]. However, these techniques usually require traffic restrictions, reducing the practical significance of the VSM for rapid bridge health monitoring under open traffic conditions. More recently, residual CP responses from two connected vehicles have been verified to be free from the influence of road surface roughness [18,27]. The potential implementation of residual CP responses in a two-axle vehicle is a fascinating prospect, achieved through a process of eliminating road surface roughness by subtracting the front and rear axle CP responses. While the theory behind this concept has been demonstrated, experimental validation is still required for practical application [28].

In the exploration of applying the VSM for indirect bridge damage identification, various studies have examined algorithms such as mode shape difference, wavelet transform, and deep learning [19–21,27]. Zhang et al. [26] introduced the metric of instantaneous amplitude squared (IAS), derived from the Hilbert transform of isolated bridge vibration signals from vehicle responses, to detect bridge damage. The spring-mass VBI model was employed in this study for illustration. Following this work, the feasibility of using the IAS for identifying bridge damage has been demonstrated using various numerical examples [16,27–29]; however, these studies lack experimental validation and do not consider more realistic road roughness conditions.

The objective of this study is to propose a VSM approach for identifying bridge damage using an IAS extracted from the residual CP responses of a two-axle passing vehicle with the consideration of road surface roughness. It fills the literature gap through the following two aspects. (1) It proposes an IAS metric extracted from residual CP responses of a two-axle passing vehicle, which simultaneously eliminates the negative influence of vehicle self-vibrations and road surface roughness. Currently, the IAS metric is derived from an oversimplified spring-mass vehicle model [26], which fails to mitigate the impact of road surface roughness. (2) It experimentally validates the utilization of the IAS and CP responses for indirect damage detection, an aspect that has not been addressed in current VSM studies, which predominantly focus on numerical validations. First, a closed-form solution for the VBI responses of a two-axle vehicle interacting with a simply supported beam was derived. Residual CP responses of the two-axle vehicle were derived and back-calculated from vehicle responses. An IAS metric was derived from the residual CP responses. Then, a numerical finite element simulation was prepared to validate theoretical derivations and verify the feasibility of the proposed VSM-based damage identification approach. Finally, laboratory tests were conducted to further validate the approach.

## 2. Theoretical Formulations of the Problem

In this section, the theoretical problem is presented by illustrating a two-axle vehicle interacting with a simply supported beam, as shown in Figure 1. The test vehicle is simplified to have two degrees of freedom of translational and rotational motions, i.e., $y_v$ and $\theta_v$. These two degrees of freedom are functions of time. The main parameters of the simply supported beam consist of the bridge length $L$, mass per unit length $m$, elastic modulus $E$, and moment of inertia $I$. The parameter $EI$ is the bending rigidity of the beam. The main parameters of the two-axle vehicle comprise the vehicle mass $M_v$ and mass moment of inertia of the vehicle $J_v$. The front and rear axle spring stiffness are $k_1$ and $k_2$, and the distance from the front and rear wheels to the center of gravity of the vehicle are $l_1$ and $l_2$, respectively. The vehicle passes over the bridge at a constant speed of $v$. In the following study, the closed-form solutions for the CP responses of the test vehicle passing over the simply supported beam are first derived. Then, the residual CP responses are obtained by subtracting the time-lagged CP response of the front axle from the CP response of the rear axle. Finally, the IAS index, which can reflect damage location, is formulated based on the Hilbert transform of the drive frequency response components of the residual CP responses.

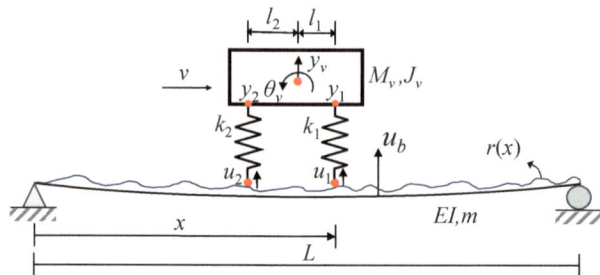

**Figure 1.** Schematic representation of a two-axle vehicle interacting with a simply supported beam.

The assumptions used for theoretical formulations are summarized as follows: (1) The simply supported beam is the Euler–Bernoulli type with a constant cross-section, where the shear deformation and rotary inertia are not considered. (2) The damping of the system and bridge road roughness are not considered. (3) The vehicle mass is assumed to be significantly less than the bridge mass, and its influence on bridge modal properties is ignored. (4) The velocity of the vehicle remains constant during its passage. (5) The vehicle–bridge coupled interaction is ignored in solving bridge responses but considered in deriving vehicle responses. These assumptions are commonly adopted in VSM studies [5–29] for theoretical derivation. Nevertheless, the full interactions of the moving vehicle with the beam, the consideration of the shear deformation and rotary inertia of the beam, damping, and non-constant vehicle velocity are meaningful for follow-up works [30,31].

### 2.1. Closed-Form Solutions of Residual CP Responses

To streamline the formulation, the vehicle mass is generally considered to be negligible with respect to the bridge, and thus, the vehicle–bridge coupling effect can be ignored. This assumption is frequently adopted in VSM studies [5–7], yet its validity may be questionable and warrants closer consideration when investigating the coupling effects [32]. Nevertheless, the vehicle–bridge coupling effects will be fully considered in the following numerical examples. Hence, the two-axle vehicle passing over the bridge can be regarded as two moving forces acting on the bridge, and the close-from solution of the bridge displacement $u_b$ can be obtained as follows [22]:

$$u_b(x,t) = \sum_{n=1}^{N}\sum_{k=1}^{2} q_k(t)\sin\left(\frac{n\pi x}{L}\right), \qquad (1)$$

where

$$q_k(t) = -\frac{2L^3(l-l_k)M_v g}{EIn^4\pi^4 l(1-S_n^2)}\left\{\begin{array}{l}\left[\sin\left(\frac{n\pi v(t-t_k)}{L}\right)-S_n\sin(\omega_{bn}(t-t_k))\right]H(t-t_k)\\ +\left[\sin\left(\frac{n\pi v(t-t_k-\Delta t)}{L}\right)-S_n\sin(\omega_{bn}(t-t_k-\Delta t))\right]H(t-t_k-\Delta t)\end{array}\right\}, \qquad (2)$$

where $H(\cdot)$ represents the unit step function, $t_k = (l_1 + l_2)(k-1)/v$ represents the entry time of the $k$th vehicle axle into the beam ($k$ = 1, 2), and $\Delta t = L/v$ denotes the time duration of the vehicle axle staying on the bridge. Moreover, $\omega_{bn}$ denotes the $n$th bridge frequency, and $S_n$ denotes the speed parameter, which can be expressed as follows:

$$\omega_{bn} = \frac{n^2\pi^2}{L^2}\sqrt{\frac{EI}{m}}, \; S_n = \frac{n\pi v}{L\omega_{bn}}. \qquad (3)$$

Furthermore, the vehicle is considered to be symmetric, i.e., $k_1 = k_2 = k$, $l_1 = l_2 = l$. This assumption is solely for the convenience of theoretical derivations and does not affect the proposed approach. Additionally, many real-world two-axle vehicles can be considered symmetric, such as train carriages. Let $x = v(t - t_k)$, and the CP displacement of the $k$th axle $u_k(t)$ at the timestamp $t$ is the superposition of the CP displacement of the bridge $u_b(x,t)|_{x=vt}$. The road surface roughness $r(x)|_{x=vt}$, given as follows:

$$u_i(t) = \sum_{n=1}^{N}\sum_{k=1}^{2} A_n\left\{\begin{array}{l}\cos\frac{n\pi v(t_k-t_i)}{L}-\cos\left(\frac{2n\pi vt}{L}-\frac{n\pi v(t_k+t_i)}{L}\right)\\ +S_n\cos\left(\left(\omega_{bn}+\frac{n\pi v}{L}\right)t-\omega_{bn}t_k-\frac{n\pi vt_i}{L}\right)\\ -S_n\cos\left(\left(\omega_{bn}-\frac{n\pi v}{L}\right)t-\omega_{bn}t_k+\frac{n\pi vt_i}{L}\right)\end{array}\right\}\times\left[\begin{array}{c}H(t-t_k)\\ -H(t-t_k-\Delta t)\end{array}\right]+r(x)|_{x=vt}, (i=1,2), \qquad (4)$$

where

$$A_n = -\frac{L^3 M_v g}{2EIn^4\pi^4(1-S_n^2)}. \qquad (5)$$

It is shown in Equations (2) and (4) that the CP response of the vehicle axle contains four components: road surface roughness $r$, the driving frequency $2n\pi v/L$, the left-shifted bridge frequencies $\omega_{bn} - n\pi v/L$, and the right-shifted bridge frequencies $\omega_{bn} + n\pi v/L$.

The CP response excludes the component of vehicle frequency but is influenced by the road surface roughness. Notably, road roughness is a broadband signal that obscures all frequency components, posing challenges in extracting bridge frequencies from the CP response.

However, the information on road surface roughness is presented in the CP responses of the front and rear axles at different moments, i.e., $t$ and $t - d/v$. Therefore, the influence of the road surface roughness can be eliminated by subtracting the time-lagged CP response of the rear axle from the CP response of the front axle. In the following study, the driving frequency component and the road roughness component in Equation (3) are selected for further derivation. To simplify the theoretical derivation, the unit step function component $H(\cdot)$ in Equation (4) is treated as 1, i.e., the vehicle axles are always in contact with the bridge. Therefore, the Equation (4) can be rewritten as follows:

$$\begin{cases} u_1(t) = \left\{\sum_{n=1}^{N} -A_n\left[\cos\left(\frac{2n\pi vt}{L}\right) + \cos\left(\frac{2n\pi vt}{L} - \frac{2n\pi l}{L}\right)\right]\right\} + r(x)|_{x=vt} + B_1 \\ u_2(t) = \left\{\sum_{n=1}^{N} -A_n\left[\cos\left(\frac{2n\pi vt}{L} - \frac{2n\pi l}{L}\right) + \cos\left(\frac{2n\pi vt}{L} - \frac{4n\pi l}{L}\right)\right]\right\} + r(x)|_{x=v(t-t_2)} + B_2 \end{cases} \tag{6}$$

where

$$\begin{cases} B_1 = \sum_{n=1}^{N} A_n \begin{bmatrix} \cos\left(\frac{2n\pi l}{L}\right) + S_n \cos\left(\omega_{bn} + \frac{n\pi v}{L}\right)t \cos\left(\left(\omega_{bn} + \frac{n\pi v}{L}\right)t - \frac{2l\omega_{bn}}{v}\right) \\ -S_n \cos\left(\omega_{bn} - \frac{n\pi v}{L}\right)t \cos\left(\left(\omega_{bn} - \frac{n\pi v}{L}\right)t - \frac{2l\omega_{bn}}{v}\right) \end{bmatrix} \\ B_2 = \sum_{n=1}^{N} A_n \begin{bmatrix} -\cos\left(\frac{2n\pi l}{L}\right) + S_n \cos\left(\left(\omega_{bn} + \frac{n\pi v}{L}\right)t - \frac{2n\pi l}{L}\right) \cos\left(\left(\omega_{bn} + \frac{n\pi v}{L}\right)t - \frac{2n\pi l}{L} - \frac{2l\omega_{bn}}{v}\right) \\ -S_n \cos\left(\left(\omega_{bn} - \frac{n\pi v}{L}\right)t + \frac{2n\pi l}{L}\right) \cos\left(\left(\omega_{bn} - \frac{n\pi v}{L}\right)t + \frac{2n\pi l}{L} - \frac{2l\omega_{bn}}{v}\right) \end{bmatrix} \end{cases} \tag{7}$$

When introducing a time lag of $2l/v$ to the CP displacement of the rear axle, $u_2(t)$ is rewritten as follows:

$$u_2\left(t + \frac{2l}{v}\right) = \left\{\sum_{n}^{N} A_n\left[\cos\left(\frac{2n\pi vt}{L}\right) + \cos\left(\frac{2n\pi vt}{L} + \frac{2n\pi l}{L}\right)\right]\right\} + r(x)|_{x=vt} + \widetilde{B}_2, \tag{8}$$

where

$$\widetilde{B}_2 = \sum_{n}^{N} A_n \begin{bmatrix} -\cos\left(\frac{2n\pi l}{L}\right) + S_n \cos\left(\left(\omega_{bn} + \frac{n\pi v}{L}\right)t + \frac{2l\omega_{bn}}{v}\right)\cos\left(\omega_{bn} + \frac{n\pi v}{L}\right)t \\ -S_n \cos\left(\left(\omega_{bn} - \frac{n\pi v}{L}\right)t + \frac{2l\omega_{bn}}{v}\right)\cos\left(\omega_{bn} - \frac{n\pi v}{L}\right)t \end{bmatrix}. \tag{9}$$

Following the CP displacement of the front axle in Equation (6) and the CP displacement of the rear axle in Equation (8), the residual CP displacement is obtained as follows:

$$\Delta u = u_2\left(t + \frac{2l}{v}\right) - u_1(t) = \left\{\sum_{n}^{N} A_n\left[\cos\left(\frac{2n\pi vt}{L} + \frac{2n\pi l}{L}\right) - \cos\left(\frac{2n\pi vt}{L} - \frac{2n\pi l}{L}\right)\right]\right\} + \widetilde{B}, \tag{10}$$

where

$$\widetilde{B} = \sum_{n}^{N} A_n \begin{bmatrix} -2\cos\left(\frac{2n\pi l}{L}\right) + S_n \cos\left(\left(\omega_{bn} + \frac{n\pi v}{L}\right)t + \frac{2l\omega_{bn}}{v}\right)\cos\left(\omega_{bn} + \frac{n\pi v}{L}\right)t \\ -S_n \cos\left(\left(\omega_{bn} - \frac{n\pi v}{L}\right)t + \frac{2l\omega_{bn}}{v}\right)\cos\left(\omega_{bn} - \frac{n\pi v}{L}\right)t \\ -S_n \cos\left(\omega_{bn} + \frac{n\pi v}{L}\right)t \cos\left(\left(\omega_{bn} + \frac{n\pi v}{L}\right)t - \frac{2l\omega_{bn}}{v}\right) \\ +S_n \cos\left(\omega_{bn} - \frac{n\pi v}{L}\right)t \cos\left(\left(\omega_{bn} - \frac{n\pi v}{L}\right)t - \frac{2l\omega_{bn}}{v}\right) \end{bmatrix}. \tag{11}$$

It is shown in Equation (10) that the influence of the road surface roughness was removed from the residual CP displacement. Only the frequency components of the driving frequency $2n\pi v/L$ and the left-shifted and right-shifted bridge frequencies $\widetilde{B}$ are retained. Considering that the acceleration is easier than the displacement for field measurements, Equation (10) is differentiated twice, and the residual CP acceleration is obtained as follows:

$$\Delta \ddot{u} = \left\{ \sum_{n=1}^{N} \frac{4n^2\pi^2 v^2 A_n}{L^2} \left[ \cos\left(\frac{2n\pi vt}{L} - \frac{2n\pi l}{L}\right) - \cos\left(\frac{2n\pi vt}{L} + \frac{2n\pi l}{L}\right) \right] \right\} + \widetilde{\ddot{B}}, \quad (12)$$

where $\widetilde{\ddot{B}}$ is the second time derivative of Equation (11).

Notably, the CP acceleration of the vehicle axles described above cannot be directly measured. This is because the above closed-form solutions require prior knowledge of the modal information of the bridge, which is what the VSM seeks to identify. However, the axle responses can be indirectly back-calculated from the vehicle responses, which are formulated as follows [26,27]:

$$\begin{cases} u_1(t) = \frac{M_v l^2 + J_v}{4kl^2} \ddot{y}_1(t) + \frac{M_v l^2 - J_v}{4kl^2} \ddot{y}_2(t) + y_1(t) \\ u_2(t) = \frac{M_v l^2 - J_v}{4kl^2} \ddot{y}_1(t) + \frac{M_v l^2 + J_v}{4kl^2} \ddot{y}_2(t) + y_2(t) \end{cases}, \quad (13)$$

where $y_1$ and $y_2$ are the vertical displacements of the vehicle body at the front and rear axles, as illustrated in Figure 1.

By substituting Equation (13) into Equation (10), the residual CP displacement can be obtained as follows:

$$\Delta u = u_2\left(t + \frac{2l}{v}\right) - u_1(t) = \left[ \begin{array}{c} \frac{M_v l^2 - J_v}{4kl^2} \ddot{y}_1\left(t + \frac{2l}{v}\right) \\ + \frac{M_v l^2 + J_v}{4kl^2} \ddot{y}_2\left(t + \frac{2l}{v}\right) + y_2\left(t + \frac{2l}{v}\right) \end{array} \right] - \left[ \begin{array}{c} \frac{M_v l^2 + J_v}{4kl^2} \ddot{y}_1(t) \\ + \frac{M_v l^2 - J_v}{4kl^2} \ddot{y}_2(t) + y_1(t) \end{array} \right]. \quad (14)$$

Furthermore, the residual CP acceleration can be formulated by differentiating Equation (14) twice, given as follows:

$$\Delta \ddot{u} = \ddot{u}_2\left(t + \frac{2l}{v}\right) - \ddot{u}_1(t) = \left[ \begin{array}{c} \frac{M_v l^2 - J_v}{4kl^2} \frac{d^2\ddot{y}_1\left(t+\frac{2l}{v}\right)}{dt^2} \\ + \frac{M_v l^2 + J_v}{4kl^2} \frac{d^2\ddot{y}_2\left(t+\frac{2l}{v}\right)}{dt^2} + \ddot{y}_2\left(t + \frac{2l}{v}\right) \end{array} \right] - \left[ \begin{array}{c} \frac{M_v l^2 + J_v}{4kl^2} \frac{d^2\ddot{y}_1(t)}{dt^2} \\ + \frac{M_v l^2 - J_v}{4kl^2} \frac{d^2\ddot{y}_2(t)}{dt^2} + \ddot{y}_1(t) \end{array} \right]. \quad (15)$$

Therefore, it is known that the residual CP acceleration of the two-axle passing vehicle can be calculated from the vehicle responses $\ddot{y}_1$ and $\ddot{y}_2$, which are practical for measurements. Notably, the above derivations ignore the vehicle–bridge coupled effect, which will be investigated in the following numerical validation section.

## 2.2. Bridge Damage Detection Using Residual CP Acceleration

In this section, the driving frequency component ($2n\pi v/L$) from the residual CP acceleration of the two-axle passing vehicle is isolated to construct the IAS for identifying bridge damage. The rationale for selecting driving frequencies rather than bridge frequencies is their low and closely distributed nature, which reduces the likelihood of contamination by high-frequency signals such as environmental noise and road roughness signals. After applying the fast Fourier transform (FFT) to the residual CP acceleration in Equation (12), the corresponding frequency spectrum is formulated as follows:

$$F(\omega) = \int_{-\infty}^{\infty} \Delta \ddot{u}(t) \cdot e^{-j\omega t} dt. \quad (16)$$

The components of driving frequencies in Equation (12) can be isolated from the residual CP acceleration by applying a multi-peak spectrum idealized filter as follows:

$$H_d(\omega) = \begin{cases} 1 & \omega = 2n\pi v/L \\ 0 & else \end{cases}. \quad (17)$$

By applying the idealized filter transfer function to the frequency function of the residual CP acceleration, the filtered amplitude frequency function is obtained as follows:

$$F_d(\omega) = F(\omega) \times |H_d(\omega)| = \int_{-\infty}^{\infty} \Delta\ddot{u}(t) \cdot e^{-j\omega t} dt, \quad \omega = 2n\pi v/L. \tag{18}$$

Then, the time-domain response of $F_d(jw)$ can be reconstructed using inverse FFT as follows:

$$R_n(t) = \frac{1}{2\pi}\int_{-\infty}^{\infty} F_d(\omega) \cdot e^{j\omega t} d\omega = \sum_{n=1}^{N} D_n \left[\cos\left(\frac{2n\pi vt}{L} - \frac{2n\pi l}{L}\right) - \cos\left(\frac{2n\pi vt}{L} + \frac{2n\pi l}{L}\right)\right], \tag{19}$$

where

$$D_n = \frac{4n^2\pi^2 v^2 A_n}{L^2}. \tag{20}$$

Therefore, the driving frequency components $R_n(t)$ in the time domain are extracted from the residual CP acceleration. The driving frequency component responses are narrow-band time series, and the Hilbert transform can be applied to obtain its pair. Consequently, the Hilbert transform of $R_n(t)$ is derived as follows:

$$\widehat{R_n}(t) = \sum_{n=1}^{N} D_n \left[\sin\left(\frac{2n\pi vt}{L} - \frac{2n\pi l}{L}\right) - \sin\left(\frac{2n\pi vt}{L} + \frac{2n\pi l}{L}\right)\right]. \tag{21}$$

According to Equations (19) and (21), the IAS index can be constructed as follows:

$$\begin{aligned}A^2(t) &= R_n^2(t) + \widehat{R_n}^2(t) \\ &= 2\left(\sum_{n=1}^{N} D_n^2 - \sum_{j=1}^{N}\sum_{i=1}^{N} D_j D_i \cos\frac{2\pi l(j+i)}{L}\right) \\ &\quad + 4\sum_{j=1}^{N}\sum_{i=1(i>j)}^{N} D_j D_i \left[\left(1 - 2\sin^2\frac{\pi v t(j-i)}{L}\right)\left(\cos\frac{2\pi l(j-i)}{L} - \cos\frac{2\pi l(j+i)}{L}\right)\right].\end{aligned} \tag{22}$$

It is acknowledged that the mode shape of the bridge for the simply supported beam is $\Phi = \sin(n\pi vt/L)$. By substituting the mode shape function into Equation (22), the relationship between the IAS and the bridge mode shape $\Phi$ is expressed as follows:

$$\begin{aligned}\text{IAS} = A^2(t) &= 2\left(\sum_{n=1}^{N} D_n^2 - \sum_{j=1}^{N}\sum_{i=1}^{N} D_j D_i \cos\frac{2\pi l(j+i)}{L}\right) \\ &\quad + 4\sum_{j=1}^{N}\sum_{i=1(i>j)}^{N} D_j D_i \left[\left(1 - 2\Phi_{j-i}^2\right)\left(\cos\frac{2\pi l(j-i)}{L} - \cos\frac{2\pi l(j+i)}{L}\right)\right],\end{aligned} \tag{23}$$

It is shown in the equation that the IAS index is closely connected with the bridge mode shape $\Phi$. It is widely understood that the presence of damage alters the bridge mode shape. This suggests that the IAS can reflect the bridge damage because the bridge mode shape $\Phi$ will be changed if damage occurs in the beam. Therefore, the IAS index can detect the existence and location of damage. Concerning the severity of the damage, the abnormality level of the IAS index can capture this severity. Therefore, the following practical procedures are proposed for identifying bridge damage using the IAS extracted from the residual CP acceleration, as follows:

- Measure the vehicle accelerations $\ddot{y}_1$ and $\ddot{y}_2$ of the vehicle body at the front and rear axles of the two-axle test vehicle;
- Calculate the residual CP acceleration $\Delta\ddot{u}$ of the front and rear vehicle axles using Equation (15);
- Analyze the frequency spectrum of $\Delta\ddot{u}$ using FFT and isolate its first few orders of driving frequencies $2n\pi v/L$ using the multi-peak spectrum idealized filter;

- Obtain the time-domain results of the driving frequency components $R_n(t)$ using the multi-point spectra idealized filter and inverse FFT and construct its instantaneous amplitude IAS index $A(t)$ by Hilbert transform.

## 3. Numerical Investigations Using Finite Element Simulation

### 3.1. Finite Element Simulation of the VBI System with Damage

In this section, the finite element simulation is conducted for a symmetric two-axle vehicle interacting with a simply supported beam (see Figure 2). The bridge is divided into $N^e$ beam units with an equal length $L_e$. The beam element has two nodes, each considering two degrees of freedom, i.e., nodding and sinking. The beam element where the vehicle axle acts is a new VBI element as it considers both the motion of the beam element and the vehicle. The equations of motion of the VBI element and normal beam element are provided in [22,30]. The vehicle axle distance $d = (l_1 + l_2)$ must be larger than the length of the beam element $L_e$ to ensure each vehicle axle acts on different beam elements. Furthermore, to facilitate the following discussions regarding vehicle damping and stiffness, a distinction is made between damping and stiffness of the front and rear axles using subscripts 1 and 2.

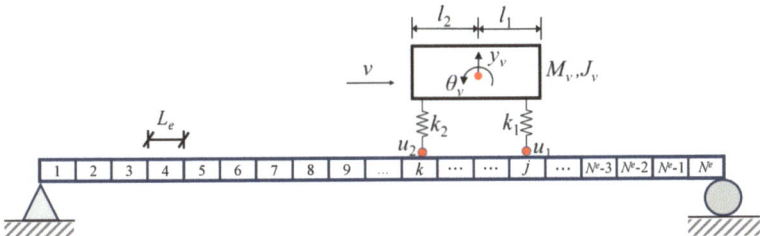

**Figure 2.** Finite element simulation of a symmetric two-axle vehicle interacting with a simply supported beam.

In addition, the beam damage is considered as the loss of element stiffness [33]. Notably, damage in beam-like structures can also be modeled in other forms, such as cracks or internal hinges [33,34]. However, the reduction in element stiffness remains the most common technique of damage modeling. Additionally, this study does not concentrate on modeling and detecting beam damage at the meso scale, including pinpointing the damage location or determining the damage direction within the beam cross-section. This study's objectives revolve around detecting and quantifying damage in field applications, with no emphasis on damage quantification at the meso scale. The following simple theoretical derivation is employed to illustrate that the decrease in structural stiffness directly causes a change in the modal vibration pattern of the bridge. For the undamped, freely vibrating beam, the characteristic equation of dynamics is as follows:

$$(\mathbf{K} - \lambda \mathbf{M})\mathbf{\Phi} = \mathbf{0}, \tag{24}$$

where $\mathbf{K}$ and $\mathbf{M}$ represent the structural stiffness and mass matrices, and $\lambda$ and $\mathbf{\Phi}$ denote the structural eigenvalues and eigenvectors, respectively.

Assuming that the beam experiences an element stiffness loss, and ignoring the change in beam mass resulting from the element stiffness loss, the characteristic equation of dynamics is as follows:

$$[(\mathbf{K} + \Delta\mathbf{K}) - (\lambda + \Delta\lambda)\mathbf{M}](\mathbf{\Phi} + \Delta\mathbf{\Phi}) = \mathbf{0}, \tag{25}$$

where $\Delta\mathbf{K}$ denotes the change in structural element stiffness, and $\Delta\lambda$ and $\Delta\mathbf{\Phi}$ denote the change of the structural eigenvalue and the change of the structural eigenvector, respectively. By left-multiplying the $\mathbf{\Phi}^T$ on both sides of Equation (15), the change in structural eigenvalue can be expressed as follows:

$$\Delta\lambda = \frac{\mathbf{\Phi}^T \Delta\mathbf{K}(\mathbf{\Phi}+\Delta\mathbf{\Phi})}{\mathbf{\Phi}^T \mathbf{M}(\mathbf{\Phi}+\Delta\mathbf{\Phi})}. \tag{26}$$

Clearly, the presence of element stiffness loss directly affects the eigenfrequencies and eigenvectors. Since the IAS index is closely related to the eigenvectors, it can be used to locate and quantify the beam damage.

### 3.2. Numerical Validation of the Residual CP Response

A numerical example with the vehicle and bridge parameters, outlined in Table 1, is investigated. These vehicle and bridge parameters are strictly selected to reflect the realistic conditions of highway bridges, consistent with widely accepted practices in VSM studies [8,10,12,16,22,23,26]. Notably, the parameter values remain constant in the following investigations unless otherwise noted. The simply supported bridge was divided into 50 elements, and the time step of the finite element simulation was 0.001 s. The number of beam elements plays a pivotal role in the VBI responses within the numerical investigation of damage. This is because the size of the damage is equated to the element size for modeling damage through element stiffness loss. In this study, the chosen size for the damaged element is 0.5 m, a dimension commonly employed in the literature [10–28]. Consequently, a total of 50 elements constitute the 25 m simply supported beam. In addition, a simulation time step of 0.001 s is also a common choice in VBI studies [10–28]. The first third frequencies of the bridge are $\omega_{b1}$ = 3.80 Hz, $\omega_{b2}$ = 15.22 Hz, and $\omega_{b3}$ = 34.24 Hz, respectively. The frequencies of the test vehicle are $\omega_v$ = 4.35 Hz and $\omega_\theta$ = 5.96 Hz. The road is assumed to have a relatively smooth surface with $G_d(n_0)$ = 0.001 × $10^{-6}$ m$^3$ [22]. To be consistent with the theoretical analysis, the bridge and vehicle damping are not considered. However, the vehicle in the numerical example is considered to be asymmetric for a general case.

**Table 1.** Parameter values of the test vehicle and bridge.

| Item | Parameters | Symbol | Unit | Value |
|---|---|---|---|---|
| Vehicle | Mass of vehicle | $M_v$ | kg | 1000 |
| | Mass moment of vehicle | $J_v$ | kg·m$^2$ | 900 |
| | Stiffness of front axle | $k_1$ | N/m | $3.5 \times 10^5$ |
| | Stiffness of rear axle | $k_2$ | N/m | $4 \times 10^5$ |
| | Distance from the front axle | $l_1$ | m | 1.35 |
| | Distance from the rear axle | $l_2$ | m | 1.25 |
| | Velocity | $v$ | m/s | 2 |
| Bridge | Length | $L$ | m | 25 |
| | Young's modulus | $E$ | MPa | $2.75 \times 10^4$ |
| | Moment of inertia | $I$ | m$^4$ | 0.20 |
| | Mass per unit length | $m$ | kg/m | 2400 |

Three methods were employed to calculate the CP displacements. The first method involves directly interpolating using the displacement responses of adjacent beam nodes based on the location of the wheel contact points in the beam element, referred to as FEM-B, which is the most accurate calculation result. The second method is back-calculating from the vehicle responses using Equation (13), referred to as FEM-V, which may be biased owing to the introduction of numerical differencing. The third method is the theoretical calculation by substituting $x = vt$ into Equation (1), referred to as "Analytical," which may be biased because it ignores the vehicle–bridge coupled interaction and considers only the first five bridge frequencies. Notably, the consideration of the first five modes of modal information for theoretical VBI analysis is a common choice in the literature [10,14,17,22,31]. The comparison of the CP response at the front axle of a two-axle vehicle calculated by the three methods is provided in Figure 3. Notably, the contact point displacement is the sum of road surface roughness and bridge displacement, as shown in Equation (4). It is shown in Figure 3a that the three methods yield consistent CP displacements, which validate the correctness of the theoretical derivation and numerical modeling. Slight deviations are observed in the results of "Analytical," owing to the ignorance of the VBI coupling effect. As can be seen in Figure 3b, only the first bridge frequency can be extracted from the spectrum of the CP acceleration at the front axle, owing to the interference of the road surface roughness. Again, as before, the spectrum of the CP acceleration calculated by the three methods yields the same results.

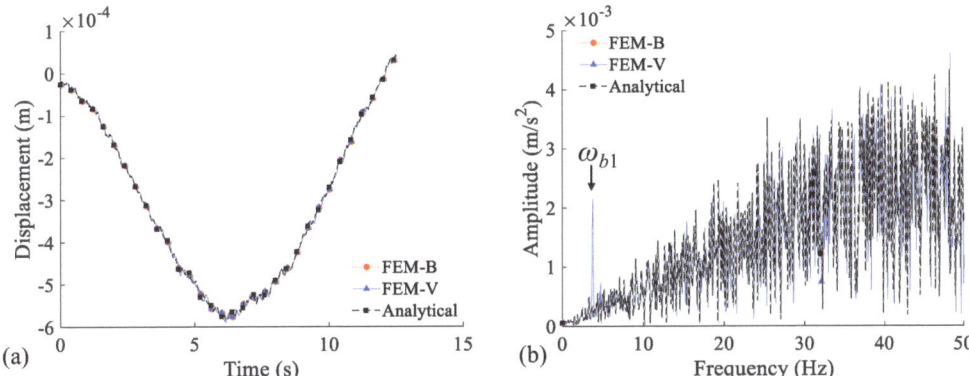

**Figure 3.** Comparison of the CP response at the front axle of a two-axle vehicle calculated by different methods: (**a**) CP displacement; (**b**) Spectrum of CP acceleration.

The influence of road surface roughness can be eliminated by using the residual CP response, according to Equation (10). Therefore, the residual CP response of the two-axle test vehicle back-calculated from the vehicle responses is provided in Figure 4. As shown in Figure 4b, the high-frequency spectra exhibit a greater complexity compared to the low-frequency spectra, owing to the anomalous vibrations shown in Figure 4a. Nevertheless, the first three bridge frequencies are still visible and easy to identify in the frequency spectra, which suggests that the residual CP responses eliminate the interference of the road surface roughness. In addition, it should be noted that the frequencies of the vehicle are also found in the spectrum of residual CP acceleration, which can be attributed to the presence of road surface roughness that renders the vehicle–bridge coupling impossible to overlook.

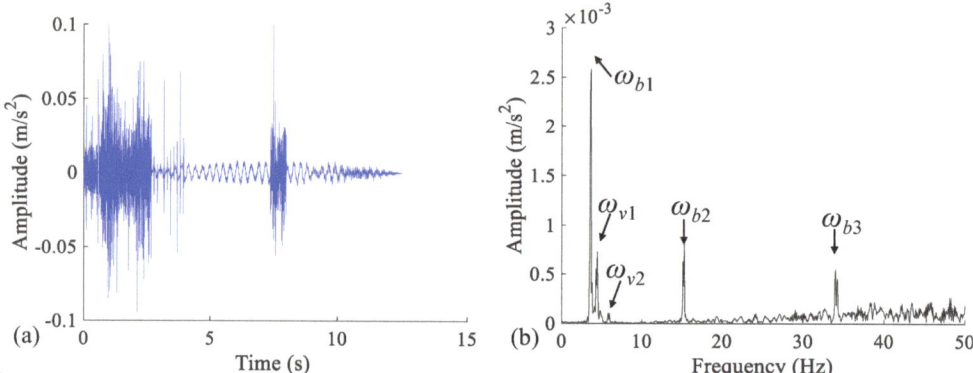

**Figure 4.** Residual CP response of the two-axle test vehicle back-calculated from the vehicle responses: (**a**) Residual CP acceleration; (**b**) Spectrum of residual CP acceleration.

### 3.3. Numerical Validation of Damage Identification

To validate the proposed IAS index for bridge damage identification, local damage with a 10% reduction in element stiffness was introduced in the 19th beam element, specifically within the range of 9.5 to 10.0 m. In this numerical case, road surface roughness was initially excluded but will be considered in subsequent parametric studies. Figure 5a illustrates the IAS index calculated using the CP acceleration of the vehicle's front axle. The initial abnormality in the IAS occurs when the front axle approaches 2.6 m, precisely where the rear axle engages with the left boundary of the bridge. The second abnormality in the IAS arises as the front axle approaches the region of 9.5 to 10.0 m, which corresponds to the location of the bridge damage. Similarly, the two anomalies in the IAS of the CP acceleration of the rear axle are observed at approximately 10 m (damage location) and 23 m (where the first axle exits the bridge), as depicted in Figure 5b. Additionally, Figure 5c presents the IAS index of the residual CP acceleration, revealing notable abnormalities near the bridge supports. The IAS of the residual CP acceleration inherits characteristics from the IAS of the CP acceleration of both the front and rear axles. Neglecting the influence of the bridge boundaries, two abnormalities in the IAS near the locations of 7 m and 12 m were roughly observed. The anomaly at 7 m is attributed to the rear axle approaching this point when the front axle is near the location of damage (9.5–10.0 m). Similarly, the front axle approaches 12 m when the rear axle is in proximity to the damaged location. In summary, for a single damage, the location of damage can be determined based on the abnormalities in the IAS for a single-axle test vehicle or the center of two adjacent abnormalities in the IAS for a two-axle test vehicle. Although the authors have marked the localization of the damage in these figures, readers can themselves assess whether these locations precisely correspond to the damage localized based on the changes in the IAS indicators. These findings validate that the proposed IAS effectively detects bridge damage.

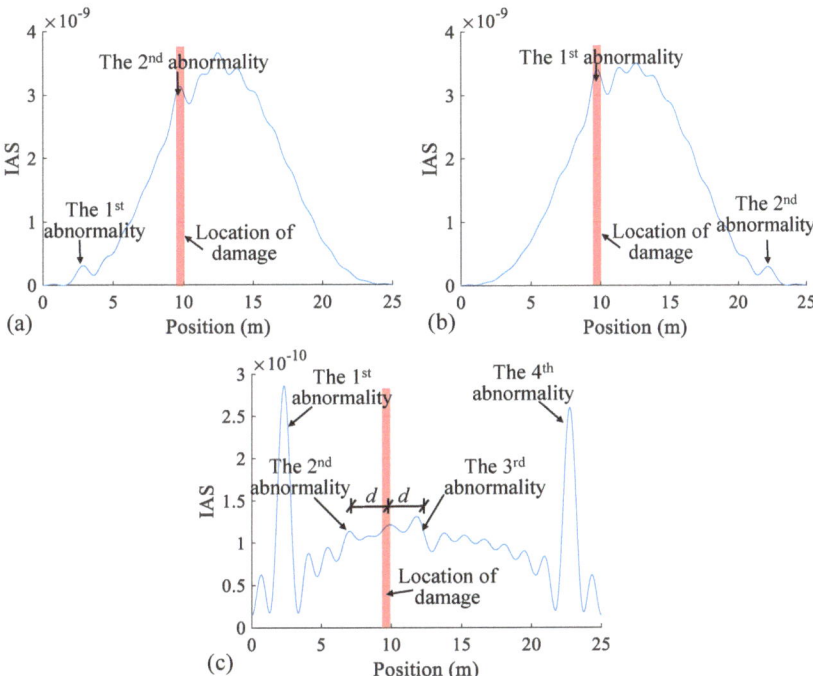

**Figure 5.** Comparison of damage identification results using the IAS calculated by various CP responses without road surface roughness: (**a**) CP acceleration of the front axle; (**b**) CP acceleration of the rear axle; (**c**) residual CP acceleration.

Furthermore, road surface roughness is introduced to illustrate the viability of the proposed IAS under such conditions, and the results are presented in Figure 6. In Figure 6a,b, the resulting IAS derived from the CP accelerations of both the front and rear axles fails to identify bridge damage due to the interference of road surface roughness on the CP accelerations. However, as shown in Figure 6c, the IAS derived from the residual CP acceleration exhibits the same capability to identify bridge damage as demonstrated in Figure 5c. Therefore, it is evident that the IAS calculated from the residual CP acceleration demonstrates superiority over the IAS calculated from single axle acceleration in identifying bridge damage in the presence of road surface roughness.

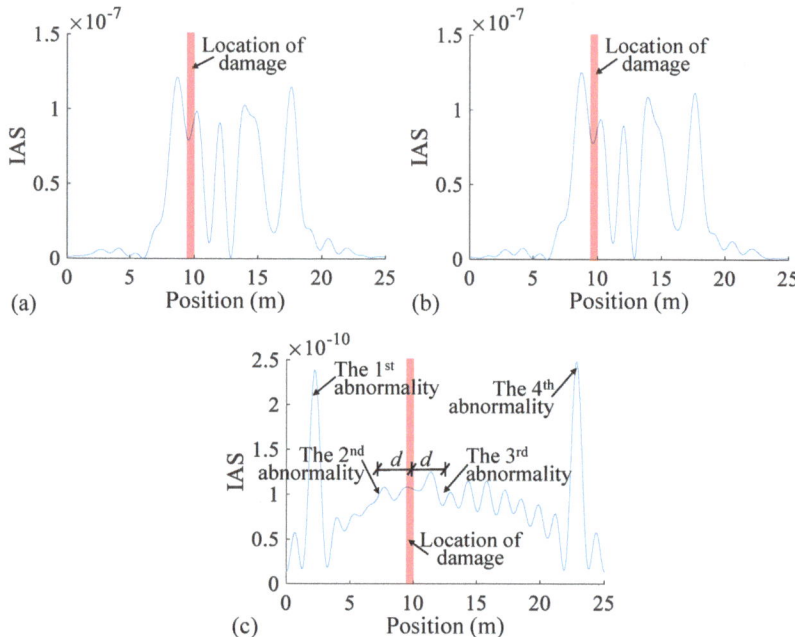

**Figure 6.** Comparison of damage identification results using the IAS calculated by various CP responses with road surface roughness of $G_d(n_0) = 0.001 \times 10^{-6} m^3$: (**a**) CP acceleration of the front axle; (**b**) CP acceleration of the rear axle; (**c**) residual CP acceleration.

*3.4. Influence of Vehicle Speed on Damage Identification*

The speed of the test vehicle is a crucial factor influencing the feasibility of the VSM for damage identification [22–28]. This is because a higher vehicle speed results in fewer vehicle records passing over the bridge, which, in turn, negatively impacts the extraction of the bridge modal information using such limited data. Three sets of vehicle speeds, namely 1 m/s, 2 m/s, and 4 m/s, are compared. For each vehicle speed, three levels of damage—10%, 20%, and 30%—were assigned to the same 19th beam element. Figure 7 presents the influence of vehicle speed on damage identification using the IAS calculated from the residual CP acceleration, where road surface roughness is not involved. It is shown in Figure 7a that all three levels of damage can be identified using the IAS calculated from the residual CP acceleration when the vehicle speed is relatively small, such as 1 m/s. However, when the vehicle speed is increased to 2 m/s, it is observed that the second IAS abnormality at a damage level of 10% becomes insignificant compared to the case with a vehicle speed of 1 m/s. However, when the damage levels are 20% and 30%, the second IAS abnormality becomes visible. Therefore, the damage location can be determined well using the proposed IAS index. When the vehicle speed is 4 m/s, as shown in Figure 7c, the IAS index fails to accurately pinpoint the location of damage across all three damage levels. Therefore, it is advisable to employ low vehicle speeds, such as 1–2 m/s, for enhanced accuracy in using the IAS index for identifying bridge damage.

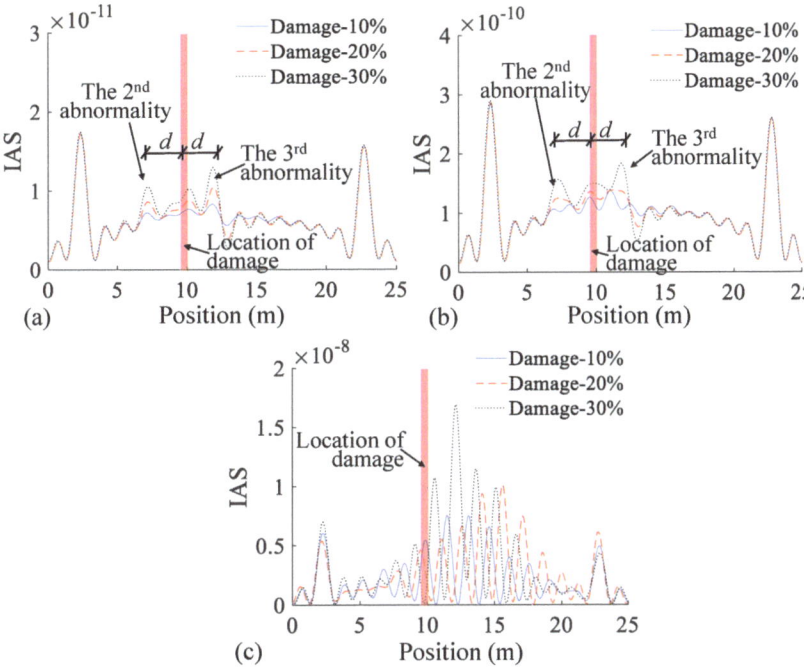

**Figure 7.** Influence of vehicle speed on damage identification using the IAS calculated from the residual CP acceleration: (**a**) 1 m/s, (**b**) 2 m/s, and (**c**) 4 m/s.

*3.5. Influence of Road Roughness on Damage Identification*

Road surface roughness is another important factor influencing the feasibility of the VSM for damage identification [22–25]. Three grades of road surface roughness are analyzed, with $G_d(n_0)$ being $0.001 \times 10^{-6}$, $2 \times 10^{-6}$, and $8 \times 10^{-6}$ m$^3$, and representing the ideal laboratory roughness: class A roughness in the ISO standard [22], and class B roughness in the ISO standard [22], respectively. Figure 8 shows the influence of road surface roughness on damage identification using the IAS calculated from the residual CP acceleration. It is shown in Figure 8a that the damage location can be directly identified through the IAS abnormalities when the road is in perfect roughness condition. Additionally, the degrees of damage can be reflected by the degree of abnormality in the IAS index. When the road roughness is set to $G_d(n_0) = 2 \times 10^{-6}$ m$^3$, as shown in Figure 8b, the damage location is almost overwhelmed by the interference of roughness when the damage levels are below 20%. However, the damage location, with a damage level of 30%, can still be identified using the IAS index. The results with $G_d(n_0) = 8 \times 10^{-6}$ m$^3$, as provided in Figure 8c, show similar findings as inferred from those in Figure 8b. These findings reveal that bridge damage can be effectively identified using the IAS index from the residual CP acceleration of a two-axle testing vehicle with the road roughness considered. If the grades of road roughness are much higher, the IAS is feasible for identifying bridge damage only when the damage is significant enough.

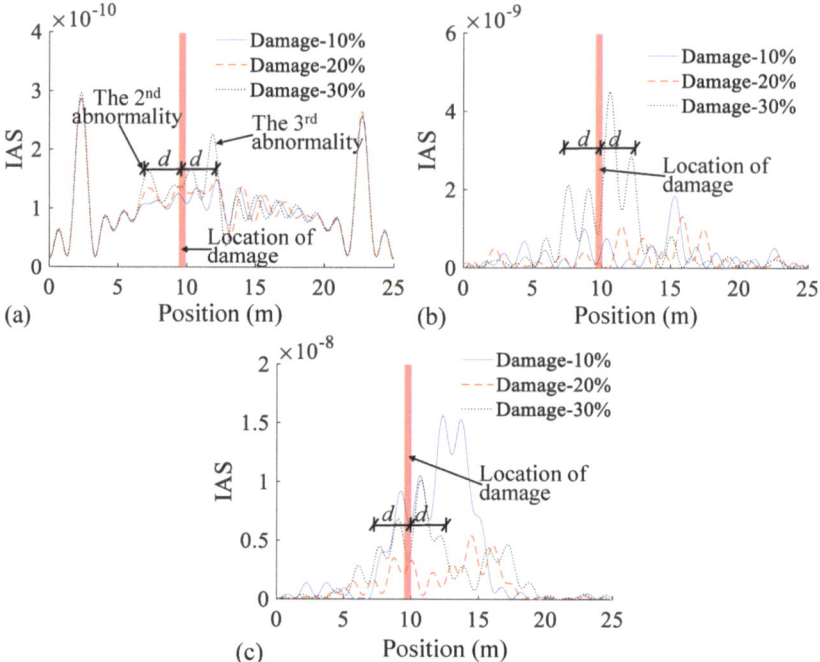

**Figure 8.** Influence of road surface roughness on damage identification using the IAS calculated from the residual CP acceleration: (**a**) $G_d(n_0) = 0.001 \times 10^{-6}$ m$^3$, (**b**) $G_d(n_0) = 2 \times 10^{-6}$ m$^3$, and (**c**) $G_d(n_0) = 8 \times 10^{-6}$ m$^3$.

## 4. Experimental Validations

### 4.1. The Laboratory VBI System

A laboratory VBI system, as shown in Figure 9, was employed for the experiment to validate the proposed IAS index for indirectly identifying bridge damage. A comprehensive description of the laboratory VBI system is available in a previous study [22]. The first two bridge frequencies were $\omega_{b,1} = 7.81$ Hz and $\omega_{b,2} = 29.29$ Hz, which were identified by direct measurements. Notably, the provided bridge frequencies are for the damaged beam. The two-axle test vehicle was composed of two axles, with each axle using a steel bar connecting two polyurethane tires on the left and right, as shown in Figure 9d. A steel plate with a thickness of 12 mm was fixed with the two steel bars. Hence, the test vehicle had relatively large vertical axle stiffnesses. Two accelerometers are mounted on the steel plate directly above the front and rear axles. Since the axle stiffness of the test vehicle is relatively large, the response of the vehicle axle can be treated as proximate to the CP response [25]. The test vehicle was pulled along the tracks across the beam at a constant speed of 0.15 m/s maintained by a winch. The test beam was equipped with two types of tracks: one made of silicone strips used to simulate the idealized perfect road surface roughness, and the other constituted by a non-slip mat on steel rails to simulate a high grade of road surface roughness. Due to the equally spaced arrangement of roughness humps with distances of 16 mm and 32 mm, the vibrational frequencies induced by these humps can be calculated with $v/l$, i.e., 0.15/0.032 = 4.69 Hz and 0.15/0.016 = 9.38 Hz. The test beam has two damage locations at 0.8 m and 1.7 m of the beam by cutting a 10 mm depth on the edge of the beam, as shown in Figure 9f. The severity of the damage corresponds to a local element stiffness loss of 17.32% with an element length of 10 mm. While this level of damage may be considered relatively severe in real-world conditions, it is quite common in laboratory SHM studies.

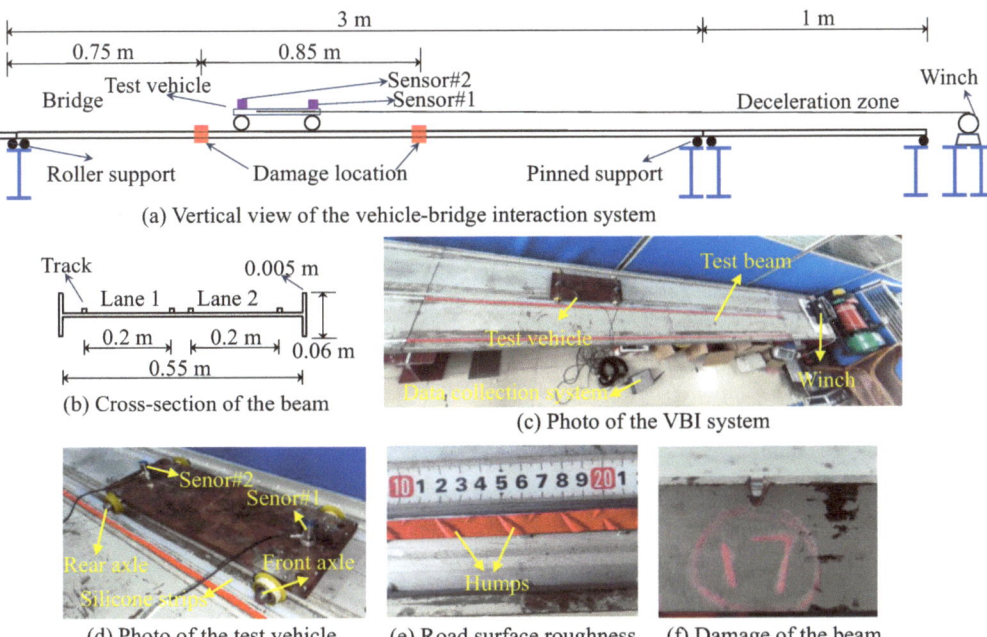

**Figure 9.** Schematic diagram and photos of the laboratory VBI system.

*4.2. Damage Detection under the Perfect Road Surface*

The perfect road surface was initially considered for the test. The test vehicle was pulled across the track made of silicone strips at a constant speed. The results are presented in Figure 10. In Figure 10a, four obvious abnormalities are observed in the IAS index obtained from the CP acceleration of the front axle, with two abnormalities directly indicating the damage locations of the beam. Similarly, in the IAS index obtained from the CP acceleration of the rear axle (Figure 10c), four abnormalities are detected, and two of them directly indicate the damaged locations of the beam. The IAS index was calculated following the practical procedures shown in Section 2.2. Sensors #1 and #2 measure the vehicle accelerations at the front and rear axles, which can be regarded as $\ddot{y}_1$ and $\ddot{y}_2$. Additionally, several abnormalities are observed in the IAS index obtained from the residual CP acceleration (Figure 10e), with the two most obvious abnormalities indicating the damage locations in the beam. The presence of other abnormalities that have no relation to the damage is not currently clear and requires further exploration. In terms of the frequency spectra, the first bridge frequency was successfully identified by the CP acceleration at the front axle in Figure 10b, the CP acceleration at the rear axle in Figure 10d, and the residual CP acceleration in Figure 10f. However, the second bridge frequency is not visible from the frequency spectra of these three responses, implying that the residual CP response does not perform better than the CP response in identifying bridge frequencies. In summary, under perfect road surface conditions, the IAS indexes calculated from both CP accelerations and residual CP acceleration were successful in identifying bridge damage. However, the residual CP acceleration does not outperform the CP acceleration, possibly because the test vehicle is too light, and as a result, the bridge vibration is not sufficiently excited.

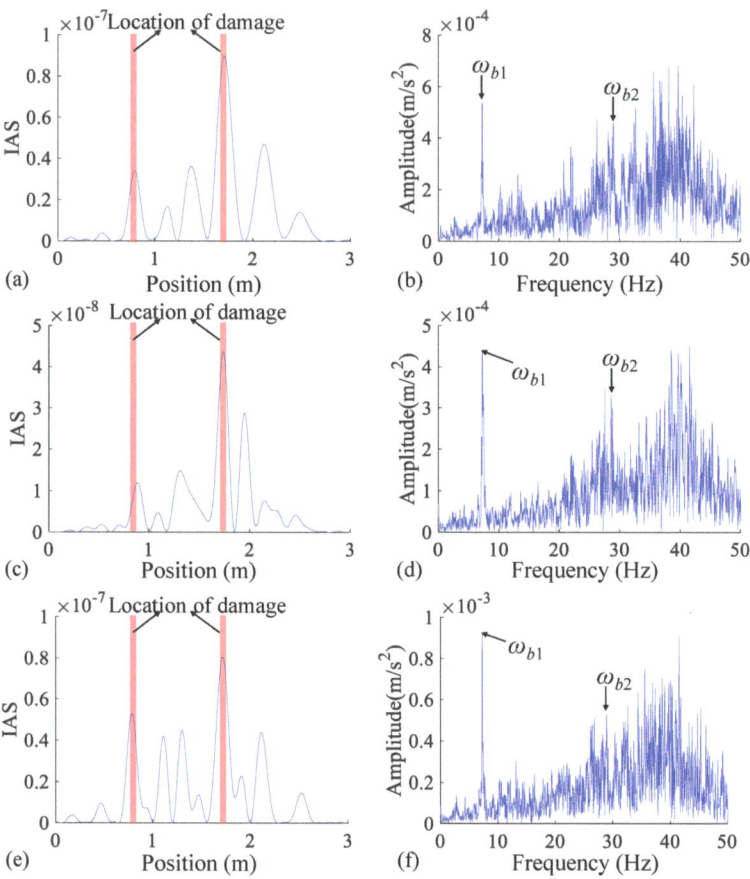

**Figure 10.** Results under the perfect road surface: (**a**) IAS of the CP acceleration at the front axle; (**b**) frequency spectra of the CP acceleration at the front axle; (**c**) IAS of the CP acceleration at the rear axle; (**d**) frequency spectra of the CP acceleration at the rear axle; (**e**) IAS of the residual CP acceleration; (**f**) frequency spectra of the residual CP acceleration.

*4.3. Damage Detection under Rough Road Surface*

To consider a rough road surface in the experiment, the test vehicle was placed on tracks with non-slip mats, as shown in Figure 9e. The same vehicle speed was maintained, and the results are shown in Figure 11. The findings indicate that the IAS of the front axle CP acceleration identifies the second location of the damage. However, due to the interference of the road surface roughness, the IAS of the front axle CP acceleration includes other irrelevant abnormalities that hinder the identification of the first bridge damage. This phenomenon is particularly evident in the IAS of the rear axle CP acceleration, as shown in Figure 11c. Both locations of damage cannot be identified by the IAS index. In terms of the IAS of the residual CP acceleration, the two damage locations are likely identified by the IAS abnormalities. However, other obvious IAS abnormalities were also presented, which have no relation to the bridge damage. In terms of the frequency spectra, the first and second bridge frequencies were all successfully identified by the CP acceleration at the front axle in Figure 11b, CP acceleration at the rear axle in Figure 11d, and residual CP acceleration in Figure 11f. Additionally, the influence of the roughness also includes introducing the roughness frequency $\omega_{roughness}$ in the spectrum of the CP responses. These interferences are inherited in the residual response, which may be another influencing factor in the recognition of damage. The reason why the second bridge frequency can be identified is that the bridge vibration is significant under the excitation of rough road roughness, making the bridge frequency easier to identify; however, such effects are not favorable for the identification of bridge damage. In conclusion, the experiments only demonstrate the weak possibility of using the IAS extracted from residual CP response for identifying bridge damage. However, further experiments should be performed to fully examine the capacity of the IAS for bridge damage identification in practical applications.

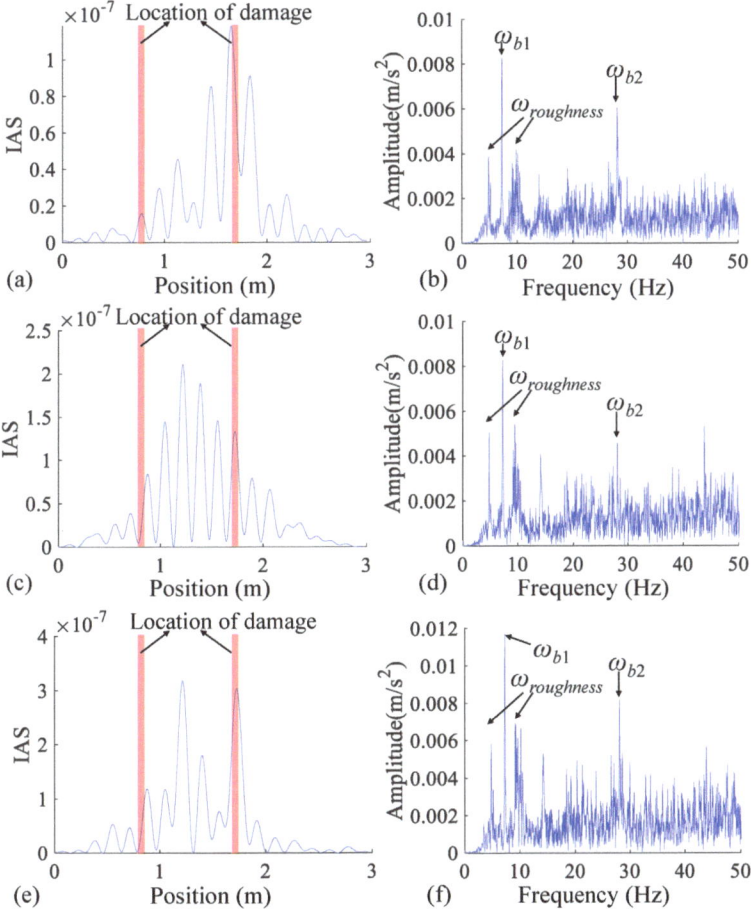

**Figure 11.** Results under the rough road surface: (**a**) IAS of the CP acceleration at the front axle; (**b**) frequency spectra of the CP acceleration at the front axle; (**c**) IAS of the CP acceleration at the rear axle; (**d**) frequency spectra of the CP acceleration at the rear axle; (**e**) IAS of the residual CP acceleration; (**f**) frequency spectra of the residual CP acceleration.

## 5. Conclusions

This study focuses on identifying bridge damage using the response of a two-axle passing vehicle. The closed solution of residual CP acceleration is derived for a two-axle vehicle interacting with a simply supported beam. The IAS index is then constructed from the driving frequency of the residual CP acceleration to identify bridge damage. Numerical investigations using finite element simulation, as well as experimental validations through laboratory VBI tests, were conducted to verify the proposed damage detection approach. The main findings are as follows:

(1) The IAS index of the residual CP acceleration can be constructed by applying a multi-peak idealized filter and the Hilbert transform to the driving frequency spectra. This index is theoretically sensitive to the bridge modal shape and can be used to identify bridge damage. Theoretically, it eliminates the influence of vehicle self-vibrations and road roughness when the vehicle–bridge coupling effect can be ignored;

(2) Numerical investigations verify the accuracy of the theoretical derivations. The bridge damage can be determined by observing IAS abnormalities, which are baseline-free. The IAS of the residual CP acceleration can identify a 10% stiffness loss in a beam element under low road surface roughness and a 30% stiffness loss under high road surface roughness. A favorable vehicle speed of no greater than 2 m/s yields good damage identification results;

(3) Laboratory tests show that it is possible to roughly identify bridge damage using the IAS extracted from residual CP acceleration under perfect road surfaces. The results of the IAS from residual CP acceleration show the same ability to locate damage as those of the IAS from CP accelerations at the front or rear axle. However, some irrelevant IAS abnormalities were observed, which have no relation to the bridge damage;

(4) Regarding rough road surfaces in the experimental setup, while both IAS indicators derived from residual CP acceleration and axle CP acceleration successfully identify multiple bridge frequencies, it is likely that they both fall short in detecting damage. Hence, further experiments should be performed to fully examine the capacity of the IAS for bridge damage identification in practical applications.

This study shows some theoretical and experimental attempts at using the IAS from residual CP responses for bridge damage identification. The feasibility of residual CP responses is not examined in the literature, and this gap was filled by this study to some extent. Based on the findings of this study, it is possible to employ an ordinary two-axle commercial vehicle for the indirect detection of bridge damage, thereby enabling the rapid estimation of structural health for a large group of bridges using only these vehicles. However, more experiments should be conducted to further validate the theoretical superiority of the residual CP response for the indirect identification of bridge modal properties. Furthermore, exploring the feasibility of the IAS index for detecting damage in beams with other boundary conditions represents a significant area for future research. Additionally, considering the incorporation of machine learning algorithms for predicting bridge damage, particularly with an expanded dataset of the IAS, represents a meaningful future endeavor. Exploring the potential of the proposed method to identify multiple damage regions through numerical investigations would also be meaningful follow-up work.

**Author Contributions:** Conceptualization, J.Z.; Methodology, Z.Z.; Software, J.Z.; Validation, S.L. and Z.Z.; Investigation, S.L.; Data curation, S.L. and Y.Z.; Writing—original draft, S.L. and Z.Z.; Writing—review & editing, J.D. and J.Z.; Supervision, J.D. and J.Z.; Project administration, Z.S.; Funding acquisition, J.Z. All authors have read and agreed to the published version of the manuscript.

**Funding:** This research was supported by the Fundamental Research Program of Guangzhou Municipal College Joint Fund (SL2023A03J00897) and the College Student Innovation and Entrepreneurship Program of Guangzhou University (S202311078055 and S202311078017).

**Data Availability Statement:** Data are available based on reasonable request from the corresponding author.

**Conflicts of Interest:** The authors declare that they have no known competing financial interests or personal relationships that could have appeared to influence the work reported in this paper.

## References

1. Sun, L.; Shang, Z.; Xia, Y.; Bhowmick, S.; Nagarajaiah, S. Review of bridge structural health monitoring aided by big data and artificial intelligence: From condition assessment to damage detection. *J. Struct. Eng.* **2020**, *146*, 04020073. [CrossRef]
2. An, Y.; Chatzi, E.; Sim, S.H.; Laflamme, S.; Blachowski, B.; Ou, J. Recent progress and future trends on damage identification methods for bridge structures. *Struct. Control Health Monit.* **2019**, *26*, e2416. [CrossRef]

3. Brownjohn, J.M.; De Stefano, A.; Xu, Y.L.; Wenzel, H.; Aktan, A.E. Vibration-based monitoring of civil infrastructure: Challenges and successes. *J. Civ. Struct. Health Monit.* **2011**, *1*, 79–95. [CrossRef]
4. Hou, R.; Xia, Y. Review on the new development of vibration-based damage identification for civil engineering structures: 2010–2019. *J. Sound Vib.* **2021**, *491*, 115741. [CrossRef]
5. Wang, Z.L.; Yang, J.P.; Shi, K.; Xu, H.; Qiu, F.Q.; Yang, Y.B. Recent advances in researches on vehicle scanning method for bridges. *Int. J. Struct. Stab. Dyn.* **2022**, *22*, 2230005. [CrossRef]
6. Shokravi, H.; Shokravi, H.; Bakhary, N.; Heidarrezaei, M.; Rahimian Koloor, S.S.; Petrů, M. Vehicle-assisted techniques for health monitoring of bridges. *Sensors* **2020**, *20*, 3460. [CrossRef]
7. Malekjafarian, A.; Corbally, R.; Gong, W. A review of mobile sensing of bridges using moving vehicles: Progress to date, challenges and future trends. *Structures* **2022**, *44*, 1466–1489. [CrossRef]
8. Yang, Y.B.; Lin, C.W.; Yau, J.D. Extracting bridge frequencies from the dynamic response of a passing vehicle. *J. Sound Vib.* **2004**, *272*, 471–493. [CrossRef]
9. Nagayama, T.; Reksowardojo, A.P.; Su, D.; Mizutani, T. Bridge natural frequency estimation by extracting the common vibration component from the responses of two vehicles. *Eng. Struct.* **2017**, *150*, 821–829. [CrossRef]
10. Xu, H.; Huang, C.C.; Wang, Z.L.; Shi, K.; Wu, Y.T.; Yang, Y.B. Damped test vehicle for scanning bridge frequencies: Theory, simulation and experiment. *J. Sound Vib.* **2021**, *506*, 116155. [CrossRef]
11. Yang, Y.; Lu, H.; Tan, X.; Wang, R.; Zhang, Y. Mode shape identification and damage detection of bridge by movable sensory system. *IEEE T. Intell. Transp.* **2022**, *24*, 1299–1313. [CrossRef]
12. Li, J.; Zhu, X.; Guo, J. Bridge modal identification based on successive variational mode decomposition using a moving test vehicle. *Adv. Struct. Eng.* **2022**, *25*, 2284–2300. [CrossRef]
13. Yin, X.; Yang, Y.; Huang, Z. Bridge frequency extraction method based on contact point response of two-axle vehicle. *Structures* **2023**, *57*, 105176. [CrossRef]
14. Hashlamon, I.; Nikbakht, E. Theoretical and numerical investigation of bridge frequency identification employing an instrumented vehicle in stationary and moving states. *Structures* **2023**, *51*, 1684–1693. [CrossRef]
15. Zhan, Y.; Au, F.T.; Zhang, J. Bridge identification and damage detection using contact point response difference of moving vehicle. *Struct. Control Health Monit.* **2021**, *28*, e2837. [CrossRef]
16. Yang, D.S.; Wang, C.M. Bridge damage detection using reconstructed mode shape by improved vehicle scanning method. *Eng. Struct.* **2022**, *263*, 114373. [CrossRef]
17. He, Y.; Yang, J.P.; Yan, Z. Enhanced identification of bridge modal parameters using contact residuals from three-connected vehicles: Theoretical study. *Structures* **2023**, *54*, 1320–1335. [CrossRef]
18. Liu, Y.; Zhan, J.; Wang, Y.; Wang, C.; Zhang, F. An effective procedure for extracting mode shapes of simply-supported bridges using virtual contact-point responses of two-axle vehicles. *Structures* **2023**, *48*, 2082–2097. [CrossRef]
19. Hajializadeh, D. Deep learning-based indirect bridge damage identification system. *Struct. Control Health Monit.* **2023**, *22*, 897–912. [CrossRef]
20. Hurtado, A.C.; Kaur, K.; Alamdari, M.M.; Atroshchenko, E.; Chang, K.C.; Kim, C.W. Unsupervised learning-based framework for indirect structural health monitoring using adversarial autoencoder. *J. Sound Vib.* **2023**, *550*, 117598. [CrossRef]
21. Li, Z.; Lin, W.; Zhang, Y. Real-time drive-by bridge damage detection using deep auto-encoder. *Structures* **2023**, *47*, 1167–1181. [CrossRef]
22. Zhou, J.; Lu, Z.; Zhou, Z.; Pan, C.; Cao, S.; Cheng, J.; Zhang, J. Extraction of bridge mode shapes from the response of a two-axle passing vehicle using a two-peak spectrum idealized filter approach. *Mech. Syst. Signal Pr.* **2023**, *190*, 110122. [CrossRef]
23. Xu, H.; Yang, M.; Yang, J.P.; Wang, Z.L.; Shi, K.; Yang, Y.B. Vehicle scanning method for bridges enhanced by dual amplifiers. *Struct. Control Health Monit.* **2023**, *2023*, 6906855. [CrossRef]
24. Yang, Y.B.; Li, Z.; Wang, Z.L.; Shi, K.; Xu, H.; Qiu, F.Q.; Zhu, J.F. A novel frequency-free movable test vehicle for retrieving modal parameters of bridges: Theory and experiment. *Mech. Syst. Signal Pr.* **2022**, *170*, 108854. [CrossRef]
25. Zhou, Z.; Zhou, J.; Deng, J.; Wang, X.; Liu, H. Identification of multiple bridge frequencies using a movable test vehicle by approximating axle responses to contact-point responses: Theory and experiment. *J. Civ. Struct. Health Monit.* **2024**. *under review*.
26. Zhang, B.; Qian, Y.; Wu, Y.; Yang, Y.B. An effective means for damage detection of bridges using the contact-point response of a moving test vehicle. *J. Sound Vib.* **2018**, *419*, 158–172. [CrossRef]
27. Feng, K.; Casero, M.; González, A. Characterization of the road profile and the rotational stiffness of supports in a bridge based on axle accelerations of a crossing vehicle. *Comput. Aided Civ. Inf.* **2023**, *38*, 12974. [CrossRef]
28. Yang, Y.B.; Xu, H.; Wang, Z.L.; Shi, K. Using vehicle–bridge contact spectra and residue to scan bridge's modal properties with vehicle frequencies and road roughness eliminated. *Struct. Control Health Monit.* **2022**, *29*, e2968. [CrossRef]
29. Hashlamon, I.; Nikbakht, E. The use of a movable vehicle in a stationary condition for indirect bridge damage detection using baseline-free methodology. *Appl. Sci.* **2022**, *12*, 11625. [CrossRef]
30. Ma, X.; Roshan, M.; Kiani, K.; Nikkhoo, A. Dynamic response of an elastic tube-like nanostructure embedded in a vibrating medium and under the action of moving nano-objects. *Symmetry* **2023**, *15*, 1827. [CrossRef]
31. Yu, G.; Kiani, K.; Roshan, M. Dynamic analysis of multiple-nanobeam-systems acted upon by multiple moving nanoparticles accounting for nonlocality, lag, and lateral inertia. *Appl. Math. Model.* **2022**, *108*, 326–354. [CrossRef]

32. Dimitrovová, Z. Dynamic interaction and instability of two moving proximate masses on a beam on a Pasternak viscoelastic foundation. *Appl. Math. Model.* **2021**, *100*, 192–217. [CrossRef]
33. Zhou, J.; Zhou, Z.; Jin, Z.; Liu, S.; Lu, Z. Comparative study of damage modeling techniques for beam-like structures and their application in vehicle-bridge-interaction-based structural health monitoring. *J. Vib. Control* **2023**, 10775463231209357. [CrossRef]
34. Xiao, J.; Huang, L.; He, Z.; Qu, W.; Li, L.; Jiang, H.; Zhong, Z.; Long, X. Probabilistic models applied to concrete corrosion depth prediction under sulfuric acid environment. *Measurement* **2024**, *234*, 114807. [CrossRef]

**Disclaimer/Publisher's Note:** The statements, opinions and data contained in all publications are solely those of the individual author(s) and contributor(s) and not of MDPI and/or the editor(s). MDPI and/or the editor(s) disclaim responsibility for any injury to people or property resulting from any ideas, methods, instructions or products referred to in the content.

*Article*

# Study of Structural Seismic Damage Considering Seasonal Frozen Soil–Structure Interaction

Xuyang Bian [1,2] and Guoxin Wang [1,2,*]

1. State Key Laboratory of Coastal and Offshore Engineering, Dalian University of Technology, Dalian 116024, China; bianxuyang@mail.dlut.edu.cn
2. Institute of Earthquake Engineering, Faculty of Infrastructure Engineering, Dalian University of Technology, Dalian 116024, China
* Correspondence: gxwang@dlut.edu.cn

**Abstract:** Frozen soil may cause structures to have different damage statuses, as revealed by earthquakes in northeastern China. ABAQUS (2019), a numerical simulation software application, was adopted to systematically and deeply study the structural seismic response, considering seasonal frozen soil–structure interaction under different ground motion intensities and soil ambient temperatures. The results showed firstly that the variation in soil ambient temperature had a great influence on the seismic response of the structure, as indicated by the damage status of the structure obtained through numerical simulation. Secondly, through further analysis of the numerical simulation results, the influence amplitude of different soil temperatures on the structural seismic response was quantitatively analyzed and systematically summarized. Finally, the structural seismic damage with negative ambient temperature could be significantly lower than that with positive temperature normally. Additionally, such an internal change mechanism was also objectively analyzed to verify the reliability of the conclusion.

**Keywords:** seasonal frozen soil; frozen soil–structure interaction; numerical simulation; structural seismic response; structural damage

## 1. Introduction

Earthquakes occur almost every year all over the world, causing huge economic losses and major casualties. In areas with four distinct seasons, such as northeastern China, where temperatures can reach +40 °C in summer and −40 °C in winter, the physical properties of soil layers change with natural seasonal variation, which can lead to a significant change in soil seismic response. The presence of a frozen soil layer in winter significantly affects the structural response during an earthquake, compared to that in summer. For example, when comparing the four earthquakes—Ms 5.0, 9 February 1986 and Ms 5.4, 1 March 1986 in Dedu, Heilongjiang Province, China, and Ms 4.8 and Ms 5.5, respectively, on 16 August in the same year, in winter, multi-story brick-concrete buildings and single-story brick-wood structures both suffered significant earthquake damage, especially brick-concrete buildings of two stories or higher. Industrial factories with brick load-bearing walls and large-span cinemas experienced relatively minor damage. In summer, rigid multi-story brick-concrete buildings and single-story brick-wood structures did not sustain severe damage after subsequent earthquakes. Conversely, industrial factories that experienced minor damage in winter can suffer significant damage [1–3]. It can be seen that the earthquakes that occurred in February and March caused minor damage to houses with flexible structures, while the earthquakes in August caused minor damage to houses with rigid structures. That is, flexible structures such as frame structures suffer less damage than rigid structures such as masonry structures when there is a frozen soil layer in winter, and the damage to flexible structures is more serious than that to rigid structures without a frozen soil layer in summer.

**Citation:** Bian, X.; Wang, G. Study of Structural Seismic Damage Considering Seasonal Frozen Soil–Structure Interaction. *Buildings* **2024**, *14*, 1493. https://doi.org/10.3390/buildings14061493

Academic Editor: Eugeniusz Koda

Received: 12 April 2024
Revised: 13 May 2024
Accepted: 16 May 2024
Published: 21 May 2024

**Copyright:** © 2024 by the authors. Licensee MDPI, Basel, Switzerland. This article is an open access article distributed under the terms and conditions of the Creative Commons Attribution (CC BY) license (https://creativecommons.org/licenses/by/4.0/).

Globally, many earthquakes occur in the same region during different seasons within the same year. For example, an Ms 6.0 earthquake struck Christchurch, New Zealand, on 13 June 2011; later that year, the city experienced another two earthquakes, on 23 November and 22 December, of Ms 6.0 and Ms 6.3, respectively. On 15 and 18 February 2023, earthquakes of Ms 4.6 and Ms 5.1, respectively, occurred in Gekesun City, Kahlamamarash Province, Turkey; on 20 August of the same year, another Ms 4.2 earthquake occurred in the area. Currently, there are no detailed damage records available to compare the damage to different structures across different seasons in the aforementioned regions. Therefore, this paper analyzes detailed damage data from the Dedu region in China and incorporates numerical simulations to preliminarily predict the damage to structures in different seasons caused by earthquakes.

Extensive research has been conducted to investigate the engineering properties of seasonally frozen soil, revealing that ice in the frozen soil layer exists in the form of ice crystals or ice layers. Due to the ever-changing structure of these two forms of ice [4–6], the mechanical properties of frozen soil differ from those of non-frozen soil and are closely related to changes in temperature and ice content [7,8]. During soil freezing, the internal structure of the soil becomes more stable due to the ice crystals, which improves its bearing capacity [9]. To study the ice crystal content change in soil voids during soil freezing, Tan et al. [10] analyzed the influencing factors of soil ice content through tests. Ladanyi et al. [11] conducted triaxial tests on frozen soil in the 1970s to analyze its strength characteristics and better understand its damage after being subjected to external loads. Chamberlain et al. [12] discovered through triaxial tests that the strength of frozen soil begins to deteriorate when the stress reaches a certain level. Zhu et al. [13] studied the mechanical properties of frozen silt and established the relationship formula between strength and temperature by analyzing the influence of temperature and other factors on its mechanical properties. Additionally, Wu et al. [14] conducted dynamic triaxial tests on frozen loess to study its strength characteristics under earthquake load, and Li et al. [15] obtained the failure mechanism of frozen soil through a soil deformation characteristics test with cyclic loading. Wang et al. [16] studied the influence of freezing time and other factors on the mechanical properties of frozen silty clay through experiments. Therefore, studying frozen soil's mechanical properties is of significant importance.

Scholars have conducted numerous studies to explore soil–structure interaction. Since the 1980s, numerical simulation has been applied to the study of soil–structure interaction with the advancement of computer technology. Toki et al. [17] used structural simulation technology to model soil mass deformation in mining disasters and transfer it to the structure. Makris et al. [18] used a simplified model to conduct a dynamic time-history analysis of soil–structure interaction. Wijaya et al. [19] used the boundary element method to simulate the interaction between piles and soil and suggested that it is a simpler method. Ilaria et al. [20] analyzed the wind-induced vibration response of high-rise buildings with soil–structure interaction using the finite element method. Renzi et al. [21] assessed the safety and cost of soil–structure interaction for the dynamic response of various structures. Zhang et al. [22] established a soil–pile–structure interaction model using the finite element software ABAQUS and analyzed the dynamic response of piles and superstructures. Xu et al. [23] analyzed the dynamic response of transmission towers considering soil–structure interaction and found that the structural displacement would increase significantly under site conditions such as soft soil. Jendoubi et al. [24] investigated the dynamic response of transmission towers under an impact load. Ma et al. [25] and Mi et al. [26] analyzed the soil–structure interaction of irregular structures and obtained the differences between numerical simulation results that considered soil–structure interaction and those that did not. Forcellini et al. [27,28] emphasized that the dynamic analysis of soil–structure interactions for structures should consider soil deformation. In the numerical simulation process, Zhao et al. [29] and Jiang et al. [30] suggested that the finite-infinite element method can better simulate the infinite domain of soil. Nielsen et al. [31] utilized the infinite element method to achieve vertical incidence of shear waves in ABAQUS. Deeks et al. [32]

proposed a two-dimensional viscoelastic artificial boundary to simulate the infinite domain of soil in the time domain. Liu et al. [33] subsequently proposed a three-dimensional viscoelastic boundary.

Although many studies have addressed soil–structure interaction, as previously discussed, research on frozen soil–structure interaction remains limited. Thus, further investigation into this area is necessary. This paper uses ABAQUS software to conduct numerical simulations of seismic damage to structures in seasonal frozen soil areas. The finite element models of a multi-story frame structure (four stories) and a high-rise frame structure (sixteen stories) were established. In the presence of a frozen soil layer, the seismic response of the frozen soil–structure interaction was analyzed in detail and compared with the structure without a frozen soil layer. This study focuses on Harbin, Heilongjiang Province, China, a region with significant annual temperature variations, making it ideal for examining how different temperatures affect structural responses. The annual temperature data for Harbin are presented in Table 1. The data originate from the China Meteorological Administration.

**Table 1.** Temperature change in Harbin.

| Month | Daily Average Maximum Temperature (°C) | Daily Average Minimum Temperature (°C) | Historical Maximum Temperature (°C) | Historical Minimum Temperature (°C) |
| --- | --- | --- | --- | --- |
| January | −14 | −25 | −1 | −34 |
| February | −8 | −20 | 6 | −30 |
| March | 3 | −9 | 22 | −24 |
| April | 15 | 2 | 32 | −7 |
| May | 22 | 11 | 34 | 1 |
| June | 28 | 17 | 38 | 9 |
| July | 29 | 20 | 35 | 14 |
| August | 27 | 19 | 35 | 8 |
| September | 22 | 11 | 29 | −2 |
| October | 12 | 1 | 25 | −12 |
| November | 0 | −9 | 16 | −24 |
| December | −11 | −21 | 7 | −32 |

According to the data presented in Table 1, the historical records indicate that the lowest temperature recorded in the Harbin region was −34 °C, while the highest temperature reached 38 °C. The daily average minimum temperature hovers around −25 °C, with the daily average maximum temperature reaching approximately 29 °C. According to the findings from the investigation, in seasonal frozen soil regions during winter, temperatures mostly fall below −20 °C. In summer, temperatures are consistently positive. During spring and autumn, temperatures generally range between positive temperatures and −15 °C. To better simulate the impact of environmental temperature changes on the seismic response of structures, this study sets the temperature for summer at 23 °C. The temperature is set to −5 °C for late spring and early autumn. For early spring and late autumn, the temperatures are set at −10 °C and −15 °C. The temperature for winter is set at −20 °C. The dynamic triaxial test is conducted to obtain the soil dynamic parameters at different temperatures, making the simulation results more consistent with reality [34]. The results show that the dynamic elastic modulus and dynamic cohesion will increase significantly when the clay is frozen; as the temperature continues to decrease, this increasing trend will gradually slow down, and the dynamic damping ratio will go down when the freezing temperature decreases.

## 2. Establishment of Finite Element Model

The numerical simulation software ABAQUS is used to establish a three-dimensional model, in which the soil, pile, and structure are modeled using solid elements. The model includes a four-story and a sixteen-story frame structure, with a story height of 3 m, column spacing of 6 m, and column section size of 0.5 m × 0.5 m. The column height is 3 m, the beam section size is 0.4 m × 0.2 m, the beam length is 6 m, the floor size is 6 m × 6 m, and the floor thickness is 0.12 m. The beams and columns are reinforced with HRB400 reinforcement with a diameter of 16 mm. The plate reinforcements are arranged in double rows, while plate reinforcement and stirrups are made of HRB400 reinforcement with a diameter of 8 mm. The yield strength of HRB400 reinforcing steel is 400 MPa, offering high strength, good ductility, excellent durability, and corrosion resistance. The reinforcement details of beams and columns are shown in Figure 1. The concrete strength grade is C30. The strength grade of C30 concrete is 30 MPa. It is known for its high strength, good durability, and ease of construction.

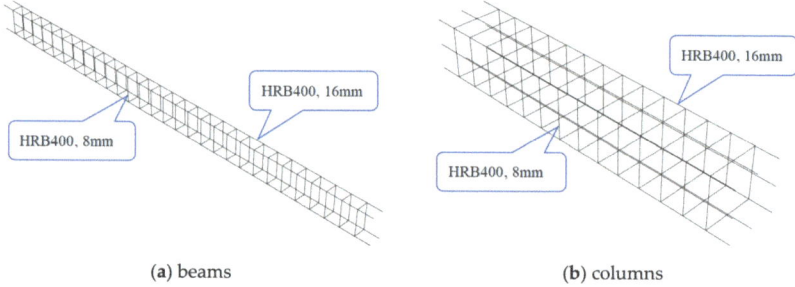

(a) beams  (b) columns

**Figure 1.** Reinforcement details.

Before establishing the soil model, a detailed analysis was conducted on the geological survey report of Harbin, Heilongjiang. The construction site is located on Xingjiang Road in Harbin City, and the entire site is flat, without adverse geological effects such as landslides or collapses that could impact stability. The distribution and characteristics of soil layers within the depth range reached by drilling are shown in Table 2.

**Table 2.** Distribution of soil layers in the geological survey report.

| Soil Type | Soil Thickness (m) | Soil Properties |
|---|---|---|
| Miscellaneous fill | 0.60–1.00 | Mixed colors, mainly composed of construction waste, including sticky soil, with black sedimentary soil at the bottom. |
| Silty clay 1 | 7.80–8.90 | Yellow-brown, plastic to rigid, with high dry strength and high toughness. |
| Silty clay 2 | 2.00–4.70 | Brown, plastic, with moderate dry strength and moderate toughness. |
| Silty clay 3 | 1.10–3.60 | Gray-yellow to gray, soft plastic to plastic, with moderate dry strength and low toughness. |
| Fine sand 1 | 1.00–1.00 | Yellow, slightly dense to moderately dense, slightly moist. |
| Fine sand 2 | 4.70–4.90 | Gray, slightly dense. |
| Medium sand | 1.70–2.00 | Gray, moderately dense. |
| Coarse sand | 4.50–5.50 | Yellow, moderately dense. |

Based on the geological survey report, the size of the soil model is 60 m × 60 m × 30 m, and there is an infinite element boundary of 30 m around the soil model. The soil layer is divided into nine layers. The first layer is frozen soil with a thickness of 2.5 m, which is more consistent with the actual frozen soil depth in Harbin. Detailed soil layer parameters are shown in Table 3. The date of the non-frozen soil layer was provided by the geological survey report. The established models are shown in Figure 2.

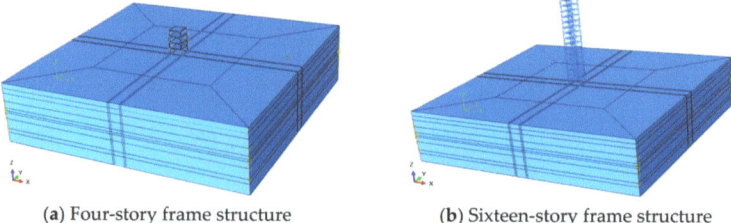

(a) Four-story frame structure  (b) Sixteen-story frame structure

**Figure 2.** Frame structure.

Table 3. Soil parameters.

| Soil Thickness (m) and Soil Type | Temperature (°C) | Density (kg/m³) | Elastic Modulus (MPa) | Cohesion (kPa) | Internal Friction Angle (°) |
|---|---|---|---|---|---|
|  | 23 | 1480 | 97.1 | 38.9 | 9.6 |
|  | −5 | 1480 | 244.7 | 173.5 | 27.4 |
| 2.5 (Clay) | −10 | 1480 | 462.1 | 343.7 | 34.1 |
|  | −15 | 1480 | 540.1 | 367.5 | 33.2 |
|  | −20 | 1480 | 568.9 | 382.4 | 32.9 |
| 6.5 (Silty clay 1) | 23 | 1930 | 204.3 | 36.1 | 15.9 |
| 3.5 (Silty clay 2) | 23 | 1890 | 173.3 | 26.8 | 11.1 |
| 1.5 (Silty clay 3) | 23 | 1860 | 140.2 | 26.6 | 10.0 |
| 1 (Fine sand 1) | 23 | 1840 | 312.1 | 6.0 | 28.0 |
| 3 (Silty clay 3) | 23 | 1860 | 140.2 | 26.6 | 10.0 |
| 5 (Fine sand 2) | 23 | 1840 | 272.9 | 6.0 | 25.0 |
| 2 (Medium sand) | 23 | 1840 | 302.5 | 3.0 | 30.0 |
| 5 (Coarse sand) | 23 | 1840 | 358.9 | 2.0 | 35.0 |

The numerical simulation uses implicit dynamic analysis for elastoplastic analysis. For selecting a model constitution, the plastic constitution of concrete uses the damaged plasticity of concrete. This constitutive model has many applications and can be used to analyze the response of frame structures under dynamic loads. Molar Coulomb plasticity is adopted as the plastic constitutive model of soil mass. When the earthquake occurs, the vibration of the seismic wave causes the soil mass to enter a plastic state. The Molar Coulomb plastic constitutive model can well reflect the soil mass's failure state and strength characteristics and is widely used in geotechnical engineering. Because the simulation in this paper adopts implicit dynamic analysis, Rayleigh damping is used to reflect the damping characteristics better.

*2.1. Selection of Ground Motions*

For ground motion selection, 12 widely used records (El-Centro, Kobe, Kocaeli, Loma Prieta, Northridge, San Francisco, Taft, Tangshan, Tianjin, QianAn, Concrete, Shanghai) were chosen for dynamic time-history analysis of the four-story frame structure. For the sixteen-story frame structure, considering many working conditions and a long calculation time, three ground motions (El-Centro, Loma Prieta, Taft) are selected for dynamic time history analysis in the simulation process, and the ground motion amplitude is adjusted to 0.1 g and 0.3 g, respectively. Before the simulation, amplitude modulation and baseline calibration were conducted for each ground motion.

*2.2. Solver and Element Types*

This paper utilizes the implicit solver available in the standard module of ABAQUS. This solver accurately simulates linear and nonlinear engineering projects, efficiently and reliably resolving various complex nonlinear issues.

ABAQUS software offers a wide range of element types for scholars to conduct diverse simulation studies, each possessing unique characteristics. The correct choice of element type directly affects the accuracy of the simulation results. In this article, both the structural and soil models employ solid elements, specifically the C3D8R element type. This type of element has excellent deformation and stress analysis capabilities, enhancing the computational convergence and precision of simulation results.

When simulating building structures, the internal reinforcement structure element type typically selected is the truss element type provided by ABAQUS. The hoop reinforcement and load-bearing reinforcement elements modeled in this paper both utilize the T3D2 element. This element type can simulate large deformations and effectively model the stress conditions of reinforcement bars.

Regarding the selection of contact types, ABAQUS includes various contact and constraint modes. In this article, the contact between reinforcement and concrete uses an embedded approach, while the contact between the structure and soil employs a surface-to-surface contact method.

## 2.3. Mesh Size and Properties

The rationality of the cell grid size directly affects the calculation results and convergence. In this paper, the grid division adopts the structured grid inherent in ABAQUS, using hexahedral elements for division. The structural grid size is 0.2 m, the reinforcement grid size is 0.1 m, and the soil minimum grid size is 0.5 m. The layout method is single precision division. This layout method results in a dense grid near the structure and a sparser grid further away. The single precision division method can improve the computer calculation speed while ensuring the accuracy of the calculation results.

## 2.4. Boundary Condition

When analyzing the interaction between soil and structure, the range of the soil is infinite. In the numerical simulation, the soil is regarded as a semi-infinite space. That is, it needs to be calculated for the limited range of soil. For the selection of soil mass range, a too-small range will lead to a scattering wave unable to cross the artificial boundary, which will reflect and affect the accuracy of the calculation results. A too-large range will lead to too many units, which requires high computer performance and will affect the operation speed. The infinite element provided by ABAQUS is used as the artificial boundary to simulate the infinite soil mass area better. Structures can generate foundation radiational damping during seismic events, affecting the dynamic characteristics of the structure. By using an infinite element boundary, the radiational damping effect of an infinite foundation can be effectively simulated [35–37]. The infinite element boundary can well absorb the scattering wave. For the bottom of the soil model, we use a fixed boundary. In this simulation, the seismic wave is assumed to propagate from the bedrock surface through the soil layer and then to the structure. The structural vibration reflects the seismic wave from the soil layer to the bedrock. Due to the effect of soil damping, the amplitude will be tiny. After being reflected by the bedrock, the amplitude will be reduced again, which has little impact on the structural dynamic response.

## 2.5. Geo-Stress Balance

Geo-stress is a kind of natural stress in the crust that is not affected by external factors. It is also called the initial stress of rock mass [38]. Balancing the geo-stress is essential in the numerical simulation of dynamic analysis. After the geo-stress is balanced, the actual situation of the site soil can be well restored, affecting the accuracy of the subsequent analysis results. ABAQUS offers several methods to balance geo-stress, including automatic balancing, extracting node stress using an inp file, and importing an ODB file for balancing. This paper uses importing an ODB file to balance the geo-stress, and good results are obtained. As shown in Figure 3, the displacement is $10^{-3}$ m when the ground stress is not balanced and $10^{-6}$ m when the ground stress is balanced. For the ground stress balance standard, when the displacement reaches $10^{-4}$ m, the result is reasonable [39], so the ground stress balance results in this paper align with the standard.

In frame structures, the characteristics of reinforced concrete components exhibit nonlinearity after experiencing seismic loads. To demonstrate the nonlinear characteristics, this paper employs suitable constitutive models and element types to represent the nonlinearity of the components. For instance, the constitutive model for concrete uses the concrete damage plasticity model available in ABAQUS. This model effectively represents the structure's nonlinearity and accurately simulates the mechanical behavior of concrete under seismic loads. The reinforcement elements use the T3D2 element type from ABAQUS, which can simulate large deformations under seismic loads, thereby reflecting its nonlinearity. Simultaneously, the definition of plastic hinges is primarily based on the plastic zone model in ABAQUS to perform nonlinear analysis. By selecting suitable constitutive models and setting appropriate element types, the components' yield criteria and hysteresis rules are reflected, forming plastic hinges at all possible regions of the component, which more accurately matches the actual damage scenarios of structures under seismic loads.

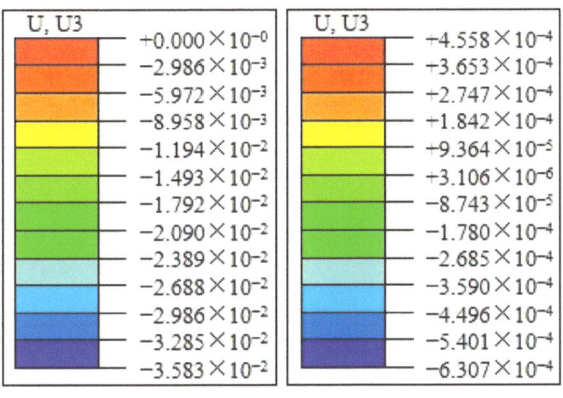

**Figure 3.** Geo-stress balance.

## 3. Numerical Simulation Results

### 3.1. Seismic Response of Four-Story Frame Structure

#### 3.1.1. Structural Response

This paper judges frame structure damage based on its maximum inter-story displacement angle and structural damage. Based on the results, it can be concluded that temperature changes significantly affect seismic damage to the structure. When the temperature drops below 0 °C, the maximum inter-story displacement angle will decrease, which indicates that the seismic damage to the four-story frame structure will be reduced with the freezing of the soil layer. Figure 4 depicts the change rule of the maximum inter-story displacement angle.

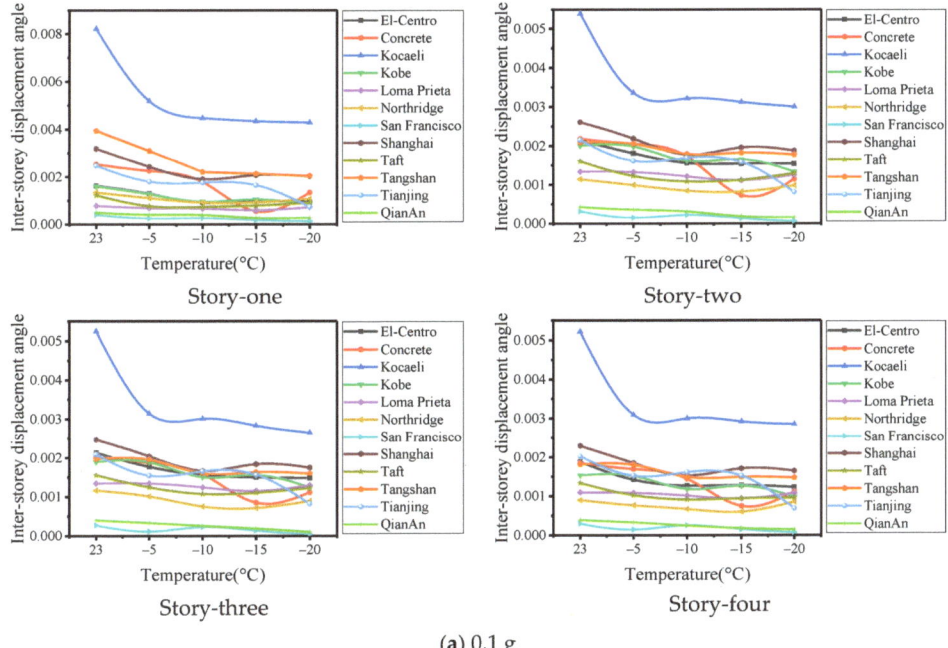

(**a**) 0.1 g

**Figure 4.** *Cont.*

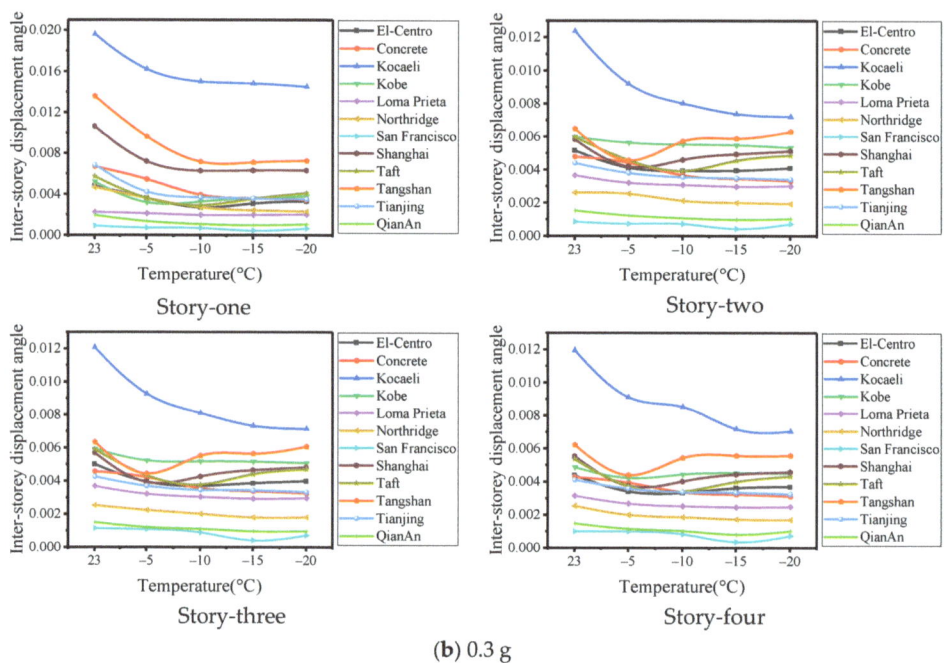

(**b**) 0.3 g

**Figure 4.** Maximum inter-story displacement angle of four-story frame structure.

Figure 4 illustrates the variation in the maximum inter-story displacement angle of the structure under 12 seismic waves. As a whole, the maximum inter-story displacement angle of the structure decreases with decreased ambient temperature. Figure 4a reveals that the maximum inter-story displacement angle of the structure occurs on the first and second floors when the ground motion amplitude is 0.1 g, and gradually decreases with an increase in the number of floors. This trend is attributed to the pile foundation, which connects the structure to the ground. Soil disturbances affect the foundation and transmit the resultant effects to the lower floors, producing maximum displacement angles there. At normal temperatures (i.e., 23 °C), the maximum inter-story displacement angle of the structure is generally greater than that under negative temperatures. At −5 °C, however, the change in the maximum inter-story displacement angle is between that at normal and lower temperatures, but with significant fluctuations. This behavior occurs because, below −5 °C, not all soil water freezes, resulting in an unstable ice crystal structure more susceptible to external disturbances. Consequently, different earthquakes may cause varying degrees of damage. As the temperature drops to −10 °C, the maximum inter-story displacement angle of the structure under different ground motions shows no discernible trend. This can be attributed to the fact that, at −10 °C, all of the free water in the soil freezes, resulting in a stable molecular structure of ice crystals. Additionally, the bond between ice crystals and soil particles becomes firmer, and the interaction between them is minimally affected as the temperature decreases further. This phenomenon has a significant impact on the behavior of the structure, and different ground motions can result in varying outcomes.

Figure 4b indicates that with a ground motion amplitude of 0.3 g, structural damage increases with earthquake intensity, more so than at 0.1 g. The seismic damage response law of the structure at different temperatures is similar to that of 0.1 g, but there are some inconsistencies in a few ground motions when the ground motion amplitude reaches 0.3 g. This is due to the enhanced ground motion, which increases the probability of cliff-type damage occurring in the structural mode between soil particles, water, and ice crystals in the frozen soil layer, resulting in inconsistent laws.

Damage levels in building structures are generally classified into five categories: intact, minor damage, moderate damage, severe damage, and collapse. Currently, there are no detailed boundaries defined for these five levels. By examining the overall trends in inter-story drift angles, corresponding damage levels can be preliminarily assessed. For instance, under cold winter temperatures, frame structures may experience minor to moderate damage after an earthquake. As temperatures rise, the structures are likely to undergo moderate to severe damage. In summer, when temperatures are positive, the damage to structures is the most severe, potentially resulting in severe damage or even collapse. The specific damage levels should be defined based on the actual post-earthquake damage scenarios observed. According to the research presented in this paper, by correlating the damage levels of building structures observed post-earthquake in specific seasons, it is possible to preliminarily predict the earthquake damage levels in other seasons.

### 3.1.2. Change Amplitude of Structural Response

From our analysis of the numerical simulation results, we propose Equation (1) to calculate the data, enhancing our understanding of how soil freezing impacts structures. This equation can be used to obtain the change amplitude of the maximum inter-story displacement angle of the structure under negative and positive temperatures.

$$R_{\frac{\Delta U_i}{h}} = \frac{\left| \frac{\Delta U_i}{h}(T_n) - \frac{\Delta U_i}{h}(T_p) \right|}{\frac{\Delta U_i}{h}(T_p)} \quad (1)$$

$$\Delta U_i = U_i - U_{i-1} \quad (2)$$

where $R_{\frac{\Delta U_i}{h}}$ is the change amplitude of maximum inter-story displacement angle, $\Delta U_i$ is the maximum inter-story displacement, $U_i$ is the displacement of the $i^{th}$ layer, $U_{i-1}$ is the displacement of the $(i-1)^{th}$ layer, $h$ is the story height, $T_n$ is the negative temperature, and $T_p$ is the positive temperature.

The processed data are summarized in Table 4.

Table 4 presents the change amplitude of the maximum inter-story displacement angle. As the ambient temperature drops to a negative value when there is a frozen soil layer, the maximum inter-story displacement angle of the structure decreases significantly compared with that of the non-frozen soil layer, whether the ground motion amplitude is 0.1 g or increased to 0.3 g. To better observe the amplitude of change, the proportion histogram is drawn as shown in Figure 5. Because the seismic response of the structure will fluctuate when the temperature of the frozen soil layer is different, different negative temperatures are considered as a whole for analysis here.

Figure 5 shows the proportion of change in the maximum inter-story displacement angle. When the ground motion amplitude is 0.1 g, the reduction amplitude on the first floor of the frame structure generally ranges from 20% to 50%, while for the entire structure, it varies from 20% to 40%. With an increase in ground motion amplitude by 0.3 g, the reduction amplitude of the first floor still accounts for between 20% to 50%. Simultaneously, the overall reduction amplitude of the structure accounts for between 10% to 30%. Moreover, it can be observed from Figure 5 that when the reduction amplitude is less than 10%, the proportion of the first floor is relatively small compared to the overall structure. This is because the first layer of the structure is in direct contact with the ground, and the surface temperature changes significantly affect the first floor, leading to a higher change amplitude.

When comparing the maximum inter-story displacement angle of the structure under negative temperature conditions, the change amplitude can be calculated from the data in Table 4. Since there is a fluctuation between negative temperatures, the increase and decrease are not considered here, and only the correlation between negative temperatures is considered. When comparing different negative temperatures with $-5\ °C$, it can be concluded that the proportion of change amplitude in the first layer of the structure is mostly less than 30%, and the overall proportion of the structure is mostly less than 20%. Compared with −10 °C, the proportion of change amplitude in the first layer is less than 20%, and the overall proportion of the structure is less than 10%.

**Table 4.** The change amplitude of maximum inter-story displacement angle (four-story structure).

| Seismic Wave | Floor | 0.1 g | | | | 0.3 g | | | |
|---|---|---|---|---|---|---|---|---|---|
| | | −5 °C | −10 °C | −15 °C | −20 °C | −5 °C | −10 °C | −15 °C | −20 °C |
| El-Centro | 1 | 0.2 | 0.43 | 0.39 | 0.43 | 0.25 | 0.44 | 0.36 | 0.32 |
| | 2 | 0.16 | 0.27 | 0.28 | 0.28 | 0.2 | 0.24 | 0.24 | 0.21 |
| | 3 | 0.17 | 0.27 | 0.3 | 0.31 | 0.21 | 0.26 | 0.23 | 0.21 |
| | 4 | 0.24 | 0.32 | 0.32 | 0.35 | 0.22 | 0.24 | 0.18 | 0.16 |
| | Average value | 19.25% | 32.25% | 32.25% | 34.25% | 22.00% | 29.50% | 25.25% | 22.50% |
| Kocaeli | 1 | 0.37 | 0.45 | 0.47 | 0.48 | 0.17 | 0.23 | 0.24 | 0.26 |
| | 2 | 0.38 | 0.40 | 0.42 | 0.44 | 0.26 | 0.35 | 0.40 | 0.42 |
| | 3 | 0.40 | 0.42 | 0.46 | 0.49 | 0.23 | 0.33 | 0.39 | 0.41 |
| | 4 | 0.41 | 0.42 | 0.44 | 0.45 | 0.24 | 0.29 | 0.40 | 0.41 |
| | Average value | 38.81% | 42.67% | 44.72% | 46.65% | 22.45% | 30.01% | 35.95% | 37.34% |
| Loma Prieta | 1 | 0.12 | 0.15 | 0.23 | 0.08 | 0.05 | 0.13 | 0.12 | 0.1 |
| | 2 | 0.01 | 0.09 | 0.16 | 0.06 | 0.12 | 0.16 | 0.19 | 0.18 |
| | 3 | 0 | 0.07 | 0.14 | 0.04 | 0.13 | 0.18 | 0.21 | 0.2 |
| | 4 | 0.01 | 0.07 | 0.14 | 0.01 | 0.15 | 0.2 | 0.22 | 0.21 |
| | Average value | 3.50% | 9.50% | 16.75% | 4.75% | 10.25% | 18.25% | 18.50% | 17.25% |
| Northridge | 1 | 0.18 | 0.31 | 0.31 | 0.21 | 0.23 | 0.42 | 0.48 | 0.5 |
| | 2 | 0.13 | 0.26 | 0.28 | 0.14 | 0.03 | 0.19 | 0.23 | 0.25 |
| | 3 | 0.13 | 0.35 | 0.38 | 0.23 | 0.11 | 0.2 | 0.29 | 0.28 |
| | 4 | 0.15 | 0.25 | 0.33 | 0.05 | 0.21 | 0.27 | 0.32 | 0.33 |
| | Average value | 14.75% | 29.25% | 32.50% | 15.75% | 14.50% | 27.00% | 33.00% | 34.00% |
| Concrete | 1 | 0.11 | 0.29 | 0.78 | 0.47 | 0.19 | 0.41 | 0.46 | 0.49 |
| | 2 | 0.06 | 0.21 | 0.66 | 0.47 | 0.08 | 0.23 | 0.28 | 0.31 |
| | 3 | 0.07 | 0.22 | 0.58 | 0.45 | 0.08 | 0.22 | 0.26 | 0.29 |
| | 4 | 0.08 | 0.22 | 0.59 | 0.39 | 0.08 | 0.21 | 0.24 | 0.27 |
| | Average value | 8.00% | 23.50% | 65.25% | 44.50% | 10.75% | 26.75% | 31.00% | 34.00% |
| Kobe | 1 | 0.2 | 0.4 | 0.34 | 0.47 | 0.38 | 0.37 | 0.31 | 0.27 |
| | 2 | 0.01 | 0.19 | 0.17 | 0.33 | 0.06 | 0.08 | 0.08 | 0.11 |
| | 3 | 0.01 | 0.21 | 0.18 | 0.34 | 0.12 | 0.13 | 0.13 | 0.14 |
| | 4 | 0.01 | 0.23 | 0.18 | 0.36 | 0.13 | 0.09 | 0.07 | 0.08 |
| | Average value | 5.75% | 25.75% | 21.75% | 37.50% | 17.28% | 16.48% | 14.70% | 14.86% |
| Shanghai | 1 | 0.24 | 0.4 | 0.35 | 0.36 | 0.32 | 0.41 | 0.41 | 0.41 |
| | 2 | 0.16 | 0.32 | 0.25 | 0.28 | 0.28 | 0.21 | 0.15 | 0.12 |
| | 3 | 0.17 | 0.32 | 0.26 | 0.29 | 0.31 | 0.25 | 0.18 | 0.15 |
| | 4 | 0.19 | 0.33 | 0.25 | 0.28 | 0.32 | 0.28 | 0.2 | 0.17 |
| | Average value | 19.00% | 34.25% | 27.75% | 30.25% | 30.75% | 28.75% | 23.50% | 21.25% |
| San Francisco | 1 | 0.37 | 0.34 | 0.53 | 0.65 | 0.2 | 0.25 | 0.52 | 0.29 |
| | 2 | 0.51 | 0.29 | 0.56 | 0.8 | 0.14 | 0.16 | 0.5 | 0.16 |
| | 3 | 0.57 | 0.16 | 0.48 | 0.82 | 0.05 | 0.22 | 0.64 | 0.37 |
| | 4 | 0.49 | 0.13 | 0.46 | 0.72 | 0.01 | 0.17 | 0.63 | 0.27 |
| | Average value | 48.50% | 23.00% | 50.75% | 74.75% | 10.00% | 20.00% | 57.25% | 27.25% |
| QianAn | 1 | 0.18 | 0.2 | 0.44 | 0.43 | 0.3 | 0.44 | 0.49 | 0.45 |
| | 2 | 0.15 | 0.26 | 0.54 | 0.62 | 0.19 | 0.3 | 0.36 | 0.32 |
| | 3 | 0.16 | 0.34 | 0.51 | 0.73 | 0.19 | 0.26 | 0.36 | 0.35 |
| | 4 | 0.15 | 0.35 | 0.52 | 0.6 | 0.21 | 0.3 | 0.44 | 0.31 |
| | Average value | 16.00% | 28.75% | 50.25% | 59.50% | 22.25% | 32.50% | 41.25% | 35.75% |
| Tangshan | 1 | 0.21 | 0.44 | 0.46 | 0.48 | 0.29 | 0.47 | 0.48 | 0.47 |
| | 2 | 0.01 | 0.14 | 0.12 | 0.15 | 0.29 | 0.12 | 0.09 | 0.03 |
| | 3 | 0.01 | 0.19 | 0.17 | 0.19 | 0.3 | 0.13 | 0.11 | 0.04 |
| | 4 | 0.01 | 0.18 | 0.18 | 0.19 | 0.29 | 0.13 | 0.1 | 0.1 |
| | Average value | 6.00% | 23.75% | 23.25% | 25.25% | 29.25% | 21.25% | 19.50% | 16.00% |
| Tianjing | 1 | 0.27 | 0.29 | 0.33 | 0.7 | 0.38 | 0.46 | 0.48 | 0.49 |
| | 2 | 0.25 | 0.21 | 0.26 | 0.62 | 0.14 | 0.19 | 0.21 | 0.22 |
| | 3 | 0.26 | 0.21 | 0.25 | 0.6 | 0.13 | 0.19 | 0.19 | 0.22 |
| | 4 | 0.25 | 0.2 | 0.25 | 0.66 | 0.13 | 0.18 | 0.19 | 0.21 |
| | Average value | 25.75% | 22.75% | 27.25% | 64.50% | 19.50% | 25.50% | 26.75% | 28.50% |
| Taft | 1 | 0.37 | 0.39 | 0.35 | 0.25 | 0.37 | 0.49 | 0.38 | 0.28 |
| | 2 | 0.24 | 0.32 | 0.3 | 0.19 | 0.23 | 0.34 | 0.24 | 0.19 |
| | 3 | 0.2 | 0.31 | 0.29 | 0.21 | 0.27 | 0.36 | 0.25 | 0.2 |
| | 4 | 0.23 | 0.31 | 0.29 | 0.28 | 0.3 | 0.36 | 0.25 | 0.19 |
| | Average value | 26.00% | 33.25% | 30.75% | 23.25% | 29.25% | 38.75% | 28.00% | 21.50% |

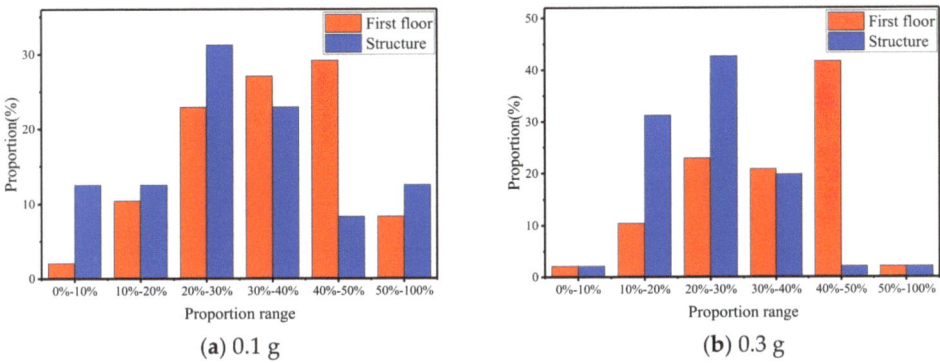

**(a)** 0.1 g  **(b)** 0.3 g

**Figure 5.** Proportion of change in maximum inter-story displacement angle (four-story).

### 3.1.3. Structural Damage

This paper provides a detailed analysis of the tensile and compressive damage to the four-story frame structure and assesses the damage under different temperature conditions. As there are many working conditions involved in this study, only the damage effect diagram of the structure is shown here under two ground motions, as shown in Figure 6.

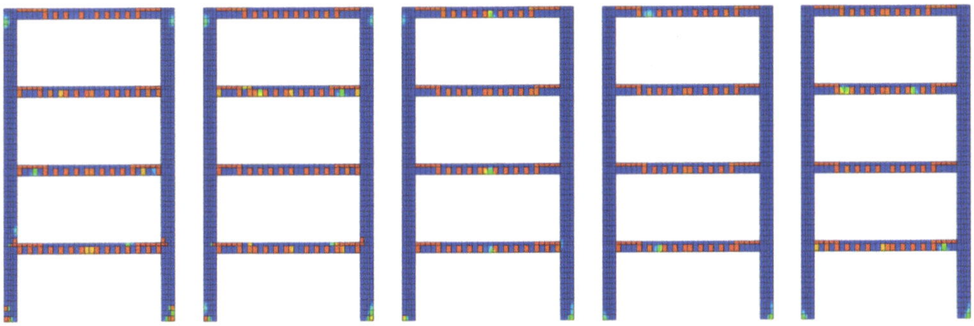

| 23 °C | −5 °C | −10 °C | −15 °C | −20 °C |

**(a)** Tensile damage (El-Centro)

| 23 °C | −5 °C | −10 °C | −15 °C | −20 °C |

**(b)** Tensile damage (Kobe)

**Figure 6.** *Cont.*

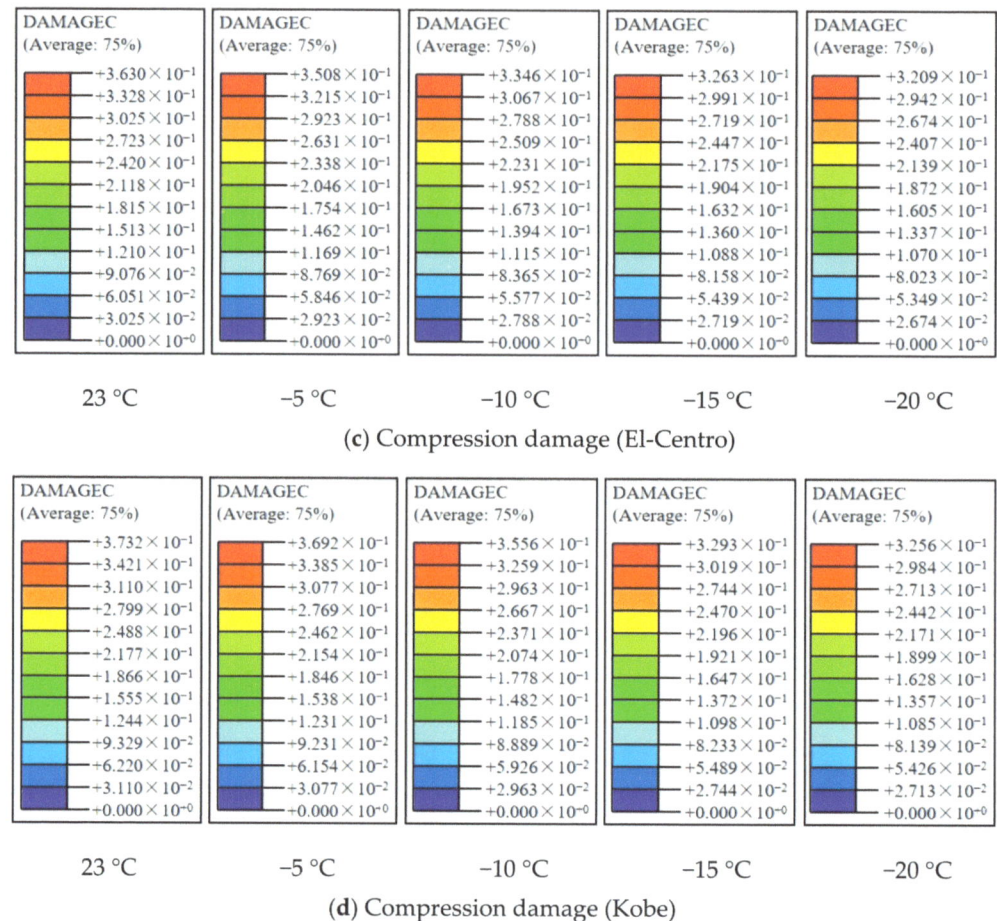

**Figure 6.** Tensile damage and compression damage to the four-story frame structure.

Figure 6a,b show the tensile damage to the structure, and Figure 6c,d show the compression damage to the structure.

As for the evaluation criteria of tensile damage, the tensile damage factors shown in the nephogram are the same. Under the same damage factors, the damage status of the structure can be intuitively seen through the tensile damage nephogram of the structure. Figure 6a,b demonstrate significant tensile damage at the base of the first-floor columns at normal temperatures, with similar damage evident at the top of the first-floor columns and the base of the second-floor columns. For the beam part, the tensile damage area of the structure at normal temperature is more significant than that at negative temperature. In summary, the tensile damage to the structure at normal temperature is more severe than that at negative temperature. For the damage to the structure under different negative temperatures, carefully observe Figure 6a,b. From the tensile damage area of the structural column bottom and beam, it can be seen that the tensile damage to the structure will gradually decrease with the decrease in temperature. For some ground motions, the tensile damage will fluctuate when the temperature reaches −10 °C. This is because when the temperature decreases to a certain extent, the content of ice crystals in the frozen soil layer will not change significantly. At the same time, the degree of cementation between soil particles and ice crystals will also tend to be stable. This change will directly affect the superstructure so that the damage will fluctuate due to different ground motions.

When evaluating compression damage, the structural compression damage cloud diagram does not directly indicate the damage status, so the degree of damage is defined by the compression damage factor. As shown in Figure 6c,d, it can be seen from the cloud diagram that the compression damage to the structure occurs at the beam end. For the compression damage, the closer the compression damage factor is to 1, the more serious the damage is. By observing the magnitude of the compression damage factor, it can be concluded that for the El-Centro seismic wave, the maximum compression damage factor of the structure at normal temperature is 0.363, 0.3508 at $-5\ °C$, 0.3346 at $-10\ °C$, 0.3263 at $-15\ °C$, and 0.3209 at $-20\ °C$. For the Kobe seismic wave, the maximum compression damage factor of the structure at normal temperature is 0.3732, 0.3692 at $-5\ °C$, 0.3293 at $-10\ °C$, 0.3556 at $-15\ °C$, and 0.3256 at $-20\ °C$. It can be concluded that the compression damage factor of the structure at normal temperature is significantly greater than that at negative temperature. That is, the compression damage to the structure at normal temperature is more serious. Concerning the compression damage to the structure at various negative temperatures, the data indicate that at $-10\ °C$, the structure's compression damage is significantly less than that at $-5\ °C$ and normal temperatures. When the temperature continues to drop, the amplitude of the change in the compression damage factor will decrease. The structural compression damage fluctuates after the temperature reaches $-10\ °C$ under some ground motions, and the principle is similar to the tensile damage.

Analysis of the damage reveals that structural damage, from both compression and tension, is more severe at normal temperatures than at negative temperatures. This indicates that seismic damage to the four-story frame structure under negative temperatures is significantly less than that under normal temperatures. The extent of seismic damage varies at different negative temperatures, with $-5\ °C$ resulting in either similar or significantly different damage compared to normal temperatures. The reason for this is that the water in the soil does not completely freeze, resulting in an unstable ice crystal structure that is more susceptible to external factors. Therefore, there are two distinct scenarios. At $-10\ °C$, all water molecules in the soil freeze into ice crystals, leading to significant differences between the seismic damage at normal temperature and that at $-10\ °C$. As the temperature drops further, the impact of temperature on the seismic damage to the structure becomes less significant.

*3.2. Seismic Response of Sixteen-Story Frame Structure*

3.2.1. Structural Response

Numerical simulation was used to obtain the changes in the maximum inter-story displacement angle in response to seismic damage for a sixteen-story frame structure. The obtained data indicate that the environmental temperature has a significant impact on the structural damage resulting from seismic activity. To better visualize the changing trend of the maximum inter-story displacement angle, the data obtained from numerical simulation are plotted in Figure 7.

Figure 7a shows that the ground motion amplitude is 0.1 g. The maximum inter-story displacement angle of the structure is smaller when the ambient temperature is negative compared to normal temperature. At $-5\ °C$, the maximum inter-story displacement angle is significantly reduced compared to the normal temperature. At $-10\ °C$, there will still be some differences in the change in the maximum inter-story displacement angle of the structure, but the amplitude is smaller than that at $-5\ °C$ and normal temperature. As the temperature continues to decrease and reaches $-15\ °C$ and $-20\ °C$, the change in maximum inter-story displacement angle of the structure becomes very small. From Figure 7a, it is also clear that for the sixteen-story frame structure, the change in the maximum inter-story displacement angle between different negative temperatures is more regular than for the four-story frame structure, with less fluctuation. This consistency is due to the significant dead weight of the sixteen-story frame structure, which increases downward pressure and friction between the piles and the soil, thereby enhancing stability. At $-5\ °C$, the mechanical parameters of the soil will undergo significant changes compared to positive temperatures, leading to a significant difference in the maximum inter-story displacement angle. As the temperature decreases, various mechanical parameters of the soil continue to change, but the lower the temperature, the smaller the trend. At this time, with increasing self-weight of the upper structure, the environmental temperature will have a smaller impact on it, resulting in a smaller difference in the maximum inter-story displacement angle of the sixteen-story structure under different negative temperature conditions.

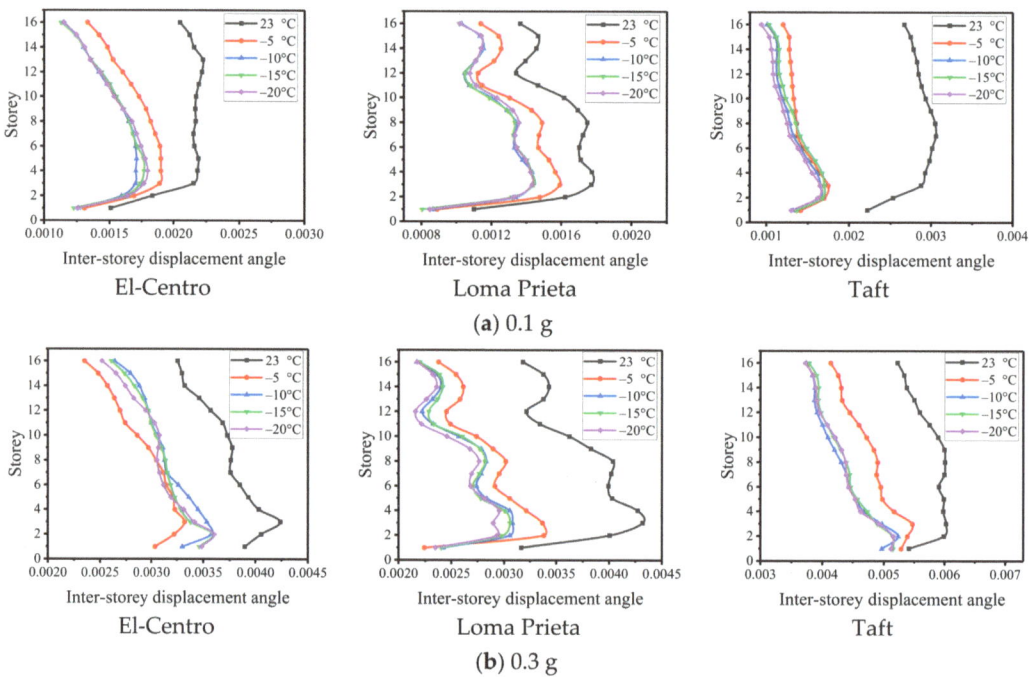

**Figure 7.** Maximum inter-story displacement angle of sixteen-story frame structure.

When the ground motion amplitude is 0.3 g, it can be seen from Figure 7b that the variation law of the maximum inter-story displacement angle under different ground motions will have certain differences. Furthermore, structural damage under certain ground motions fluctuates significantly with temperature changes. This fluctuation is due to enhanced ground motion, which likely causes cliff-type damage within the interactions of soil particles, water, and ice crystals in the frozen soil. At the same time, the longitudinal dimension of the structure is high. The fluctuation will produce a flexible swing phenomenon with the increase in floors. The higher the floors are, the less impact the frozen soil layer will have, leading to large fluctuations. However, the rule is evident for the bottom layer of the structure. The maximum inter-story displacement angle of the structure's bottom layer is significantly smaller at negative temperatures than at normal temperatures. This is because the bottom layer directly contacts the ground through the piles, which are greatly affected by the soil layer.

3.2.2. Change Amplitude of Structural Response

From Figure 7, it can be seen that for high-rise structures, although the maximum inter-story displacement angle of the structure will exhibit varying degrees of flexible oscillation with the increase in floors under different environmental temperatures, it can be seen that the maximum inter-story displacement angle of the structure is significantly greater at positive temperatures than at negative temperatures. To compare the seismic damage to high-rise structures in different seasons, Equation (1) can also be used to calculate the amplitude of maximum inter-story displacement angle changes under positive and negative temperatures. Due to the large amount of data and occupying a considerable amount of space, the average values of the calculated data were taken. The results are shown in Table 5.

Table 5. The change amplitude of maximum inter-story displacement angle (sixteen-story structure).

| Seismic Wave | Position | 0.1 g | | | | 0.3 g | | | |
|---|---|---|---|---|---|---|---|---|---|
| | | −5 °C | −10 °C | −15 °C | −20 °C | −5 °C | −10 °C | −15 °C | −20 °C |
| El-Centro | First floor | 13.13% | 16.45% | 18.44% | 16.45% | 21.96% | 15.25% | 11.15% | 10.37% |
| | Entire structure | 20.00% | 28.00% | 27.56% | 26.81% | 22.00% | 15.88% | 16.69% | 17.63% |
| Loma Prieta | First floor | 19.09% | 21.52% | 26.97% | 23.03% | 29.34% | 23.66% | 24.29% | 25.87% |
| | Entire structure | 14.75% | 21.94% | 22.50% | 21.38% | 24.38% | 29.31% | 29.25% | 31.31% |
| Taft | First floor | 36.49% | 40.54% | 38.29% | 41.44% | 2.40% | 8.32% | 4.81% | 5.36% |
| | Entire structure | 49.88% | 53.75% | 51.94% | 55.19% | 16.63% | 25.06% | 24.19% | 24.50% |

Upon analyzing Table 5, it can be concluded that when the ground motion amplitude is 0.1 g and the temperature drops to negative values, the maximum inter-story displacement angle change of the overall structure will be greatly reduced. For the overall structure, the inter-story displacement angle decreases by up to 50% at negative temperatures compared to positive temperatures. For the first floor of the structure, the maximum reduction can reach 40%. When the ground motion amplitude is 0.3 g, the overall reduction of the structure can reach a maximum of 30%, with the first floor experiencing a maximum reduction of 20%. It is evident that high-rise structures are highly sensitive to environmental temperature changes; thus, seasonal variations must be fully considered in structural design.

Based on the simulation results of this paper, it is concluded that changes in environmental temperature caused by seasonal changes will significantly affect the damage to structures after earthquakes. Whether it is a multi-layer structure or a high-rise structure, this impact cannot be ignored. Figure 5 in this paper shows that the reduction in damage to structures after earthquakes under negative temperatures is mostly between 20% and 50% compared to that under positive temperatures. In light of this, we propose incorporating this conclusion into the design of the structure, based on the original seismic code. When building structures under negative temperatures, it is possible to accurately predict the damage to the structure following an earthquake at positive temperatures, thereby enhancing the design details of the structure based on the original design and guaranteeing its safety. When building structures under positive temperatures, it is possible to adjust the structural design to ensure the economic efficiency of the building structure.

## 4. Conclusions

In this paper, using the numerical simulation software ABAQUS, a detailed analysis of frozen soil–structure interaction is conducted for a four-story frame structure and a sixteen-story frame structure, respectively, and the earthquake damage under different ambient temperatures and different earthquake intensities is obtained. The following conclusions were drawn:

(1) For the frame structure under the ground motion of 0.1 g and 0.3 g, the structure's maximum inter-story displacement angle in the presence of frozen soil layer is significantly reduced compared to the case without frozen soil layer.
(2) When the ambient temperature is −5 °C, the seismic damage to the structure fluctuates wildly and will be close to that at the normal temperature and the lower negative temperature. When the ambient temperature is −10 °C, −15 °C, or −20 °C, the damage levels fluctuate relative to each other.
(3) For the first floor of a four-story frame structure, when the temperature drops below 0 °C, the maximum inter-story displacement angle reduction amplitude is mostly between 20 and 50%. For the overall structure, the reduction amplitude is mainly between 20 and 40%. When the ground motion amplitude is increased to 0.3 g, the reduction amplitude of the first floor is also between 20 and 50%, and that for the overall structure is between 10 and 30%.

(4) For the sixteen-story frame structure, when the temperature drops below 0 °C, the first floor's maximum inter-story displacement angle reduction amplitude can reach 40%. For the overall structure, the reduction amplitude can reach 50%.

(5) When the ambient temperature is negative, the tensile damage and compression damage to the frame structure are relatively minor. When the ambient temperature is positive, the damage will be more serious. The tensile damage to the structure mainly occurs at the column end (more severe at the bottom) and the whole beam, while the compressive damage to the structure mainly occurs at the beam end.

(6) By analyzing the evolutionary patterns of damage status of the structure in the sequence of seasonal changes in spring, summer, autumn, and winter, it is observed that the damage status demonstrates an increasing trend followed by a decreasing trend.

**Author Contributions:** X.B.: Conceptualization, Methodology, Validation, Software, Writing—original draft. G.W.: Methodology, Writing—review and editing, Supervision, Funding acquisition. All authors have read and agreed to the published version of the manuscript.

**Funding:** This work was supported by the National Key Research and Development Program of China [2018YFD1100405].

**Data Availability Statement:** Data generated or analyzed during this study are available from the corresponding author upon reasonable request.

**Conflicts of Interest:** The authors declare there are no conflicts of interest.

# References

1. Guo, D.M. Preliminary analysis of the impact field and seismic geological conditions of the 1986 Dedu earthquake. *Northeast. Seismol. Res.* **1987**, *3*, 57–68.
2. Zhang, F.M.; Yi, F.L. Source parameters of Dedu moderate earthquake of Heilongjiang province in 1986. *Seismol. Res. Northeast China* **1995**, *11*, 34–38.
3. Liu, H.X.; Sun, Y.F.; Chen, Y.M.; Xu, X.Y.; Yin, Y.H. Influence of seasonally frozen ground on the seismic damages of buildings. *J. Glaciol. Geocryol.* **1998**, *20*, 46–50.
4. Wu, L.B.; Qi, W.; Niu, F.J.; Niu, Y.H. A review of studies on roadbed frozen damage and countermeasures in seasonal frozen ground regions in China. *J. Glaciol. Geocryol.* **2015**, *37*, 1283–1293.
5. Osama, A.; Sameer, A.D. Comparison of solar thermal and solar electric space heating and cooling systems for buildings in different climatic regions. *Sol. Energy* **2019**, *11*, 545–560.
6. Li, N.; Chen, B.; Chen, F.; Xu, X. The coupled heat-moisture-mechanic model of the frozen soil. *Cold Reg. Sci. Technol.* **2000**, *31*, 199–205. [CrossRef]
7. Evans, S.G.; Ge, S.; Voss, C.I.; Molotch, N.P. The role of frozen soil in groundwater discharge predictions for warming alpine watersheds. *Water Resour. Res.* **2018**, *54*, 1599–1615. [CrossRef]
8. Zhang, Z.Q.; Wu, Q.B.; Xun, X.Y.; Wang, B.X.; Xu, N. Climate change and the distribution of frozen soil in 1980–2010 in northern northeast China. *Quat. Int.* **2018**, *467*, 203–241. [CrossRef]
9. Chen, S.S.; Zang, S.Y.; Sun, L. Permafrost degradation in northeast China and its environmental effects: Present situation and prospect. *J. Glaciol. Geocryol.* **2018**, *40*, 298–306.
10. Tan, L.; Wei, C.F.; Tian, H.H.; Zhou, J.Z.; Wei, H.Z. Experimental study of unfrozen water content of frozen soils by low-field nuclear magnetic resonance. *Rock Soil Mech.* **2015**, *36*, 1566–1572.
11. Ladanyi, B. An engineering theory of creep of frozen soils. *Can. Geotech. J.* **1972**, *9*, 63–80. [CrossRef]
12. Chamberlain, E.; Groves, C.; Perham, R. The mechanical behaviour of frozen earth materials under high pressure triaxial test conditions. *Geotechnique* **1972**, *23*, 136–147. [CrossRef]
13. Zhu, Y.; Carbee, D.L. Uniaxial compressive strength of frozen silt under constant deformation rates. *Cold Reg. Sci. Technol.* **1984**, *9*, 3–15. [CrossRef]
14. Wu, Z.J.; Ma, W.; Wang, L.M.; Cheng, J.J.; Feng, W.J. Laboratory study on the effect of temperature and confining pressure on strength of frozen soil under seismic dynamic loading. *J. Glaciol. Geocryol.* **2003**, *25*, 648–652.
15. Li, X.L.; Wang, H.J.; Zou, S.J.; Ma, H.C.; Niu, Y.H. Research state of deformation characteristics of frozen soil under cyclic loading and problems in frozen soil excavation. *J. Glaciol. Geocryol.* **2017**, *39*, 92–101.
16. Wang, R.M.; Ma, Q.Y. Experimental analysis of the influence of freezing time on compressive strength of frozen silty clay. *J. Anhui Univ. Sci. Technol. (Nat. Sci.)* **2019**, *39*, 74–79.
17. Toki, K.; Miura, F. Non-linear seismic response analysis of soil-structure interaction systems. *Earthq. Eng. Struct. Dyn.* **1983**, *11*, 77–89. [CrossRef]

18. Makris, N.; Badoni, D.; Delis, E.; Gazetas, G. Prediction of observed bridge response with soil-pile-structure interaction. *J. Struct. Eng.* **1994**, *120*, 2992–3011. [CrossRef]
19. Wijaya, P.K. Boundary element model coupled with finite element model for dynamic soil-pile interaction. In Proceedings of the 2009 Third Asia International Conference on Modelling and Simulation, Bundang, Indonesia, 25–29 May 2009; pp. 491–496.
20. Ilaria, V.; Diana, S.; Claudio, T. The effect of soil-foundation-structure interaction on the wind-induced response of tall buildings. *Eng. Struct.* **2014**, *7*, 117–130.
21. Renzi, S.; Madiai, C.; Vannucchi, G. A simplified empirical method for assessing seismic soil-structure interaction effects on ordinary shear-type buildings. *Soil Dyn. Earthq. Eng.* **2013**, *55*, 100–107. [CrossRef]
22. Zhang, Y.X.; Wang, X.X.; Zhuang, H.Y. Fine numerical modeling of nonlinear soil-pile-frame structure interaction system and its verification. *J. Disaster Prev. Mitig. Eng.* **2010**, *30*, 558–566.
23. Xu, J. *Seismic Response Analysis of Transmission Tower-Line System Considering SSI*; Dalian University of Technology: Dalian, China, 2008.
24. Jendoubi, A.; Legeron, F. Effect of the dynamic soil-structure interaction on rigid transmission line towers subjected to wind and impulse loads. *Electr. Transm. Substation Struct.* **2012**, *27*, 250–261.
25. Ma, M.J. *The Seismic Performance Simulation Analysis of the Irregular of Castle Hotel of Dalian Considering the SSI Effect*; Liaoning Technical University: Fuxin, China, 2013.
26. Mi, P. *Adverse Impact on Seismic Performance Analysis of Frame Structure Considering Soil-Structure Interaction*; Guangzhou University: Guangzhou, China, 2016.
27. Forcellini, D. Seismic assessment of a benchmark based isolated ordinary building with soil structure interaction. *Bull. Earthq. Eng.* **2017**, *12*, 2021–2042. [CrossRef]
28. Forcellini, D. Cost assessment of isolation technique applied to a benchmark bridge with soil structure interaction. *Bull. Earthq. Eng.* **2016**, *15*, 51–69. [CrossRef]
29. Zhao, C.; Valliappan, S. A dynamic infinite element for three-dimensional infinite-domain wave problems. *Int. J. Numer. Methods Eng.* **1993**, *36*, 2567–2580. [CrossRef]
30. Jiang, X.L.; Xu, Y.; Zheng, G. Finite element and infinite element coupling method for seismic analysis of soil-underground tunnel system. *Earthq. Eng. Eng. Vib.* **1999**, *19*, 22–26.
31. Nielsen, A.H. Towards a complete framework for seismic analysis in ABAQUS. *Eng. Comput. Mech.* **2014**, *167*, 3–12. [CrossRef]
32. Deeks, A.J.; Randolph, M.F. Axisymmetric time-domain transmitting boundaries. *J. Eng. Mech.* **1994**, *120*, 25–42. [CrossRef]
33. Liu, J.B.; Wang, Z.Y.; Du, X.L.; Du, Y.X. Three-dimensional visco-elastic artificial boundaries in time domain for wave motion problems. *Eng. Mech.* **2005**, *22*, 46–51.
34. Bian, X.Y.; Wang, G.X.; Li, Y.D. Experimental research on dynamic characteristics of frozen clay considering seasonal variation. *Geomech. Eng.* **2024**, *36*, 391–406.
35. Li, Z.Q.; Du, C.B.; Ai, Y.M. Effect of radiation damping on seismic response of structures. *J. Hohai Univ. (Nat. Sci.)* **2009**, *37*, 400–404.
36. Huang, S.; Chen, W.Z.; Wu, G.J.; Guo, X.H.; Qiao, C.J. Study of method of earthquake input in aseismic analysis for underground engineering. *Chin. J. Rock Mech. Eng.* **2010**, *29*, 1254–1262.
37. Song, J.K.; Liu, Z.X.; Zhou, X.J. Analysis of the nonlinear earthquake responses of the Hong Kong-Zhuhai-Macao immersed tunnel. *Chin. J. Undergr. Space Eng.* **2015**, *11*, 323–331.
38. Cai, M.F.; Qiao, L. *Geostress Measurement Principle and Technology*; Science Press: Beijing, China, 1995.
39. Dai, R.L.; Li, Z.F.; Wang, J. Research on initial geo-stress balance method based on ABAQUS. *J. Chongqing Technol. Bus. Univ. (Nat. Sci. Ed.)* **2012**, *9*, 76–81.

**Disclaimer/Publisher's Note:** The statements, opinions and data contained in all publications are solely those of the individual author(s) and contributor(s) and not of MDPI and/or the editor(s). MDPI and/or the editor(s) disclaim responsibility for any injury to people or property resulting from any ideas, methods, instructions or products referred to in the content.

# Investigating Large-Scale Tuned Liquid Dampers through Real-Time Hybrid Simulations

Ali Ashasi Sorkhabi [1,*], Barry Qiu [2] and Oya Mercan [2]

1 BBA Consultants, 99 Great Gulf Dr Unit #2, Concord, ON L4K 5W1, Canada
2 Department of Civil Engineering, University of Toronto, 35 St. George Street, Toronto, ON M5S 1A4, Canada
* Correspondence: ali.ashasi@bba.ca

**Abstract:** As buildings become taller and slenderer, managing their vibrational response and mitigating it pose significant challenges in design. Tuned liquid dampers (TLDs) are liquid (usually water)-filled tanks that can mitigate structural vibrations by leveraging the sloshing motion of the contained fluid. However, the dynamic behavior of TLDs and their interaction with structures is complex. While most research on TLDs has focused on mitigating wind-induced vibrations, less attention has been paid to their seismic control of structural responses. Moreover, existing literature on the experimental research involving TLDs mostly pertains to small-scale models. This study aims to experimentally explore the effectiveness of large-scale TLDs in mitigating vibrations in both linear and nonlinear structures under seismic loads. A real-time hybrid simulation is employed as the experimental method, where only the TLD is physically constructed and tested, while the rest of the system is simulated numerically in a coupled manner, allowing for obtaining the dynamic response of the structure equipped with the TLD in real time. This approach offers the flexibility to significantly scale up the TLD size for physical testing while exploring various TLD-structure scenarios by numerically adjusting the structural properties within the simulation.

**Keywords:** tuned liquid dampers; experimental testing; real-time hybrid simulation; seismic response; nonlinear structures

## 1. Introduction

In recent years, there has been a notable shift in the architectural landscape toward the construction of high-rise buildings. These structures are typically characterized by their slender and flexible design, often exhibiting low damping properties. As a result, engineers have been compelled to seek effective and cost-efficient methods to manage the vibrations of these buildings. As a response, several passive energy dissipators have been introduced to control hazards associated with tall buildings under dynamic loads, such as wind or seismic forces. Examples of these devices include friction dampers [1], tuned liquid dampers [2,3], viscoelastic dampers [4], metallic dampers [5], shape memory alloy-based reusable hysteretic dampers [6], and magneto-rheological fluid dampers [7,8].

Tuned liquid dampers have gained significant attention due to their minimal maintenance requirements, cost-effectiveness, and ease of installation [9,10]. As TLDs only require the liquid itself and a tank for which they can slosh inside, water storage tanks in high-rise structures can be repurposed into a TLD or serve dual functionality [9]. This allows for space saving and without the need to perform extensive remodeling to improve a building's structural system [9]. In comparison to other damping systems, such as tuned mass dampers (TMDs), TLDs offer advantages, such as easier control over the natural frequency of a building [10], and may be more cost effective as TMDs generally require more work and materials to implement in structures [11]. TLDs are supplemental devices designed to mitigate the effects of dynamic forces, such as wind or seismic loads, on buildings. TLDs work by utilizing a sloshing liquid mass inside a container, which is tuned to oscillate at the same frequency as the frequency of the structure. This synchronized motion helps to dissipate energy and reduce the amplitude of vibrations, thereby improving the overall stability and safety of the structure. When a TLD undergoes a high-amplitude motion, the horizontal component of liquid velocity, associated with wave motion, causes wave crests to descend as the amplitude rises. This phenomenon is referred to as wave breaking [12]. As wave breaking occurs, simple linear models become inadequate to describe the liquid behavior, and the sloshing frequency of the liquid is altered [12]. Furthermore, this complex nonlinear effect impacts the shear force at the interface of the TLD with the structure, which opposes the structure's motion, posing challenges for accurate modeling.

The mass ratio (MR), defined as the ratio of water mass to structural mass, significantly impacts the TLD-structure system's performance. Existing literature suggests mass ratios ranging from 1% [13,14] to 4% [15], yet experimental validation for higher ratios remains sparse, with previous studies predominantly relying on numerical simulations. TLDs, with lower mass ratios, can effectively reduce structural displacement and acceleration without significantly adding to system inertia. Furthermore, the liquid sloshing frequency plays a crucial role in TLD behavior. Experimental findings [13,16] indicate optimal TLD effectiveness when the liquid frequency aligns closely with the excitation frequency, reaching resonance with the tank motion. However, past studies provide limited and scattered data on these influential parameters.

Several configurations of TLDs (e.g., rectangular, cylindrical, annular, and column-shaped) have been proposed and studied by researchers around the world. Most studies on TLDs have primarily concentrated on mitigating wind-induced vibrations in structures, with comparatively less attention paid to employing them for the seismic control of structural responses. More recently, researchers have begun to explore the effectiveness of these dampers in mitigating vibrations of structures under seismic loads [17–19].

The application of rectangular TLDs to mitigate the seismic response of structures was studied analytically and, in some cases, experimentally (on a small scale) by Banerji et al. [15], Malekghasemi et al. [20], Novo et al. [21], Rai et al. [22], Shad et al. [23], and Wang et al. [24]. Also, Jin et al. [25] studied the effectiveness of cylindrical TLDs as a passive control device to improve the seismic response of offshore platforms. Gaemmaghami et al. [26,27] numerically evaluated the performance of annular liquid tanks as a variant of TLDs in the vibration mitigation of wind turbines due to earthquake loads. Additionally, the seismic performance of tuned liquid column dampers (TLCDs) was investigated experimentally on a small scale by Zhu et al. [28].

Understandably, there is a lack of studies/discussion on nonlinear structures equipped with TLDs. This is because it can become quite costly and time-consuming to build and test nonlinear structures as the experiment can only be run once and a new specimen must be built to run the test again. However, in recent years, some effort has been put into characterizing the effectiveness of TLDs in nonlinear structures, such as the work by Das and Choudhury [29]. Das and Choudhury investigated the performance of a quarter-scale reinforced concrete building equipped with a TLD [29]. More research into nonlinear substructure models is important as buildings may not always stay within the elastic range. With the use of the testing methodology employed here (i.e., real-time hybrid simulation), since the nonlinear structure can be modeled numerically, it allows for a much more cost-effective method of investigating the performance of TLDs placed onto structures that experience nonlinear behavior.

The size of TLDs that are investigated in a laboratory is generally governed by the size of the test equipment available to the researcher(s), for example the size of the shake table available. However, the scale effect of structures and liquid dampers can have a significant impact on the behavior and performance, as noted by Wang et al. [24]. This aspect is further confirmed by Zhu et al. [30] in their investigation of the size effects of TLDs in RTHS tests. They reached the conclusion that downsized models tend to overstate the effectiveness of TLDs, emphasizing the need for full-scale experiments to obtain more accurate results [30].

## 2. Objectives

As mentioned in the Introduction Section, there is a sparse inventory of the experimental data on the performance of TLDs. It is mostly focused on wind applications and limited to only experiments on the interaction of small-scale TLD-structure setups that is feasible in the lab environment. Also, more research into nonlinear substructure models is crucial, as buildings may not always remain within the elastic range.

This study aims to experimentally investigate the performance of large-scale TLDs in suppressing the vibrations of both linear and nonlinear structures under seismic loading. This is carried out using a state-of-the-art experimental testing method, namely a real-time hybrid simulation (RTHS), where only the TLD is built and tested physically, and the rest of the system is simulated numerically. This testing method provides the flexibility to significantly increase the TLD size as the sole physically tested component of the setup. Additionally, it allows for the consideration of various TLD-structure scenarios by numerically altering the structural properties within the computer program. Utilizing the RTHS, which allows the nonlinear structure to be modeled numerically, offers a cost-effective method for investigating the performance of TLDs in structures that exhibit nonlinear behavior. The RTHS experiments are conducted using the computational/control platform that was previously developed and verified by the authors at the University of Toronto [31].

To the best of the authors' knowledge, the TLD studied in this paper is the largest TLD that was coupled with the response of a nonlinear structure at the time of the experiments. The total mass of the TLD tested in this study is nearly 600 kg, while previously tested TLDs were in the range of 60 to 200 kg [24,32–35].

Given its comparable size to TLDs used in real-world applications, the findings from this study offer a more accurate and realistic insight into the interaction between TLDs and structures, including linear and nonlinear structural responses. Additionally, the experimental data obtained could be instrumental in refining existing analytical models for more dependable performance predictions of TLDs.

## 3. Real-Time Hybrid-Simulation Experimental Setup

*3.1. Methodology: Real-Time Hybrid Simulation (RTHS)*

In a hybrid simulation, as an experimental testing method, physical testing is combined with a numerical simulation. This technique is, in fact, considered a variation in the traditional pseudo-dynamic testing (PSD) method [36]. In this approach, the structure being tested is divided into two parts. The experimental substructure includes critical components of the structure that either lack a reliable analytical model or are difficult to accurately simulate using computer models. These components are physically tested in a laboratory setting. The analytical substructure comprises the remaining portion of the structure, which is simulated using computer models and analyzed numerically. By combining physical testing with computer simulation, hybrid testing allows researchers to study the behavior of complex structures more effectively and accurately [37].

If the test structure possesses properties that are dependent on the rate of loading, the experiments must be carried out in real time. This facilitates an accurate representation of the structure's dynamic behavior and ensures the effective capture of load-rate-dependent characteristics [38–40]. The RTHS relies heavily on robust and effective computational resources and well-synchronized data communication [40]. The RTHS involves physically testing only critical components of the structures, while modeling the rest analytically. This approach enables the cost-effective and timely consideration of various influential parameters, loading scenarios, and structural configurations [41]. As a result, by employing the RTHS method, the dynamic performance of complex structures, including passive, active, and semi-active control devices, such as base isolators, tuned liquid, mass, and magneto-rheological dampers [20,42], can be accurately assessed. In this study, the RTHS method is adopted to experimentally investigate the performance of large-scale TLDs installed on linear and nonlinear structures subjected to seismic loading.

## 3.2. Mechanical Setup for Tests

This study utilized a 2.0 m × 1.5 m uniaxial shaking table with a 1.5-ton payload to move the large-scale TLD during the RTHS experiments. The shaking table simulated the roof floor of the test structure, and replicated real-life roof displacements. It was powered by a servo hydraulic actuation system, which included a hydraulic service manifold (HSM) capable of a continuous flow rate of 450 L/min (120 gpm) at a pressure of 20 mPa (3000 psi). Two fatigue-rated hydraulic actuators with a stroke length of ±127 mm (±5 inches) and a maximum force capacity of ±33 kN (7500 lbf) were driven by electro servo-valves with a flow capacity of 63 L/min (16.5 gpm) at 7 mPa (1000 psi). Each actuator was equipped with a ±127 mm (±5 inches) AC linear variable differential transformer (LVDT) sensor for displacement feedback and a dynamic load cell with a ±50 kN (±12,500 lbf) capacity for force feedback. The two actuators were mechanically linked to double the force capacity of the testing platform.

## 3.3. Real-Time Hybrid Simulator

The authors previously developed, implemented, and verified the user reconfigurable computational/control platform that is used in this study to conduct the RTHS experiments [31]. The key components of the developed real-time hybrid simulator include a quad-core real-time processor and a field programmable gate array (FPGA). Figure 1 shows the architecture of the platform, as well as all the signal routings amongst the system components. As shown in the figure, the simulation consists of two nested loops: an inner loop and an outer loop. The outer loop of the platform aims to solve the second-order ordinary equation of motion associated with the test structure that is expressed by:

$$M\ddot{x}(t) + C\dot{x}(t) + R(x, \dot{x}, \ddot{x}, t) = F(t) \tag{1}$$

where, $M$ denotes the mass matrix, $C$ represents the damping matrix (reflecting inherent structural damping), $R$ stands for the restoring force vector, and $F$ is the effective or applied external force vector. During iterations of the outer loop, a numerical integration algorithm is employed to compute the command displacements to be imposed on the test structure. Additionally, the outer loop encompasses all the tasks associated with determining the state of the analytical substructure and manipulating the input/output files.

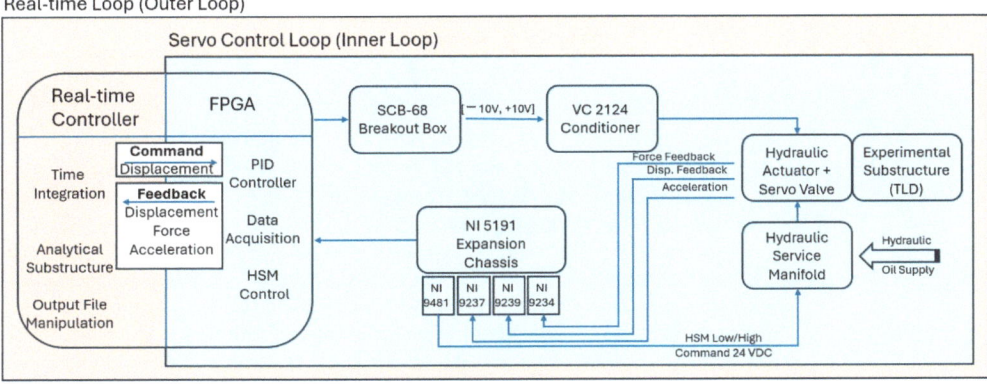

**Figure 1.** RTHS platform system setup.

The inner loop serves as the servo-control mechanism of the system. It is responsible for applying command displacements to the experimental substructure via the hydraulic actuators. Within this loop, all data communication occurs between the controller and the hardware components, including the servo valves, LVDTs, and load cells [31]. It needs to be noted that, in Figure 1, the experimental substructure is represented as a spring element.

However, as previously explained, in this study, the experimental substructure consists of a large-scale TLD driven by two dynamic actuators, which are coupled to enhance the force capacity.

### 3.4. Software

Unlike turnkey RTHS platforms, the controller of the current setup has been designed like an empty canvas, requiring user configuration to execute specific tasks for each application. This design enhances platform flexibility, allowing for various experiments and compatibility with different loading systems. For this application, in addition to the servo-control laws, multiple tasks are addressed and incorporated to ensure the safe startup, optimal performance, and secure shutdown of the shake table. The user interface of the RTHS platform, which manages computational, data acquisition, control, and safety-related tasks (such as displacement and force limit switches), was developed using LabVIEW (2009), MATLAB (2010), and Simulink (2010) programming tools. The core of the program comprises a multi-state Host VI (VI being the term for codes developed in LabVIEW (2009)), referred to as real-time VI, connected to an FPGA VI and several sub-VIs (similar to subfunctions in MATLAB), all coordinated within a LabVIEW project [31]

### 3.5. Ground Motions

In this RTHS investigation, a selection of seven earthquake records constitutes the ground motion suite. The significant features of these selected ground motions are outlined in Table 1.

**Table 1.** Ground motions utilized in this study (re-produced from Ashasi-Sorkhabi and Mercan [43]).

| # | Ground Motion | Magnitude | Location | Distance (km) | PGA (g) | Duration (s) |
|---|---|---|---|---|---|---|
| EQ1 | Erzincan Turkey 1992 | 6.69 | 95 Erzincan | 8.97 | 0.496 | 20.78 |
| EQ2 | Nahanni Canada 1985 | 6.76 | 6095 site 1 | 6.8 | 2.0508 | 20.56 |
| EQ3 | Kocaeli Turkey 1999 | 7.51 | Duzce | 98.22 | 0.312 | 27.185 |
| EQ4 | Duzce Turkey 1999 | 7.14 | Bolu | 41.27 | 0.728 | 55.9 |
| EQ5 | Chi-Chi Taiwan 1999 | 7.62 | CHY028 | 32.67 | 0.822 | 90 |
| EQ6 | Imperial Valley 1940 | 6.95 | El Centro, Array 09 | 12.99 | 0.3129 | 40.00 |
| EQ7 | Northridge 1994 | 6.69 | Simi Valley-Katherine | 12.18 | 0.8774 | 24.99 |

### 3.6. Analytical and Experimental Substructures

In this study, a single-story shear building equipped with a large-scale TLD was tested using the RTHS platform explained in Sections 3.2 and 3.3. The main structure, herein called the analytical substructure, was modeled numerically in a computer, and the TLD was tested physically (experimental substructure) in the lab.

A large-scale water tank with dimensions shown on Table 2 was constructed from $\frac{1}{4}$ inch-thick transparent plexiglass sheets and was used as the experimental TLD during the RTHS experiments. To the best of authors' knowledge, this experimental water tank is the largest TLD that has ever been tested in a lab environment to study the structure-TLD interaction. The height of the water in the tank was adjusted such that its sloshing frequency was tuned to the natural frequency of the analytical substructure. Equation (2) is employed to obtain the sloshing frequency of rectangular TLDs [13].

$$f_{TLD} = \frac{1}{2\pi}\sqrt{\frac{\pi g}{L}\tanh\left(\frac{\pi h_w}{L}\right)} \tag{2}$$

where $L$, $h_w$, and $g$ are the tank length, water height, and acceleration of gravity, respectively. In this study, the TLD was filled with 300 mm of water that resulted in a sloshing frequency of 0.418 Hz. Table 2 summarizes the geometrical and sloshing characteristics of the TLD.

Table 2. Characteristics of the experimental substructure (TLD) (re-produced from Ashasi-Sorkhabi and Mercan [43]).

| Net Length (mm) | Net Width (mm) | TLD Height (mm) | TLD MASS (kg) | Height of Water (mm) | Water Mass (kg) | Sloshing Frequency (Hz) |
|---|---|---|---|---|---|---|
| 1978 | 779 | 1200 | 125 | 300 | 462 | 0.418 |

A total of six single-degree-of-freedom (SDOF) structures with properties shown in Table 3 were considered as the analytical substructure. The properties of the main structure in different cases are designed such that three TLD/structure mass ratios of 1%, 3%, and 5% could be obtained. In the first three cases shown on Table 3, the main structure is modeled with linear stiffness assumption in the lateral direction, and in the last three, the single-story buildings are modeled as elastic–perfectly plastic systems with a mass $M$, lateral stiffness, $K_f$, and yield strength, $V_y$. The inherent damping, $C$, of the analytical substructure is computed assuming a 2.0% damping ratio. The properties of the nonlinear structures are set so that, in all three cases, the structure yields when the roof displacements reach 55 mm.

Table 3. Structural properties of the analytical substructure (1-storey structure).

| Case # | M (kg) | $K_f$ (N/m) | C (N.s/m) | Linear or Nonlinear | Vy N | MR % |
|---|---|---|---|---|---|---|
| 1 | 46,200 | 318,660 | 4853.4 | Linear | /// | 1 |
| 2 | 15,400 | 106,220 | 1617.8 | Linear | /// | 3 |
| 3 | 9240 | 63,732 | 970.67 | Linear | /// | 5 |
| 4 | 46,200 | 318,660 | 4853.4 | Nonlinear | 17,526 | 1 |
| 5 | 15,400 | 106,220 | 1617.8 | Nonlinear | 5842.1 | 3 |
| 6 | 9240 | 63,732 | 970.67 | Nonlinear | 3505.2 | 5 |

Figure 2 shows the schematic of the RTHS experiments carried out in this study. During the tests, the TLD was physically isolated and tested on the shake table, serving as the experimental substructure in the RTHS. It represents a portion of the building's roof. Meanwhile, the remaining structure was simulated numerically within the real-time controller. In each iteration of the outer control loop, displacement commands were computed and applied to both the analytical and experimental substructures. Following this, the restoring forces obtained from the TLD and computed for the analytical substructure were utilized to generate the subsequent command. To simulate the effects of ground motion records on the test structure, corresponding effective floor forces were computed and applied laterally during the experiments. Four experiments were conducted per each of the ground motions: structure without TLD, structure with TLD with a 1% mass ratio, structure with TLD with a 3% mass ratio, and structure with TLD with a 5% mass ratio. Throughout all the experiments conducted in this study, ground accelerations were scaled enough to achieve a peak roof displacement of approximately 80 mm in the uncontrolled structure. A picture of the actual specimen (experimental substructure) is shown in Figure 3.

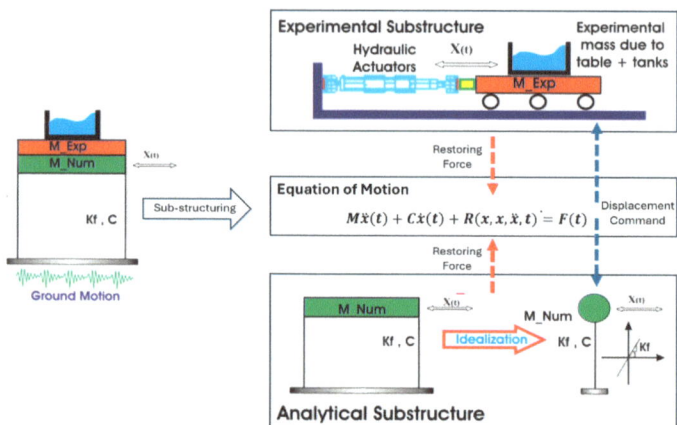

**Figure 2.** Schematic view of the RTHS test setup.

**Figure 3.** Experimental substructure.

## 4. RTHS of Linear/Nonlinear SDOF Equipped with Large-Scale TLD Subjected to Seismic Loading

This section presents the RTHS experiment results on the seismic performance of SDOF structures equipped with a large-scale TLD on the roof. For completeness, multiple frequencies were investigated; however, since the TLDs are only tuned to the resonance of 0.418 Hz, only those results are considered. Here, for brevity, only a representative sample of the more than 30 tested configurations is presented. The results corresponding to EQ2 (i.e., Nahanni 1985), and resonance are provided; however, the entire performance envelope for all tests are presented at the end of each section. In Figure 4, the time history of the ground motion is provided, along with its Fast Fourier Transform (FFT) in Figure 5.

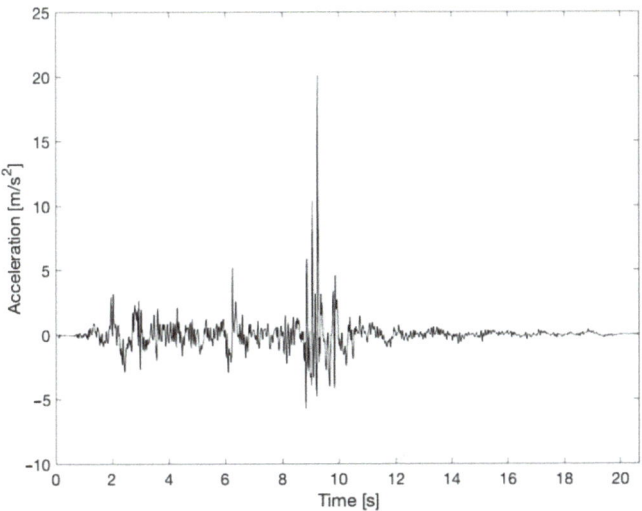

**Figure 4.** Time history of the 1985 Nahanni Earthquake.

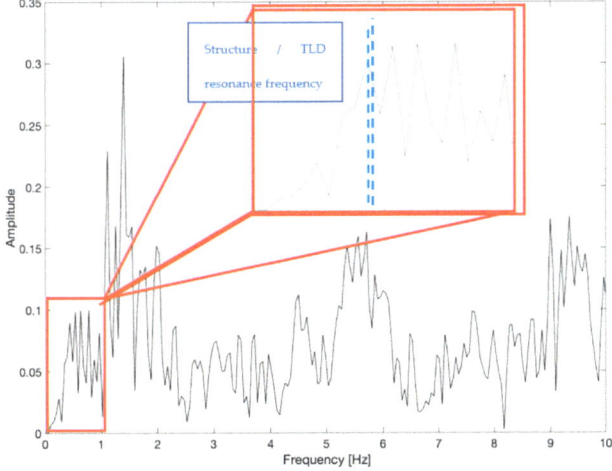

**Figure 5.** FFT analysis of the 1985 Nahanni Earthquake, with an enlarged view focusing on frequencies below 1 Hz, encompassing the structural and sloshing frequencies.

## 5. Linear Substructure Results

Multiple RTHSs were conducted for each earthquake event detailed in Table 1. These simulations were carried out using a linear structure with three distinct mass ratios: 1%, 3%, and 5%. Before summarizing all the results as trend charts, to illustrate the reduction in displacements in both the time and frequency domains, Figures 6–11 specifically focus on the Nahanni Earthquake, showcasing the influence of varying mass ratios of the TLD. Specifically, reductions of 19%, 36%, and 43% were recorded for the respective mass ratios of 1%, 3%, and 5%. The root mean square (RMS) values were also calculated for each of the tests. The RMS of the displacements were reduced by 30%, 53%, and 63% respectively for each of the three mass ratios. Furthermore, each RTHS test was extended by 20 s beyond the duration of the ground motion to analyze the amplitude reduction in the free vibration region. The results indicate significant reductions in amplitude in the controlled response compared to the uncontrolled response across the free vibration region. Specifically, these reductions were 56%, 94%, and 99% for the mass ratios of 1%, 3%, and 5% respectively. To further assess the impact of the TLDs, FFT analysis was conducted on the obtained results. This analysis revealed reductions in the FFT spectrum amplitude of 36%, 47%, and 56% for the Nahanni Earthquake simulations. These findings indicate the positive effects of increasing mass ratios on various performance indicators.

The reductions in peak displacement across all earthquakes were compiled into a trend chart and provided in Figure 12. Analysis of the data reveals that, for a mass ratio of 1%, the effectiveness of the TLD ranges from −2% to 19%. Negative values indicate instances where the peak displacement increased for certain ground motions. Similarly, for a mass ratio of 3%, the effectiveness varied between −2% and 36%, while for a mass ratio of 5%, it ranged from −2% to 44%. The slight increase in peak displacement observed in some scenarios suggests that the TLD may be ineffective under certain ground motion conditions, possibly due to a mismatch between the structural/TLD frequency and the frequency content of the earthquake.

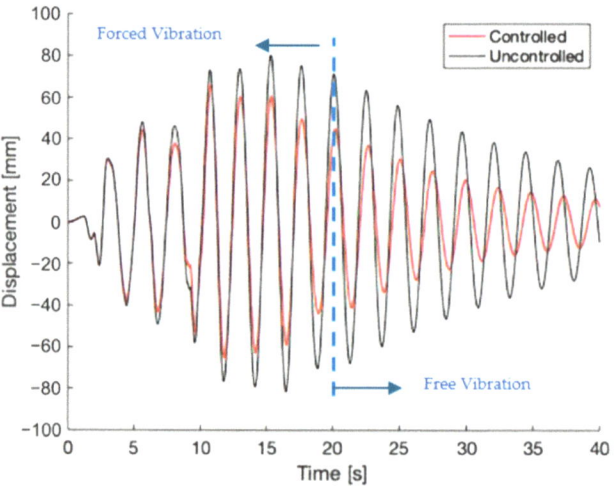

**Figure 6.** Structural displacement response history for EQ#2-MR1%—0.418 Hz (Linear Substructure).

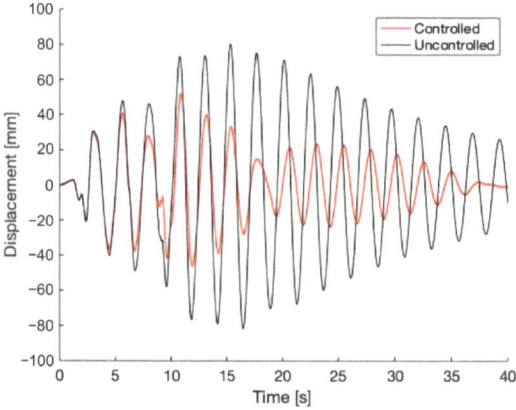

**Figure 7.** Structural displacement response history for EQ#2-MR3%—0.418 Hz (Linear Substructure).

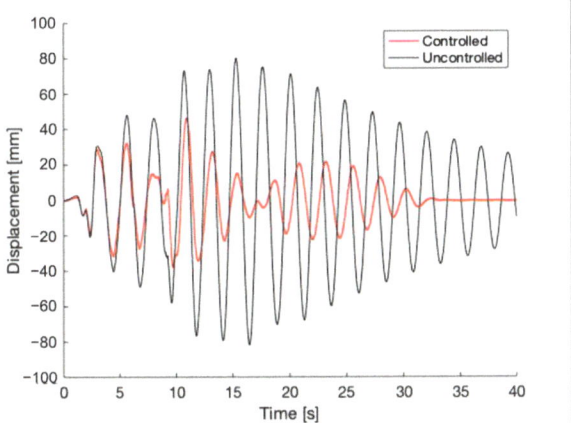

**Figure 8.** Structural displacement response history for EQ#2-MR5%—0.418 Hz (Linear Substructure).

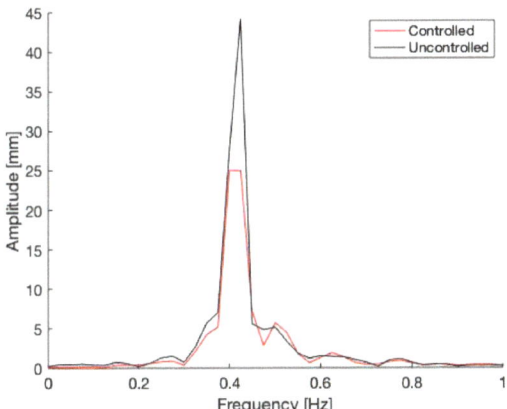

**Figure 9.** FFT analysis of structural displacement response for EQ#2-MR1%—0.418 Hz (Linear Substructure).

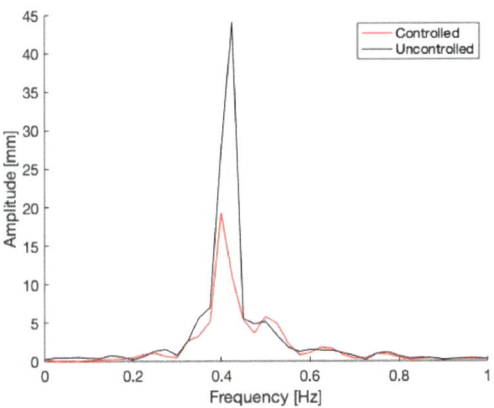

**Figure 10.** FFT analysis of structural displacement response for EQ#2-MR3%—0.418 Hz (Linear Substructure).

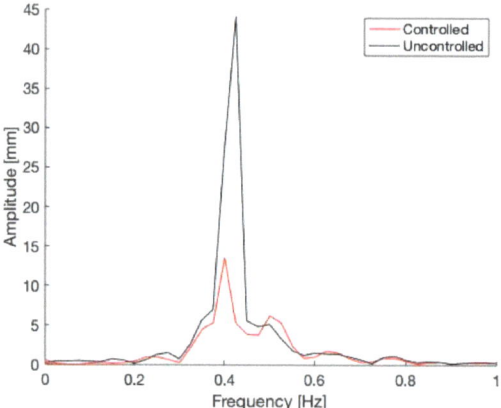

**Figure 11.** FFT analysis of structural displacement response for EQ#2-MR5%—0.418 Hz (Linear Substructure).

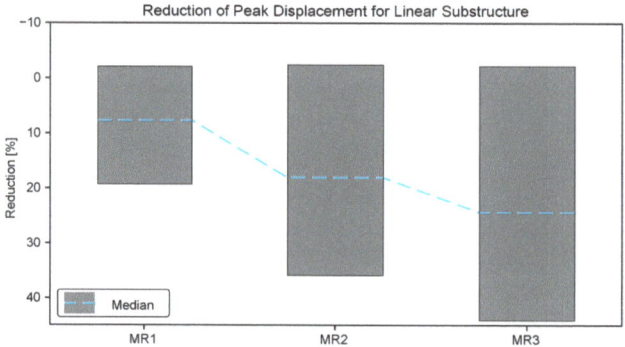

**Figure 12.** Peak displacement reduction trend chart for linear substructure.

Furthermore, a similar analysis was conducted for the reduction in FFT amplitudes, as illustrated in Figure 13. For a mass ratio of 1%, the reduction ranged from 20% to 43%, for 3% it was between 30% and 47%, and for 5% it ranged from 33% to 59%.

In conclusion, the findings demonstrate a positive correlation between the increase in mass ratio and the overall performance enhancement of the TLD.

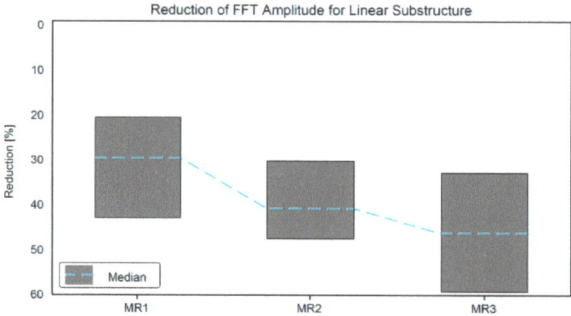

**Figure 13.** FFT amplitude reduction trend chart for linear substructure.

## 6. Nonlinear Substructure Results

Multiple RTHSs were conducted with a nonlinear substructure for the same three mass ratios, with the properties listed on Table 3. As mentioned earlier in Section 3.6 in the paper, the ground accelerations were scaled to limit the peak roof displacements to approximately 80 mm in the uncontrolled structure. Consequently, the test structures entered a nonlinear state, once the roof displacements exceeded the 55 mm yield displacement limit. This scaling enabled the assessment of TLD efficiency during the nonlinear behavior of the system.

The peak displacements were reduced by 11%, 19%, and 21% respectively for the three different mass ratios under the Nahanni ground motion. The RMS values of the displacements were reduced by 22%, 33%, and 41%. The free vibration amplitude measured 20 s after the duration of the earthquake was measured to have been reduced by 44%, 87%, and 84%. Again, the response was analyzed using FFT, revealing reductions in amplitude of 18%, 23%, and 27%. In the case of the nonlinear substructure, an additional performance indicator was also compared, since the nonlinearity in the structure allowed for residual displacements if/when the earthquake yielded the structure. The liquid damper was found to have reduced the residual displacement by 97%, 70%, and 77%. The increase in mass ratio has once again shown a positive effect on the performance indicators considered. Figures 14–19 provide the time histories and FFTs for the test cases involving a nonlinear substructure subjected to the Nahanni ground motion.

Trend charts for the nonlinear substructure were created and are presented in Figures 20 and 21. For a mass ratio of 1%, the effectiveness of the TLD was between −9 and 11%. For a mass ratio of 3%, the effectiveness was between −2 and 24%. Finally, for a mass ratio of 5%, the effectiveness was between 0 and 33%. For FFT amplitude reduction, the mass ratio of 1% had a 0 to 48% reduction, the mass ratio of 3% had a reduction of 5 to 44%, and the mass ratio of 5% had a reduction of 7 to 50%.

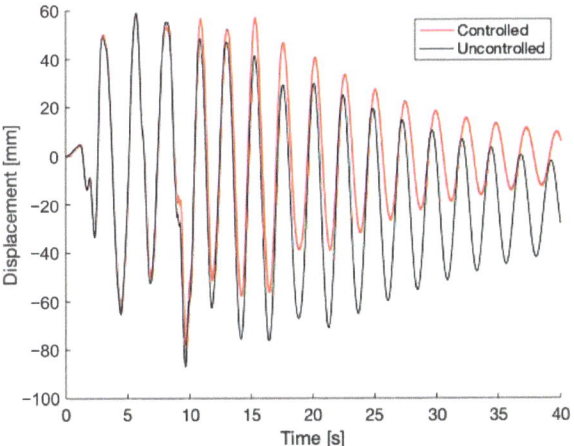

**Figure 14.** Structural displacement response history for EQ#2-MR1%—0.418 Hz (Nonlinear Substructure).

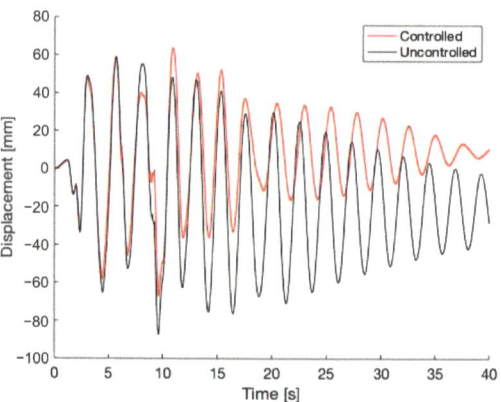

**Figure 15.** Structural displacement response history for EQ#2-MR3%—0.418 Hz (Nonlinear Substructure).

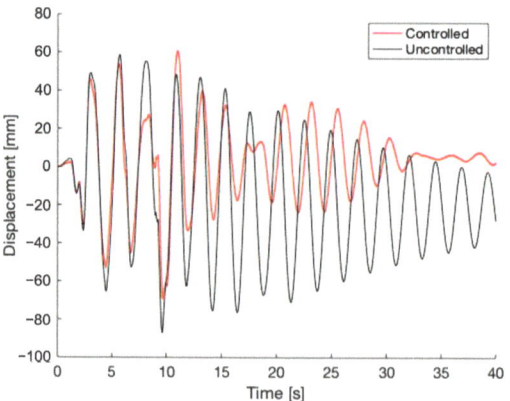

**Figure 16.** Structural displacement response history for EQ#2-MR5%—0.418 Hz (Nonlinear Substructure).

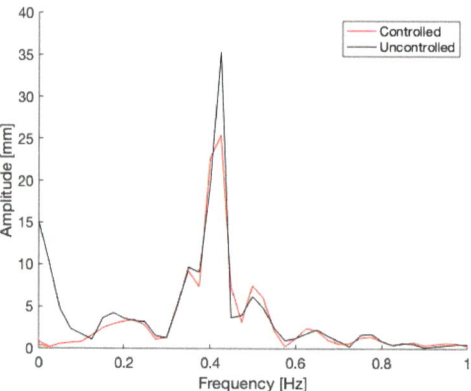

**Figure 17.** FFT analysis of structural displacement response for EQ#2-MR1%—0.418 Hz (Nonlinear Substructure).

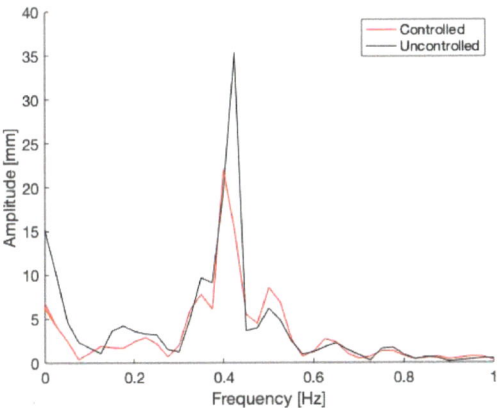

**Figure 18.** FFT analysis of structural displacement response for EQ#2-MR3%—0.418 Hz (Nonlinear Substructure).

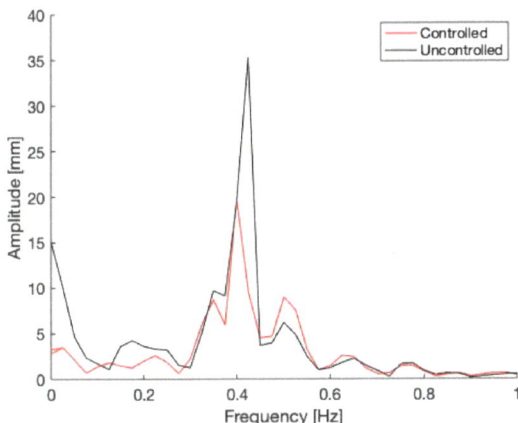

**Figure 19.** FFT analysis of structural displacement response for EQ#2-MR5%—0.418 Hz (Nonlinear Substructure).

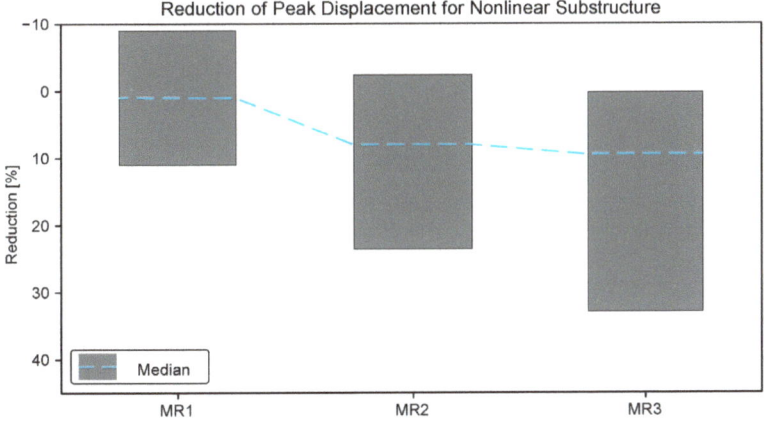

**Figure 20.** Peak displacement reduction trend chart for nonlinear substructure.

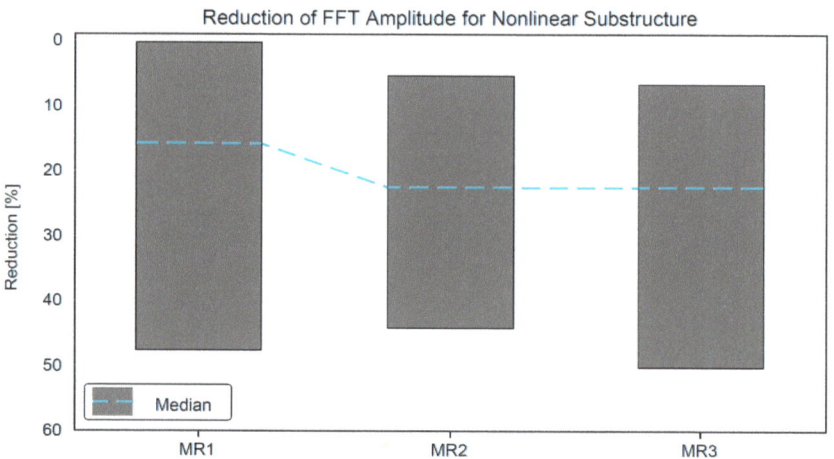

**Figure 21.** FFT amplitude reduction trend chart for nonlinear substructure.

The linear and nonlinear trend charts are combined in Figures 22 and 23. The results reveal a wider range of performance in peak displacement reduction for the linear substructure, yet they also indicate greater reductions compared to the nonlinear substructure. When examining the reduction in FFT peaks, it becomes evident that the nonlinear substructure exhibits significantly higher spreads in performance compared to the linear case. Nonetheless, the linear substructure continues to demonstrate greater efficiency relative to the nonlinear counterpart. It seems that, in scenarios where the structure remains within the linear–elastic range, the TLD proves more effective than in nonlinear structures.

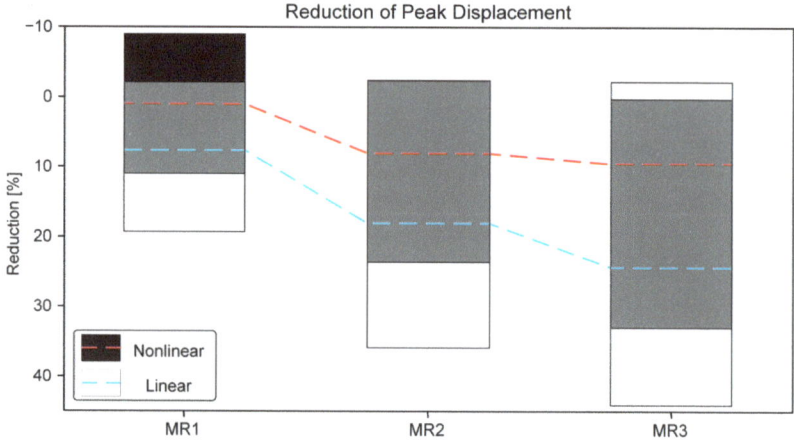

**Figure 22.** Peak displacement reduction trend chart comparison.

It is observed that the type of earthquake influences the performance of the TLD. For example, while the second load case, i.e., EQ2 (i.e., Nahanni 1985), as shown above, has a favorable performance, the third load case, i.e., EQ3 (i.e., Northridge 1994), exhibits a less favorable performance. In some cases, the results of this ground motion show a slight increase in peak values, especially for the nonlinear substructure. Based on these observations, it can be concluded that the frequency content of the earthquake is a crucial factor that affects the performance of the TLD. Moreover, certain types of earthquakes, such as pulse-type earthquakes, may diminish effectiveness as they do not allow the TLD to engage properly before the peak displacements occur. While TLDs may not be as effective in nonlinear structures compared to linear structures, they were still able to provide some effectiveness in controlling displacements. Additionally, in nearly all cases, the TLD was also able to reduce the residual displacement when compared to the uncontrolled case (the test structure only subjected to the same seismic loading).

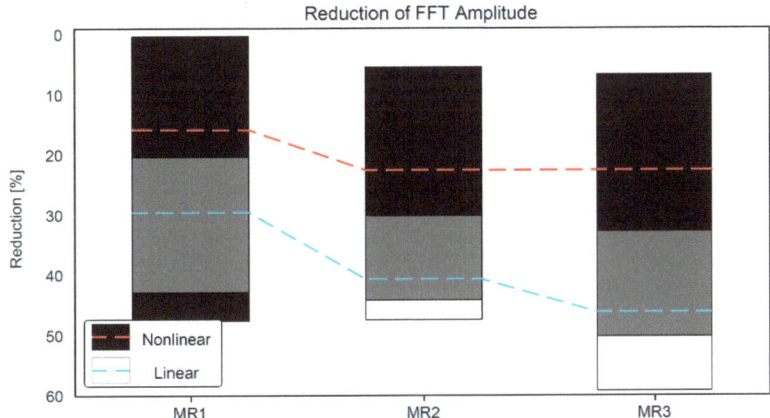

Figure 23. FFT amplitude reduction trend chart comparison.

## 7. Summary and Conclusions

This study has provided insights into the performance of tuned liquid dampers in suppressing vibrations of structures under seismic loading conditions. Through a series of real-time hybrid-simulation experiments, the effectiveness of TLDs was investigated on both linear and nonlinear substructures. The experimental setup, which utilized a large-scale TLD and state-of-the-art RTHS methodology, allowed for the accurate assessment of TLD performance in mitigating structural vibrations.

The results from the experiments demonstrate significant reductions in peak displacements, RMS values, and FFT spectrum amplitudes when TLDs are employed, particularly for linear structures. The effectiveness of TLDs varied depending on factors such as the mass ratio, earthquake type, and structural nonlinearity. While TLDs showed promising results in controlling displacements and reducing residual displacements, it was noted that their effectiveness could be influenced by the frequency content of the earthquake and the structural characteristics. It is important to note that these experiments with large-scale TLDs were conducted in a laboratory environment; actual structures may exhibit different dynamic behaviors due to factors such as scale, shape, and materials.

As a prospective avenue, the authors intend to investigate the utilization of multiple TLDs tuned to different operational frequencies to broaden the effectiveness range of TLDs in attenuating structural vibrations under seismic loading. Another future topic is to use the experimental results obtained in this study to validate and calibrate existing theoretical models, thereby improving their accuracy in capturing the realistic performance of TLDs under seismic loading. Additionally, a more comprehensive and systematic study to understand the effects of different earthquakes is part of the authors' future research plans.

**Author Contributions:** Conceptualization, A.A.S. and O.M.; methodology, A.A.S.; software, A.A.S.; validation, A.A.S. and O.M.; formal analysis, A.A.S. and B.Q.; investigation, A.A.S.; resources, A.A.S. and O.M.; data curation, A.A.S. and B.Q.; writing—original draft preparation, A.A.S. and B.Q.; writing—review and editing, A.A.S., B.Q. and O.M.; visualization, A.A.S. and B.Q.; supervision, O.M.; project administration, O.M.; funding acquisition, O.M. All authors have read and agreed to the published version of the manuscript.

**Funding:** This research received no external funding.

**Data Availability Statement:** The data presented in this study are available upon request from the corresponding author.

**Acknowledgments:** The financial support from NSERC Discovery and NSERC RTI programs, as well as the Edwin Edward Hart Professorship Award are gratefully acknowledged. Any opinions, findings, conclusions, and recommendations expressed here are those of the authors and do not necessarily reflect the views of the sponsors.

**Conflicts of Interest:** The authors declare no conflict of interest.

## References

1. Xu, Y.; Chen, B. Integrated vibration control and health monitoring of building structures using semi-active friction dampers: Part I—Methodology. *Eng. Struct.* **2008**, *30*, 1789–1801. [CrossRef]
2. Fujino, Y.; Pacheco, B.M.; Chaiseri, P.; Sun, L.M. Parametric studies on tuned liquid damper (TLD) using circular containers by free-oscillation experiments. *Doboku Gakkai Ronbunshu* **1988**, *5*, 381–391. [CrossRef]
3. Tamura, Y.; Fujii, K.; Sato, T.; Wakahara, T.; Kosugi, M. Wind-induced vibration of tall towers and practical applications of tuned sloshing dampers. In Proceedings of the Workshop on Serviceability of Buildings (Movements, Deformations, Vibrations), Ottawa, ON, Canada, 16–18 May 1988.
4. Shen, K.; Soong, T.; Chang, K.; Lai, M. Seismic behavior of reinforced concrete frame with added visco-elastic dampers. *EnGineering Struct.* **1995**, *17*, 372–380. [CrossRef]
5. Ghabraie, K.; Chan, R.; Huang, X.; Xie, Y.M. Shape optimization of metallic yielding devices for passive mitigation of seismic energy. *Eng. Struct.* **2010**, *32*, 2258–2267. [CrossRef]
6. Zhang, Y.; Zhu, S. A shape memory alloy-based reusable hysteretic damper for seismic hazard mitigation. *Smart Mater. Struct.* **2007**, *16*, 1603–1613. [CrossRef]
7. Ni, Y.; Chen, Y.; Ko, J.; Cao, D. Neuro-control of cable vibration using semi-active magneto-rheological dampers. *Eng. Struct.* **2003**, *24*, 295–307. [CrossRef]
8. Yang, G.; Spencer, B.; Carlson, J.; Sain, M. Large-scale MR fluid dampers: Odeling and dynamic performance considerations. *Eng. Struct.* **2002**, *24*, 309–323. [CrossRef]
9. Chen, Y.; Hwang, W.; Chiu, L.; Sheu, S. Flexibility of TLD to high-rise building by simple experiment and comparison. *Comput. Struct.* **1995**, *57*, 855–861. [CrossRef]
10. Kim, Y.-M.; You, K.-P.; Ko, N.-H.; Yoon, S.-W. Use of TLD and MTLD for control of wind-induced vibration of tall buildings. *J. Mech. Sci. Technol.* **2006**, *20*, 1346–1354. [CrossRef]
11. NatHaz Research. tuned Liquid Dampers (TLDs) and Tuned Liquid Column Dampers (TLCDs) Research at NatHaz Modeling Laboratory. Available online: https://nathaz.nd.edu/research/liquid/liq_damp.html (accessed on 30 May 2024).
12. Reed, D.; Yu, J.; Yeh, H.; Gardarsson, S. Investigation of Tuned Liquid Dampers under Large Amplitude Excitation. *J. Eng. Mech.* **1998**, *124*, 405–413. [CrossRef]
13. Sun, L.M.; Fujino, Y.; Pacheco, B.M.; Chaiseri, P. Modelling of tuned liquid damper (TLD). *J. Wind Eng. Ind. Aerodyn.* **1992**, *43*, 1883–1894. [CrossRef]
14. Yu, J.; Wakahara, T.; Reed, D.A. A non-linear numerical model of the tuned liquid damper. *Earthq. Eng. Struct. Dyn.* **1999**, *28*, 671–686. [CrossRef]
15. Banerji, P.; Murudi, M.; Shah, A.; Popplewell, N. Tuned liquid dampers for controlling earthquake response of structures. *Earthq. Eng. Struct. Dyn.* **2000**, *29*, 587–602. [CrossRef]
16. Kosaka, H.; Noji, T.; Yoshida, H.; Tatsumi, E.; Yamanaka, H.; Agrawal, A. Damping effects of a vibration control damper using sloshing of water. In Proceedings of the 10th World Conference on Earthquake Engineering, Madrid, Spain, 19–24 July 1992.
17. Xiao, C.; Wu, Z.; Chen, K.; Tang, Y.; Yan, Y. An experimental study on the equivalent nonlinear model for a large-sized tuned liquid damper. *J. Build. Eng.* **2023**, *73*, 106754. [CrossRef]
18. Ocak, A.; Nigdeli, S.M.; Bekdaş, G.; Kim, S.; Geem, Z.W. Adaptive Harmony Search for Tuned Liquid Damper Optimization under Seismic Excitation. *Appl. Sci.* **2022**, *12*, 2645. [CrossRef]
19. Tang, Z.; Sheng, J.; Dong, Y. Effects of tuned liquid dampers on the nonlinear seismic responses of high-rise structures using real-time hybrid simulations. *J. Build. Eng.* **2023**, *70*, 106333. [CrossRef]
20. Malekghasemi, H.; Ashasi-Sorkhabi, A.; Ghaemmaghami, A.R.; Mercan, O. Experimental and numerical investigations of the dynamic interaction of tuned liquid damper–structure systems. *J. Vib. Control.* **2013**, *21*, 2707–2720. [CrossRef]
21. Novo, T.; Varum, H.; Teixeira-Dias, F.; Rodrigues, H.; Falcao-Silva, M.; Cost, A.; Guerreiro, L. Tuned liquid dampers simula-tion for earthquake response control of buildings. *Bull. Earthq. Eng.* **2013**, *12*, 1007–1024. [CrossRef]
22. Rai, K.; Reddy, G.; Venkatraj, V. Tuned liquid sloshing water damper: A robust device for seismic retrofitting. *Int. J. Environ. Sci. Dev. Monit.* **2013**, *4*, 36–44.
23. Shad, H.; Bin Adnan, A.; Behbahani, H.P. Performance Evaluation of Tuned Liquid Dampers on Response of a SDOF System Under Earthquake Excitation and Harmonic Load. *Res. J. Appl. Sci. Eng. Technol.* **2013**, *6*, 3018–3021. [CrossRef]
24. Wang, J.-T.; Gui, Y.; Zhu, F.; Jin, F.; Zhou, M.-X. Real-time hybrid simulation of multi-story structures installed with tuned liquid damper. *Struct. Control Health Monit.* **2015**, *23*, 1015–1031. [CrossRef]

25. Jin, Q.; Li, X.; Sun, N.; Zhou, J.; Guan, J. Experimental and numerical study on tuned liquid dampers for controlling earth-quake response of jacket offshore platform. *Mar. Struct.* **2007**, *20*, 238–254. [CrossRef]
26. Ghaemmaghami, A.; Kianoush, M.; Mardukhi, J. Numerical study on annular tuned liquid dampers for controlling the re-sponse of wind towers subjected to seismic loads. In Proceeding of the 15th World Conference on Earthquake Engineering, Lisbon, Portugal, 24–28 September 2012.
27. Ghaemmaghami, A.R.; Kianoush, R.; Mercan, O. Numerical modeling of dynamic behavior of annular tuned liquid dampers for the application in wind towers under seismic loading. *J. Vib. Control* **2015**, *22*, 3858–3876. [CrossRef]
28. Zhu, F.; Wang, J.; Jin, F.; Altay, O. Real-time hybrid simulation of single and multiple tuned liquid column dampers for con-trolling seismic-induced response. In Proceedings of the 6th International Conference on Advances in Experimental Structural Engineering, Illinoi, IL, USA, 19–21 October 2015.
29. Das, S.; Choudhury, S. Seismic response control by tuned liquid dampers for low-rise RC frame buildings. *Aust. J. Struct. Eng.* **2017**, *18*, 135–145. [CrossRef]
30. Zhu, F.; Wang, J.-T.; Jin, F.; Lu, L.-Q.; Gui, Y.; Zhou, M.-X. Real-time hybrid simulation of the size effect of tuned liquid dampers. *Struct. Control Health Monit.* **2017**, *24*, e1962. [CrossRef]
31. Ashasi-Sorkhabi, A.; Mercan, O. Development, Implementation, and Verification of a User Configurable Platform for Re-al-time Hybrid Simulation. *Smart Struct. Syst.* **2014**, *14*, 1151–1172. [CrossRef]
32. Ashasi-Sorkhabi, A. Implementation, Verification and Application of Real-Time Hybrid Simulation. ProQuest Dissertations & Theses, University of Toronto, Toronto, ON, Canada, 2015.
33. Lee, S.-K.; Park, E.C.; Min, K.-W.; Lee, S.-H.; Chun, L.; Park, J.-H. Real-time hybrid shaking table testing method for the per-formance evaluation of a tuned liquid damper controlling seismic response of building structures. *J. Sound Vi-Bration* **2006**, *302*, 596–612. [CrossRef]
34. Banerji, P. Tuned Liquid Dampers for Control of Earthquake Response. In Proceedings of the 13th World Conference on Earthquake Engineering, Vancouver, BC, Canada, 1–6 August 2004.
35. Ruiz, R.; Taflanidis, A.; Lopez-Garcia, D. Characterization and design of tuned liquid dampers with floating roof considering abitrary tank cross-sections. *J. Sound Vib.* **2016**, *368*, 36–54. [CrossRef]
36. Mahin, S.; Shing, P. Pseudodynamic method for seismic testing. *J. Struct. Eng. (ASCE)* **1985**, *111*, 1482–1503. [CrossRef]
37. Dermitzakis, S.; Mahin, S. *Development of Substructuring Techniques for On-Line Computer Controlled Seismic Performance Testing*; Report UBC/EERC-85/04; Earthquake Engineering Research Center: Berkeley, CA, USA, 1985.
38. Nakashima, M.; Kato, H.; Takaoka, E. Development of real-time pseudodynamic testing. *Earthq. Eng. Struct. Dyn.* **1995**, *21*, 79–92. [CrossRef]
39. Horiuchi, T.; Inoue, M.; Konno, T.; Namita, Y. Real-time hybrid experimental system with actuator delay compensation and its application to a piping system with energy absorber. *Earthq. Eng. Struct. Dyn.* **1999**, *28*, 1121–1141. [CrossRef]
40. Mercan, O.; Ricles, J. Experimental Studies on real-time pseudodynamic (PSD) and hybrid PSD testing of structures with elastomeric dampers. *J. Struct. Eng.* **2009**, *135*, 1124–1133. [CrossRef]
41. Ashasi-Sorkhabi, A.; Malekghasemi, H.; Mercan, O. Implementation and verification of real-time hybrid simulation (RTHS) using a shake table for research and education. *J. Vib. Control* **2012**, *21*, 1459–1472. [CrossRef]
42. Christenson, R.; Lin, Y.Z.; Emmons, A.; Bass, B. Large-Scale Experimental Verification of Semiactive Control through Real-Time Hybrid Simulation. *J. Struct. Eng.* **2008**, *134*, 522–534. [CrossRef]
43. Ashasi-Sorkhabi, A.; Mercan, O. Experimental investigations of large scale TLD-structure interaction via real-time hybrid simulation. In Proceedings of the Resilient Infrastructure, CSCE, London, ON, Canada, 1–4 June 2016.

**Disclaimer/Publisher's Note:** The statements, opinions and data contained in all publications are solely those of the individual author(s) and contributor(s) and not of MDPI and/or the editor(s). MDPI and/or the editor(s) disclaim responsibility for any injury to people or property resulting from any ideas, methods, instructions or products referred to in the content.

Article

# Static and Dynamic Response Analysis of Flexible Photovoltaic Mounts

Yibing Lou, Jian Zhang * and Yuxin Pan

School of Shipbuilding and Ocean Engineering, Jiangsu University of Science and Technology, Zhenjiang 212100, China; 13270323596@163.com (Y.L.); pyx18360735895@163.com (Y.P.)
* Correspondence: justzj@just.edu.cn

**Abstract:** Traditional rigid photovoltaic (PV) support structures exhibit several limitations during operational deployment. Therefore, flexible PV mounting systems have been developed. These flexible PV supports, characterized by their heightened sensitivity to wind loading, necessitate a thorough analysis of their static and dynamic responses. This study involves the development of a MATLAB code to simulate the fluctuating wind load time series and the subsequent structural modeling in SAP2000 to evaluate the safety performance of flexible PV supports under extreme wind conditions. The research explores the critical wind speeds relative to varying spans and prestress levels within the system. Modal analysis reveals that the flexible PV support structures do not experience resonant frequencies that could amplify oscillations. The analysis also provides insights into the mode shapes of these structures. An analysis of the wind-induced vibration responses of the flexible PV support structures was conducted. The results indicated that the mid-span displacements and the axial forces in the wind-resistant cables are greater under wind-pressure conditions compared to wind-suction conditions. Conversely, for mid-span accelerations, the wind-suction conditions resulted in higher values than the wind-pressure conditions. Furthermore, the wind-induced vibration coefficients were computed, with findings suggesting a recommended coefficient range of 1.5 to 2.52. To mitigate wind-induced vibrations, structural reinforcement strategies were assessed. The results indicate that the introduction of support beams at the mid-span is the most effective measure to attenuate wind-induced vibrational responses. Conversely, increasing the diameter of the tensioned cables exhibited a negligible effect in reducing these responses. On the other hand, implementing stabilizing cables at the mid-span demonstrated a substantial reduction in wind-induced vibrational responses under suction wind-load conditions.

**Keywords:** flexible photovoltaic mounts; wind-vibration response; static response; fluctuating wind; wind-vibration coefficient

**Citation:** Lou, Y.; Zhang, J.; Pan, Y. Static and Dynamic Response Analysis of Flexible Photovoltaic Mounts. *Buildings* **2024**, *14*, 2037. https://doi.org/10.3390/buildings14072037

Academic Editor: Humberto Varum

Received: 11 June 2024
Revised: 26 June 2024
Accepted: 29 June 2024
Published: 4 July 2024

**Copyright:** © 2024 by the authors. Licensee MDPI, Basel, Switzerland. This article is an open access article distributed under the terms and conditions of the Creative Commons Attribution (CC BY) license (https://creativecommons.org/licenses/by/4.0/).

## 1. Introduction

Since the 18th National Congress of the Communist Party of China, China has entered a new phase of development, and the energy sector has likewise reached a critical period of transformation [1]. Renewable energy, particularly solar PV power, is increasingly becoming a key focus in the global energy structure transition. China boasts exceptionally favorable conditions for PV power generation [2,3], with more than 66% of its regions receiving over 200 h of sunlight annually [4]. The traditional rigid PV support systems face several issues and limitations, such as the requirement for large land areas, which constrain their deployment and development, especially in eastern regions [5]. In response to these challenges, flexible PV support systems have rapidly developed. Compared to conventional rigid PV supports, flexible PV supports offer advantages such as flexibility, adaptability, shorter construction periods, lower costs, and higher land utilization rates [6].

Previous research has primarily focused on simulating wind loads on PV panels, with numerous numerical simulations conducted by researchers [7–12]. Additionally, various scholars have examined rooftop PV structures, exploring the effects of the tilt angle, array spacing, building type, and parapet on the wind action on rooftop PV arrays [13–16].

Fluctuating wind is caused by the irregularity of the wind, with its intensity randomly varying over time. There are many methods to simulate wind load time series, such as the linear filter method [17,18], harmonic superposition method [19,20], inverse Fourier transform method [21], wavelet analysis method [22,23], and artificial neural network method [24,25]. Among these methods, the autoregressive (AR) model is widely used in stochastic vibration and time series analysis due to its high computational efficiency and simplicity. The AR model generates a random process for wind speed by constructing one or more autoregressive terms to describe the relationship between the current wind speed value and its historical values. When simulating the fluctuating wind speed time series for flexible PV supports, the AR model's characteristics can be used to generate time series data that match the actual wind speed characteristics, providing a basis for wind load analysis of the structure.

Flexible PV supports are highly sensitive to fluctuating wind, and thus numerous scholars have studied the wind-induced response of flexible PV supports. Guo Tao [26] and others, in conjunction with actual engineering projects, discovered that the maximum amplitude of the wind-induced response of PV arrays was approximately 8.0 cm. Cai Yuan [27] and colleagues researched the wind resistance design methods for flexible PV support structures, deriving a formula to estimate the standard deviation of the wind-induced dynamic response by using the standard deviation of the quasi-static response of the structure, and validated the accuracy of this formula. Xie Dan [28], Wang Zeguo [29], and their respective teams used finite element software to study the natural vibration characteristics and wind-induced response of single-layer cable-supported flexible PV support structures. They found that the structure is prone to vertical vibration and torsional deformation, and that fluctuating wind vibration has little effect on structural deflection under transverse wind loads. Xu [30] and others conducted a series of wind tunnel tests on flexible PV supports and found that the torsional vibration of flexible PV supports is significant, with PV modules being most at risk when the wind direction angle is 180°. Xu [31] and his team further conducted wind tunnel tests using aeroelastic and rigid models, showing that the vertical vibration of flexible cable-supported PV systems increases significantly with the tilt angle, and that the gust load coefficient of PV panels with a tilt angle of 10° ranges between 1.2 and 2.5. Liu [32] and colleagues investigated the wind-induced response and critical wind speed of a 33-m span flexible PV support structure through wind tunnel tests based on elastic models, finding that 180° and 0° are the most unfavorable wind directions, with a critical wind speed of approximately 18.5 m/s, and examined the effectiveness of three measures to mitigate wind-induced vibrations. Li [33] and his team studied the instability mechanisms and failure criteria of large-span flexible PV supports, concluding that triangular and cross diagonal braces fail at critical wind speeds of 51 m/s and 46 m/s, respectively.

## 2. Materials and Methods

### 2.1. Flexible PV Mounting Structure Geometric Model

The constructed flexible PV support model consists of six spans, each with a span of 2 m. The spans are connected by struts, with the support cables having a height of 4.75 m, directly supporting the PV panels. The wind-resistant cables are 4 m high and are connected to the lower ends of the struts. The end support beams are 4 m high, with tie rods connected to the end support beams at a 45° angle, each measuring 5.657 m in length. There are six sets of struts, spaced 2 m apart.

In accordance with the "Steel Strand for Prestressed Concrete" (GB/T 5224-2014) [34], we selected 1 × 7 unbonded prestressed hot-dip galvanized steel strands as the load-bearing cables, which have the following properties: tensile strength $R_m$ = 1860 MPa, elastic modulus $E_0$ = 1.95 × $10^5$ MPa, linear expansion coefficient $\alpha_T$ = 1.17 × $10^{-5}$/°C, and Poisson's ratio $\nu$ = 0.3. The diameter of the support cables is 0.0127 m, while the wind-resistant cables have a diameter of 0.0152 m. The end support beams are made of HPB300 steel, with cross-sectional dimensions of 0.2 m in length and width, and a wall thickness of 0.01 m. The columns are constructed from Q355 seamless steel pipes, having an outer diameter of 0.2 m and an inner diameter of 0.05 m, with an elastic modulus of $2.06 \times 10^5$ N/mm$^2$. The struts are solid HPB300 steel rods with a diameter of 0.05 m. To simulate the PV panels, a virtual surface was employed, applying a uniform distributed load of 0.15 kN/m$^2$ to represent the self-weight of the PV modules. The geometric model of the flexible PV support system and the nomenclature of its components are illustrated in Figure 1.

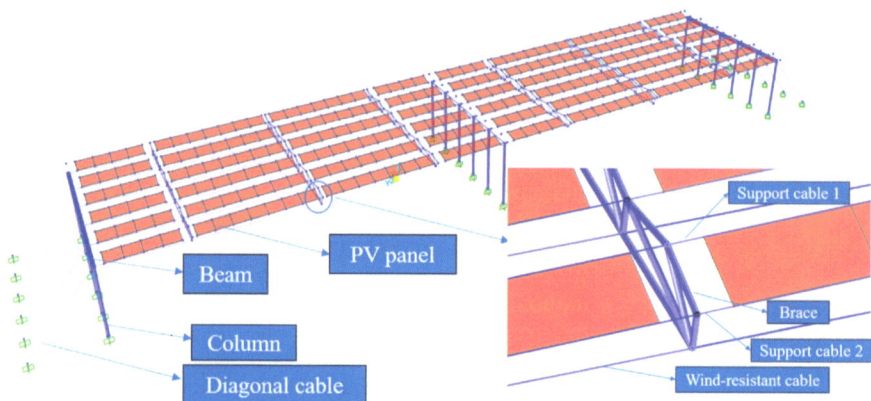

**Figure 1.** Geometric modeling and naming of flexible PV mounts.

*2.2. Boundary Condition Configuration*

For all components connected to the ground, the nodes are constrained in all six degrees of freedom (DOFs): translational in the $x$, $y$, and $z$ directions, and rotational about the $x$, $y$, and $z$ axes. The nodes along the upper edges on both sides of the flexible PV support structure are also fixed in all six DOFs. For the nodes on the middle support beams of the flexible PV structure, constraints are applied in the $x$ and $z$ directions. The sections of the columns interfacing with the ground are modeled using fixed supports to simulate full constraint conditions. Given the significant geometric nonlinearity inherent in the flexible PV support system, the analysis incorporates nonlinear approaches, specifically selecting the $P$-$\Delta$ effect and large displacement effects. The time step is set to 1000, with a time interval of 0.1 s. Given that the direct integration method is used for time–history analysis, Rayleigh damping is applied. Calculations yield a modal damping ratio of 0.02 for the first two modes, with the proportional damping coefficients $\alpha = 0.304$ and $\beta = 0.00132$.

*2.3. Simulation of Fluctuating Wind Load Time History*

The fluctuating wind speed time series $v(t)$ at time $t$ is represented as a linear combination of the time series from several previous moments, plus an independent stochastic process at time $t$. The expression is as follows:

$$v(t) = \sum_{k=1}^{p} \varphi \cdot v(t - k\Delta t) + N(t) \tag{1}$$

where $v(t)$ is the fluctuating wind speed at time $t$; $\varphi_k$ is the autoregressive coefficient; $p$ is the order of the AR model; $v(t - k\Delta t)$ is the fluctuating wind speed at $k$ previous time steps; $\Delta t$ is the time step of the fluctuating wind speed; and $N(t)$ is an independent stochastic process with a mean of 0 and variance $\sigma_N^2$. Multiplying both sides of Equation (2) by $v(t - k\Delta t)$ gives:

$$v(t)v(t - j\Delta t) = \sum_{k=1}^{p} \varphi \cdot v(t - j\Delta t)(t - k\Delta t) + N(t) \cdot v(t - j\Delta t) \tag{2}$$

In Equation (3), $j = 1, 2,\ldots, p$. Taking the mathematical expectation on both sides of Equation (2)

$$E(v(t)v(t)) = \sum_{k=1}^{p} \varphi_k \cdot E(v(t - k\Delta t) \cdot v(t)) + \sigma_N^2 \qquad (3)$$

Considering the properties of the autocorrelation function: the autocorrelation function of a stochastic process $X(t)$ is defined as the mean of $x(t)x(t + \tau)$. If the process is a stationary stochastic process, its mean $E[x(t)x(t + \tau)]$ is independent of the absolute value of time, and only depends on the time difference, that is:

$$R(j \cdot \Delta t) = E[v(t) \cdot v(t - j\Delta t)] \qquad (4)$$

Since the mean of $N(t)$ is 0 and is independent of $v(t)$, the relationship between the correlation function $R(j \cdot \Delta t)$ and the autoregressive coefficient $\varphi_k$ is:

$$R(j \cdot \Delta t) = \sum_{k=1}^{p} \varphi_k \cdot R[(t - k) \cdot \Delta t] \qquad (5)$$

The autoregressive coefficients $\varphi_k$ in the equation can be determined by the following system of equations:

$$\begin{cases} R(\Delta t) = \sum_{k=1}^{p} \varphi_k \cdot R[(1 - k) \cdot \Delta t] \\ R(2\Delta t) = \sum_{k=1}^{p} \varphi_k \cdot R[(2 - k) \cdot \Delta t] \\ \vdots \\ R(j\Delta t) = \sum_{k=1}^{p} \varphi_k \cdot R[(j - k) \cdot \Delta t] \end{cases} \qquad (6)$$

where $R(j \cdot \Delta t)$ is the correlation function of the fluctuating wind speed at $t = j\Delta t$, which can be obtained by Fourier transform from the target power spectral density function, and can be calculated as follows:

$$R(\tau) = \int_0^\infty S(f) \cos(2\pi f \cdot t) dn \qquad (7)$$

In Equation (6), $f$ is the frequency of the fluctuating wind speed. Substituting the obtained autoregressive coefficients $\varphi_k$ and the independent stochastic process $N(t)$ at time $t$ into Equation (1), the single-point fluctuating wind speed time series can be obtained.

In MATLAB (2021b), programming was conducted to simulate the fluctuating wind speed time series for a single node based on the Davenport wind spectrum, utilizing the auto-regressive (AR) technique. The simulation does not account for the correlation of fluctuating wind speeds between different nodes. The duration of the fluctuating wind speed time series was set to 100 s with a time step of 0.1 s, and the AR model was configured with a fourth-order process. The standard wind speed was set to 30 m/s, and the frequency integration range was chosen from 0.001 Hz to 10 Hz [35]; the simulation results of the fluctuating wind flow are shown in Figure 2. As depicted in Figure 3, the simulated fluctuating wind speeds predominantly vary within the range of −10 m/s to 10 m/s, with a mean value oscillating around zero, indicating that the simulation results for the fluctuating wind are realistic and satisfactory. Furthermore, as shown in Figure 4, the simulated spectrum closely aligns with the target spectrum, demonstrating the efficacy of the AR method in replicating the desired wind speed characteristics.

The fluctuating wind speed time series for the flexible PV support structure was simulated using the linear filtering method. This time series was then converted into a fluctuating wind load time series. The relationship between wind speed and wind pressure is given by the following equation:

$$\omega = \frac{1}{2}\rho v^2 \qquad (8)$$

In Equation (8), $\omega$ denotes the wind pressure corresponding to the wind speed; $\rho$ represents the air density, assumed to be 1.225 kg/m$^3$ in this context; and $v$ stands for the instantaneous wind speed. Utilizing the given equation and the relationship between the mean wind speed $\bar{v}$ and the fluctuating wind speed $v_t$, the time history of the fluctuating wind load can be derived.

$$F_t = \frac{1}{2}\rho\mu_s A\bar{v}^2 + \frac{1}{2}\rho\mu_s A\left(v_t^2 + 2\bar{v}v_t\right) \tag{9}$$

In Equation (9), $\mu_s$ is the shape coefficient, taken as 1.4 [36], and $A$ represents the area of the PV panel. Figure 5 illustrates the time history of the fluctuating wind load. After this conversion, fluctuating wind can be added to SAP2000. The obtained data can be directly utilized for structural dynamic analysis in SAP2000.

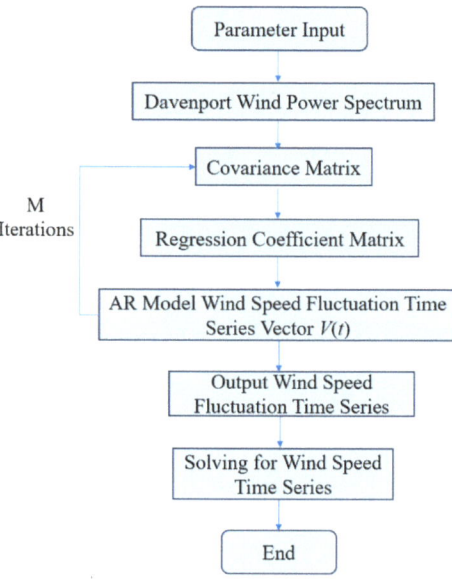

**Figure 2.** Fluctuating wind simulation process.

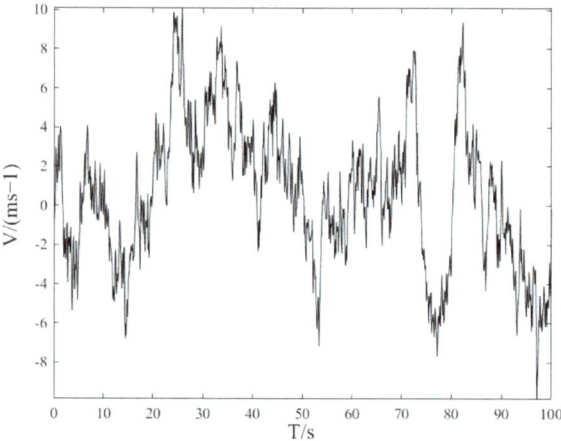

**Figure 3.** Fluctuating wind speed simulation spectrum.

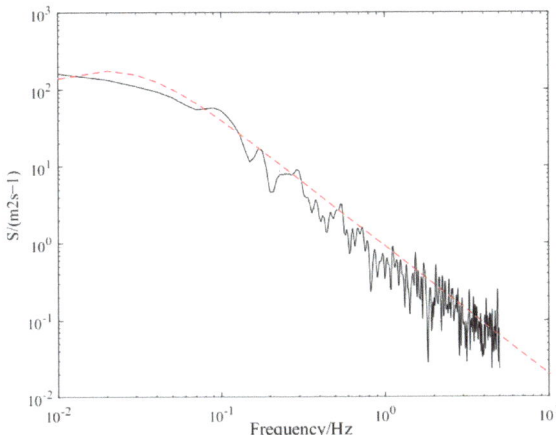

**Figure 4.** Fluctuating wind power spectrum vs. target spectrum.

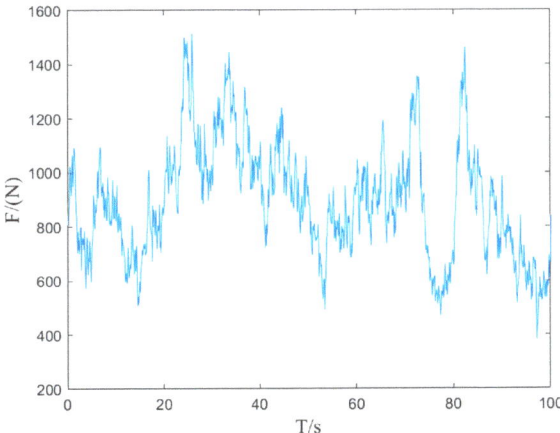

**Figure 5.** Fluctuating wind load time course.

## 3. Static Analysis of Flexible PV Racks for Extreme Working Conditions

To validate the accuracy of the numerical simulation, a comparative analysis with Li's [33] wind tunnel experiments was conducted. Wind speeds of 24 m/s, 28 m/s, 32 m/s, 36 m/s, 40 m/s, 44 m/s, 48 m/s, 49 m/s, and 50 m/s were selected for validation, and the results are depicted in the accompanying Figure 6. The maximum deviation occurs at 50 m/s, with an error of 16.8%. The mean error is calculated to be 9.1%, thereby demonstrating that the employed methodology can simulate the conditions with a high degree of accuracy.

### 3.1. Safety Analysis under Extreme Operating Conditions

For flexible PV brackets, the allowable deflection value adopted in current engineering practice is 1/100 of the span length [32]. To ensure the safety of PV modules under extreme static conditions, a detailed analysis of a series of extreme scenarios will be conducted. Given that the self-weight of the PV panels and flexible cables has a minimal impact on the flexible PV brackets, seismic loads are not considered. According to GB 50797-2012 "Code for Design of PV Power Stations" [37], the design value of the load effect combination should be calculated as follows:

$$S = \gamma_G S_{GK} + \gamma_w \psi_w S_{wk} + \gamma_S \psi_S S_{sk} + \gamma_t \psi_t S_{tk} \tag{10}$$

In Equation (10), $S$ is the design value of the load effect combination; $\gamma_G$, $\gamma_W$, $\gamma_S$, $\gamma_T$ are permanent load sub-factors, wind load sub-factors, snow load sub-factors, and temperature load sub-factors, respectively; $\Psi_W$, $\Psi_S$, $\Psi_T$ are the coefficients of the combined values of wind load, snow load, and temperature load, respectively; $S_{GK}$, $S_w$, $S_{sk}$, $S_{tk}$ are the standard values of permanent load, wind load, snow load, and temperature load, respectively.

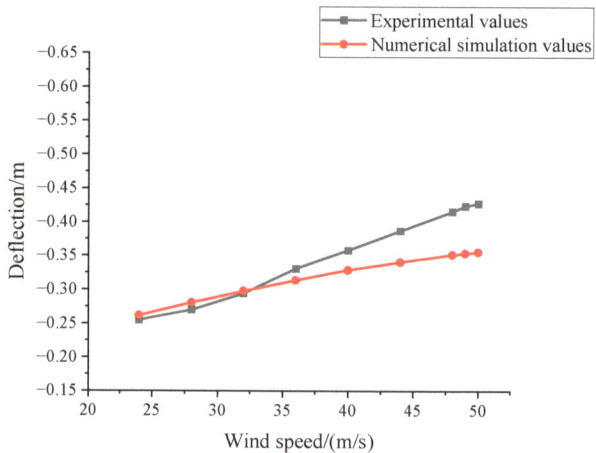

**Figure 6.** Comparison of maximum deflection values at different wind speeds.

According to the requirements of the aforementioned code, four types of ultimate limit state load combinations are presented in Table 1. Due to the unfavorable effects of permanent loads on the structure, $\gamma_G$ is 1.2 for all four conditions.

**Table 1.** Extreme operating condition combinations.

| Combination of Operating Conditions | $\gamma_W \Psi_W$ | $\gamma_S \Psi_S$ | $\gamma_T \Psi_T$ |
|---|---|---|---|
| 1 | 1.4 × 1 | 0 | 1.4 × 0.6 |
| 2 | 0 | 1.4 × 1 | 1.4 × 0.6 |
| 3 | 1.4 × 0.6 | 0 | 1.4 × 1 |
| 4 | 0 | 1.4 × 0.6 | 1.4 × 1 |

Taking a flexible PV bracket with a span of 30 m and a cable axial force of 75 kN as the research object, we investigate the variation patterns of the support cables and wind-resistant cables under temperature decrease and increase scenarios. The calculation results shown in Figure 7 indicate that, regardless of a temperature decrease or increase, the axial force of the wind-resistant cables is greater than that of the support cables. Additionally, the axial force of the flexible cables during a temperature increase is less than that during a temperature decrease.

Selecting Case 1, with the deflection limit at the mid-span of the wind-resistant cable under temperature decrease conditions set to 1/100 of the span length as the standard, we investigate the prestress and span limits under extreme conditions. Spans of 15 m, 25 m, 30 m, 35 m, and 45 m were selected, along with various levels of prestress for plotting. As shown in Figure 8, when the span exceeds 30 m, the rate of deflection increase accelerates with the increase in the span length.

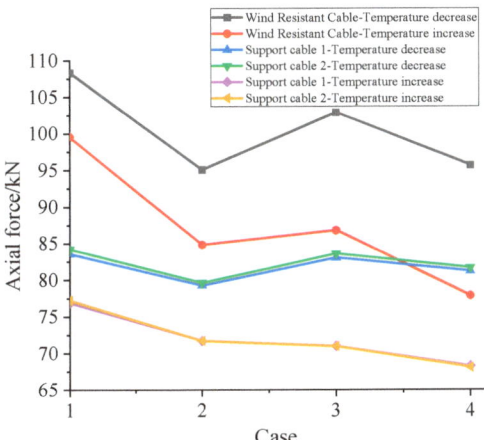

**Figure 7.** Comparison of axial forces in wind-resistant cables and support cables under different conditions of temperature increase and decrease.

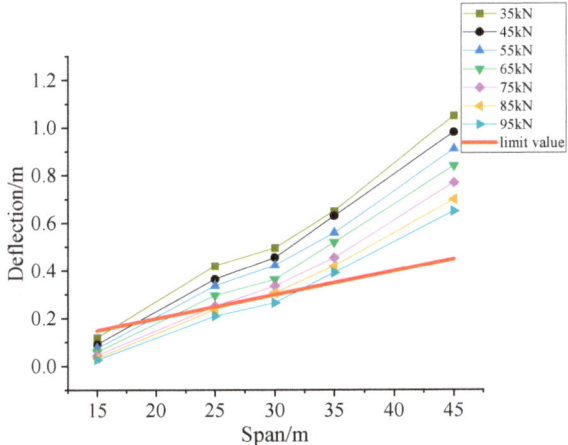

**Figure 8.** Comparison of mid-span deflections with different spans and prestresses.

Table 2 presents the prestress limits for different spans under extreme conditions. It is essential to consider the minimum prestress value corresponding to each span length when designing flexible PV brackets.

**Table 2.** The prestress limits under different span lengths.

| Span/m | 15 | 25 | 30 | 35 | 45 |
|---|---|---|---|---|---|
| Limit value of prestress/kN | 27 | 75 | 85 | 105 | 154 |

### 3.2. Critical Wind Speed Study

In summary, the study on the critical wind speed of flexible photovoltaic brackets uses the mid-span deflection limit at the wind-resistant cables under cooling conditions as the standard, set at 1/100 of the span length. Figure 9 illustrates the critical wind speed for distinct prestressing and span combinations. As illustrated in Figure 8, the critical wind speed exhibits a linear increase with increasing prestress, while the rate of increase diminishes with the increasing span. When the span of the flexible PV bracket is 45 m and the prestressing force is 35 kN, the critical wind speed decreases significantly due to the fact that the self-weight of the flexible PV bracket represents a considerable proportion of the pre-stressing cords, which are insufficient to cope with the wind load while counteracting the self-weight. Therefore, it is essential to ensure that the prestressing force of the flexible cords is greater than 45 kN in order to prevent failure.

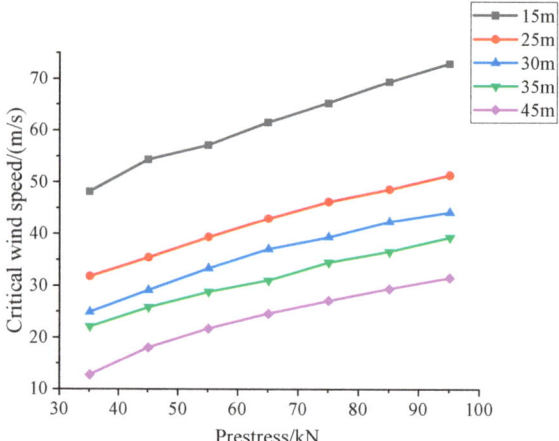

**Figure 9.** Critical wind speed for different spans and prestress combinations.

Table 3 presents the specific values of critical wind pressure for different spans and prestressing combinations. It is of paramount importance to exercise particular caution when designing flexible PV mounts in accordance with the specific characteristics of the local environment. This approach will ensure the safety of the mounting system while simultaneously reducing costs.

**Table 3.** The critical wind pressure values under different combinations of span lengths and prestress levels (kN/m²).

|  | Span/m | 15 | 25 | 30 | 35 | 45 |
| --- | --- | --- | --- | --- | --- | --- |
|  | 35 | 1.42 | 0.62 | 0.38 | 0.30 | 0.1 |
|  | 45 | 1.81 | 0.77 | 0.52 | 0.41 | 0.2 |
|  | 55 | 2.00 | 0.95 | 0.60 | 0.51 | 0.29 |
| Prestress/kN | 65 | 2.32 | 1.13 | 0.64 | 0.59 | 0.37 |
|  | 75 | 2.61 | 1.31 | 0.76 | 0.73 | 0.45 |
|  | 85 | 2.95 | 1.45 | 1.1 | 0.82 | 0.53 |
|  | 95 | 3.26 | 1.62 | 1.2 | 0.95 | 0.61 |

Based on the data in Figure 8, the critical wind speed equations are given for prestressing of 35 kN to 95 kN (not applicable when the span is 45 m and prestressing is 35 kN):

$$V_{\max} = A_1 x + B_1 \quad (11)$$

In Equation (11), $V_{\max}$ is the critical wind speed, $x$ is the span, and the values of a and b are given in Table 4 below:

**Table 4.** Values of $A$ and $B$ in different spans.

| Span/m | 15 | 25 | 30 | 35 | 45 |
| --- | --- | --- | --- | --- | --- |
| $A_1$ | 0.413 | 0.327 | 0.323 | 0.288 | 0.270 |
| $B_1$ | 33.700 | 20.375 | 13.614 | 12.067 | 5.931 |

## 3.3. Modal Analysis of Flexible PV Mounts

The eigenvector method in SAP2000 was employed to analyze the natural vibration characteristics of a flexible PV support structure after the application of prestress. The frequencies of the first 12 modes are shown below. Given that fluctuating wind load is a type of random load that varies randomly over time, with a period of 1 to 2 s and a frequency of 0.5 Hz to 1 Hz, the minimal natural frequency, as indicated in Table 5, is 1.460 Hz. This frequency is higher than that of the fluctuating wind, and the structure's natural frequencies are 1.460 to 6.032 times greater than the fluctuating wind frequency. According to vibration theory, resonance does not occur when the frequency of external excitation differs by more than 25% from the natural frequency of the structure. Therefore, resonance will not occur in the flexible PV support structure.

**Table 5.** Frequency of the first 12 orders of vibration pattern of flexible PV mounts.

| Modal Step | Natural Period/s | Natural Frequency/Hz |
|---|---|---|
| 1 | 0.685 | 1.460 |
| 2 | 0.646 | 1.547 |
| 3 | 0.641 | 1.560 |
| 4 | 0.635 | 1.575 |
| 5 | 0.629 | 1.589 |
| 6 | 0.613 | 1.630 |
| 7 | 0.598 | 1.673 |
| 8 | 0.587 | 1.702 |
| 9 | 0.553 | 1.807 |
| 10 | 0.460 | 2.172 |
| 11 | 0.353 | 2.835 |
| 12 | 0.331 | 3.016 |

As shown in Table 6, the first mode primarily exhibits translational vibration in the $x$-direction, while the fourth and eighth modes primarily exhibit translational vibration in the $z$-direction. The second, third, fifth, sixth, seventh, ninth, tenth, eleventh, and twelfth modes primarily exhibit torsional vibration.

**Table 6.** Modal participation factors.

| Modal Step | UX | UY | UZ | RZ |
|---|---|---|---|---|
| 1 | −2.413318 | 0.000583 | 0.095626 | −1.116369 |
| 2 | −0.079541 | −0.010703 | −0.250148 | 5.499972 |
| 3 | 0.258653 | 0.002853 | 0.424804 | −27.059293 |
| 4 | −0.023301 | 0.001903 | −1.546522 | −1.364577 |
| 5 | 0.118711 | 0.004366 | 0.383939 | 30.625138 |
| 6 | −0.086721 | 0.004188 | −1.00108 | −1.768091 |
| 7 | −0.00158 | −0.006285 | −0.237825 | −2.309102 |
| 8 | 0.046369 | −0.000467 | 1.035485 | −0.556642 |
| 9 | −0.196866 | 0.000431 | 0.502407 | −5.998283 |
| 10 | 0.104026 | −0.001627 | −0.165358 | −2.266144 |
| 11 | 0.004583 | 0.000024 | 0.000638 | −0.086253 |
| 12 | −0.000871 | 0.003654 | 0.000046 | −2.483576 |

## 3.4. Wind Vibration Response of Flexible PV Mounting Structures

To investigate the impact of fluctuating wind loads on the flexible PV support structure, the previously obtained wind load time histories were applied to a flexible PV support structure with a span of 30 m and a prestress of 50 kN. Analysis of the calculation results shows that the maximum deflection and acceleration occur at the mid-span, and the axial force in the wind-resistant cables is greater than that in the supporting cables. Figure 10 presents the time histories of mid-span deflection, acceleration, and wind-resistant cable axial force under wind-suction and wind-pressure conditions. The axial force in the wind-resistant cables is greater under wind-pressure conditions than under wind-suction conditions. The displacement time history at the mid-span is greater under wind-pressure conditions than under wind-suction conditions. However, for mid-span acceleration, the wind suction condition results in greater values than the wind-pressure condition. Overall, it can be concluded that the flexible PV support structure exhibits a consistent response trend under both wind-suction and wind-pressure conditions.

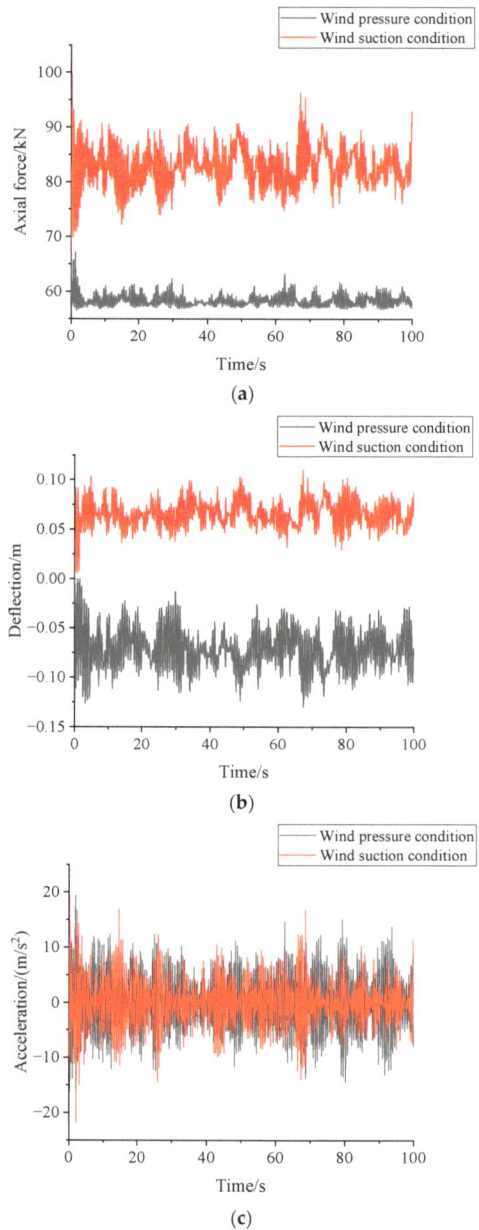

**Figure 10.** Wind-induced vibration response of the flexible PV mounting structure under wind-suction and wind-pressure conditions. (**a**) Time history of axial force of wind-resistant cables. (**b**) The mid-span deflection time history. (**c**) The mid-span acceleration time history.

To investigate the distribution patterns of maximum deflection, axial force, and acceleration in a flexible PV array group, Tables 7 and 8, respectively, present the comparisons of average deflection, average axial force, and absolute average acceleration at the mid-span under wind-suction and wind-pressure conditions. The tables indicate that the maximum wind-induced vibration responses in the flexible PV array group occur at the mid-span under both wind suction and wind-pressure conditions, with the responses gradually decreasing towards the edges under wind-pressure conditions.

Table 7. Comparison of deflection, axial force, and acceleration at mid-span of different rows for wind-pressure conditions.

|  | First Row | Second Row | Third Row | Fourth Row | Fifth Row | Sixth Row |
|---|---|---|---|---|---|---|
| Axial force/kN | 76.99 | 78.75 | 79.04 | 77.15 | 78.97 | 77.6 |
| Deflection/m | −0.287 | −0.295 | −0.303 | −0.310 | −0.288 | 0.07 |
| Acceleration/(m/s$^2$) | 3.97 | 3.54 | 4.86 | 3.67 | 3.49 | 4.93 |

Table 8. Comparison of deflection, axial force, and acceleration at mid-span of different rows under wind-suction conditions.

|  | First Row | Second Row | Third Row | Fourth Row | Fifth Row | Sixth Row |
|---|---|---|---|---|---|---|
| Axial force/kN | 48.55 | 48.26 | 49.28 | 48.41 | 49.01 | 47.88 |
| Deflection/m | 0.213 | 0.212 | 0.184 | 0.205 | 0.186 | −0.08 |
| Acceleration/(m/s$^2$) | 4.93 | 3.96 | 5.24 | 3.96 | 4.55 | 4.90 |

Based on the summarized results, in subsequent reinforcement of the flexible PV mounting structure, it is recommended to focus on the mid-span of the central rows for the analysis of deflection, axial force, and acceleration. For axial force analysis, focus on the axial force in the wind-resistant cables.

## 4. Wind-Induced Vibration Coefficient for Flexible PV Mounting Structure

Although the finite element method can quantitatively analyze the dynamic response of flexible PV support structures under fluctuating wind loads, this method's time consumption is highly dependent on computer performance and is often impractical for actual engineering design. To better meet practical application needs, it is necessary to consider using static calculation methods to determine the dynamic response of structures.

In practical engineering design, equivalent static wind loads are commonly used to account for the dynamic effects of wind. The equivalent static wind load is represented by the product of the static wind load $P_s$ and the wind vibration coefficient $\beta$. According to the Chinese "Building Structural Load Specification" [38], the wind vibration coefficient $\beta$ can be taken as the load wind-vibration coefficient $\beta_{Li}$, which is expressed as follows:

$$\beta_L = 1 + \frac{P_d}{P_s} = 1 + \frac{\mu \sigma_F}{P_s} \tag{12}$$

$$\sigma_F = \sqrt{\frac{\sum_{n=1}^{N}(P_d - P_s)^2}{n}} \tag{13}$$

In Equation (12), $P_d$ represents the nodal dynamic wind load. $P_s$ is the nodal static wind load. $\mu$ is the peaking factor, which takes the value of 3.5, according to the wind-resistant design calculation manual [39]. $\sigma_F$ is the mean square deviation of the fluctuating wind response.

In addition to the load wind-vibration coefficient, which is a commonly used wind-vibration coefficient, there is also a displacement wind-vibration coefficient and a displacement of the structure in the time domain. The displacement of the structure in the time domain is made up of static displacement caused by the average wind and dynamic displacement caused by fluctuating wind. The displacement wind-vibration coefficient is calculated using the following formula:

$$\beta_u = \frac{\overline{u} + \hat{u}}{\overline{u}} = 1 + \frac{\hat{u}}{\overline{u}} = 1 + \frac{\mu \sigma_w}{\overline{u}} \quad (14)$$

In Equation (14), $\beta_{ui}$ is the displacement wind-vibration coefficient, $\hat{u}$ is the peak displacement due to the fluctuating wind, $\overline{u}$ is the static displacement due to the mean wind, and $\sigma_w$ is the mean square deviation of the displacement response to the fluctuating wind.

$$\sigma_w = \sqrt{\frac{\sum_{n=1}^{N}(\hat{u} - \overline{u})^2}{n}} \quad (15)$$

Given that the fluctuating wind load time duration is in the hundreds of seconds, with a time step of 0.1 s, the value of $N$ is taken to be 1000.

To minimize the error between the load wind-vibration coefficient and the displacement wind-vibration coefficient, 10 different sets of fluctuating wind speed time histories were used to calculate the load wind-vibration coefficient and the displacement wind-vibration coefficient under wind-suction and wind-pressure conditions. The simulation was conducted with a span of 30 m, and axial forces of 50 kN in both the supporting cables and the wind-resistant cables. Refer to previous for other material properties and settings.

Table 9 indicates that the displacement wind-vibration coefficients under both wind-suction and wind-pressure conditions are generally higher than the load wind-vibration coefficients. This suggests that the deflection of the flexible PV support structure is more sensitive to fluctuating wind loads compared to the axial force. Considering the safety of flexible PV support structures, it is reasonable to use the displacement wind-vibration coefficient rather than the load wind-vibration coefficient. For the flexible PV arrays with wind-resistant cables discussed in this study, a recommended range for the wind-vibration coefficient is 1.5 to 2.52. This range aligns well with the suggested wind-vibration coefficient values of 1.2 to 2.5 obtained from wind tunnel tests [31], thereby further validating the accuracy of the numerical simulations presented in this paper.

**Table 9.** Comparison of load wind-vibration coefficients and displacement wind-vibration coefficients for different fluctuating wind speeds with range wind pressure and wind suction conditions.

| Group Number | Wind Pressure Condition | | Wind Suction Condition | |
| --- | --- | --- | --- | --- |
| | $\beta_L$ | $\beta_u$ | $\beta_L$ | $\beta_u$ |
| 1 | 1.256 | 1.564 | 1.159 | 2.173 |
| 2 | 1.218 | 1.556 | 1.112 | 2.110 |
| 3 | 1.243 | 1.604 | 1.118 | 2.230 |
| 4 | 1.248 | 1.626 | 1.123 | 2.294 |
| 5 | 1.225 | 1.571 | 1.114 | 2.133 |
| 6 | 1.224 | 1.611 | 1.114 | 2.132 |
| 7 | 1.235 | 1.586 | 1.110 | 2.149 |
| 8 | 1.217 | 1.540 | 1.125 | 2.179 |
| 9 | 1.228 | 1.561 | 1.114 | 2.148 |
| 10 | 1.193 | 1.490 | 1.103 | 2.046 |

## 5. Reinforcement Scheme for Wind-Induced Vibration Resistance in Flexible PV Mounting Structures

Given the sensitivity of flexible PV support structures to wind loads and their pronounced wind-induced vibration responses in large-span settings, the development of effective vibration control measures is of paramount importance. This study proposes and evaluates several reinforcement strategies for flexible PV support structures.

The baseline, unreinforced flexible PV support structure is designated as F. The first reinforcement strategy involves increasing the diameter of the prestressed cables to 17.8 mm and 21.6 mm, respectively. These configurations are named F1-1 and F1-2 for ease of comparison. The second strategy (F2) introduces a support beam at mid-span, constructed from Q355 seamless steel pipes with an outer diameter of 0.2 m and an inner diameter of 0.05 m. The third strategy (F3) involves adding a stabilizing cable at mid-span, with a diameter of 0.0287 m and a horizontal tension of 15.9 kN. The structural response varies depending on the reinforcement strategy and loading conditions. For strategy F2, the support beam directly impacts the mid-span, causing the maximum deflection and acceleration to occur at the 3/4L or 1/4L positions of the middle row. Conversely, in strategy F3, the stabilizing cable causes the maximum deflection and acceleration to appear at the L/4 or 3L/4 positions of the middle row under wind-suction conditions. However, under wind-pressure conditions, the maximum deflection and acceleration remain at mid-span. The remaining material properties and setup are simulated according to the parameters detailed in Section 2. Geometric schematics of the wind-induced vibration control strategies F2 and F3 are shown in Figures 11 and 12.

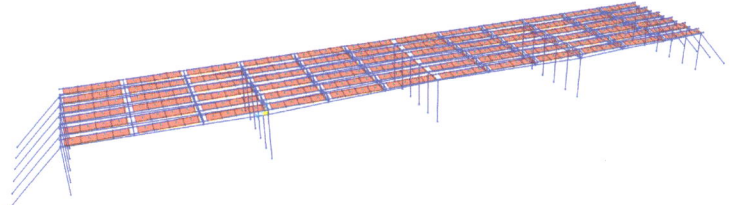

**Figure 11.** F2 Geometric model of wind-vibration resistance scheme.

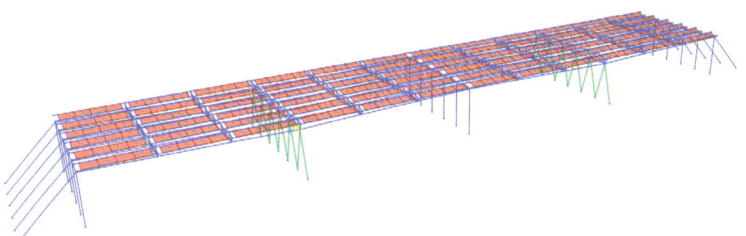

**Figure 12.** F3 Geometric model of wind-vibration resistance scheme.

Figures 13 and 14 illustrate the dynamic responses of a flexible PV support structure under wind-pressure and wind-suction conditions, respectively. Under wind-pressure conditions: For the axial force in the flexible cables of the structure, the hierarchy is as follows: F1-2 > F1-1 > F > F3 > F2. Increasing the diameter of the prestressed cables significantly enhances the axial force in the flexible cables. Regarding the maximum deflection of the structure, the order is: F3 > F > F1-1 > F1-2 > F2. The deflection in F3 is greater than in the unstiffened flexible PV support structure because the stabilizing cables in F3 are tensioned but not compressed. For structural acceleration, the ranking is: F3 > F > F1-1 > F1-2 > F2.

Under wind-suction conditions: For the axial force in the flexible cables, the sequence is: F3 > F2 > F > F1-1 > F1-2. The presence of stabilizing cables increases the axial force. Regarding the maximum deflection of the structure, the order is: F > F1-1 > F1-2 > F3 > F2. For structural acceleration, the ranking is: F3 > F > F1-1 > F1-2.

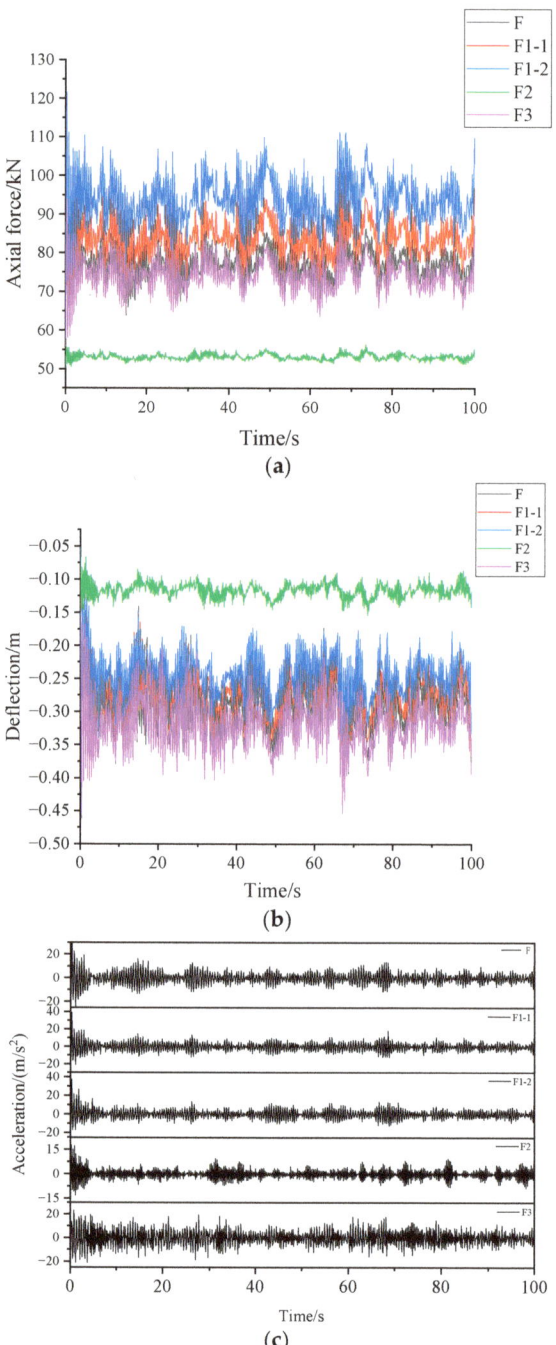

**Figure 13.** A comparative analysis of the wind-pressure response time history of various structural strengthening schemes. (**a**) Comparison of axial force. (**b**) Deflection comparison. (**c**) Acceleration comparison.

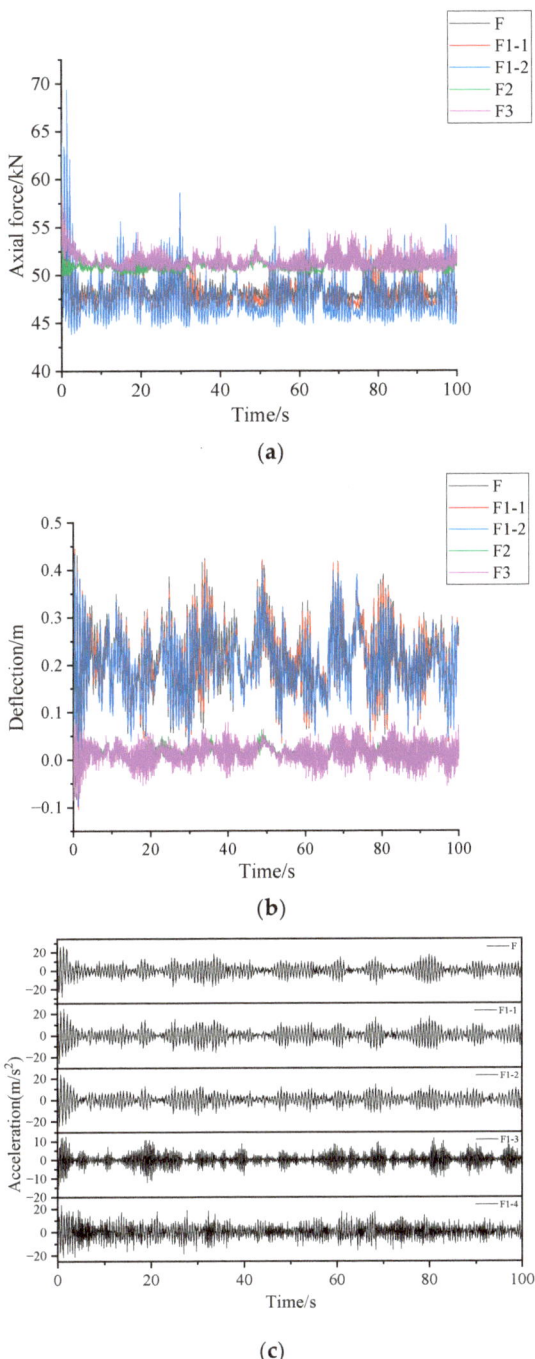

**Figure 14.** A comparative analysis of the wind-absorption response time histories of different structural reinforcement schemes. (**a**) Comparison of axial force. (**b**) Deflection comparison. (**c**) Acceleration comparison.

Figures 15 and 16 illustrate the ratios of wind-induced vibration responses—namely, axial force, deflection, and acceleration—under wind-pressure and wind-suction conditions, compared to the unreinforced flexible PV mounting structure. To better demonstrate the effectiveness of each reinforcement scheme, Tables 10 and 11 provide the specific ratios of each scheme relative to the unreinforced case. The F2 scheme is the most effective in reducing the wind-induced vibration response of the structure. In contrast, the F3 scheme is less beneficial, as it may even be detrimental in reducing the structural wind-induced vibration response. Although the F1-1 and F1-2 schemes do contribute to reducing the response, their impact is not significant. Similarly, under wind-suction conditions, the F2 scheme remains the most effective in mitigating the structural wind-induced vibration response, followed by the F3 scheme. The F1-1 and F1-2 schemes also help to reduce the wind-induced vibration response, but their effectiveness is even less pronounced under wind-suction conditions. These findings highlight that while F2 provides the most substantial reduction in wind-induced vibration for both conditions, the F3 scheme, though less effective for wind pressure, offers a cost-efficient and space-saving alternative with better performance under wind-suction conditions. Conversely, the F1-1 and F1-2 schemes, although slightly effective, do not provide significant benefits in either condition.

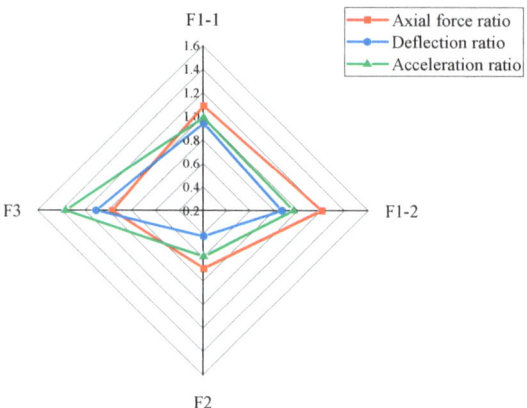

**Figure 15.** Comparison of wind vibration response of optimization schemes for wind-pressure conditions.

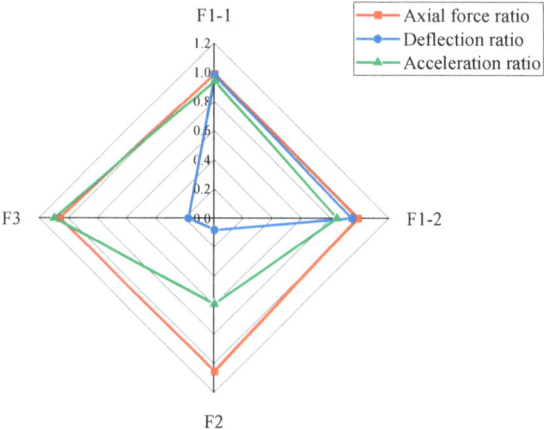

**Figure 16.** Comparison of wind vibration response of optimization schemes for wind suction condition.

Table 10. Comparison of wind-pressure conditions by scenario.

|                    | F1-1 | F1-2  | F2    | F3   |
|--------------------|------|-------|-------|------|
| Axial force ratio  | 1.09 | 1.20  | 0.69  | 0.97 |
| Deflection ratio   | 0.94 | 0.861 | 0.418 | 1.11 |
| Acceleration ratio | 0.99 | 0.96  | 0.59  | 1.37 |

Table 11. Comparison of wind suction scenarios.

|                    | F1-1 | F1-2 | F2   | F3   |
|--------------------|------|------|------|------|
| Axial force ratio  | 0.99 | 0.98 | 1.05 | 1.06 |
| Deflection ratio   | 0.98 | 0.94 | 0.08 | 0.18 |
| Acceleration ratio | 0.94 | 0.84 | 0.59 | 1.1  |

In summary, although the F2 scheme is the most effective in reducing the wind-induced vibration response of the structure, it requires more land area and typically incurs higher costs. The F1-1 and F1-2 schemes, while capable of mitigating the wind-induced vibration response, do not significantly reduce the response under both wind-pressure and wind-suction conditions. The F3 scheme effectively reduces the structural wind-induced vibration response under wind-suction conditions, but it is less effective for wind-pressure conditions. Compared to F2, F3 has a lower cost and is more land-efficient.

## 6. Conclusions

Using MATLAB, we developed a program to generate the fluctuating wind-speed time series, and then created a model in SAP2000 to conduct both static analysis under extreme conditions and wind-induced vibration response analysis. This research focused on the safety and critical wind speed of flexible PV mounting structures, as well as the calculation of wind-vibration coefficients, and proposed reinforcement strategies for wind-induced vibration resistance. The results indicate the following:

(1) Under the combined effect of extreme conditions, the axial force of the wind-resistant cable during a temperature rise is lower than that of the flexible cable during a temperature drop. Extreme conditions dominated by wind have a greater impact on the flexible PV mounting structures compared to those dominated by snow. For structures with spans of 15 m, 25 m, 30 m, 35 m, and 45 m, the prestress limits under extreme conditions are 27 kN, 75 kN, 85 kN, 105 kN, and 154 kN, respectively.

(2) Modal analysis reveals that the structure does not resonate under fluctuating wind loads, with the dominant vibration mode being torsional. The mid-span displacement and axial force in the wind-resistant cables are greater under wind-pressure conditions than under wind-suction conditions. In contrast, the mid-span acceleration is higher under wind-suction conditions compared to wind-pressure conditions.

(3) The calculation of displacement and load wind-vibration coefficients indicates that using the displacement wind-vibration coefficient is more appropriate than using the load wind-vibration coefficient. It is recommended that the wind-vibration coefficient be in the range of 1.5 to 2.52.

(4) Four structural reinforcement schemes were proposed for enhancing the wind-induced vibration resistance of flexible PV mounting structures. The analysis suggests that adding a support beam at the mid-span is the most effective measure to reduce the structural wind-vibration response. However, this approach requires more land and usually entails higher costs. Increasing the cable diameter can reduce the structural wind-vibration response, but the reduction is not significant when considering both the wind-pressure and wind-suction conditions. Adding a stabilizing cable at the mid-span effectively reduces the wind-vibration response under wind-suction conditions but is less effective for wind-pressure conditions. Compared to adding support beams, this method can be more cost-effective and requires less land area.

**Author Contributions:** Conceptualization, Y.L.; methodology, Y.L.; software, Y.L.; validation, Y.L. and J.Z.; formal analysis, J.Z.; investigation, Y.L. and Y.P.; resources, J.Z.; data curation, Y.L. and Y.P.; writing—original draft preparation, Y.L.; writing—review and editing, J.Z. and Y.P.; visualization, Y.L.; supervision, J.Z.; project administration, J.Z.; funding acquisition, J.Z. All authors have read and agreed to the published version of the manuscript.

**Funding:** This research was funded by the National Natural Science Foundation of China (Grant No. 52201323).

**Data Availability Statement:** The data presented in this study are available on request from the corresponding author.

**Acknowledgments:** This work is supported by the National Natural Science Foundation of China. This support is gratefully appreciated.

**Conflicts of Interest:** The authors declare no conflicts of interest.

# References

1. Liu, H.J.; Shi, J.; Guo, L.X.; Qiao, L.C. China's Energy Reform in the New Era: Process, Achievements and Prospects. *J. Manag. World* **2022**, *38*, 6–24. [CrossRef]
2. Wang, C.; Shuai, J.; Ding, L.; Lu, Y.; Chen, J. Comprehensive benefit evaluation of solar PV projects based on multi-criteria decision grey relation projection method: Evidence from 5 counties in China. *Energy* **2022**, *238*, 121654. [CrossRef]
3. Wang, L. Photovoltaic industry is expected to usher in a new round of outbreak. *China Bus. News*, 10 November 2020; p. 005. [CrossRef]
4. Ren, G.; Wan, J.; Liu, J.; Yu, D. Spatial and temporal assessments of complementarity for renewable energy resources in China. *Energy* **2019**, *177*, 262–275. [CrossRef]
5. Wang, Y. PV module flexible bracket technical solution. *Sol. Energy* **2018**, 37–40.
6. Liu, X.J.; Cui, G.Q.; Yu, K. Research on Solar Photovoltaic Flexible Racking System. *New Technol. New Prod. China* **2020**, 79–81. [CrossRef]
7. Aly, A.; Bitsuamlak, G. Aerodynamics of ground-mounted solar panels: Test model scale effects. *J. Wind Eng. Ind. Aerodyn.* **2013**, *123*, 250–260. [CrossRef]
8. Aly, A.; Bitsuamlak, G. Wind induced pressures on solar panels mounted on residential homes. *J. Archit. Eng.* **2014**, *20*, 04013003. [CrossRef]
9. Kopp, G.A.; Banks, D. Use of wind tunnel test method for obtaining design wind loads on roof-mounted solar arrays. *J. Struct. Eng.* **2013**, *139*, 284–287. [CrossRef]
10. Pratt, R.N.; Kopp, G.A. Velocity measurements around low-profile, tilted, solar arrays mounted on large flat-roofs, for wall normal wind directions. *J. Wind Eng. Ind. Aerodyn.* **2013**, *123*, 226–238. [CrossRef]
11. Stathopoulos, T.; Zisis, I.; Xypnitou, E. Local and overall wind pressure and force coefficients for solar panels. *J. Wind Eng. Ind. Aerodyn.* **2014**, *125*, 195–206. [CrossRef]
12. Warsido, W.P.; Bitsuamlak, G.T.; Barata, J. Influence of spacing parameters on the wind loading of solar array. *J. Fluids Struct.* **2014**, *48*, 295–315. [CrossRef]
13. Shafique, M.; Luo, X.; Zuo, J. Photovoltaic-green roofs: A review of benefits, limitations, and trends. *Sol. Energy* **2020**, *202*, 485–497. [CrossRef]
14. Trindade, A.; Cordeiro, L. Automated formal verification of stand-alone solar photovoltaic systems. *Sol. Energy* **2019**, *193*, 684–691. [CrossRef]
15. Glick, A.; Smith, S.E.; Ali, N.; Bossuyt, J.; Recktenwald, G.; Calaf, M.; Cal, R.B. Influence of flow direction and turbulence intensity on heat transfer of utility-scale photovoltaic solar farms. *Sol. Energy* **2020**, *207*, 173–182. [CrossRef]
16. Naeiji, A.; Raji, F.; Zisis, I. Wind loads on residential scale rooftop photovoltaic panels. *J. Wind. Eng. Ind. Aerodyn.* **2017**, *168*, 228–246. [CrossRef]
17. Mignolet, M.P.; Spanos, P.D. Simulation of Homogeneous Two-Dimensional Random Fields: Part IAR and ARMA Models. *J. Appl. Mech.* **1992**, *59*, S260–S269. [CrossRef]
18. Owen, J.S.; Eccles, B.J.; Choo, B.S.; Woodings, M.A. The application of auto-regressive time series modelling for the: Time-frequency analysis of civil engineering structures. *Eng. Struct.* **2001**, *23*, 521–536. [CrossRef]
19. Borgman, L.E. *Ocean Wave Simulation for Engineering Design*; American Society of Civil Engineers: Reston, VA, USA, 1967; p. 95.
20. Shinozuka, M. Simulation of Multivariate and Multidimensional Random Processes. *J. Acoust. Soc. Am.* **1971**, *49*, 357–368. [CrossRef]
21. Shinozuka, M.; Jan, C.M. Digital simulation of random processes and its applications. *J. Sound Vib.* **1972**, *25*, 111–128. [CrossRef]
22. Yamada, M.; Ohkitani, K. Orthonormal wavelet analysis of turbulence. *Fluid Dyn. Res.* **1991**, *8*, 101–115. [CrossRef]
23. Kitagawa, T.; Nomura, T. A wavelet-based method to generate artificial wind fluctuation data. *J. Wind. Eng. Ind. Aerodyn.* **2003**, *91*, 943–964. [CrossRef]
24. Tang, S.L.; Luo, Y.F. Development and application of artificial neural network technology. *Comput. Dev. Appl.* **2009**, *2*, 10.

25. Mao, J.; Zhao, H.D.; Yao, J.J. Application and prospect of Artificial Neural Network. *Electron. Des. Eng.* **2011**, *19*, 6265.
26. Guo, T.; Yang, Y.; Huang, G.Q.; Zhang, J.M. Wind-induced vibration analysis of flexible photovoltaic support structure under mountain canyon terrain. *Acta Energiae Solaris Sin.* **2023**, *44*, 31–40. [CrossRef]
27. Cai, Y.; Deng, H.; Li, B.Y. Wind-resistant design method of cable-suspended photovoltaic module support structures. *J. Vib. Shock* **2022**, *41*, 69–77.
28. Xie, D.; Fan, J. Wind vibration analysis of prestressed flexible photovoltaic support systems. *Build. Struct.* **2021**, *51*, 15–18.
29. Wang, Z.G.; Zhao, F.F.; Ji, C.M.; Peng, X.F.; Lu, H.Q. Wind-induced vibration analysis of multi-row and multi-span flexible photovoltaic support. *Eng. J. Wuhan Univ.* **2021**, *54*, 75–79.
30. He, X.-H.; Ding, H.; Jing, H.-Q.; Zhang, F.; Wu, X.-P.; Weng, X.-J. Wind-induced vibration and its suppression of photovoltaic modules supported by suspension cables. *J. Wind. Eng. Ind. Aerodyn.* **2020**, *206*, 104275. [CrossRef]
31. Xu, H.; Ding, K.; Shen, G.; Du, H.; Chen, Y. Experimental investigation on wind-induced vibration of photovoltaic modules supported by suspension cables. *Eng. Struct.* **2024**, *299*, 117125. [CrossRef]
32. Liu, J.; Li, S.; Luo, J.; Chen, Z. Experimental study on critical wind velocity of a 33-meter-span flexible photovoltaic support structure and its mitigation. *J. Wind. Eng. Ind. Aerodyn.* **2023**, *236*, 105355. [CrossRef]
33. Li, W.; Ke, S.; Cai, Z.; Ji, C.; Wang, W.; Wang, L.; Ren, H. Instability mechanism and failure criteria of large-span flexible PV support arrays under severe wind. *Sol. Energy* **2023**, *264*, 112000. [CrossRef]
34. GB/T 5224-2014; Steel Strand for Prestressed Concrete. China Standard Publishing House: Beijing, China, 2015.
35. Zhang, Z.H. Simulation of wind loading. *J. Build. Struct.* **1994**, 44–52.
36. Zhang, J.; Lou, Y. Study of Wind Load Influencing Factors of Flexibly Supported Photovoltaic Panels. *Buildings* **2024**, *14*, 1677. [CrossRef]
37. GB 50797-2012; Code for Design of Photovoltaic Power Station. Standardization Administration of the People's Republic of China: Beijing, China, 2012.
38. GB 50009-2012; Building Structural Load Specification. Standardization Administration of the People's Republic of China: Beijing, China, 2012.
39. Zhang, X.T. *Engineering Wind Design Calculation Manual*; China Construction Industry Press: Beijing, China, 1998.

**Disclaimer/Publisher's Note:** The statements, opinions and data contained in all publications are solely those of the individual author(s) and contributor(s) and not of MDPI and/or the editor(s). MDPI and/or the editor(s) disclaim responsibility for any injury to people or property resulting from any ideas, methods, instructions or products referred to in the content.

*Article*

# Physically Guided Estimation of Vehicle Loading-Induced Low-Frequency Bridge Responses with BP-ANN

Xuzhao Lu [1,2], Guang Qu [1,2,*], Limin Sun [1,2], Ye Xia [1,2], Haibin Sun [1] and Wei Zhang [3]

1. Department of Bridge Engineering, Tongji University, Shanghai 200092, China; luxuzhao_1992@tongji.edu.cn (X.L.); lmsun@tongji.edu.cn (L.S.); yxia@tongji.edu.cn (Y.X.); 2232472@tongji.edu.cn (H.S.)
2. Shanghai Qi Zhi Institute, Shanghai 200232, China
3. Fujian Provincial Construction Engineering Quality Testing Center Co., Ltd., Fujian Academy of Building Research Co., Ltd., Fuzhou 350109, China; fjjkyzw@163.com
* Correspondence: qug@tongji.edu.cn

**Citation:** Lu, X.; Qu, G.; Sun, L.; Xia, Y.; Sun, H.; Zhang, W. Physically Guided Estimation of Vehicle Loading-Induced Low-Frequency Bridge Responses with BP-ANN. *Buildings* **2024**, *14*, 2995. https://doi.org/10.3390/buildings14092995

Academic Editor: Fabrizio Gara

Received: 31 August 2024
Revised: 17 September 2024
Accepted: 18 September 2024
Published: 21 September 2024

**Copyright:** © 2024 by the authors. Licensee MDPI, Basel, Switzerland. This article is an open access article distributed under the terms and conditions of the Creative Commons Attribution (CC BY) license (https://creativecommons.org/licenses/by/4.0/).

**Abstract:** The intersectional relationship in bridge health monitoring refers to the mapping function that correlates bridge responses across different locations. This relationship is pivotal for estimating structural responses, which are then instrumental in assessing a bridge's service status and identifying potential damage. The current research landscape is heavily focused on high-frequency responses, especially those associated with single-mode vibration. When it comes to low-frequency responses triggered by multi-mode vehicle loading, a prevalent strategy is to regard these low-frequency responses as "quasi-static" and subsequently apply time-series prediction techniques to simulate the intersectional relationship. However, these methods are contingent upon data regarding external loading, such as traffic conditions and air temperatures. This necessitates the collection of long-term monitoring data to account for fluctuations in traffic and temperature, a task that can be quite daunting in real-world engineering contexts. To address this challenge, our study shifts the analytical perspective from a static analysis to a dynamic analysis. By delving into the physical features of bridge responses of the vehicle–bridge interaction (VBI) system, we identify that the intersectional relationship should be inherently time-independent. The perceived time lag in quasi-static responses is, in essence, a result of low-frequency vibrations that are aligned with driving force modes. We specifically derive the intersectional relationship for low-frequency bridge responses within the VBI system and determine it to be a time-invariant transfer matrix associated with multiple mode shapes. Drawing on these physical insights, we adopt a time-independent machine learning method, the backpropagation–artificial neural network (BP-ANN), to simulate the intersectional relationship. To train the network, monitoring data from various cross-sections were input, with the responses at a particular section designated as the output. The trained network is now capable of estimating responses even in scenarios where time-related traffic conditions and temperatures deviate from those present in the training data set. To substantiate the time-independent nature of the derived intersectional relationship, finite element models were developed. The proposed method was further validated through the in-field monitoring of a continuous highway bridge. We anticipate that this method will be highly effective in estimating low-frequency responses under a variety of unknown traffic and air temperature conditions, offering significant convenience for practical engineering applications.

**Keywords:** bridge health monitoring; low-frequency responses; vehicle–bridge interaction (VBI) system; BP-ANN

## 1. Introduction

Simulating an intersectional relationship is a key area of focus in bridge health monitoring. By utilizing historical monitoring data from multiple cross-sections, it is possible to model the intersectional relationship [1] that exists between these locations. This model can then be used to estimate the current response at a specific cross-section by multiplying the relationship with the responses recorded at other cross-sections. If there is a significant discrepancy between the actual current monitoring data and the estimated results, it could be an indication of potential damage in the vicinity of that particular cross-section. This approach provides a valuable tool for identifying structural issues and ensuring the ongoing safety and integrity of a bridge.

The majority of the current research concentrates on the intersectional relationship associated with high-frequency responses [2], with scant attention given to low-frequency responses. It has been demonstrated that the intersectional relationship acts as a transfer matrix determined by mode shapes. Consequently, it is essential to initially identify a bridge's mode shapes. Subsequently, several explicit mode shape identification methods may become available, such as Stochastic Subspace Identification (SSI) [3,4], Independent Component Analysis (ICA) [5,6], and other general physical parameter-identification methods [7–9]. With these methods, the intersectional relationship can be further estimated. However, for typical low-frequency responses induced via vehicle loading, the corresponding frequencies not only are low but also vary with a vehicle's moving speed. Moreover, the differences between these frequencies are minimal, making it challenging to identify bridge-mode shapes using most of the aforementioned methods [10,11].

In place of the term for "low-frequency" responses, existing research often employs the descriptor of "quasi-static" responses [12,13] to circumvent the challenges associated with identifying bridge-mode shapes. From a static structural analysis perspective, quasi-static responses are considered to be time-dependent functions. According to the conventional static deflection calculation method, such as the influence line [14], the vertical displacement time–history curve should trace a piecewise cubic function, with inflection points occurring at the moments when a vehicle passes over the observed cross-section. Moreover, the timing of the maximum displacement correlates with the vehicle's travel speed, as well as its entry and exit times. Specifically, a temporal lag [15] is observed between the quasi-static displacement time histories at different cross-sections. Consequently, it has been assumed that the intersectional relationship is inherently time-dependent. Building on this intuition, the simulation of the intersectional relationship for low-frequency responses has typically been framed as a time-series prediction challenge [16].

To predict time-varying responses at specific bridge locations, a variety of time-series forecasting methods have been naturally adopted, including long and short-term memory (LSTM) networks [17], convolutional neural networks (CNNs) [18], and generative adversarial networks (GANs) [19]. Zhao et al. [20] employed LSTM to establish a mapping model among diverse data sources, such as temperature-induced strains and those induced via vehicle loading, concluding that these influences are nonlinear in nature. Along similar lines, Xin et al. [21] integrated TVFEMD with LSTM to retrieve missing monitoring data, essentially addressing a multi-input time-series forecasting task. Wang and Wang [22] utilized LSTM to infer vehicle loading from bridge responses, using a range of traffic conditions for network training. Li et al. [23] trained a CNN network with multiple inputs and outputs to generate comprehensive bridge responses in conjunction with finite element models. Pamuncak et al. [24] leveraged a CNN network to estimate the structural responses of the Suramadu Bridge under varying environmental conditions. Furthermore, Du et al. [25] introduced a Heterogeneous Structural Response Recovery (HSRR) method, which includes two CNNs designed to capture the spatial and temporal correlations within structural health monitoring (SHM) data. The HSRR also incorporates a parallel optimization technique to refine the network structure and expedite the computational speed. Zhang et al. [26] used a GAN to reconstruct the strain measurements at two sensors from data collected via ten other strain gauges. Zhuang et al. [27] similarly harnessed a GAN to fill in missing data within a bridge weigh-in-motion system. Fan et al. [28] trained a segment-based GAN to reconstruct the responses of a linear steel frame structure during earthquakes, achieving precise estimations.

Quasi-static analysis fundamentally requires the collection of data pertaining to time-dependent factors, notably fluctuating external traffic conditions and air temperature, which significantly influence material stiffness. To this end, there is a necessity to harness long-term monitoring data that capture variations in these time-related temperature and traffic conditions, which is especially crucial for ongoing monitoring projects. The reality, however, poses a challenge, particularly with newly deployed monitoring systems, for which securing extensive historical data is a formidable task. Moreover, compiling comprehensive monitoring data is further complicated by the potential for equipment malfunctions and the impact of external environmental elements.

To address the aforementioned challenge, this study introduces a physically guided approach to estimating low-frequency bridge responses without relying on time-dependent information regarding traffic conditions or air temperatures. Initially, we diverged from quasi-static analysis and instead conducted a theoretical examination of low-frequency bridge responses through the lens of dynamic analysis within the vehicle–bridge-interaction (VBI) system framework. As a vehicle traverses a bridge, a VBI system is established, encompassing the vehicle itself, the bridge structure, and the interactions between the tires and the road surface. Drawing from the works of Yang and Lin [29,30], we considered a simplified VBI system composed of a simply supported beam and a moving sprung mass, which can be abstracted into a driving force model. This simplification is valid, especially when the vehicle's mass is negligible compared to the mass of the bridge. Within this model, low-frequency bridge responses are predominantly dictated by the modes associated with the driving force. This insight is corroborated by Biggs's research in 1964 [31]. Furthermore, Fryba [32] has theoretically demonstrated that low-frequency bridge responses can be approximated as quasi-static responses.

Building on the aforementioned research, we analyzed theoretical low-frequency responses and confirmed that the seemingly time-dependent intersectional relationship should, in fact, be time-independent, even amidst varying traffic conditions. Specifically, the perceived "time lag" is essentially a cumulative effect of responses that correspond to the driving force mode. Moreover, we formulated a transfer matrix for the estimation of intersectional responses, which is invariant, time-independent, and solely reliant on a bridge's mode shapes.

Leveraging physical insights derived from the intersectional relationship, this study reconceptualized the simulation of this relationship as a time-independent regression issue. Significantly, we posit that a time-independent intersectional relationship simulated from short-term monitoring data should maintain its applicability in long-term monitoring scenarios despite fluctuations in traffic conditions and temperature variations. To this end, we employed the backpropagation–artificial neural network (BP-ANN) method [33], which is renowned for its efficacy in addressing regression challenges across diverse domains and has demonstrated impressive accuracy [34–36]. Utilizing historical monitoring data, we successfully estimated low-frequency responses following the simulation of intersectional relationships via the BP-ANN approach.

A defining aspect of the method proposed in our study is the departure from a "quasi-static" analysis in favor of a dynamic analysis approach that uncovers the time-invariant nature of the transfer matrix associated with low-frequency responses across different bridge cross-sections. This time-invariant characteristic was instrumental in our choice of the BP-ANN method. We anticipate that, compared to SSI and SSI-COV, BP-ANN is better equipped to tackle the identification of mode shapes at very low frequencies. In the context of existing research that employs time-series prediction methods, such as LSTM [17] and CNN [18], the architectures of these algorithms typically incorporate time-related factors. During training, these factors require careful design, testing, and weight adjustment, which can be quite time-consuming. However, in our study, the time-invariant feature of the transfer matrix, as derived and validated, indicated that there is no necessity to account for unreal time-related factors, even when estimating time-series data. This is the rationale behind selecting BP-ANN, as it is a time-independent method that circumvents the unnecessary consideration of time-related factors, thereby offering greater time efficiency compared to traditional time-series prediction methods. Most importantly, for practical engineering applications, our method eliminates the need to gather traffic condition or air temperature data, which simplifies the process considerably. This convenience is a significant advantage in real-world engineering scenarios.

Section 2 delineates the physical features of a bridge low-frequency responses, with a particular focus on the constant transfer function between low-frequency displacements at various cross-sections. This section also elaborates on the structure and application methodology of the BP-ANN. Moving forward, Section 3 presents the validation of the target relationship and the robustness of our proposed method with numerical simulations. Subsequently, Section 4 employs monitoring data from a field-tested bridge monitoring system to substantiate the precision of the constructed BP-ANN network. The results demonstrate that our method is capable of accurately estimating low-frequency bridge responses without relying on information about external traffic loading conditions or air temperatures.

## 2. Methodologies

### 2.1. Dynamics of a Typical VBI System

#### 2.1.1. Dynamic Equations and Modal Responses

A schematic representation of a typical simple vehicle–bridge interaction (VBI) system is depicted in Figure 1, comprising a simply supported beam and a moving sprung mass traverses at a uniform velocity, $v$. The dynamic equations governing the system's behavior are articulated as follows [30]:

For the vehicle,

$$m_v \ddot{q}_v + k_v q_v = k_v \left. u \right|_{x=vt} \tag{1}$$

For the bridge,

$$\overline{m}\ddot{u} + EI u'''' = p(x,t) \tag{2}$$

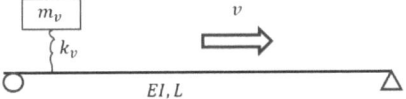

**Figure 1.** A typical, simple VBI system.

Elaborations of the symbols and abbreviations of all these equations are listed in the Appendix A. Road roughness was excluded from the analysis due to its minimal impact on bridge dynamics [37]. As Yang posited [30], in scenarios where the vehicle's mass is significantly lower compared to the bridge's mass, the force exerted via the vehicle, denoted as $p(x,t)$, can be approximated as the moving vehicle's gravitational force. Consequently, the dynamic responses of the bridge can be resolved as indicated [30]:

$$u(x,t) = \sum_n \frac{\Delta_{stn}}{1 - S_n^2} \left\{ \sin\frac{n\pi x}{L} \left[ \sin\frac{n\pi v t}{L} - S_n \sin\omega_{bn} t \right] \right\} \tag{3}$$

where [30]

$$\Delta_{st,n} = \frac{-2 m_v g L^3}{n^4 \pi^4 EI} \tag{4}$$

$$S_n = \frac{n\pi v}{L \omega_{b,n}} \tag{5}$$

$$\omega_{b,n} = \frac{n^2 \pi^2}{L^2} \sqrt{\frac{EI}{\overline{m}}} \tag{6}$$

The $u(x,t)$ in Equation (3) can be divided into two parts: the low-frequency part, $u_{low}(x,t)$, and the high-frequency part, $u_{high}(x,t)$ (shown in Equations (7) and (8)) [30].

$$u_{low}(x,t) = \sum_n \frac{\Delta_{stn}}{1-S_n^2}\left[\sin\frac{n\pi x}{L}\sin\frac{n\pi vt}{L}\right] \quad (7)$$

$$u_{high}(x,t) = \sum_n \frac{\Delta_{stn}}{1-S_n^2}\left[-\sin\frac{n\pi x}{L}S_n\sin\omega_{bn}t\right] \quad (8)$$

It is important to highlight that the scope of this study, including the finite element simulations and field tests presented in subsequent sections, was primarily concentrated on long and slender beams, which are more representative of those commonly found in typical bridges. Consequently, in this theoretical segment, our analysis is confined to the Euler–Bernoulli beam model. Timoshenko beams, whose shear deformation plays a considerably significant role, are beyond the purview of this investigation.

2.1.2. Time Lag in Low-Frequency Bridge Displacement

The concept of a time lag is traditionally perceived as a time-dependent phenomenon in the context of quasi-static bridge responses to vehicular loading. However, in this study, we delved into the examination of quasi-static bridge responses through the lens of low-frequency dynamic behavior.

As demonstrated by Fryba in [32], the low-frequency dynamic response $u_{low}(x,t)$ corresponds to the static deflection of the bridge, as depicted in Equation (9) [32], when subjected to a constant moving force, $m_v g$, when $S_n$ approaches zero.

$$u_{low}(x,t) = u_{static}(x,a)$$
$$= \begin{cases} \frac{-m_v g x(L-a)}{6EIL}\left(L^2 - x^2 - (L-a)^2\right) & (a > x) \\ \frac{-m_v g(L-a)}{6EIL}\left(\frac{L}{L-a}(x-a)^3 + x\left(L^2 - (L-a)^2\right) - x^3\right) & (a < x) \end{cases} \quad (9)$$

where

$$a = vt \quad (10)$$

As noted by Paultre et al. [38], $S_n$ approaches zero for typical highway bridges. Consequently, Equation (9) can be regarded as approximately valid under such conditions. It is important to recognize that the calculation of $u_{static}(x,a)$ is based on a static mechanical perspective, which assumes the absence of bridge damping. Accordingly, in this study, the computation of $u_{low}(x,t)$ intentionally disregarded the potential impacts arising from damping effects.

The "time-lag" phenomenon can be inferred from the right-hand side of Equation (9), where the temporal instances corresponding to the maximum bridge deflection vary for sensors situated at distinct locations. While the function $u_{static}(x,a)$ is piecewise, with its inflection point and the moment of peak deflection being time-dependent, Equation (7) illustrates that $u_{low}(x,t)$ is a superposition of sinusoidal time functions, specifically $\sin\frac{n\pi vt}{L}$. It is crucial to observe that these sinusoidal functions in the time domain are uniform across different locations, such as $x_1$ and $x_2$. The disparity in the responses at $x_1$ and $x_2$ should be attributable to the modal coordinates, that is, $\sin\frac{n\pi x}{L}$. Hence, the time lag can be elucidated with the divergence in modal coordinates.

For instance, as depicted in Figure 2a, the low-frequency vertical displacement of the bridge at the 1/4, 1/2, and 3/4 points of the beam length is presented for the first mode ($n$ = 1 in Equation (7)). Figure 2b displays the low-frequency bridge displacement in the second mode at the same three locations. Figure 2c demonstrates the combined effect of the displacements from the first and second modes. Moreover, Equation (7) indicates that higher modes contribute minimally to the displacement, $u_{low}(x,t)$. The displacement amplitude ratio for each low-frequency mode follows a pattern of (1, $1/2^4$, $1/3^4$, ...

$1/n^4$). Figure 2c reveals that the aggregate displacement is approximately equivalent to $u_{low}(x,t)$. Figure 3 provides a comparative analysis of the cumulative displacement. The time-lag phenomenon can thus be confirmed as an aggregate of multiple low-frequency modal vibrations.

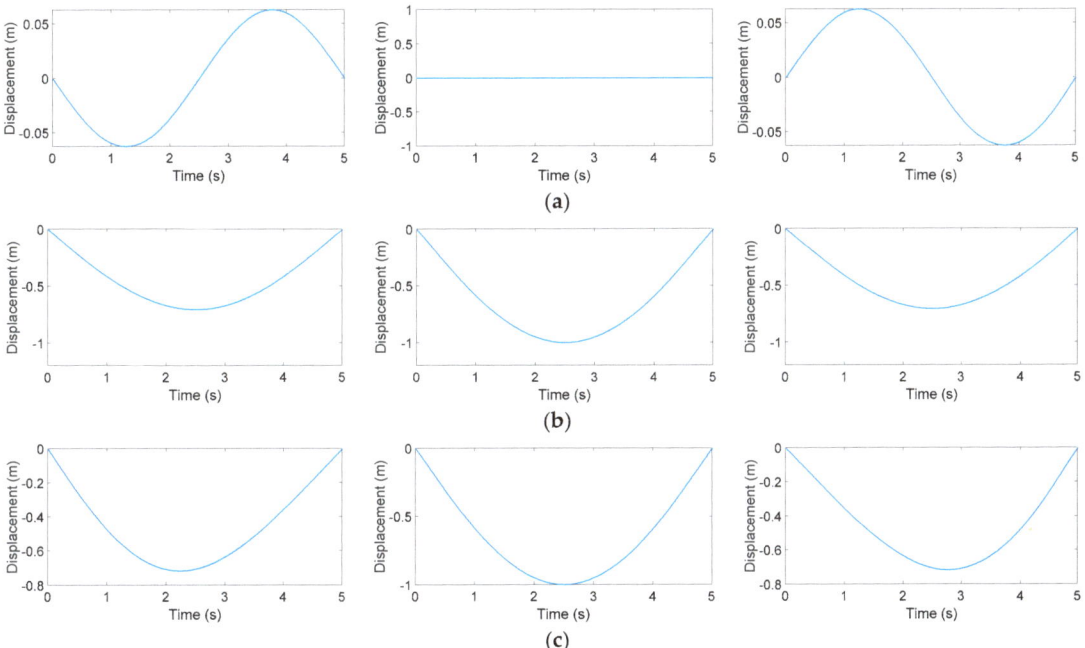

**Figure 2.** Responses corresponding to the first and second modes at three cross-sections. (**a**) First-mode responses; (**b**) second-mode responses; (**c**) summation of the first- and second-mode responses (left column: 1/4-beam responses; middle column: mid-beam responses; right column: 3/4-beam responses).

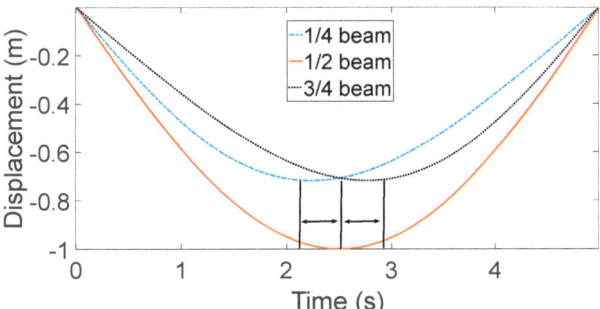

**Figure 3.** Comparison between responses at three locations on the beam. (The "double arrow" denotes the observed time lag.)

2.1.3. Intersectional Relationship for the Simple VBI System

Specifically, the intersectional relationship for the aforementioned simple VBI system was derived. Sensors positioned at three distinct cross-sections, denoted as $x_1$, $x_2$, and $x_3$ were selected. The low-frequency bridge displacements at the N+1 time points were assumed to be the sequences $\{u_{x_1,t_0}, u_{x_1,t_1}, \ldots u_{x_1,t_N}\}$, $\{u_{x_2,t_0}, u_{x_2,t_1}, \ldots u_{x_2,t_N}\}$, and $\{u_{x_3,t_0}, u_{x_3,t_1}, \ldots u_{x_3,t_N}\}$. In the case of medium-span and short-span bridges, the first two modes typically represent the global modes of the entire bridge and are the most significant contributors to the bridge's dynamic responses. Consequently, the subsequent matrix equations (Equations (11) and (12)) can be deduced from Equation (7).

$$\begin{bmatrix} \sin\frac{\pi x_1}{L} & \sin\frac{2\pi x_1}{L} \\ \sin\frac{\pi x_2}{L} & \sin\frac{2\pi x_2}{L} \end{bmatrix} \begin{bmatrix} \frac{\Delta_{st,1}}{1-S_1^2}\sin\frac{\pi v t_0}{L} & \frac{\Delta_{st,1}}{1-S_1^2}\sin\frac{\pi v t_1}{L} & \cdots & \frac{\Delta_{st,1}}{1-S_1^2}\sin\frac{\pi v t_N}{L} \\ \frac{\Delta_{st,2}}{1-S_2^2}\sin\frac{2\pi v t_0}{L} & \frac{\Delta_{st,2}}{1-S_2^2}\sin\frac{2\pi v t_1}{L} & \cdots & \frac{\Delta_{st,2}}{1-S_2^2}\sin\frac{2\pi v t_N}{L} \end{bmatrix} = \begin{bmatrix} u_{x_1,t_0} & u_{x_1,t_1} & \cdots & u_{x_1,t_N} \\ u_{x_2,t_0} & u_{x_2,t_1} & \cdots & u_{x_2,t_N} \end{bmatrix} \quad (11)$$

$$\begin{bmatrix} \sin\frac{\pi x_2}{L} & \sin\frac{2\pi x_2}{L} \\ \sin\frac{\pi x_3}{L} & \sin\frac{2\pi x_3}{L} \end{bmatrix} \begin{bmatrix} \frac{\Delta_{st,1}}{1-S_1^2}\sin\frac{\pi v t_0}{L} & \frac{\Delta_{st,1}}{1-S_1^2}\sin\frac{\pi v t_1}{L} & \cdots & \frac{\Delta_{st,1}}{1-S_1^2}\sin\frac{\pi v t_N}{L} \\ \frac{\Delta_{st,2}}{1-S_2^2}\sin\frac{2\pi v t_0}{L} & \frac{\Delta_{st,2}}{1-S_2^2}\sin\frac{2\pi v t_1}{L} & \cdots & \frac{\Delta_{st,2}}{1-S_2^2}\sin\frac{2\pi v t_N}{L} \end{bmatrix} = \begin{bmatrix} u_{x_2,t_0} & u_{x_2,t_1} & \cdots & u_{x_2,t_N} \\ u_{x_3,t_0} & u_{x_3,t_1} & \cdots & u_{x_3,t_N} \end{bmatrix} \quad (12)$$

The responses at $x_3$ can then be calculated from Equation (13).

$$\begin{bmatrix} u_{x_2,t_0} & u_{x_2,t_1} & \cdots & u_{x_2,t_N} \\ u_{x_3,t_0} & u_{x_3,t_1} & \cdots & u_{x_3,t_N} \end{bmatrix} = \begin{bmatrix} \sin\frac{\pi x_2}{L} & \sin\frac{2\pi x_2}{L} \\ \sin\frac{\pi x_3}{L} & \sin\frac{2\pi x_3}{L} \end{bmatrix} \begin{bmatrix} \sin\frac{\pi x_1}{L} & \sin\frac{2\pi x_1}{L} \\ \sin\frac{\pi x_2}{L} & \sin\frac{2\pi x_2}{L} \end{bmatrix}^{-1} \begin{bmatrix} u_{x_1,t_0} & u_{x_1,t_1} & \cdots & u_{x_1,t_N} \\ u_{x_2,t_0} & u_{x_2,t_1} & \cdots & u_{x_2,t_N} \end{bmatrix} \quad (13)$$

The transform matrix is then defined as $T$. For this simple VBI system,

$$T = \begin{bmatrix} \sin\frac{\pi x_2}{L} & \sin\frac{2\pi x_2}{L} \\ \sin\frac{\pi x_3}{L} & \sin\frac{2\pi x_3}{L} \end{bmatrix} \begin{bmatrix} \sin\frac{\pi x_1}{L} & \sin\frac{2\pi x_1}{L} \\ \sin\frac{\pi x_2}{L} & \sin\frac{2\pi x_2}{L} \end{bmatrix}^{-1} \quad (14)$$

The matrix $T$ represents the target intersectional relationship, which is utilized to derive the displacement $\{u_{x_3,t_N}\}$ from the measured $\{u_{x_1,t_N}\}$ and $\{u_{x_2,t_N}\}$. This matrix, $T$, is solely dependent on the bridge's mode shapes, and it is invariant with time. Furthermore, $T$ is independent of traffic conditions, which are characterized by the term $\{\frac{\Delta_{st,n}}{1-S_n^2}\}$. Additionally, while fluctuations in air temperatures may influence the global material stiffness of the bridge, $T$ retains its time-invariant property as long as the mode shapes remain unchanged. In the context of the estimation process, it is advisable to employ monitoring data from a minimum of two cross-sections. This ensures that the information obtained encompasses at least the first two principal modes of the bridge's dynamic behavior.

2.1.4. From a Simple Model to a General Bridge Structure

In typical bridge structures, the solution derived from Equation (3) can be generalized as a product of the modal shapes and their corresponding modal coordinates, as articulated in Equation (15).

$$u(x,t) = \sum_n \varnothing_n(x) q_{b,n}(t) \quad (15)$$

For example, we chose two arbitrary observation points, $x_1$ and $x_2$. In accordance with Equation (15), the vertical displacements at $x_1$ and $x_2$ should be

$$u(x_1,t) = \sum_n \varnothing_n(x_1) q_{b,n}(t) \quad (16)$$

$$u(x_2,t) = \sum_n \varnothing_n(x_2) q_{b,n}(t) \quad (17)$$

Equations (16) and (17) can be reformatted into matrix form, as presented in Equations (18) and (19).

$$u(x_1,t) = \varnothing_n(x_1) q_{b,n}(t) \quad (18)$$

$$u(x_2,t) = \varnothing_n(x_2) q_{b,n}(t) \quad (19)$$

where are corresponding matrices or vectors. The intersection relationship is represented as $T$, which transforms $u(x_1,t)$ into $u(x_2,t)$ (as shown in Equation (20)).

$$u(x_2,t) = Tu(x_1,t) \tag{20}$$

Substituting Equations (18) and (19) into Equation (20), one can confirm that

$$T = \{\varnothing_n(x_1)\}^+ \varnothing_n(x_2) \tag{21}$$

where the + denotes the generalized inverse. Equation (21) illustrates that the matrix $T$ is independent of time and is solely associated with the mode shapes. Furthermore, Equations (18) and (19) indicate that the dynamic responses $x_1$ and $x_2$ should share the same time-domain coordinate, $q_{b,n}(t)$. Although $q_{b,n}(t)$ may change under varying traffic conditions, vehicle characteristics, and moving speeds, this time-domain coordinate remains consistent across different cross-sections. Consequently, $T$ should be exempt from the influence of time-varying traffic conditions. Additionally, it is postulated that the time-independent nature of the intersectional relationship should also extend to complex bridge structures, provided that the dynamic responses can be articulated through Equation (21) in conjunction with the time-independent mode shape function, $\varnothing_n(x)$.

It is important to note that Equation (21) also highlights the distinction between the current study and existing research. In prior studies, low-frequency bridge responses, referred to as "quasi-static responses," were analyzed from a static perspective. These quasi-static responses are influenced by time-varying factors, including external loading, which is dictated by traffic conditions, and material stiffness, which can be affected by air temperatures. Moreover, as suggested in the right side of Equation (9), the transfer function between responses at different cross-sections appears to be time-dependent. However, in this study, we adopted a dynamic analysis approach to treat low-frequency responses. As demonstrated in Equations (14) and (21), the transfer matrix should remain time-invariant, regardless of changes in traffic conditions and air temperatures. This fundamental difference also informed our choice of the subsequent response-estimation method.

## 2.2. BP-ANN for Intersection Responses Prediction

The hypothesis was that the intersectional relationship, as per Equation (21), should remain time-independent under fluctuating temperatures and vehicle loading conditions. Consequently, diverging from the time-series prediction methods employed in previous studies, it was assumed that there was no necessity to account for time-related factors in the response estimation process. To simulate the target relationship and subsequently estimate the responses at a specific cross-section, a BP-ANN was utilized for training. It is crucial to emphasize that the BP-ANN network was designed with a time-invariant structure, aligning with the time-independent relationship established in Equation (21). Furthermore, the adoption of BP-ANN was expected to eliminate the need to train any superfluous time-related factors, which are typically associated with time-series prediction methods in existing research. This approach was anticipated to be more time-efficient compared to traditional time-series prediction techniques.

In the process of training the network, responses from several cross-sections were configured as multiple inputs, whereas the responses at a particular section served as the output. A mapping relationship was subsequently trained to emulate the intersectional relationship. This trained network, informed by Equation (21), should be able to capture long-term intersectional dynamics under varying traffic conditions and air temperatures, effectively utilizable even without traffic condition or air temperature information.

A typical backpropagation neural network structure [33] consists of artificial neuron units, as shown in Figure 4, where $x_i (i = 1, 2, \ldots n)$ denotes the input of the current unit,

$j$. $w_{ij}$ is the weight corresponding to each input. Then, the output, $y$, of the unit, $j$, can be calculated as follows:

$$s = \sum_{i=1}^{n} w_{ij} x_i + b \tag{22}$$

$$y = F(s) = \frac{1}{1 + e^{-s}} \tag{23}$$

in which $b$ is the bias term.

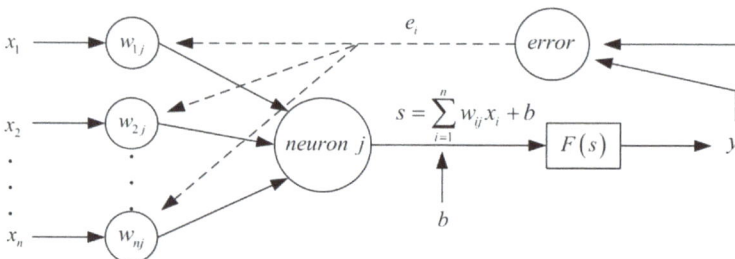

**Figure 4.** Artificial neuron unit [33].

Backpropagation neural networks are composed of input layers, output layers, and hidden layers, as depicted in Figure 5. Each layer is made up of one or more artificial neuron units. During model training, these units take in the output from the preceding layer and process it to produce the input for the subsequent layer. The weights and biases are adjusted through an iterative process aimed at minimizing the overall error, in accordance with Equations (24) and (25) [33].

$$w(k+1) = w(k) - \alpha \frac{\partial E(k)}{\partial w(k)} \tag{24}$$

$$b(k+1) = b(k) - \alpha \frac{\partial E(k)}{\partial b(k)} \tag{25}$$

in which,

$$E(k) = \sqrt{\frac{1}{N} \sum_{i=1}^{N} |e_i|^2} \tag{26}$$

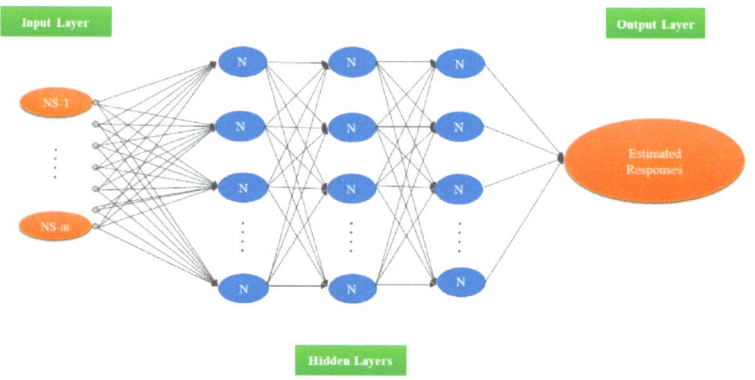

**Figure 5.** ANN structure for responses' estimation (NS-1, ..., and NS-m represent the input data from the m-th cross-sections).

The network architecture is depicted in Figure 5. For instance, let us consider a scenario where responses at $m + 1$ cross-sections are measured. The time-series responses at the first $m$ cross-sections are then employed as $m$ inputs, while the responses at the $m + 1$ cross-section are designated as the output. Specifically, for each set of inputs and outputs, each neuron contains a single time-point value. Under the guidance of Equation (21), the network does not incorporate time-dependent information regarding traffic conditions and temperature. Moreover, the mode shapes represented in all of these inputs should include the mode shape component present in the output. If there exists a unique mode in the output that is orthogonal to all the modes in the input, it is anticipated that the model may not yield satisfactory results.

The network configuration is detailed as follows. The network comprises two hidden layers: the first layer consists of 128 neurons, and the second layer contains 32 neurons. The output layer is designed with a single neuron, which corresponds to the monitoring data at sensor 02-S01. The learning rate is configured at 0.001, the batch size is set to 100, and the number of epochs is 500. The activation function employed is the rectified linear unit (ReLU) function. During the training phase of the BP-ANN network, the sequential order of the time-series data is not taken into account. Data batches are formed randomly and used for training, which deviates from the conventional time-series prediction methods. This random batching approach ensures that no time-dependent characteristics are considered for the intersectional relationship. In the subsequent validation processes, as specifically outlined in Sections 3.4 and 4.3.2, the network with this straightforward structure demonstrates its capability of providing accurate estimations for both finite element simulation and field-test data.

## 3. Numerical Analysis

### 3.1. Numerical Models

In this study, a typical VBI system model [30] employed in a previous study was used. This model consists of a simply supported beam and a sprung mass as the moving vehicle. The beam span is $L = 25$ m. The unit beam mass per meter is $\overline{m} = 4800$ kg/m. $EI = 3.33 \times 10^9$ N/m$^2$. The first three bending frequencies of the beam are 2.08 Hz, 8.33 Hz, and 18.75 Hz, respectively. The sprung mass is $m_v = 1200$ kg, and the spring stiffness is $k_v = 500{,}000$ N/m. The vibration frequency of the vehicle is 3.25 Hz.

The commercial software ABAQUS 2020 [39] was employed to construct a finite element model, as depicted in Figure 6, in order to simulate the VBI system. The model utilized three-dimensional solid elements to represent the beam, sprung mass, and wheel components. The element types, quantities, and mesh sizes for these components are detailed in Table 1 as follows:

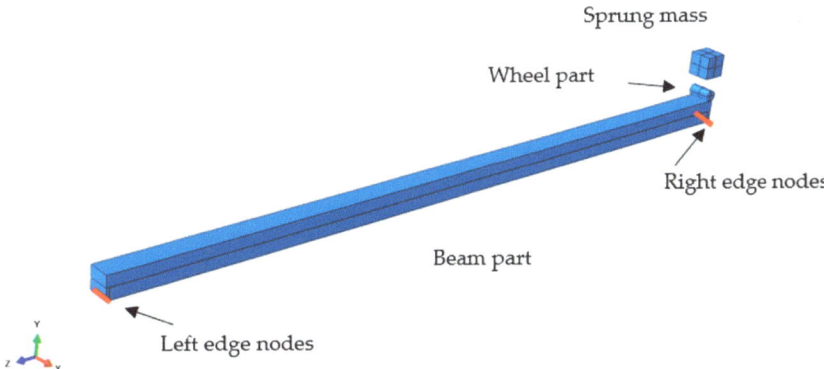

**Figure 6.** Finite element model for the simple VBI system built with ABAQUS 2020 (left and right edge nodes are marked in red).

**Table 1.** Element properties of the finite element model.

| Component | Type | Amount | Size (m × m × m) |
|---|---|---|---|
| Beam | C3D8R | 16,128 | 0.1 × 0.1 × 0.1 |
| Wheel | C3D8R | 320 | 0.08 × 0.08 × 0.08 |
| Sprung mass | C3D8R | 8000 | 0.04 × 0.04 × 0.04 |

The element size for the beam was set to 0.1 m × 0.1 m × 0.1 m, a decision informed by a mesh convergence study. As illustrated in Figure 7, the mid-span displacement exhibits minimal variation when the mesh size is finer than 0.15 m × 0.15 m × 0.15 m. The boundary conditions for the simply supported beam were established by restricting the appropriate degrees of freedom at the beam's edge nodes, as indicated in Figure 6. For the left edge nodes, translations along the X, Y, and Z axes, as well as rotations about the Y and Z axes, were fixed. Similarly, translations along the X and Y axes and rotations around the Y and Z axes were restricted for the right edge nodes. Interaction was modeled with penalty method, and the interaction force was implicitly calculated and applied to the beam surface in contact with the wheel. Additionally, a spring element was employed to represent the spring constant between the sprung mass and the wheel. Road roughness was excluded from this model due to its minimal impact on low-frequency beam responses. The model responses were obtained using the Hilber–Hughes–Taylor $\alpha$-method in the implicit calculation mode, which involves two main stages. The first stage involves applying gravity to the entire system, known as the "Static, Implicit" step, during which the vehicle is positioned at one end of the beam. The second stage is the "Dynamic, Implicit" step, during which time integration is performed with a time step of 0.01 s to compute the dynamic responses of the system. In this stage, the vehicle is moved from the initial position to the opposite end at a constant velocity [40].

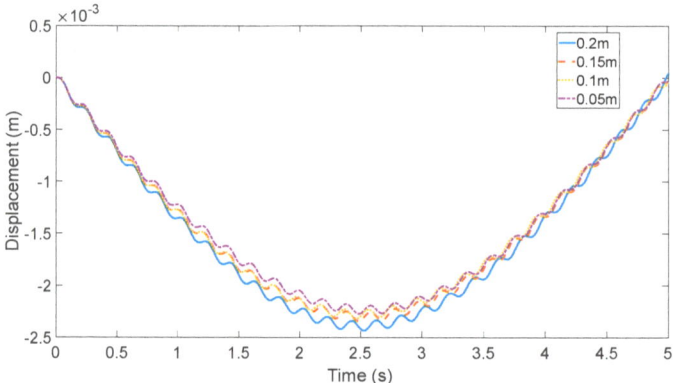

**Figure 7.** Comparison of mid-span displacement with different mesh densities.

*3.2. Cases' Configuration*

This study was designed to validate the consistent intersectional relationship between low-frequency responses at different locations along the beam. In prior research focusing on "quasi-static" responses [12,13], the adoption of time-related time-series prediction methods is conventional, given that "quasi-static" responses, as depicted in Equation (9), are influenced by time-dependent traffic conditions. Furthermore, in practical engineering, the three principal factors of traffic conditions are vehicle weight, vehicle speed, and vehicle volume. However, in this study, we shifted our focus from "quasi-static" responses to the transfer matrix of low-frequency responses, which demonstrated independence from fluctuating traffic conditions. Therefore, it is essential to confirm the time-irrelevant, time-independent physical characteristic of the transfer matrix, as well as the efficacy of the proposed method. Consequently, four scenarios were devised to encompass variations in moving speed, vehicle weight, and vehicle volume, as shown in Figure 8:

(1) Reference case, where the moving speed was set to 5 m/s;
(2) High-speed case, where the moving speed was set to 10 m/s;
(3) Half-mass vehicle case, where the sprung mass was half that of the reference case;
(4) Dual-vehicle case: The half-mass vehicle and the reference vehicle were running on the beam simultaneously. The high-frequency vehicle was moving at a speed of 3 m/s, while the reference vehicle was moving at a speed of 5 m/s.

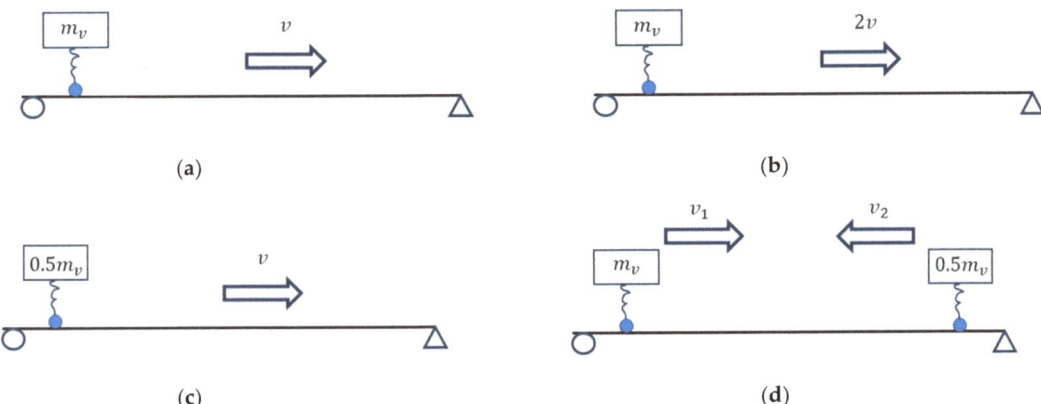

**Figure 8.** Cases for validation. (**a**) Reference; (**b**) high-speed; (**c**) light-mass; and (**d**) dual vehicles.

*3.3. Simulation Result Analysis*

The phenomenon of a "time lag" was initially investigated. Figure 9, panels (a) to (d), depict the time history of the vertical displacement of the beam at three cross-sections: the 3/4 point, the 1/2 point, and the 1/4 point of the beam's length, across the four cases. It is apparent that the primary cause of the bridge's displacement is the low-frequency responses associated with the driving force, a finding that aligns with Yang's research [30]. Moreover, the time-lag phenomenon is quite pronounced. In Figure 9, the dashed lines highlight the time lag between the responses at different cross-sections, especially for the first three cases.

The consistently time-independent relationship between cross-sections was subsequently scrutinized. Specifically, the low-frequency vertical displacement time history at the 1/4 point of the beam was estimated using the data from the 1/2 and 3/4 points. The transfer matrix, derived from Equation (14), was employed to predict the low-frequency responses at the 1/4 point of the beam across all four cases. It is important to note that the same transfer matrix was applied to all scenarios. A cut-off frequency of 1 Hz was used to isolate the low-frequency displacement components. As evidenced in Figure 10, the estimated low-frequency vertical displacement at the 1/4 point of the beam closely aligns with the simulation outcomes in all four cases. Thus, it can be concluded that the intersectional relationship under scrutiny is indeed time-independent and remains constant across varying traffic conditions, including vehicle mass, speed, and passage time. Furthermore, since the transfer matrix is dictated by the bridge's mode shape, and since alterations in global material stiffness do not modify the mode shape, changes in temperature, which might affect the bridge's material stiffness, should not influence the intersectional relationship. Consequently, this section does not delve into potential numerical simulations associated with temperature variations.

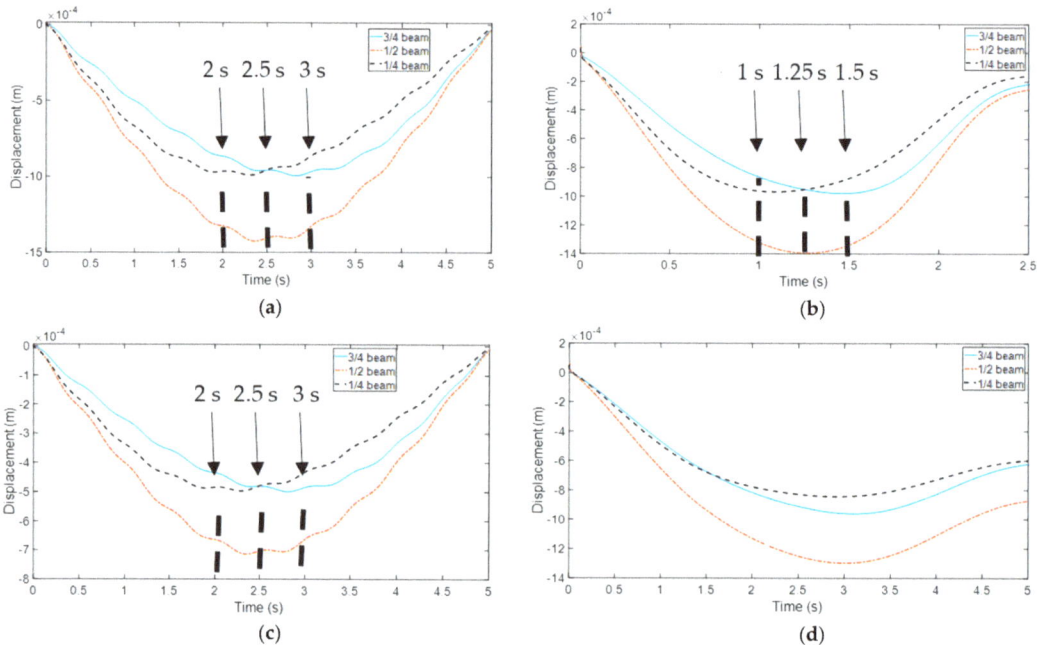

**Figure 9.** Vertical displacement time history at three cross-sections in four cases. (Dashed line: the time instance when the largest displacement occurs on each curve. The left dashed line corresponds to the 1/4 beam. The middle dashed line corresponds to the 1/2 beam, and the right dashed line corresponds to the 3/4 beam). (**a**) Reference case; (**b**) high-speed case; (**c**) light-mass case; and (**d**) dual vehicles.

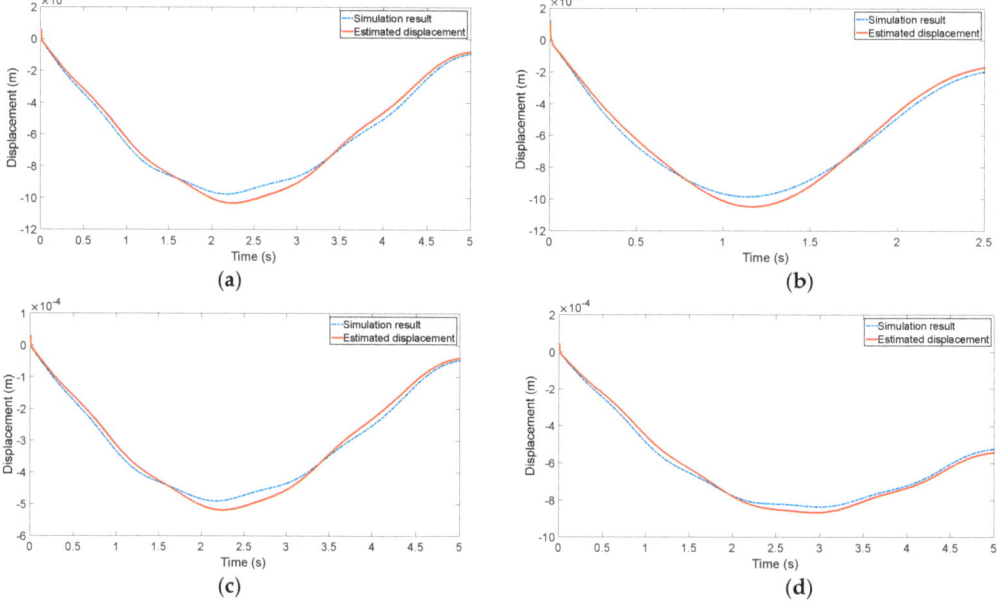

**Figure 10.** Comparison of vertical displacement time history at 1/4 of the beam between the estimation and simulation results. (**a**) Reference case; (**b**) high-speed case; (**c**) light-mass case; and (**d**) double-vehicle case (solid curve: estimated displacement; dashed line curve: simulation results).

*3.4. Validation of the BP-ANN with the Simulation Data*

To substantiate the effectiveness of BP-ANN and assess its robustness, simulated data from the first three cases were used to train a BP-ANN model, while data from the fourth case were employed to evaluate the model's performance. It is important to note that these simulations incorporated 5% white noise.

The network architecture includes an input layer with two neurons, corresponding to the displacements at the 1/2 and 3/4 points of the beam. Figure 11 presents a comparison between the noisy displacement of the simulation results and the displacement estimates derived from the BP-ANN. Both the peak values and the complete time history records show a close match. Thus, it can be concluded that the proposed method demonstrates robustness and performs effectively even in the presence of noise.

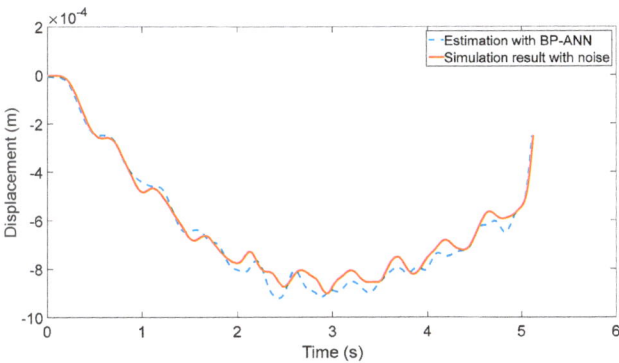

**Figure 11.** Comparison between the estimation result with BP-ANN and the simulation result with white noise.

## 4. Validation with Field Test on a Continuous Bridge

In the preceding sections, we detailed the theoretical derivations and finite element simulations specifically for a simply supported bridge. However, in accordance with Equation (21), the proposed estimation method is not limited to this bridge type and can be extended to various other types of bridges. Furthermore, while our previous analysis focused solely on low-frequency displacement, the method we propose is also applicable to a broader range of bridge response indicators. In this section, we proceed to validate the proposed method using field test data measured on a real continuous bridge..

*4.1. Target Bridge and SHM System*

The target bridge is a concrete highway overpass situated in Hebei Province, China. It is a separate bridge structure on Baofu Highway, with distinct left and right sides. The left side comprises four continuous spans measuring 133 m (32 m + 32 m + 37 m + 32 m), and it is constructed with prestressed box girders, as depicted in Figure 12a [36]. The total length of the right side spans 179 m, consisting of a 75-m section (3 × 25 m) made up of prestressed concrete T-beams and a 104-m section (35 m + 37 m + 32 m) of a continuous prestressed box girder [41]. For more comprehensive geometric details of the bridge, reference [41] can be consulted.

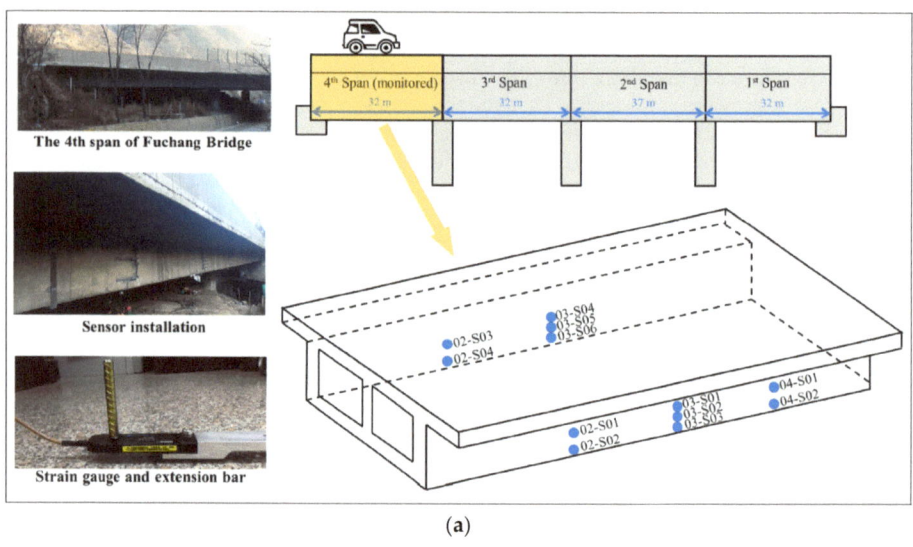

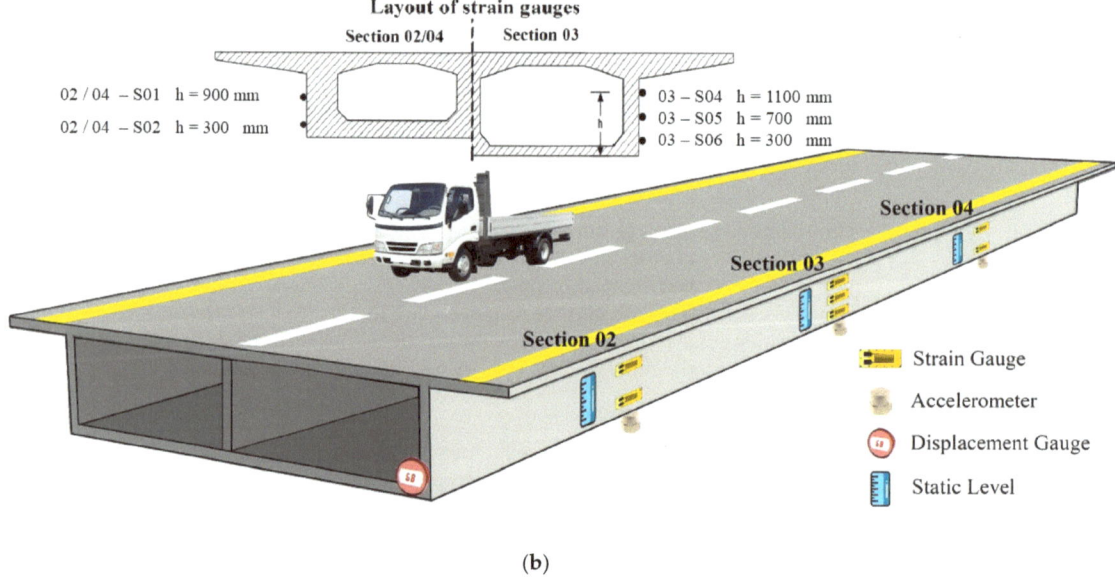

**Figure 12.** Target Bridge and the SHM system. (**a**) Fuchang Bridge [41]; (**b**) SHM system [42].

In 2018, a structural health monitoring (SHM) system was installed to monitor responses of the target bridge, as illustrated in Figure 12b. The first two natural vibration frequencies of the bridge were previously determined using the stochastic subspace identification (SSI) method, measuring 3.906 Hz and 5.01 Hz, respectively [41]. The structural health monitoring (SHM) system is equipped with an array of sensors, including strain gauges, thermometers, accelerometers, and so on. For the purposes of this study, we utilized only the strain gauges mounted on Section 02, which is approximately at the 1/4 point of the fourth span, Section 03 (the midpoint section), and Section 04 (the 3/4 point of the fourth span). There are a total of twelve strain gauges installed across these three cross-sections (02, 03, and 04), with strain data being sampled at a frequency of 50 Hz. Further details regarding the SHM system can be found in the referenced study [42]. Although the previous section focused exclusively on bridge displacement and the intersectional relationship of displacement, it was anticipated that the strain time history would exhibit characteristics similar to those of the low-frequency bridge displacement. This expectation was grounded in the fact that the low-frequency bridge displacement under vehicular loading closely mimics the static displacement under a moving force. Moreover, in static scenarios, a relationship exists between the bending moment at a cross-section and the displacement at that section,

$$M(x) = -EI\frac{d^2u}{dx^2} \tag{27}$$

where $M(x)$ is the moment. Also, the moment is linearly proportional to the strain. Therefore, similar to Equation (3), the following function (Equation (28)) can be generated.

$$\varepsilon(x,t) = \sum_{n} \varnothing_{\varepsilon,n}(x) q_{\varepsilon,n}(t) \tag{28}$$

The strain mode shape function is represented by $\varnothing_{\varepsilon,n}(x)$, and the corresponding coefficient in the time domain is $q_{\varepsilon,n}(t)$. Additionally, the physical properties of the intersection displacement relationship, including the time-independent and constant properties, should also be available for the intersectional bridge strain under vehicular loading.

*4.2. Monitoring Data*

Figure 13 presents a typical piece of monitoring data. The strain variations depicted in Figure 13a are predominantly due to temperature fluctuations. Notably, there are several local "peaks" on the curve in Figure 13a, which are attributable to passing vehicles (with zoomed-in views provided in Figure 13b,c). It is evident that the strain induced via temperature changes exhibits a significantly higher amplitude compared to that caused by vehicle loading. Figure 13b illustrates that the amplitude of the low-frequency strain, induced via vehicle loading, is substantially greater than that of the high-frequency strain. This observation is further supported by Figure 13c, which shows numerous high-frequency, low-amplitude peaks in the strain time history. It is important to note that this study concentrated solely on low-frequency responses. As documented in prior research [37,38], the low frequencies associated with driving forces are considerably lower than the natural vibration frequencies of bridges. Moreover, the typical natural frequencies of short- and medium-span bridges exceed 1 Hz. To eliminate high-frequency strains, a low-pass filter [43] with a cutoff frequency of 1 Hz was employed in this study. The bridge's natural vibration frequencies, while relevant, were not essential for the current investigation. The temperature-induced strain was estimated using a moving-mean method [43] and subsequently removed. This process yielded the low-frequency strain induced via vehicle loading. It should be mentioned that, in this study, the bridge strain was measured at only three cross-sections, which is insufficient for determining bridge-mode shapes using conventional methods such as SSI [3,4]. However, as outlined in the introduction, the proposed method addresses this limitation, as detailed below.

In this research, we utilized monitoring data from Section 03 and Section 04 to estimate the dynamic responses at Section 02. Specifically, data from sensors 03-S01 and 04-S01 were employed to forecast the data at 02-S01. Consequently, the input layer of the BP-ANN features two neuron units, each corresponding to the monitoring data from 03-S01 and 04-S01, respectively. When training the network, instead of inputting time-series data directly into the input layer's neuron units, the BP-ANN processed discrete data points measured at specific time intervals. In more elaborate terms, with two input neuron units, each set of input data, comprising two values, was assigned to one neuron unit each. This approach marks a significant departure from the time-series prediction methods used in previous studies [17–28]. Although the estimation outcomes in this study are presented as time series of monitoring data, they are, in essence, a collection of discrete output values derived from the BP-ANN using discrete input data sets. A key advantage of this method is that it circumvents the need to calculate time-related factors, which are often required in traditional time-series prediction models.

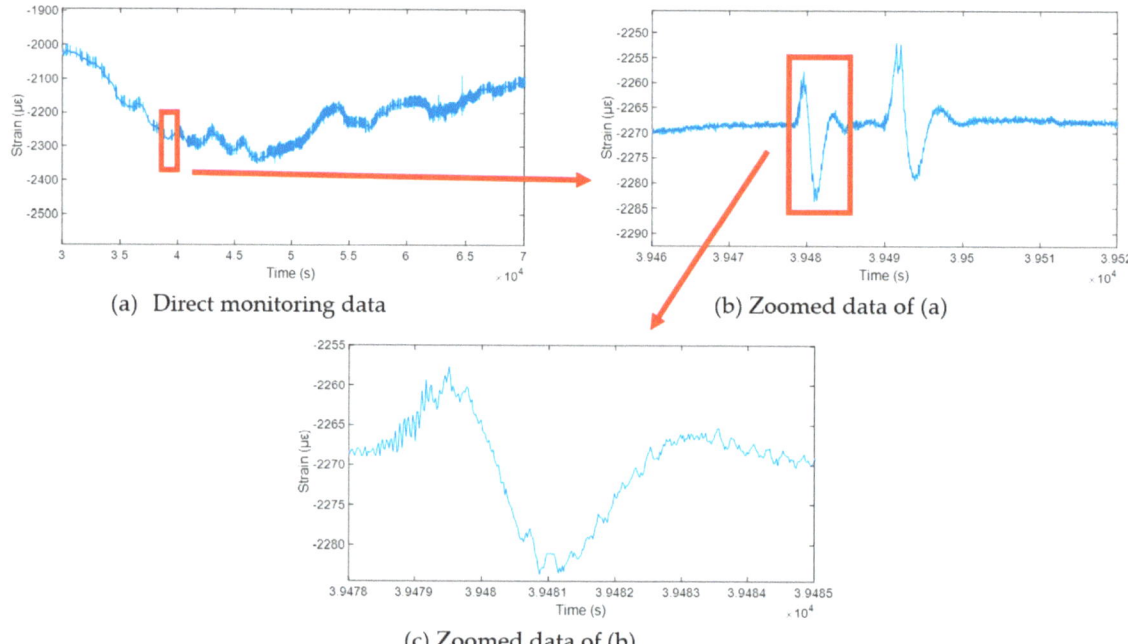

**Figure 13.** A piece of typical strain monitoring data. (Rectangle marked data in (**a**) is zoomed in on and illustrated as (**b**), and Rectangle marked data in (**b**) is zoomed in on and illustrated as (**c**)).

*4.3. Scenarios and Data Configuration*

4.3.1. Confirmation of Time Lag, Random Traffic Condition, and Temperature Effect

The time-lag phenomenon was evident in the time history of low-frequency strain induced via vehicle loading. Figure 14 illustrates the time history of low-frequency strain at these three cross-sections within a monitored segment. Similar to the observations in Figure 13b, a distinct peak, attributed to the passage of a vehicle, is visible in the strain time history. The time histories from the three gauges were superimposed, revealing discernible differences in the time instances at which peak amplitudes occurred. This observation confirms the presence of the time-lag phenomenon.

Traffic conditions were not specifically documented; however, the test data set encompassed scenarios featuring both single and multiple vehicles traversing the bridge, as depicted in Figures 14 and 15, respectively. In Figure 15, the duration of the recorded vibration data significantly exceeds the typical transit time for a standard vehicle, suggesting that multiple vehicles were crossing the bridge during the monitoring interval. For these scenarios, details such as the number of vehicles, their mass, the frequency of passage, and the speed were unknown and anticipated to fluctuate. This variability ensures the broad applicability of the proposed method across a range of traffic conditions.

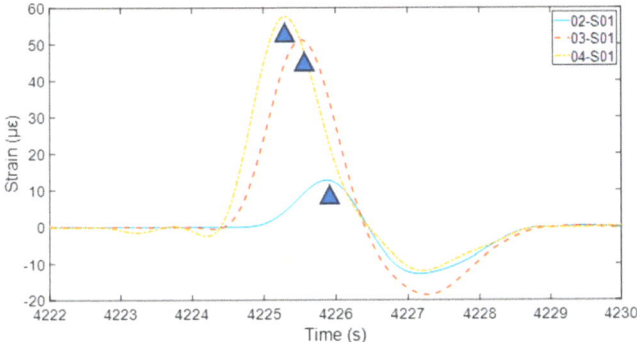

**Figure 14.** Time-lag phenomenon in the strain time history between different cross-sections. (Triangle marks denote the highest amplitude for each strain time–history curve.)

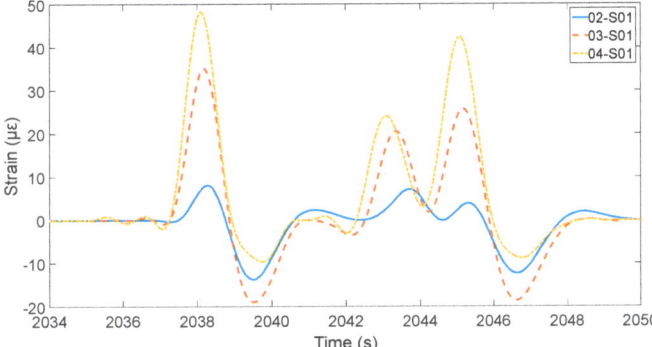

**Figure 15.** Strain time histories at three cross-sections with multiple passing vehicles.

The monitoring data set also accounts for varying temperature conditions. For illustration, two segments of monitoring data were selected: one from 28 August (summer) and another from 6 October (autumn) in 2018. According to the recorded local weather data, the daily air temperature fluctuated between 22 to 31 degrees Celsius in summer and 13 to 22 degrees Celsius in autumn. During each monitoring period, a single vehicle was observed crossing the bridge. Figure 16 presents the time history of the high-frequency bridge strain at 02-S01, with the corresponding frequency spectrum. The frequency spectra indicate that the first bridge vibration frequency (notably the peak around 3.5 Hz) undergoes minor changes under different air temperatures. This observation suggests that fluctuations in air temperature could potentially influence the stiffness of the bridge's structural materials.

It is important to note that, while Figure 13 demonstrates that temperature changes can cause significant strain variations, and Figure 16a,b show that these changes can slightly affect the bridge's natural frequency, the impact of temperature on the mode shapes of small- and medium-span bridges was expected to be minimal. Consequently, temperature was considered an unnecessary factor to include in the proposed BP-ANN model. Furthermore, as observed in the right columns of Figure 16a,b, there were differences in the amplitudes of the corresponding frequencies. These discrepancies were attributed to the unknown and varying traffic conditions. As Equation 8 indicates, the amplitudes of the bridge frequencies are determined by the number of vehicles, their weight, and their speed. Since the traffic conditions are likely to differ between the two monitoring periods, the amplitudes associated with the bridge frequencies will also vary. However, it is crucial to emphasize that, as shown in Equations (7), (8) and (14), changing traffic conditions do not alter the bridge's mode shape or the transfer matrix. Therefore, traffic conditions were not included in the proposed BP-ANN model. This approach ensures that the model remains focused on the primary factors influencing the bridge's dynamic responses without being confounded by the complexities of variable traffic patterns.

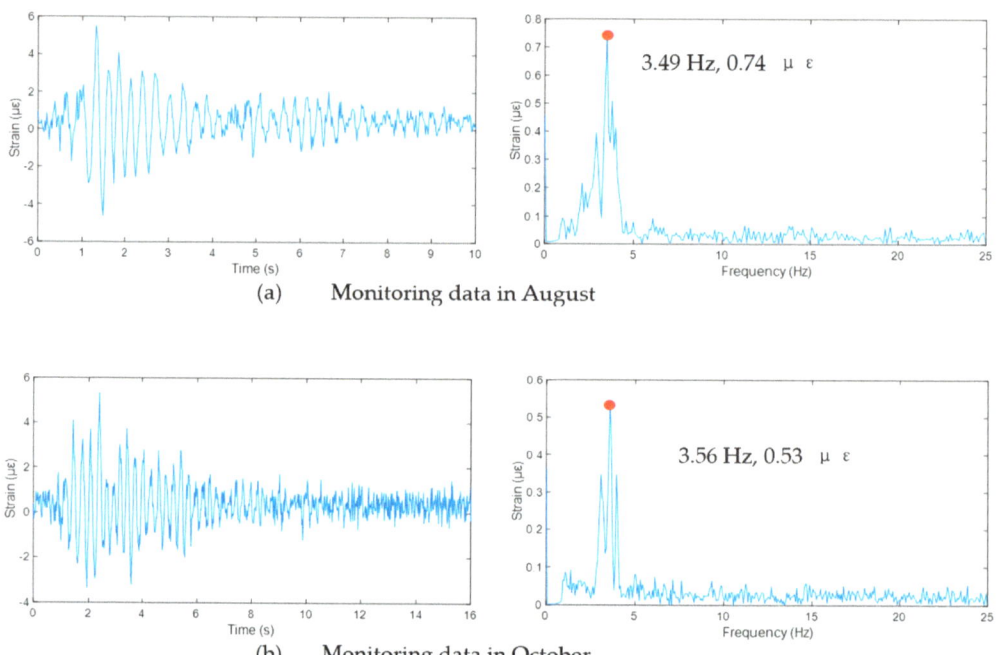

**Figure 16.** High-frequency bridge strain at 02-S01 under vehicular loading in August and October. (**a**) Monitoring data in August; (**b**) monitoring data in October. (Left column: strain time history; right column: frequency spectrum.)

4.3.2. Case Configuration

This study incorporated monitoring data from three distinct days as a case study. Air temperature records from a local meteorological station indicated that the daily temperature ranges for these days were non-overlapping. The rationale behind this selection was to evaluate the robustness of a BP-ANN model trained under specific temperature conditions and to determine its applicability under varying temperature scenarios. The ANN model was constructed to account for random traffic conditions, with the goal of creating a model that is universally applicable with varying traffic conditions and air temperatures.

The data set for each day spanned a duration of 30 min. Two experimental cases were devised. The first case, depicted in Figure 17a, utilizes the monitoring data from the initial day. In this setup, 80% of the data was allocated to training the BP-ANN model, while 20% was earmarked for assessing the model's predictive accuracy. The second case, as illustrated in Figure 17b, took into account the potential influence of temperature. To this end, 30-min segments of monitoring data from the three distinct days were amalgamated to form a composite data set. For this data set, 33% of the data was dedicated to training the model, and 67% was utilized to test the model's accuracy. The training and testing data sets for this comparison adhered to the distribution outlined in the second case, as shown in Figure 17b.

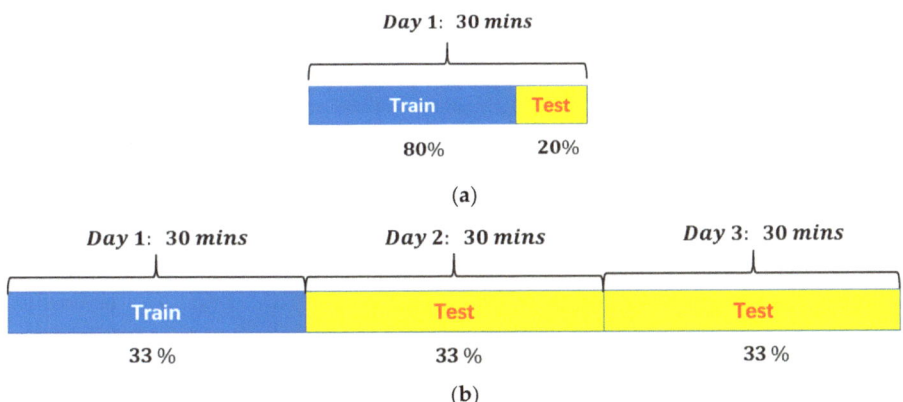

**Figure 17.** Training and testing data sets in the case study. (**a**) First case; (**b**) second case.

*4.4. Result Discussion*

Figure 18 illustrates the estimation of low-frequency bridge strain for the first case. It can be observed that, from 660 s to 700 s, there were multiple peaks in the time history of bridge strain, which indicates that multiple vehicles passed the target span in the monitoring period. The detailed conditions of these vehicles, including their number, mass, speed, and passing lanes, are unknown. However, as illustrated in Figure 18, the time instances corresponding to the peak amplitudes align closely between the estimated values and the actual monitoring data. Moreover, the highest estimated amplitudes correspond well with the periods when vehicles were passing, as observed in the monitoring data. This concurrence suggests that the proposed method effectively captured the relationship between the bridge's strain and the vehicle interactions.

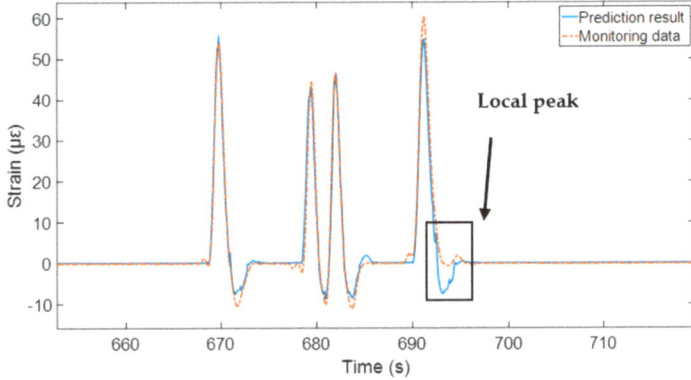

**Figure 18.** Comparison for low-frequency strain at 02-S01 (First case).

In certain time instances, the strain estimation could display a degree of imprecision, with the estimates exhibiting sudden peaks (indicated by rectangles in Figure 18) that were at odds with the more continuous curve observed in the monitoring data. This variance was thought to stem from the randomness inherent in batch processing and from measurement noise. Specifically, random batch processing does not ensure continuity in amplitudes between consecutive time points. Additionally, when the response amplitudes are relatively low, the method may not effectively separate the actual responses from noise, potentially leading to imperfect estimations. Nevertheless, these sudden peaks have a negligible effect on the estimated local peak values and the general shape of the time–history curve. It is conceivable that future modifications could be made to refine the model and yield a smoother estimation. However, such enhancements fall outside the scope of the current paper and will not be discussed further.

Additionally, the estimation results for the second case are depicted in Figure 19. Similar to Figure 18, the traffic conditions for the multiple passing vehicles in the second case are also known. Additionally, the temperatures for the training data set and the testing data set are different, which indicates a potential change in bridge-material stiffness. Figure 19 shows that the vehicle-passing periods, the highest amplitudes, and the time instances of these peaks, as observed in the monitoring data and the estimation results, match very well. It was inferred that temperature changes exert a negligible impact on the trained strain–vehicle interaction relationship. Furthermore, it is reasonable to assume that the primary mode shapes of the bridge remain stable over several months.

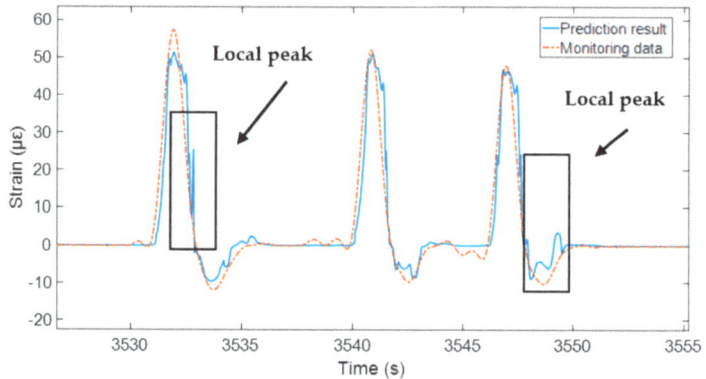

**Figure 19.** Comparison for low-frequency strain at 02-S01 (Second case).

Another noteworthy aspect is the seven-month interval between the first and third monitoring days. The estimation results presented in Figure 19 indicate that the proposed method offers several advantages. Firstly, it eliminates the need to collect traffic condition or temperature data. Secondly, for long-term bridge health monitoring, it is practical to develop a long-term strain-interaction model using a minimal data set from a short monitoring period. This approach is especially beneficial for practical engineering applications, streamlining the process of bridge health assessment and reducing the resources required for data collection and analysis.

## 5. Conclusions

This paper introduces a physically guided machine learning approach to predicting low-frequency bridge responses at a particular cross-section, leveraging responses from other cross-sections under the influence of vehicle loading. The theoretical derivation of the physical characteristics of low-frequency bridge dynamics within a typical VBI system served as the foundation. Utilizing these physical insights, a time-independent BP-ANN was trained to estimate the time-series of low-frequency bridge responses. The proposed method was rigorously validated through a combination of numerical simulations and field experiments. The analysis led to the following key conclusions:

(1) A theoretical analysis established that, for typical highway VBI systems, the commonly employed "quasi-static" approach to bridge responses closely approximates low-frequency responses, which are primarily dictated by the driving force modes. More significantly, the target strain–vehicle interaction relationship is time-independent. Specifically, the transfer matrix is solely dependent on the bridge's mode shapes, and it remains constant across varying temperature and traffic conditions.

(2) Finite element simulations were initially conducted to validate the physical characteristics of the transfer matrix. It was confirmed that the transfer matrix remains stable under fluctuating traffic conditions, including variations in vehicle mass, quantity, and speed. Furthermore, the robustness of the proposed method was demonstrated through tests involving artificially introduced noise in the simulation data.

(3) In the field tests, the proposed method was validated across two scenarios. Despite varying and unknown traffic conditions and temperatures, the method exhibited excellent performance. The estimated low-frequency responses were found to align well with the monitoring data. Additionally, it was demonstrated that the proposed method has the potential to construct an effective estimation model for long-term monitoring, utilizing a small data set collected over a short monitoring period.

Compared to previous studies, this novel approach adeptly overcomes the challenges associated with extracting modal information from low-frequency responses. Moreover, it effectively circumvents the difficulties of obtaining comprehensive traffic and temperature data, which are essential for accurate structural health assessments. Consequently, we believe this method is poised to be highly applicable in real-world engineering scenarios.

It is important to note that the current study focuses solely on linear bridge structures. The applicability of this method to large-span bridges with significant nonlinear dynamics or bridges that have been potentially damaged and exhibit nonlinear behavior has yet to be determined. Specifically, traffic conditions and temperature may impact the modal characteristics of these nonlinear structures. Therefore, it is imperative to consider these factors in our analyses. These considerations are among the areas we intend to investigate more deeply in our future research.

**Author Contributions:** Conceptualization, methodology, software, validation, and writing—original draft preparation, X.L.; writing—review and editing and supervision, G.Q.; resources and data curation, Y.X. and L.S.; investigation and writing—original draft preparation, H.S. and W.Z. All authors have read and agreed to the published version of the manuscript.

**Funding:** The authors disclose the receipt of the following financial support for the research, authorship, and publication of this article: the Technology Cooperation Project of Shanghai Qi Zhi Institute (No. SQZ202310), the Fujian Provincial Department of Science and Technology, China (Optimization design and key technology research of urban bridge cluster monitoring, Grant No. 2023Y0040), National Natural Science Foundation of China (Grant No. 52278313) and National Natural Science Foundation of China (Grant No. 5231101864).

**Data Availability Statement:** The data presented in this study are available upon request from the corresponding author, Guang Qu.

**Conflicts of Interest:** Author Wei Zhang was employed by the company Fujian Provincial Construction Engineering Quality Testing Center Co., Ltd., Fujian Academy of Building Research Co., Ltd. The remaining authors declare that the research was conducted in the absence of any commercial or financial relationships that could be construed as a potential conflict of interest.

## Appendix A. Main Symbols and Abbreviations

| | |
|---|---|
| $m_v$ | Vehicle mass. |
| $k_v$ | Spring stiffness. |
| $q_v$ | Vehicle vertical displacement. |
| $u(x,t)$ | Vertical bridge displacement. |
| $\overline{m}$ | Bridge unit mass. |
| $E$ | Material elastic modulus. |
| $I$ | Moment of inertia of the beam cross-section. |
| $p(x,t)$ | Interaction force. |
| $\varnothing_n(x)$ | Modal shapes. |

| | |
|---|---|
| $q_{b,n}(t)$ | Time-domain coordinate. |
| $w(k+1)$ & $b(k+1)$ | Weight and bias of the $(k+1)$-th iteration. |
| $\alpha$ | Learning rate. |
| $e_i$ | The error between the true value and the simulated result. |
| $\varepsilon(x,t)$ | Bridge strain. |

## References

1. Tian, Y.; Xu, Y.; Zhang, D.; Li, H. Relationship Modeling between Vehicle-Induced Girder Vertical Deflection and Cable Tension by BiLSTM Using Field Monitoring Data of a Cable-Stayed Bridge. *Struct. Control Health Monit.* **2021**, *28*, e2667. [CrossRef]
2. Oh, B.K.; Yoo, S.H.; Park, H.S. A Measured Data Correlation-Based Strain Estimation Technique for Building Structures Using Convolutional Neural Network. *Integr. Comput. Aided Eng.* **2023**, *30*, 395–412. [CrossRef]
3. Lu, L.-J.; Zhou, H.-F.; Ni, Y.-Q.; Dai, F. Output-Only Modal Analysis for Non-Synchronous Data Using Stochastic Sub-Space Identification. *Eng. Struct.* **2021**, *230*, 111702. [CrossRef]
4. Dosiek, L.; Zhou, N.; Pierre, J.W.; Huang, Z.; Trudnowski, D.J. Mode Shape Estimation Algorithms under Ambient Conditions: A Comparative Review. *IEEE Trans. Power Syst.* **2013**, *28*, 779–787. [CrossRef]
5. Poncelet, F.; Kerschen, G.; Golinval, J.-C.; Verhelst, D. Output-Only Modal Analysis Using Blind Source Separation Techniques. *Mech. Syst. Signal Process* **2007**, *21*, 2335–2358. [CrossRef]
6. Zhou, W.; Chelidze, D. Blind Source Separation Based Vibration Mode Identification. *Mech. Syst. Signal Process* **2007**, *21*, 3072–3087. [CrossRef]
7. Xiao, F.; Sun, H.; Mao, Y.; Chen, G.S. Damage Identification of Large-Scale Space Truss Structures Based on Stiffness Separation Method. *Structures* **2023**, *53*, 109–118. [CrossRef]
8. Xiao, F.; Yan, Y.; Meng, X.; Mao, Y.; Chen, G.S. Parameter Identification of Multispan Rigid Frames Using a Stiffness Separation Method. *Sensors* **2024**, *24*, 1884. [CrossRef]
9. Gulgec, N.S.; Takáč, M.; Pakzad, S.N. Structural Sensing with Deep Learning: Strain Estimation from Acceleration Data for Fatigue Assessment. *Comput.-Aided Civ. Infrastruct. Eng.* **2020**, *35*, 1349–1364. [CrossRef]
10. Xu, W.; Shi, X. Machine-Learning-Based Predictive Models for Punching Shear Strength of FRP-Reinforced Concrete Slabs: A Comparative Study. *Buildings* **2024**, *14*, 2492. [CrossRef]
11. Cheng, M.-C.; Bonopera, M.; Leu, L.-J. Applying Random Forest Algorithm for Highway Bridge-Type Prediction in Areas with a High Seismic Risk. *J. Chin. Inst. Eng.* **2024**, *47*, 597–610. [CrossRef]
12. Li, S.; Liang, Z.; Guo, P. A FBG Pull-Wire Vertical Displacement Sensor for Health Monitoring of Medium-Small Span Bridges. *Measurement* **2023**, *211*, 112613. [CrossRef]
13. Hidehiko, S.; Kosaku, K.; Chitoshi, M. Simplified Portable Bridge Weigh-in-Motion System Using Accelerometers. *J. Bridge Eng.* **2018**, *23*, 04017124. [CrossRef]
14. Breccolotti, M.; Natalicchi, M. Bridge Damage Detection through Combined Quasi-Static Influence Lines and Weigh-in-Motion Devices. *Int. J. Civ. Eng.* **2022**, *20*, 487–500. [CrossRef]
15. Zhao, H.; Uddin, N.; O'Brien, E.J.; Shao, X.; Zhu, P. Identification of Vehicular Axle Weights with a Bridge Weigh-in-Motion System Considering Transverse Distribution of Wheel Loads. *J. Bridge Eng.* **2014**, *19*, 04013008. [CrossRef]
16. Yu, E.; Wei, H.; Han, Y.; Hu, P.; Xu, G. Application of Time Series Prediction Techniques for Coastal Bridge Engineering. *Adv. Bridge Eng.* **2021**, *2*, 6. [CrossRef]
17. Hochreiter, S.; Jürgen, S. Long short-term memory. *Neural Comput.* **1997**, *9*, 1735–1780. [CrossRef]
18. Albawi, S.; Bayat, O.; Al-Azawi, S.; Ucan, O.N.; Lefevre, E. Social Touch Gesture Recognition Using Convolutional Neural Network. *Intell. Neurosci.* **2018**, *2018*, 6973103. [CrossRef]
19. Goodfellow, I.; Pouget-Abadie, J.; Mirza, M.; Xu, B.; Warde-Farley, D.; Ozair, S.; Courville, A.; Bengio, Y. Generative Adversarial Networks. *Commun. ACM* **2020**, *63*, 139–144. [CrossRef]
20. Zhao, H.; Ding, Y.; Li, A.; Sheng, W.; Geng, F. Digital Modeling on the Nonlinear Mapping between Multi-Source Monitoring Data of in-Service Bridges. *Struct. Control Health Monit.* **2020**, *27*, e2618. [CrossRef]
21. Xin, J.; Zhou, C.; Jiang, Y.; Tang, Q.; Yang, X.; Zhou, J. A Signal Recovery Method for Bridge Monitoring System Using TVFEMD and Encoder-Decoder Aided LSTM. *Measurement* **2023**, *214*, 112797. [CrossRef]
22. Wang, Z.; Wang, Y. Bridge Weigh-in-motion Through Bidirectional Recurrent Neural Network with Long Short-term Memory and Attention Mechanism. *Smart Struct. Syst.* **2021**, *27*, 241–256.
23. Li, Y.; Ni, P.; Sun, L.; Zhu, W. A Convolutional Neural Network-Based Full-Field Response Reconstruction Framework with Multitype Inputs and Outputs. *Struct. Control Health Monit.* **2022**, *29*, e2961. [CrossRef]
24. Pamuncak, A.P.; Salami, M.R.; Adha, A.; Budiono, B.; Laory, I. Estimation of Structural Response Using Convolutional Neural Network: Application to the Suramadu Bridge. *Eng. Comput.* **2021**, *38*, 4047–4065. [CrossRef]
25. Du, B.; Wu, L.; Sun, L.; Xu, F.; Li, L. Heterogeneous Structural Responses Recovery Based on Multi-Modal Deep Learning. *Struct. Health Monit.* **2023**, *22*, 799–813. [CrossRef]
26. Zhang, H.; Xu, C.; Jiang, J.; Shu, J.; Sun, L.; Zhang, Z. A Data-Driven Based Response Reconstruction Method of Plate Structure with Conditional Generative Adversarial Network. *Sensors* **2023**, *23*, 6750. [CrossRef]

27. Zhuang, Y.; Qin, J.; Chen, B.; Dong, C.; Xue, C.; Easa, S.M. Data Loss Reconstruction Method for a Bridge Weigh-in-Motion System Using Generative Adversarial Networks. *Sensors* **2022**, *22*, 858. [CrossRef]
28. Fan, G.; Li, J.; Hao, H.; Xin, Y. Data Driven Structural Dynamic Response Reconstruction Using Segment Based Generative Adversarial Networks. *Eng. Struct.* **2021**, *234*, 111970. [CrossRef]
29. Yang, Y.B.; Li, Y.C.; Chang, K.C. Constructing the Mode Shapes of a Bridge from a Passing Vehicle: A Theoretical Study. *Smart Struct. Syst.* **2014**, *13*, 797–819. [CrossRef]
30. Yang, Y.B.; Lin, C.W. Vehicle—Bridge Interaction Dynamics and Potential Applications. *J. Sound Vib.* **2005**, *284*, 205–226. [CrossRef]
31. Biggs, J.M. *Introduction to Structural Dynamics*; McGraw-Hill: New York, NY, USA, 1964.
32. Frýba, L. *Vibration of Solids and Structures under Moving Loads*; ICE Publishing: London, UK, 1999.
33. Huang, L.; Chen, J.; Tan, X. BP-ANN Based Bond Strength Prediction for FRP Reinforced Concrete at High Temperature. *Eng. Struct.* **2022**, *257*, 114026. [CrossRef]
34. Nurunnahar, S.; Talukdar, D.B.; Rasel, R.I.; Sultana, N. A Short Term Wind Speed Forcasting Using SVR and BP-ANN: A Comparative Analysis. In Proceedings of the 2017 20th International Conference of Computer and Information Technology (ICCIT), Dhaka, Bangladesh, 22–24 December 2017; pp. 1–6.
35. Huang, X.; You, Y.; Zeng, X.; Liu, Q.; Dong, H.; Qian, M.; Xiao, S.; Yu, L.; Hu, X. Back Propagation Artificial Neural Network (BP-ANN) for Prediction of the Quality of Gamma-Irradiated Smoked Bacon. *Food Chem.* **2024**, *437*, 137806. [CrossRef] [PubMed]
36. Al-Jarrah, R.; AL-Oqla, F.M. A Novel Integrated BPNN/SNN Artificial Neural Network for Predicting the Mechanical Performance of Green Fibers for Better Composite Manufacturing. *Compos. Struct.* **2022**, *289*, 115475. [CrossRef]
37. Yang, Y.-B.; Li, Y.C.; Chang, K.C. Effect of Road Surface Roughness on the Response of a Moving Vehicle for Identification of Bridge Frequencies. *Interact. Multiscale Mech.* **2012**, *5*, 347–368. [CrossRef]
38. Paultre, P.; Chaallal, O.; Proulx, J. Bridge Dynamics and Dynamic Amplification Factors—A Review of Analytical and Experimental Findings. *Can. J. Civ. Eng.* **1992**, *19*, 260–278. [CrossRef]
39. Dassault Systèmes. *Abaqus 6.11 Analysis User's Manual*; Dassault Systemes Simulia Corporation: Providence, RI, USA, 2011.
40. Lu, X.; Kim, C.-W.; Chang, K.-C. Finite Element Analysis Framework for Dynamic Vehicle-Bridge Interaction System Based on ABAQUS. *Int. J. Str. Stab. Dyn.* **2020**, *20*, 2050034. [CrossRef]
41. Lei, X.; Sun, L.; Xia, Y. Lost Data Reconstruction for Structural Health Monitoring Using Deep Convolutional Generative Adversarial Networks. *Struct. Health Monit.* **2021**, *20*, 2069–2087. [CrossRef]
42. Xia, Y.; Lei, X.; Wang, P.; Liu, G.; Sun, L. Long-Term Performance Monitoring and Assessment of Concrete Beam Bridges Using Neutral Axis Indicator. *Struct. Control Health Monit.* **2020**, *27*, e2637. [CrossRef]
43. MATLAB. Signal Processing Toolbox (Version R2022a). *MathWorks*. Available online: https://www.mathworks.com/help/signal/ref/highpass.html#mw_dcf4bbd2-1e29-4f0f-819f-39d872f77a14_seealso (accessed on 30 August 2024).

**Disclaimer/Publisher's Note:** The statements, opinions and data contained in all publications are solely those of the individual author(s) and contributor(s) and not of MDPI and/or the editor(s). MDPI and/or the editor(s) disclaim responsibility for any injury to people or property resulting from any ideas, methods, instructions or products referred to in the content.

Article

# Dynamic Testing and Finite Element Model Adjustment of the Ancient Wooden Structure Under Traffic Excitation

Xin Wang [1,*], Zhaobo Meng [2], Xiangming Lv [1] and Guoqiang Wei [1]

1. School of Civil Engineering, Tianshui Normal University, Tianshui 741001, China; lxm19791223@tsnu.edu.cn (X.L.); ceweigq@126.com (G.W.)
2. School of Architecture & Civil Engineering, Liaocheng University, Liaocheng 252000, China; mengzhaobo@lcu.edu.cn
* Correspondence: wangxin01234@aliyun.com

**Abstract:** In situ dynamic testing is conducted to study the dynamic characteristics of the wooden structure of the North House main hall. The velocity response signals on the measurement points are obtained and analyzed using the self-interaction spectral method and stochastic subspace method, yielding natural frequencies, mode shapes, and damping ratios. This study reveals that the natural frequencies and damping ratios are highly consistent between the two methods. Therefore, to eliminate errors, the average of the results from both modal identification methods is taken as the final measured modal parameters of the structure. The natural frequencies of the first and second order in the X direction were 2.097 Hz and 3.845 Hz and in the Y direction were 3.955 Hz and 5.701 Hz. The modal frequency in the Y direction of the structure exceeds that in the X direction. Concurrently, a three-dimensional finite element model was established using ANSYS 2021R1, considering the semi-rigid properties of mortise–tenon connections, and validated based on in situ dynamic testing. The sensitivity analysis indicates adjustments to parameters such as beam–column elastic modulus, tenon–mortise joint stiffness, and roof mass for finite element model refinement. Modal parameter calculations from the corrected finite element model closely approximate the measured modal results, with maximum errors of 9.41% for the first two frequencies, both within 10% of the measured resonant frequencies. The adjusted finite element model closely matches the experimental results, serving as a benchmark model for the wooden structure of North House main hall. The validation confirms the rationality of the benchmark finite element model, providing valuable insights into ancient timber structures along transportation routes.

**Keywords:** traffic excitation; ancient wooden structure; dynamic testing; modal parameter; finite element model

**Citation:** Wang, X.; Meng, Z.; Lv, X.; Wei, G. Dynamic Testing and Finite Element Model Adjustment of the Ancient Wooden Structure Under Traffic Excitation. *Buildings* 2024, 14, 3527. https://doi.org/10.3390/buildings14113527

Academic Editors: Shaohong Cheng and Haijun Zhou

Received: 23 September 2024
Revised: 25 October 2024
Accepted: 27 October 2024
Published: 5 November 2024

**Copyright:** © 2024 by the authors. Licensee MDPI, Basel, Switzerland. This article is an open access article distributed under the terms and conditions of the Creative Commons Attribution (CC BY) license (https://creativecommons.org/licenses/by/4.0/).

## 1. Introduction

The popularity of Tianshui's spicy hot pot has captivated the city, showcasing its role not only as a culinary hub but also as a city with rich cultural heritage. Designated as a National Famous Historical and Cultural City, Tianshui houses one World Cultural Heritage site and has a total of 470 units of various levels of cultural relic protection. Among others, the wooden structures of ancient residential buildings in Tianshui were announced as one of the endangered heritage sites by the World Cultural Heritage Foundation in 2006 [1].

The Hu Family Ancient Residence, commonly known as the Nanbei Courtyard, was an ancient architectural structure from the Ming Dynasty. The North Courtyard was originally the residence of Hu Xin, who served as the Minister of Rites during the Wanli period of the Ming Dynasty. Built in 1615, it has a history of over 400 years. On 25 June 2001, it was designated as a National Key Cultural Relic Protection Unit. It is one of the outstanding representatives of existing Ming Dynasty residential buildings in Tianshui City and is the only surviving official residence from the Ming Dynasty in Northwest China. The site holds significant historical, cultural, and artistic value, and its scale is also quite rare among ancient residences in the country.

The North House main hall in the middle court features a unique and grand design, serving as the core component of the North Courtyard. It embodies the exquisite architectural artistry and profound cultural significance of the Ming Dynasty. The plane of North House main hall is rectangular, oriented north–south. It spans five rooms with a total width of 20.05 m and a depth of three rooms totaling 14.41 m. The ridge height reaches 11.4 m, featuring a double-eave two-story pavilion-style brick and wood structure with a rigid roof. Figure 1 depicts the elevation plan of North House main hall. The North House main hall is located on Minzhu West Road in the Qinzhou District of Tianshui City, Gansu Province. It is only slightly over 40 m away from major traffic arteries within the city. Following the May 12 earthquake, the wooden structure of North House main hall suffered severe damage. Figure 2 shows the location schematic of North House main hall. With the economic development and population growth in Tianshui, ground traffic flow has continued to increase. Persistent ground traffic vibrations year-round have caused damage to the wooden structures. Over time, this cumulative damage has led to fatigue, the loosening of joints, and structural deformation and posed severe threats to safety and lifespan. Urgent research is needed to assess the dynamic response and safety of the wooden structures of North House main hall under traffic-induced conditions. This research will provide the basis for the maintenance, repair, and management of the wooden structures in Tianshui's ancient residences.

**Figure 1.** Elevation plan of North House main hall.

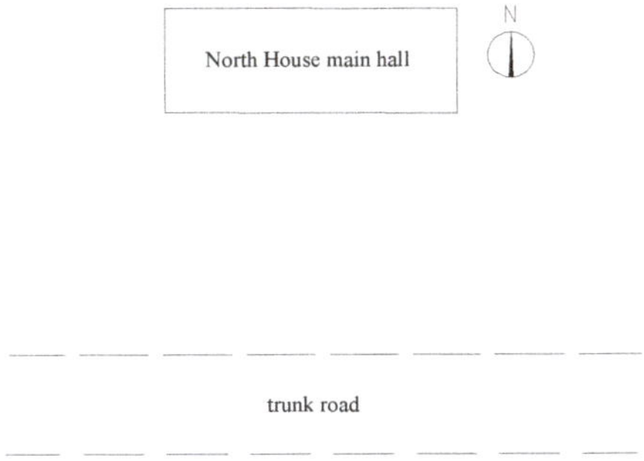

**Figure 2.** Location schematic of North House main hall.

The impact of traffic-induced vibrations on ancient architecture has received significant attention from domestic and international scholars, leading to extensive research efforts and relevant achievements in this field. To study the seismic performance of timber structures, many researchers have conducted shaking table tests on scaled models [2–5]. Due to the high costs of testing and the lack of general applicability, many researchers have adopted a cost-effective approach. This method involves the dynamic property testing of timber structures and the establishment of finite element models, which are validated through dynamic testing. Fang et al. [6,7] conducted on-site measurements and model tests on the North Gate of the Xi'an City Wall to study the basic characteristics of the timber structures. Multipoint excitation tests on the wooden models validate that the first and second modes obtained by the on-site full-scale test are the vibration modes of the tower. Wu et al. [8] and Pan et al. [9] established finite element models of timber structures and validated the model accuracy with the data from on-site tests to study the dynamic characteristics and seismic responses of the timber-frame structures. Che et al. [10] conducted on-site dynamic testing to analyze the dynamic characteristics and damage mechanics of the Yingxian Wooden Pagoda in Shanxi. Altunisik A. C. et al. [11] studied the structural condition of a restored historical timber mosque, conducting the finite element analysis, ambient vibration tests, and model updating to minimize the differences and reflect the current situation. Ahmet C. A. et al. [12] conducted eight ambient vibration tests on historical masonry armory buildings and determined the nonlinear dynamic response of historical masonry armory buildings using a validated finite element model.

This paper establishes a finite element model of the wooden structure of the North House main hall, which accurately reflects its vibration characteristics. Modal parameters of the structure are obtained using modal identification techniques based on traffic-induced excitation. A parameter correction method based on sensitivity analysis is applied to revise the original finite element model. The revised model effectively represents the dynamic characteristics of the actual structure, providing a foundational model for the seismic performance research of wooden structures of ancient buildings along traffic routes.

## 2. Vibration Testing of the Wooden Structure of North House Main Hall Underground Traffic Excitation

*2.1. Testing Instrument*

"Technical Code for Protection of Ancient Buildings against Industrial Vibration" uses the horizontal vibration velocity of the top column as the evaluation criterion [13]. In this test, vibration velocities in three directions at various measurement points of the wooden structure of the North House main hall are tested. Sensors are deployed on the roadway and at each floor level of the wooden structure. Vibration induced by vehicle loads generally exhibits low-frequency characteristics. According to the specifications, the sampling frequency is set to 50 Hz.

The Donghua DH5907A wireless environmental excitation test and analysis system is utilized, equipped with built-in sensors and a data analysis system. Online monitoring focuses primarily on the beams and columns of the main load-bearing components of the wooden structure. The vibration testing equipment includes one laptop computer, ten sensors, one GPS signal transmitter, ten GPS antennas, modeling clay, et al.

*2.2. Measurement Point Layout*

According to Section 7.1.2 of "Technical Code for Protection of Ancient Buildings against Industrial Vibration", the dynamic characteristics and response of the ancient building structure are tested. When the structure is symmetrical, testing can be conducted along any principal horizontal axis. When the structure is asymmetrical, testing should be conducted separately along each principal horizontal axis [13]. Due to the complex construction of the wooden structure of North House main hall, including vulnerable areas such as beam–column joints, column bases, and mid-span beams, and variations in damage conditions throughout the structure, factors such as the number of sensors and site conditions limit the testing scope. To address this, one reference point is selected at the base of columns 1–2 on each floor, and testing is conducted in batches per floor. Three batches are planned, with measurement points located at column bases, column heads, and adjacent floor slabs, totaling 27 measurement points. The testing conditions are detailed in Table 1.

**Table 1.** Testing conditions.

| Condition | Measurement Point Number | Direction | Sampling Target |
|---|---|---|---|
| 1 | 1–1, 1–2, 1–3, 1–4, 1–5, 1–6, 1–7, 1–8, 1–9, 1–10 | X, Y, Z | velocity |
| 2 | 2–1, 2–3, 2–4, 2–5, 2–6, 2–8, 2–9, 2–10 | X, Y, Z | velocity |
| 3 | 3–1, 3–3, 3–4, 3–5, 3–6, 3–8, 3–9, 3–10 | X, Y, Z | velocity |

Note: Reference point 1–2 is also included in each measurement condition.

Three-axis velocity sensors are installed at each measurement point, with each test duration not less than 20 min and conducted at least twice. The layout of measurement points is as shown in Figure 3, with north at the top, south at the bottom, west on the left, and east on the right. Ten measurement points are placed at the base of columns on the first floor of the timber structure, designated as 1–1 to 1–10. Eight measurement points are positioned at the base of columns on the second floor of the timber structure, labeled as 2–1 to 2–10. Eight measurement points are located at the tops of columns on the second floor of the timber structure, denoted as 3–1 to 3–10.

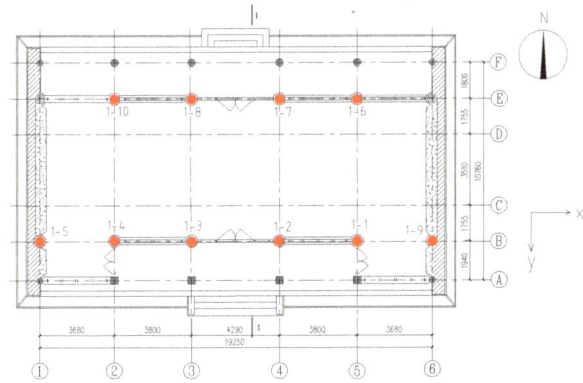

(**a**) The bottom of the first-floor column.

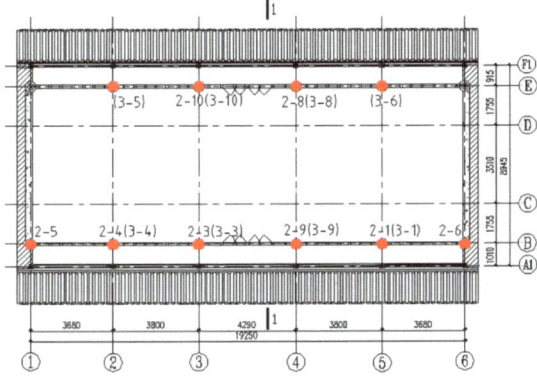

(**b**) The bottom and top of the second-floor column.

**Figure 3.** *Cont.*

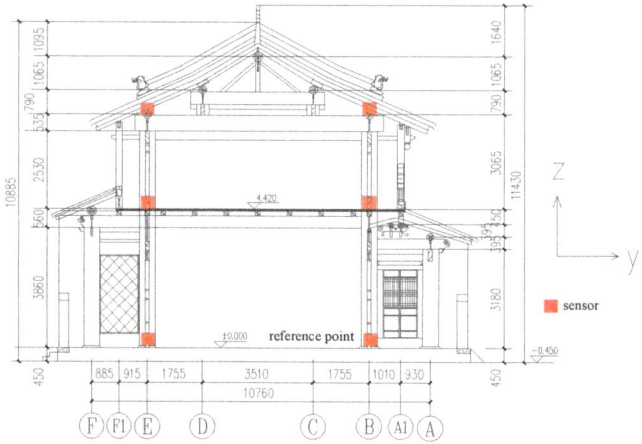

(c) 1–1 section.

**Figure 3.** The layout of measurement points.

The on-site testing process is illustrated in Figures 4–6. Due to the extended monitoring duration and high daytime visitor traffic, each measurement point is manned to ensure uninterrupted monitoring and to prevent unnecessary external interference with the sensors.

**Figure 4.** Preliminary preparation.

**Figure 5.** Data acquisition.

(a) The bottom of the second-floor column.

(b) The top of the second-floor column.

**Figure 6.** The layout of measurement points at the bottom and top of the second-floor column.

## 3. Test Data Pre-Processing

The signals obtained from vibration testing using sensors, amplifiers, and other data acquisition instruments are contaminated with unwanted components due to various external and internal factors during the testing process. To mitigate the effects of interference signals, data preprocessing is necessary. This pre-processing in MATLAB R2021b software includes eliminating trend terms, smoothing, and frequency domain filtering.

*3.1. Elimination of Trend Items*

The vibration signals collected during vibration testing often deviate from the baseline due to zero drift caused by amplifier temperature changes, instability in low-frequency performance outside the sensor's frequency range, and environmental interference around the sensor. The magnitude of deviation from the baseline over time refers to the trend of the signal [14,15]. The most commonly used method to remove the trend is polynomial least squares fitting. Taking the example of the Y-direction at measurement point 2–3 on the second-floor column base, Figure 7 shows the comparison of the velocity time history curve before and after removing the trend in the Y-direction at measurement point 2–3 on the second-floor column base.

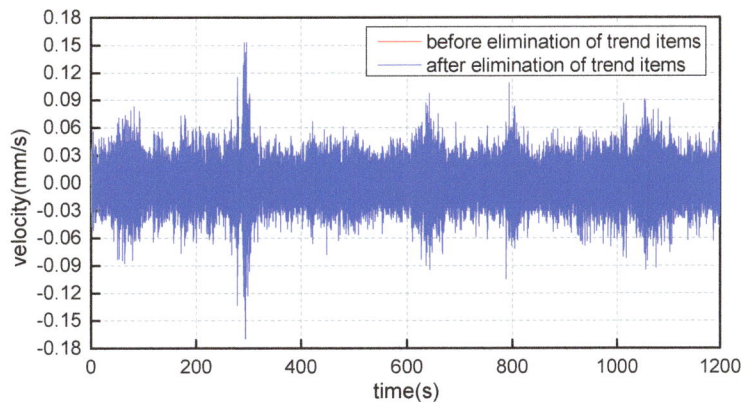

**Figure 7.** The velocity time history curve before and after eliminating the trend term in the y-direction at measurement point 2–3 on the second-floor column base.

From Figure 7, it can be observed that the deviation of the raw signal from the baseline is not significant. After removing the trend component, the data did not show significant changes.

## 3.2. Smoothing

During vibration testing, occasional unexpected disturbances to the testing instruments can lead to irregular shapes and significant deviations from the baseline in the sampled signals at individual measurement points. To address such signals, multiple rounds of data smoothing can be applied using a moving average method. By subtracting the trend component from the original signal, irregular trends in the signal are eliminated, resulting in a smooth trend curve [15]. This study employs the averaging method for processing.

Figure 8 shows the comparison of the velocity time–history curve before and after smoothing in the Y-direction at measurement point 2–3 on the second-floor column base.

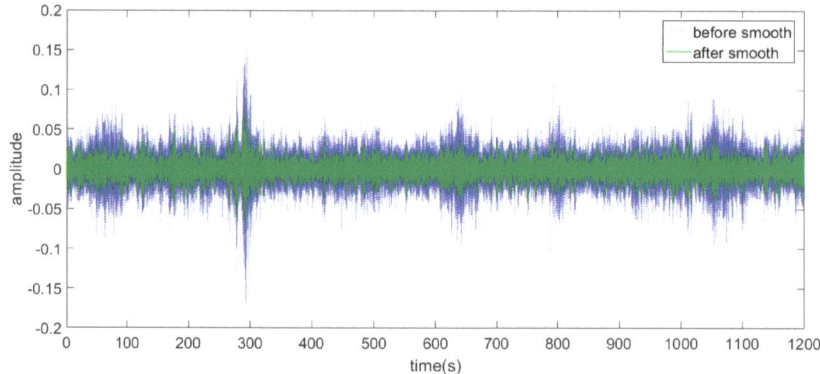

**Figure 8.** The velocity time–history curve before and after smooth in the Y-direction at measurement point 2–3 on the second floor column base.

From Figure 8, it is evident that the collected vibration signal, after undergoing smoothing, has eliminated many irregular spikes. This has resulted in smoother test data, enhancing the accuracy of subsequent processing outcomes.

## 3.3. Digital Filtration

Digital filtering applies mathematical operations to selectively remove or retain certain frequency components of collected signals, thereby filtering out noise or spurious components of test signals, improving signal-to-noise ratio, smoothing analytical data, suppressing interference signals, and separating frequency components.

Figure 9 depicts the comparison of the velocity time–history curves in the Y-direction at measurement point 2–3 on the second-floor column base before and after filtering. From Figure 9, it is evident that interference largely masks the true signal amplitude. After applying a low-pass filter, some spikes are removed, thereby attenuating the influence of interference signals.

After the elimination of trend items, applying smoothing, and performing filtration, the collected velocity signals were effectively purified. This significantly reduced noise interference, thereby enhancing the precision of the data analysis.

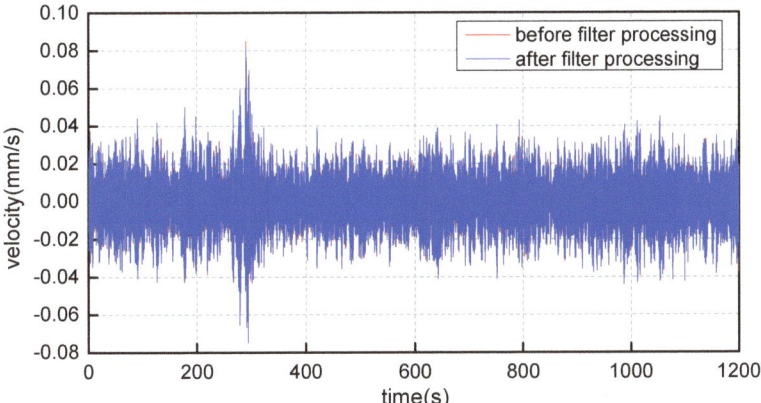

**Figure 9.** The velocity time–history curves before and after filter processing in the Y-direction at measurement point 2–3 on the second-floor column base.

## 4. Modal Parameter Identification

Modal identification methods based on environmental excitation can be classified into two categories: frequency domain methods and time domain methods. Based on the applicability of these two methods, the modal parameter identification of the wooden structures of North House main hall is conducted using the peak picking method from the frequency domain theory and the stochastic subspace identification method from the time domain theory [16].

### 4.1. The Peak Picking Method for Modal Parameter Identification

#### 4.1.1. The Peak Picking Method

The peak picking method, based on the Welch method principle, is used to determine the frequencies of the structure. The modal parameters of the system are identified based on the principle that peaks appear in the power spectral density function at the natural frequencies of the system [17]. The Welch method is employed to sequentially estimate the power spectral density functions of response signals at each measurement point, obtaining the self-power spectral density in both the X and Y directions at each layer measurement point, as shown in Figure 10.

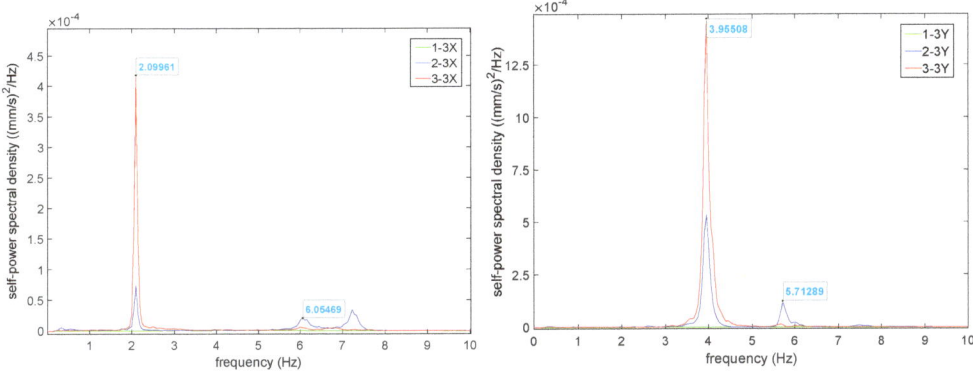

**Figure 10.** *Cont.*

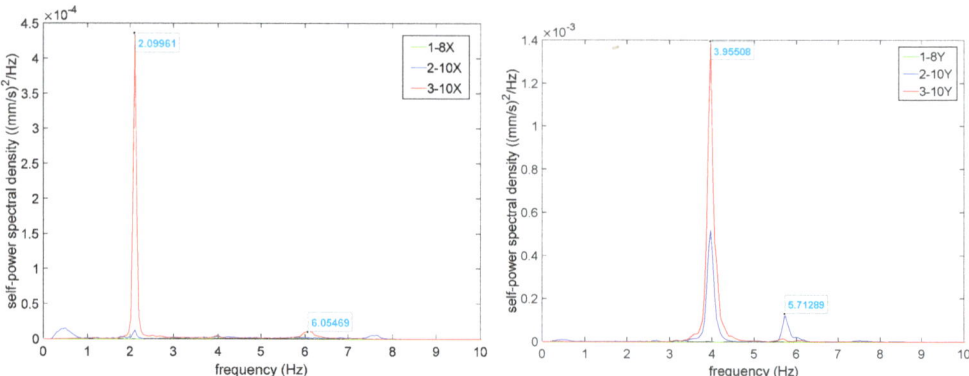

**Figure 10.** Self-power spectral density in X and Y directions at each layer's measurement points.

Figure 10 presents the self-power spectral density curves of X and Y direction at each layer measurement point of the timber frame structure. It is observed that the self-power spectral density peaks at the same location are similar, while the curves at other measurement points exhibit distinct peaks, indicating good identification performance. Additionally, as the frequency increases, the corresponding self-power spectral density peaks gradually decrease, suggesting that the coefficients of the participation of the initial vibration modes of the structure are higher, and these lower-order modes constitute the primary vibration forms of the structure.

The self-power spectral density of X and Y direction vibrations at measurement points under conditions 1 to 3 is shown in Figures 11–13.

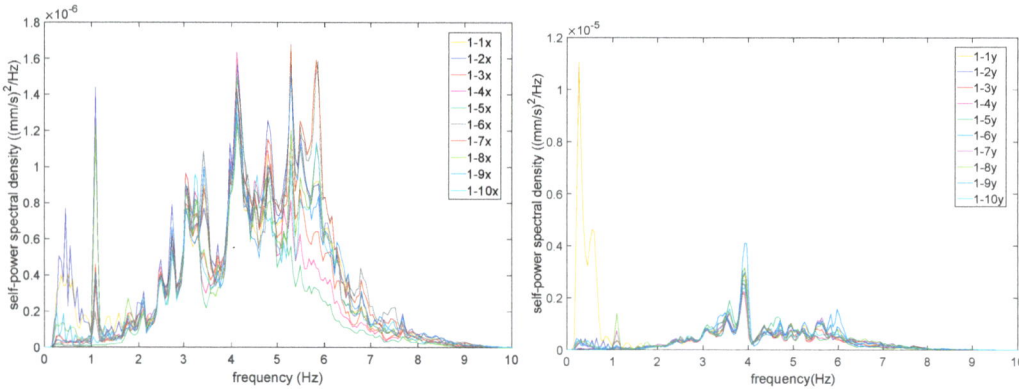

**Figure 11.** Self-power spectral density in X and Y directions at the measurement points for condition 1.

According to the self-power spectral density peaks at measurement points in Figures 11–13, points X and Y on the roof level exhibit the highest peaks. As the floors descend, the self-power spectral density peaks gradually decrease at each level, reaching near-zero values at the base of the columns on the first floor for points X and Y. Due to the proximity of the front eaves to the driveway, the self-power spectral density peaks at the front eave measurement points are greater than those at the rear eave measurement points, indicating greater vibration energy at the front eaves. Within the same floor level, vibrations are more pronounced at the front eaves.

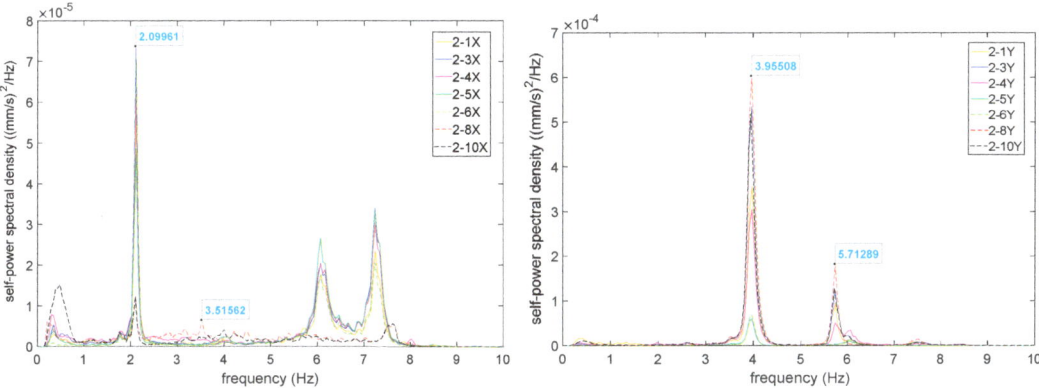

**Figure 12.** Self-power spectral density in X and Y directions at the measurement points for condition 2.

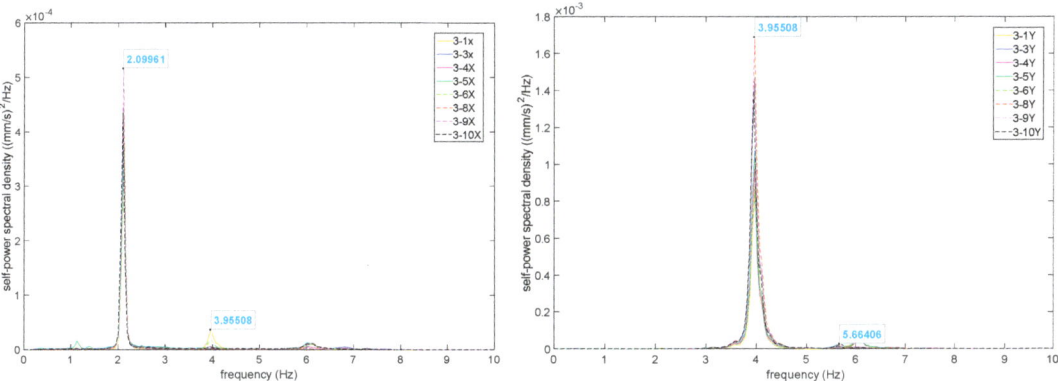

**Figure 13.** Self-power spectral density in X and Y directions at the measurement points for condition 3.

4.1.2. Natural Frequency and Damping Ratio Identification

Based on the peak frequency of the self-power spectral density curves of the self at each measurement point, the natural frequencies of each floor are calculated. Considering variations in damage conditions at different locations, there are differences in measurement results at each point. The resonant frequencies in the X and Y directions are taken as the average of the identified results from various points on the same floor. The calculated frequencies for the first two modes in the X and Y directions are shown in Table 2.

**Table 2.** Natural frequencies of the wood structure.

| Order | X Direction | | | Y Direction | | |
|---|---|---|---|---|---|---|
| | Condition 2 | Condition 3 | Average | Condition 2 | Condition 3 | Average |
| 1 | 2.099 | 2.099 | 2.099 | 3.955 | 3.955 | 3.955 |
| 2 | 3.515 | 3.955 | 3.735 | 5.713 | 5.664 | 5.689 |

The damping ratio is calculated using the half-power bandwidth method [4], as shown in Formula (1). The calculation results are presented in Table 3.

$$\zeta = \frac{f_2 - f_1}{2f_i} \times 100\% \tag{1}$$

**Table 3.** The damping ratio calculation results.

| Order | X Direction | Y Direction |
|---|---|---|
|  | Average | Average |
| 1 | 1.67 | 1.83 |
| 2 | 2.18 | 1.75 |

In the formula, $\zeta$: damping ratio; $f_i$: the peak frequency of the ith structural mode; $f_2$, $f_1$: frequencies at which the peak intersects $1/\sqrt{2}$ amplitude level line of the curve ($f_2 > f_1$).

*4.2. Random Subspace Method for Modal Parameter Identification*

The random subspace method is a time-domain technique for modal parameter identification that utilizes spatial projection for filtering, effectively denoising the modal signals. To enhance the accuracy of modal identification, the random subspace method is combined with the stability diagram theory [18,19]. Applying the stability diagram theory allows for indeterminate system order, eliminating spurious eigenvalues and directly extracting genuine physical modal parameters [20]. During data processing, it is necessary to determine the number of rows (i) of the Hankel matrix and the system order (N); in this study, (i = 100) for the Hankel matrix and (N = 50) for the system order [21–23].

For each of the three operating conditions tested, random subspace analysis was conducted, resulting in stability diagrams of the SSI calculations, as shown in Figure 14. In these diagrams, the letter "o" represents the pole characteristics obtained from structural modeling computations. Each condition exhibits distinct peaks in the curves, with clustered "o" symbols at frequencies indicating stable characteristics of frequency, damping, and mode shape, indicating clear genuine modes.

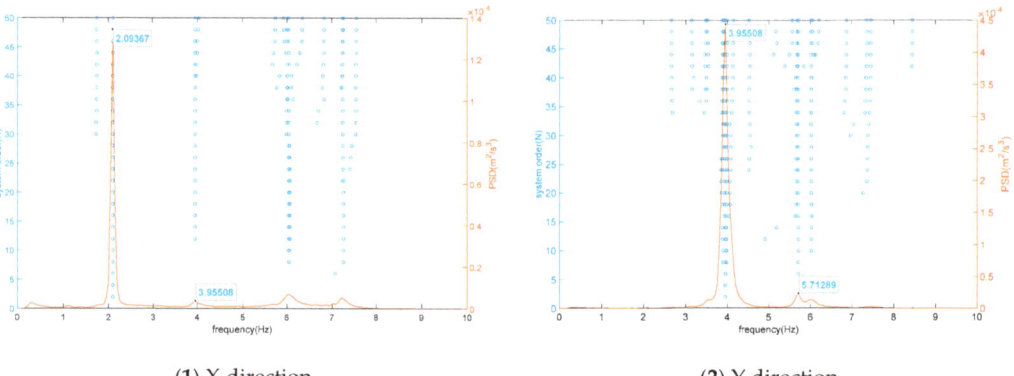

(**1**) X direction.  (**2**) Y direction.

**Figure 14.** Stability diagram.

From Figure 14, it is evident that the peaks in the stability diagram correspond to the natural frequencies of the system. Modal frequencies obtained from the structural stability diagram using the random subspace method are presented in Table 4.

**Table 4.** Modal frequencies of wood structures.

| Order | X Direction | Y Direction |
|---|---|---|
|  | Frequency (Hz) | Frequency (Hz) |
| 1 | 2.094 | 3.955 |
| 2 | 3.955 | 5.713 |

In the stability diagram shown in Figure 14, the damping ratio of the system can be inferred by analyzing the shape and width of the vibration peaks. Damping ratios of the identified structure calculated using the random subspace method are presented in Table 5.

Table 5. Damping ratio of wood structures.

| Order | X Direction | Y Direction |
|---|---|---|
| | Damping Ratio (%) | Damping Ratio (%) |
| 1 | 1.09 | 1.59 |
| 2 | 1.73 | 1.12 |

From Table 5, it is observed that the damping ratios identified using the random subspace method exhibit low variability. The damping ratios for each frame structure range from 1.09% to 1.73%, all falling within the category of low-damping structures.

Based on the results of modal parameter identification using the auto-spectral method and the random subspace method, the first two modal shapes in the east–west and north–south directions of the wooden structure of North House main hall are obtained, as shown in Figure 15. The analysis of Figure 15 indicates that the first-order modes in both X and Y directions exhibit bending behavior, with greater amplitudes observed at higher floors. The second-order modes display a bending–shear behavior, indicating that the structure experiences bending and shear movements during vibration.

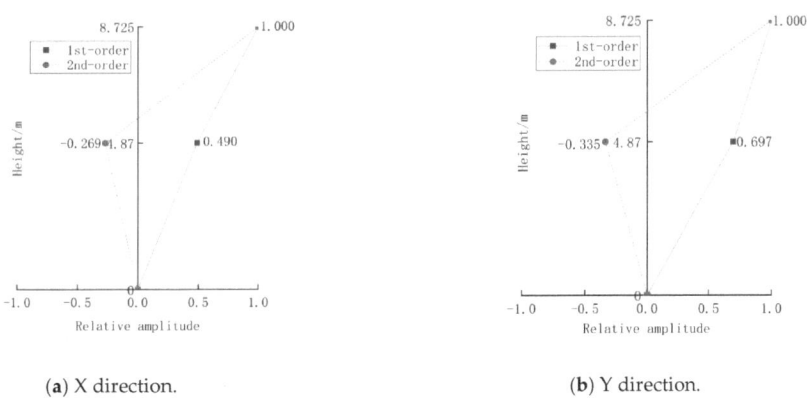

(a) X direction.  (b) Y direction.

Figure 15. The first and second-order mode shapes of North House main hall.

### 4.3. Comparison of Modal Parameter Identification Results

A comparison of Tables 2 and 4 reveals that the modal identification results for natural frequencies are highly consistent between the two methods. Therefore, the average of the results from both modal identification methods is taken as the final measured modal parameters of the structure. The computed results are presented in Table 6.

Table 6. Comparison of natural frequency identification results for timber structures.

| Order | X Direction | | | Y Direction | | |
|---|---|---|---|---|---|---|
| | Spontaneous Spectrum | SSI | Average | Spontaneous Spectrum | SSI | Average |
| 1 | 2.099 | 2.094 | 2.097 | 3.955 | 3.955 | 3.955 |
| 2 | 3.735 | 3.955 | 3.845 | 5.689 | 5.713 | 5.701 |

From Table 6, it is observed that the modal frequency in the Y direction of the structure exceeds that in the X direction. Modal frequency is an inherent property of the structure, influenced by its stiffness and mass. Through comparative analysis, it is noted that the main beams of the wooden structure of North House main hall are oriented along the north–south direction, resulting in increased stiffness in the north–south direction of the structure.

A comparison of Tables 3 and 5 reveals that the modal identification results for the damping ratio are highly consistent between the two methods. Therefore, the average of the results from both modal identification methods is taken as the final measured modal parameters of the structure. The computed results are presented in Table 7.

Table 7. Comparison of damping ratio identification results for timber structures.

| Order | X Direction | | | Y Direction | | |
|---|---|---|---|---|---|---|
| | Spontaneous Spectrum | SSI | Average | Spontaneous Spectrum | SSI | Average |
| 1 | 1.67 | 1.09 | 1.38 | 1.83 | 1.59 | 1.71 |
| 2 | 2.18 | 1.73 | 1.96 | 1.75 | 1.12 | 1.44 |

## 5. Baseline Finite Element Model

### 5.1. Initial Finite Element Model

(1) Using ANSYS software to establish a finite element model of the wooden structure of North House main hall, due to its construction time being close to that of the Bell Tower in Xi'an, material parameters are referenced from the literature [24] as shown in Table 8.

Table 8. Wooden parameters.

| Materials | Elasticity Modulus (MPa) | Density (kg/m$^3$) | Poisson Ratio |
|---|---|---|---|
| wood | 8307 | 410 | 0.25 |

According to the construction period of North House main hall and the actual damage to the timber structure, taking into account the long-term effects of loads and aging of wood, the dynamic modulus of elasticity of timber beams and columns should be reduced based on the flexural modulus of elasticity given in Table 8, as specified in Table 9 [25].

Table 9. Adjustment coefficients for the performance of the ancient wood building under long-term load and wood aging.

| Date of Building Construction (Year) | Adjustment Coefficients | | |
|---|---|---|---|
| | Compressive Strength of Smooth Grain | Flexural and Smooth Grain Shear Strength | Flexural Modulus of Elasticity |
| 100 | 0.95 | 0.90 | 0.90 |
| 300 | 0.85 | 0.80 | 0.85 |
| >500 | 0.75 | 0.70 | 0.75 |

The North House main hall, with a history of over 300 years, has a flexural modulus of elasticity adjustment factor of 0.85, equivalent to 7060.95 MPa.

(2) Wood beams and columns are simulated using the 3D elastic element Beam188, capable of withstanding tension, compression, and torsion. Each node has six degrees of freedom: translation along the x, y, and z directions and rotation about the x, y, and z axes. The large roof is simulated using the Mass21 mass element, which has six degrees of freedom: translation along the x, y, and z directions and rotation about the x, y, and z axes. Each direction can have a different mass and moment of inertia. The beam–column joints are simulated using the Combinl4 element, which can model one-dimensional, two-dimensional, and three-dimensional longitudinal or torsional spring effects. Establish

multiple coincident finite element nodes at the mortise and tenon joints of beams and columns, applying spring elements only at the beam and column connections. The spring stiffness coefficients are $K_x = K_z = 1.71 \times 10^7$ N/m, $K_y = 2.08 \times 10^8$ N/m, $k_{\theta x} = k_{\theta y} = k_{\theta z} = 6.244 \times 10^8$ N·m/rad [26], as shown in Figure 16.

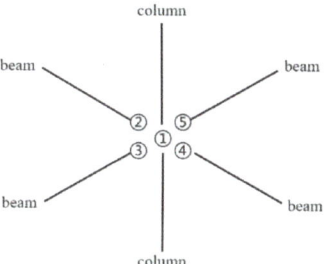

**Figure 16.** The simulation of beam and column mortise and tenon.

(3) Using the area equivalent method to concentrate roof loads at respective column ends, the roof load G is determined to be 1.925 kN/m² [27].

(4) Establish a finite element model of the timber structure of North House main hall, as shown in Figure 17. The columns are placed on pedestal bases with grooves, which do not fully restrict column rotation, thus the column base nodes are simplified to pinned connections.

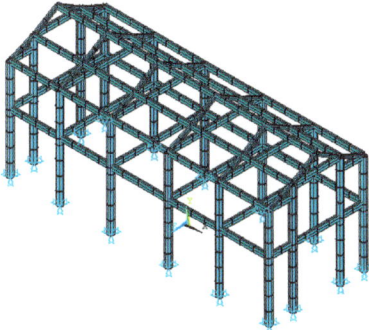

**Figure 17.** The finite element model of the wooden structure of North House main hall.

Perform modal analysis on the initial finite element model of the wooden structure of North House main hall using the Block Lanczos method. Calculate the first two natural frequencies of the timber structure. Use the experimentally measured modal frequencies as the objective function for refining the finite element model. Compare the structural natural frequencies obtained from numerical simulation and on-site testing as shown in Table 10.

**Table 10.** Comparison of natural frequencies of timber structures (Hz).

| Order | X Direction | | | Y Direction | | |
|---|---|---|---|---|---|---|
| | Test Value | Simulated Value | Inaccuracy (%) | Test Value | Simulated Value | Inaccuracy (%) |
| 1 | 2.097 | 1.832 | 12.64 | 3.955 | 3.264 | 17.47 |
| 2 | 3.845 | 3.368 | 12.41 | 5.701 | 4.740 | 16.86 |

Note : inaccuracy = $\frac{|\text{simulated value} - \text{measured value}|}{\text{measured value}} \times 100\%$.

According to Table 10, the first two natural frequencies in the east–west direction of the timber structure model are 1.832 Hz and 3.368 Hz, with relative errors to measured frequencies ranging from 12.41% to 12.64%. In the east–west direction, the first two natural frequencies are 3.264 Hz and 4.740 Hz, with relative errors to measured frequencies ranging from 16.86% to 17.47%. The finite element model shows errors greater than 10% compared to the measured values, which may be attributed to (1) the simplification of wall and floor stiffness in the model; (2) inaccuracy in the elastic modulus of wood; (3) inaccurate stiffness values at beam–column joints; (4) onaccuracy in roof weight estimation. These areas require focused correction in the finite element model.

*5.2. Finite Element Model Correction and Analysis*

5.2.1. Modal Correlation Analysis

Modal frequency criterion is established based on the error ratio formula, assessing conformity based on the magnitude of the ratio. Compliance is considered satisfactory when the ratio is less than 10%. The calculation formula is as follows:

$$e = \frac{\omega_m - \omega_n}{\omega_m} \times 100\% \quad (2)$$

where $\omega_m$ and $\omega_n$, respectively, represent the measured frequencies and finite element analysis frequencies of the structure.

5.2.2. Finite Element Model Correction

Based on the design drawings, there are inevitably discrepancies between the initial finite element model and the actual structure. These differences and inaccuracies are addressed by adjusting model parameters using field-measured natural frequencies as references to revise the ANSYS finite element model. Adjustments include modifications to material elastic modulus, joint stiffness at tenon and mortise connections, and roof mass.

(1) Material property adjustment: The elastic modulus serves as the primary parameter for model refinement. Due to multiple reinforcements and repairs in the wooden structure of North House main hall, particularly in certain beams and columns, the dynamic elastic modulus of wooden beams and columns continues to adhere to the data in Table 1. The revised elastic modulus of the timber structure is determined to be 8307 MPa.
(2) Joint stiffness adjustment: Spring elements are applied at tenon and mortise connections of beams and columns, with stiffness values set as $k_x = 1.26 \times 10^9$ KN/m, $k_y = k_z = 1.41 \times 10^9$ KN/m, and $k_{\theta x} = k_{\theta y} = k_{\theta z} = 1.5 \times 10^{10}$ KN·m/rad [28].
(3) Roof mass adjustment: The roof load is revised to G = 1.160 kN/m².

5.2.3. Modal Results Comparison

A comparison of test and simulated modal frequencies is tabulated in Table 11, and mode shapes are depicted in Figure 18.

**Table 11.** Comparison of test and simulated modal frequencies (Hz).

| Order | X Direction | | | Y Direction | | |
|---|---|---|---|---|---|---|
| | Test Value | Simulated Value | Inaccuracy (%) | Test Value | Simulated Value | Inaccuracy (%) |
| 1 | 2.097 | 1.965 | 6.29 | 3.955 | 3.583 | 9.41 |
| 2 | 3.845 | 3.674 | 4.45 | 5.701 | 5.236 | 8.16 |

Table 11 presents the comparison between modal parameters obtained from the corrected finite element model and those measured experimentally. Through analysis, it was found that modal parameter calculations from the corrected finite element model closely approximate the measured modal results, with maximum errors of 9.41% for the first two frequencies, both within 10% of the measured resonant frequencies. Numerical simulations show that each modal frequency is lower than the experimental results because the modeling process did not account for components such as doors, windows, and partition walls that contribute to the overall lateral stiffness of the structure. The corrected finite element model better reflects the true dynamic characteristics of the timber structure.

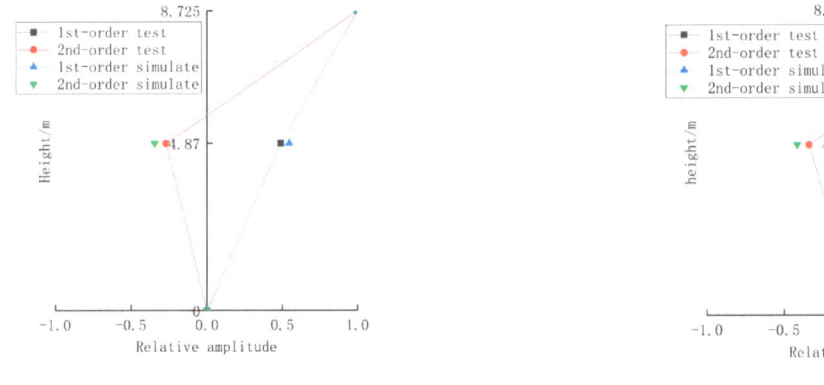

(a) X direction

(b) Y direction

**Figure 18.** Comparison of North House main hall tests and simulation mode shapes.

Figure 18 illustrates that the first and second mode shapes of the finite element model in the east–west and north–south directions align with the experimental results, further validating the accuracy of the corrected finite element model of North House main hall.

## 6. Conclusions

In situ dynamic testing was conducted in this paper, and modal parameters of the wooden structure of North House main hall were obtained using the self-interaction spectral method and stochastic subspace method. A finite element model of the wooden structure of North House main hall was developed and validated using the dynamic test results. The following conclusions can be drawn:

(1) The natural frequencies of the first and second order in the X direction were 2.097 Hz and 3.845 Hz and in the Y direction were 3.955 Hz and 5.701 Hz. The modal frequency in the Y direction of the structure exceeds that in the X direction.
(2) The finite element model of the wooden structure of North House main hall is adjusted based on measured modal parameters. Sensitivity analysis indicates adjustments to parameters such as beam–column elastic modulus, tenon–mortise joint stiffness, and roof mass for finite element model refinement.
(3) Modal parameter calculations from the corrected finite element model closely approximate the measured modal results, with maximum errors of 9.41% for the first two frequencies, both within 10% of the measured resonant frequencies. The adjusted finite element model closely matches the experimental results, serving as a benchmark model for the wooden structure of North House main hall.

**Author Contributions:** Conceptualization, X.W. and Z.M.; methodology, X.L.; software, G.W.; validation, X.W. and Z.M.; formal analysis, G.W.; data curation, X.L.; writing—original draft preparation, X.W.; writing—review and editing, Z.M.; supervision, X.L. and G.W. All authors have read and agreed to the published version of the manuscript.

**Funding:** This research was funded by National Natural Science Foundation of China (Grant No. 52068063), Natural Science Foundation Research Program of Shandong Province (Grant No. ZR 2020 ME 240), Higher Education Innovation Fund Project of Gansu Province (Grant No. 2022A-107), Technology support plan project in Qinzhou District, Tianshui City, Gansu Province (Grant No.

2023-SHFZG-2921, 2023-SHFZG-2044), Maijishan Grottoes Art Research Project of Tianshui Normal University (Grant No. MJS2021-06), and Fuxi Scientific Research Innovation Team Project of Tianshui Normal University (Grant No. FXD2020-13).

**Data Availability Statement:** The data supporting this study's findings are available from the corresponding author upon reasonable request.

**Conflicts of Interest:** The authors declare that they have no known competing financial interests or personal relationships that could have appeared to influence the work reported in this paper.

## References

1. Sun, T. The refection to the status and conservation of Tianshui historical residences. *Mod. Urban Stud.* **2008**, *11*, 20–25. (In Chinese)
2. Zhang, X.-C.; Xue, J.-Y.; Zhao, H.-T.; Sui, Y. Experimental study on Chinese ancient timber-frame building by shaking table test. *Struct. Eng. Mech.* **2011**, *40*, 453–469. [CrossRef]
3. Xie, Q.; Wang, L.; Li, S.; Zhang, L.; Hu, W. Influence of wood infill walls on the seismic performance of Chinese traditional timber structure by shaking table tests. *Bull. Earthq. Eng.* **2020**, *18*, 5009–5029. [CrossRef]
4. Xue, J.; Xu, D. Shake table tests on the traditional column-and-tie timber structures. *Eng. Struct.* **2018**, *175*, 847–860. [CrossRef]
5. Wu, Y.; Song, X.; Gu, X.; Luo, L. Dynamic performance of a multi-story traditional timber pagoda. *Eng. Struct.* **2018**, *159*, 277–285. [CrossRef]
6. Fang, D.P.; Iwasaki, S.; Yu, M.H.; Shen, Q.P.; Miyamoto, Y.; Hikosaka, H. Ancient Chinese timber architecture. I: Experimental study. *J. Struct. Eng.* **2001**, *127*, 1348–1357. [CrossRef]
7. Fang, D.P.; Iwasaki, S.; Yu, M.H.; Shen, Q.P.; Miyamoto, Y.; Hikosaka, H. Ancient Chinese timber architecture. II: Dynamic characteristics. *J. Struct. Eng.* **2001**, *127*, 1358–1364. [CrossRef]
8. Wu, C.; Xue, J.; Zhou, S.; Zhang, F. Seismic performance evaluation for a traditional Chinese timber-frame structure. *Int. J. Archit. Herit.* **2021**, *15*, 1842–1856. [CrossRef]
9. Pan, Y.; Yi, D.; Khennane, A.; Chen, J. Seismic performance of a historic timber structure on a slope. *J. Build. Eng.* **2023**, *71*, 106434. [CrossRef]
10. Che, L.A.; Ge, R.X.; Iwatate, T. Evaluation of Dynamic Behaviors and Damage Mechanism of Ancient Timber Architectures. *Key Eng. Mater.* **2007**, *63*, 277–282. [CrossRef]
11. Altunişik, A.C.; Karahasan, O.; Okur, F.Y.; Kalkan, E.; Ozgan, K. Finite Element Model Updating and Dynamic Analysis of a Restored Historical Timber Mosque Based on Ambient Vibration Tests. *J. Test. Eval.* **2019**, *47*, 20180122. [CrossRef]
12. Altunişik, A.C.; Genç, A.F.; Günaydin, M.; Okur, F.Y.; Karahasan, O.Ş. Dynamic response of a historical armory building using the finite element model validated by the ambient vibration test. *J. Vib. Control* **2018**, *24*, 5472–5484. [CrossRef]
13. GB/T50452-2008; Technical Specifications for Protection of Historic Buildings Against Man-Made Vibration. China Construction Industry Press: Beijing, China, 2008. (In Chinese)
14. Li, Y.C.; Cheng, H. Identification and diagnostic analysis of the vibrating screen's faults. *Mech. Eng. Autom.* **2008**, *3*, 119–121. (In Chinese)
15. Zhou, H.X. Research on the damage identification of reinforced concrete simple beams based on damping characteristics. *Beijing Univ. Technol.* **2011**, 1–81. (In Chinese)
16. Liu, Y.F.; Xin, K.G.; Fan, J.S. A review of structure modal identification methods through ambient excitation. *Eng. Mech.* **2014**, *31*, 46–53. (In Chinese)
17. Welch, P. The use of fast Fourier transform for the estimation of power spectra: A method based on time averaging over short, modified periodograms. *IEEE Trans. Audio Electroacoust.* **1967**, *15*, 70–73. [CrossRef]
18. Chang, J.; Zhang, Q.W.; Sun, L.M. Application of stabilization diagram for modal parameter identification using stochastic subspace method. *Eng. Mech.* **2007**, *24*, 47–52. (In Chinese)
19. Sun, X.H.; Hao, M.M.; Zhang, L.M. Research on broadband modal parameters identification under ambient excitation. *J. Build. Struct.* **2011**, *32*, 151–156. (In Chinese)
20. Li, H.L. Research on Methods of Structural Modal Parameter Identification Under Ambient Excitation. Master's Thesis, Chongqing University, Chongqing, China, 2012; pp. 1–101. (In Chinese)
21. Yang, C.; Ou, J.P. Order estimation for subspace system identification methods. *J. Vib. Shock* **2009**, *28*, 13–16. (In Chinese)
22. Wang, Y.; Hang, X.C.; Jiang, D. Selection method of Toeplitz matrix row number based on covariance driven stochastic subspace identification. *J. Vib. Shock* **2015**, *34*, 71–73. (In Chinese)
23. Rainieri, C.; Fabbrocino, G. Influence of model order and number of block rows on accuracy and precision of modal parameter estimates in stochastic subspace identification. *Int. J. Lifecycle Perform. Eng.* **2014**, *1*, 317–334. [CrossRef]
24. Meng, Z.B. Analysis and Assessment of the Vibration Response Traffic-Induced of Xi'an Bell Tower. Ph.D. Thesis, Xi'an University of Architecture and Technology, Xi'an, China, 2009; pp. 1–194. (In Chinese)
25. GB50165-92; Liang, T.; Wang, Y.W.; Ni, S.Z. National Standard of the People's Republic of China. Technical Code for Maintenance and Strengthening of Ancient Timber Buildings. China Architecture & Building Press: Beijing, China, 1992; pp. 1–84. (In Chinese)

26. Cao, Y. Study of Dynamic Analysis Models for Ancient Architectural Timber Structures Under Traffic-Induced Excitations. Master's Thesis, Liaocheng University, Liaocheng, China, 2015; pp. 1–59. (In Chinese)
27. Gao, D.F.; Zhu, S.T.; Ding, X.J. Analysis of structural and seismic performance of Yongning Gate embrasured watchtower of Xi'an City Wall. *J. Shandong Univ.* **2013**, *43*, 62–69.
28. Fang, D.-p.; Yu, M.-h.; Miyamoto, Y.; Iwasaki, S.; Hikosaka, H. Numerical analysis on structural characteristics of ancient timber architecture. *Eng. Mech.* **2001**, *18*, 137–144. (In Chinese)

**Disclaimer/Publisher's Note:** The statements, opinions and data contained in all publications are solely those of the individual author(s) and contributor(s) and not of MDPI and/or the editor(s). MDPI and/or the editor(s) disclaim responsibility for any injury to people or property resulting from any ideas, methods, instructions or products referred to in the content.

MDPI AG
Grosspeteranlage 5
4052 Basel
Switzerland
Tel.: +41 61 683 77 34

*Buildings* Editorial Office
E-mail: buildings@mdpi.com
www.mdpi.com/journal/buildings

Disclaimer/Publisher's Note: The title and front matter of this reprint are at the discretion of the Guest Editors. The publisher is not responsible for their content or any associated concerns. The statements, opinions and data contained in all individual articles are solely those of the individual Editors and contributors and not of MDPI. MDPI disclaims responsibility for any injury to people or property resulting from any ideas, methods, instructions or products referred to in the content.

www.ingramcontent.com/pod-product-compliance
Lightning Source LLC
LaVergne TN
LVHW072329090526
838202LV00019B/2376